PERVASIVE COMPUTING

Technology and Architecture of Mobile Internet Applications

PERVASIVE COMPUTING

Technology and Architecture of Mobile Internet Applications

Jochen Burkhardt

Dr Horst Henn

Stefan Hepper

Klaus Rindtorff

Thomas Schäck

Addison-Wesley

An Imprint of Pearson Education

Boston • San Fransisco • New York • Toronto • Montreal
London • Munich • Paris • Madrid
Cape Town • Sydney • Tokyo • Singapore • Mexico City

Technical specialist	Jukka Heiska, Nokia WAP Server -Iuvun osalta
Illustrations	Tomi Mainen
Cover Designer	Frank Chaumont

PEARSON EDUCATION LIMITED

Head Office:	*London Office:*
Edinburgh Gate	128 Long Acre
Harlow	London WC2E 9AN
Essex CM20 2JE	Tel: +44 (0)20 7447 2000
Tel: +44 (0)1279 623623	Fax: +44 (0)20 7240 5771
Fax: +44 (0)1279 431059	

Website: www.aw.com/cseng/

_____

First published in Great Britain 2002

© Pearson Education Limited 2002

The rights of Jochen Burkhardt, Horst Henn, Stefan Hepper, Klaus Rindtorff and Thomas Schäck to be identified as the Authors of this Work have been asserted by them in accordance with the Copyright, Designs and Patents Act 1988.

ISBN 0-201-72215-1

British Library Cataloguing in Publication Data
A CIP catalogue record for this book can be obtained from the British Library.

Library of Congress Cataloging in Publication Data
Applied for.

10 9 8 7 6 5 4 3 2 1

Typeset by Pantek Arts Ltd, Maidstone, Kent.
Printed and bound in Great Britain by Biddles Ltd, Guildford and King's Lynn.

The Publishers' policy is to use paper manufactured from sustainable forests.

Contents

Foreword

We are at the beginning of a new era of computing, one that will change our lives dramatically. While the personal computer, the Internet, and the World Wide Web have already changed many aspects of business, and signs of a bigger convergence of industries like media, entertainment, consumer electronics, telecommunications, and information technology are evident, the next wave of technological revolution will create much greater changes in every part of our daily lives.

Where are we heading? The twenty-first century will likely be less characterized, as previous popular predictions described it, by the colonization of the moon, cities on the floors of the oceans, and cars powered by nuclear energy – all of which require huge infrastructure efforts – but more by applications of miniaturized and, therefore, nearly invisible technologies like biotechnology, nanotechnology, and, last but not least, microelectronics as the base of computer science. We can look excitedly forward to see the synergies between these realms!

Advances in microelectronics are not new to us. On the contrary, Moore's law, which states that processor performance doubles every 18 months, has held true with surprising precision and persistence ever since Gordon Moore postulated it in the late 1960s. A similarly high exponential growth has also applied to some other technology parameters, such as storage density or communication bandwidth. At the same time, prices for the same level of performance have decreased radically. We expect that this will continue for a few years, which makes it all very exciting, because now it becomes obvious that our near future will be full of tiny, spontaneously communicating processors that, because of their small size and low price, will be integrated in almost all everyday items.

There will also be interesting developments in materials ('light-emitting polymers' or 'electronic ink', for example) that will make computers less perceptible by seamlessly blending them into their environment. An example of this is 'smart paper', unfortunately still very early in its development, which eventually might give computers the appearance of an interactive foldable map. While smart paper may still sound like science fiction, the results from microsystem technologies that lead to extremely small sensors capable of detecting a multitude of different environmental parameters are more solid. Also, significant advances in communication technology and electronics bring into reach small and energy-efficient modules for short-distance wireless communication, the current Bluetooth standard being a prominent example. The progress in these disciplines continues to accelerate.

Taken together, these advances draw a picture of our not-so-distant future. Many everyday items will become 'smarter' through integrated processors, memory, sensors, and communication capabilities, and will be able to serve us by tackling additional tasks beyond their normal function. In the long run, we are talking about everyday items like pencils that are capable of digitizing everything written with them, clothes that remember the places they have been to, or umbrellas that subscribe to an Internet weather information service and will trigger a friendly reminder from the door if your shoes report that you attempt to leave without an umbrella. Soon every advanced item – from the calendar to the electronic book, from the car to the kitchen appliance – will be connected to the Internet and will use them to accomplish its tasks, often without the user's knowledge. An extension of the Internet into all everyday items, however, is of course a formidable exercise, even for experts.

All of this leads us to the current topic: information technology becoming omnipresent and entering all aspects of our life – which is exactly what 'pervasive computing' means. WAP-capable mobile phones, game consoles that are connected to the Internet, and personal digital assistants that communicate wirelessly with other devices in their vicinity are only the first signs of the smarter items of the coming 'post-PC era'. This era manifests itself primarily by the migration of classical PC applications into smaller, more specialized 'information appliances'. These information appliances are being integrated into a common infrastructure that takes care of the synchronization of the distributed and replicated data, guarantees the necessary security, creates interoperability, and offers many other useful services. In the end, it is all about offering adequate access to all kinds of information in any place possible.

We are at the very beginning of this new era of technology, and currently only media artists and scientists are thinking of intelligent umbrellas and similar scenarios that promise to change the physical world into one big interactive computing platform. More concrete are the current efforts to integrate mobile and wearable 'information appliances', like mobile phones or other 'digital assistants' into Web-based business processes and electronic commerce scenarios, and to enable ubiquitous access to the applications behind them through these devices. However, scalability, flexibility, mobility, security, and heterogeneity are major challenges in the realization of adequate systems and require an appropriate integration into powerful back-end systems as well as a whole suite of modern concepts and standards.

These concepts, technologies and standards are summarized here by the term 'pervasive computing'. Software architects, application developers, and students are strongly recommended to focus on this topic. While much is changing in this fast-paced domain, with continuously-generated standards proposals (sometimes dominated more by the market than by pure insight or scientific perception), it is important to know the technologies and their strengths – and their weaknesses – as well as the general potential of the whole field. This is crucial for current practice, where more and more large, complex infrastructures for applications utilizing mobile devices at the front end are being created based on these technologies, as well as for long-term preparation for the emerging era of the invisible but pervasive computer, also called 'ubiquitous computing'.

One thing is for certain: the trend is towards control and integration of all things in a network. Completely new applications will be created around the many smart devices, and the maintenance and development of the necessary infrastructure – including the measures to satisfy the increased need for security and privacy – may keep a whole industry busy. Completely open, however, is how a technology that so profoundly influences all aspects of our life will affect our way of living and even the structure of our society. Truly, we have an exciting future in front of us!

Friedemann Mattern
ETH Zürich
January 2001

Preface

The Internet has grown into a global infrastructure causing a major restructuring of the economy. Pervasive computing will add a new dimension to the Web society. People will be able to interact with the Web everywhere and at any time using mobile devices with speech, pen, and other tailored human–machine interfaces. The World Wide Web will now reach people that have not even considered using a PC before. Existing businesses will be able to offer superior services to their customers, and exciting new businesses for mobile consumers will emerge. Technology will be the major driver for this new mobile society. Understanding the potential of the technology and its impact on society is one of the keys to developing new applications and services.

Part I Technologies

In the first part of this book, we give an introduction to technologies used by pervasive computing. This part is relevant for everybody who wants to get an overview of pervasive computing – consultants, students, IT architects, and developers. We begin with a brief discussion of the past, present, and our view of the future of pervasive computing, and give a motivation for pervasive computing by showing several typical areas where pervasive computing is introduced in a series of example applications. We give an extensive technology overview, including current man-machine interfaces, devices, operating systems, and standards.

Chapter 1: Past, present, future

Pervasive computing has three major driving forces. First, the microelectronic technology providing smaller devices and displays with lower energy consumption. Second, the communication technology providing higher bandwidth and higher data transfer rates at lower cost. The third key component is the ongoing standardization of all components in the system by international standardization committees and industry associations. Without standardization the technology cannot be exploited on a large scale. We describe the base technologies and standards, such as

Global System for Mobile Communications (GSM), Universal Mobile Telecommunications System (UMTS), Wireless Application Protocol (WAP), infrared (IR), Bluetooth, Internet Protocol (IP), Hyper Text Markup Language (HTML), Extensible Markup Lanuage (XML), VoiceXML, and Application Standards. Then we discuss the key infrastructure elements and the associated service infrastructure. Finally, we evaluate the future trends and directions.

Chapter 2: Application examples

There are already a lot of different pervasive devices available on the market, ranging from personal digital assistants (PDAs) to WAP phones. Now the question is how to use these devices effectively in business applications. In this chapter, we explore how pervasive computing devices enable exciting new ways of conducting business. We present a series of real-life application examples showing how businesses can benefit from pervasive computing. The examples will give you an overview of what is possible and what is required, and should inspire you to think of tomorrow's applications today.

Chapter 3: Device technology

This chapter gives an overview of the rapidly evolving technologies that influence the evolution of mobile devices. The key technologies are presented in three parts. The first part describes the advances in hardware technologies. The second part presents the key software technologies used for the human–machine interaction. The third part gives an introduction to some of the operating systems and Java platforms available for PDAs today. A brief discussion of each technology is given, followed by an outlook into the future direction.

Chapter 4: Device connectivity

Pervasive computing devices do not develop their full potential unless connected to applications and services through the Internet. In this chapter, protocols for device-to-device and device-to-server interactions that are relevant in the pervasive computing domain will be covered: wireless protocols, mobile phone technologies, Bluetooth, the Mobile Internet Protocol, synchronization protocols like SyncML, as well as transaction protocols and protocols enabling distributed services like Jini. In addition to those protocols, a deeper look at algorithms and protocols that address security issues is presented. Because system and device management will become a big challenge to support millions of devices, the last section will discuss device management in the pervasive space.

Chapter 5: Web application concepts

In this chapter we explain how PCs can be connected to Web applications through the Internet. Although some concepts and technologies described here can be considered classical and are well known, we want to revisit them briefly. This way, they can serve as references to be compared with the newer concepts and technologies presented in subsequent chapters.

We give an overview of the history of the World Wide Web, as well as the relevant concepts, protocols, and standards for communication between Web clients and servers via the Internet. One special topic we cover here is transcoding, the transformation of content to device-specific markup.

We discuss Web application security issues and present possible solutions ranging from use of the standard Hypertext Transfer Protocol over SSL (HTTPS) protocol to client-authentication schemes for the Internet. Apart from the typical client-authentication methods supported by today's browsers, we discuss smart cards for secure user authentication in detail.

Chapter 6: WAP and beyond

WAP has become a synonym for new wireless Internet services. This chapter describes the basics of WAP e-business implementation, device characteristics, protocol stack, security issues, products, and tools currently available on the market.

Chapter 7: Voice technology

In this chapter we will cover the basics of speech recognition and describe two important standards in the area of voice-based user interfaces: VoiceXML, a markup language for speech, and Java Speech, a Java application programming interface (Java API) to provide speech capability to Java applications. Typical speech applications, such as speech recognition on the PC, speech recognition over a telephone line, and text-to-speech translation, will be covered next. Finally, we take a closer look at speech recognition in pervasive computing and at security when using speech as a user interface method.

Chapter 8: Personal digital assistants

Today we are on the edge of an explosion of mobile devices with hitherto unprecedented connectivity and processing power. These devices replace traditional tools like pen and paper, the address book, or the calendar, and integrate all of them in a single, convenient, mobile package. What makes mobile devices so attractive is not so much the fact that they deliver new functions, but that they mimic well-known processes, combine their data and make it available everywhere and at any time. This chapter first takes a brief look at the history of PDAs. A categorization of device types and their connectivity characteristics is given. Finally, the available standards and typical software components for PDAs are explained.

Part II: Architectures

In the second part of this book, we present an end-to-end architecture for pervasive computing applications that support different kinds of devices and communication protocols. We explain how applications adhering to this architecture can be implemented, especially elaborating on the implementation of the application server and integration of WAP phones, classical telephones via voice gateways, PDAs and PCs. As a continuous example, we use the Uncle Enzo's Web shop application, which allows for ordering and payment of goods via the Internet, and later extend it to allow logon and viewing of the previous transactions through the different devices. This part is especially interesting for IT architects, consultants, and developers who face the challenge of actually implementing pervasive computing solutions.

Chapter 9: Server-side programming in Java

This chapter gives an overview of the concepts and technologies that we consider the most important in development of Web applications in general and pervasive computing Web applications in particular. We start with an overview of the Java 2 Enterprise Edition architecture, followed by a more detailed description of some key technologies, including Java Servlets, Enterprise Java Beans, and Java Server Pages. Given the importance of XML, we dedicate a major part of this chapter to this technology. We present technologies for building Web services that are based on XML, including the Simple Object Access Protocol (SOAP), and Universal Description, Discovery and Integration (UDDI). We conclude with an overview of the model–view–controller pattern and its use in the development of Web applications.

Chapter 10: Pervasive Web application architecture

In this chapter, we propose an architecture for pervasive computing applications that support multiple different devices like PCs, WAP phones, PDAs, and voice-only phones enabled to access Web servers through voice gateways. The architecture addresses the special problems associated with pervasive computing, such as diversity of devices, markup languages, and authentication methods. We especially show how pervasive computing applications based on this architecture can be secured.

Chapter 11: Example application

Here we present an example application that will be used to show how Java applications that adhere to the architecture presented in Chapter 10 can be extended to support different kinds of devices. As an example that is both simple and instructive, we chose a shopping application, including registration, login, a main menu, self-care, purchasing goods, and purchase history. The application is designed for an imaginary Italian restaurant named Uncle Enzo's that sells via the Internet. In the subsequent chapters, we will show how this application can be enabled for access from a PC using smart-card authentication, from WAP phones, from PDAs, and from a voice-only phone via a voice gateway.

Chapter 12: Access from PCs

In this chapter, we show how the shop application can be extended to allow for access from PCs, using a smart card for authentication via the Internet, as presented in Chapter 5. We explain how to implement the required components, including an authentication applet and the corresponding authentication servlet, and how to integrate them into the shop application. Finally, we present the controller for PC access and the Java Server Pages (JSPs) that it uses to interact with consumers.

Chapter 13: Access via WAP

This chapter demonstrates how the example application is extended to allow for access using mobile devices with a WAP browser, especially mobile phones. We describe how the functionality supported for WAP fits into the overall architecture and discuss the infrastructure needed to connect mobile devices to Uncle Enzo's application server. We provide some source code fragments for parts of the WAP-specific functionality of the example application. At the end of the chapter, we outline some extensions that improve speed or usability of Uncle Enzo's shop.

Chapter 14: Access from personal digital assistants

In this chapter, we show how users connecting to the Internet with a PDA can use the example application. We will do that in three steps. The first version of our application will simply synchronize the menu of Uncle Enzo's to the PDA. The user can use it as a reference and then order via the phone. In the second version, we will use a local database and native application to handle the menu and compose an order. The user will be connected only when synchronizing the data and submitting the order. In the third version, we will use the WAP to show the actual menu. The user will be connected while browsing the menu and submitting an order. The chapter is concluded with a comparison of all three approaches.

Chapter 15: Access via voice

With the steadily increasing computing power of PCs and advances in voice-recognition research, speech-recognition, and speech-synthesis software has now reached a level acceptable for commercial use. The fundamentals of speech recognition and speech synthesis are described in Chapter 7.

This chapter explains how an e-business application can communicate with users over a normal telephone line, and how a voice gateway is integrated into the sample application. The voice gateway processes and recognizes voice input to generate appropriate requests for application servers, and converts responses containing VoiceXML into voice output for the user. Finally, we show you how to enable the sample application from ordinary telephones via a voice gateway.

Acknowledgements

To work on this book while at the same time being involved in real-life customer engagements and development projects was a unique opportunity that helped us gain and broaden our experience in pervasive computing technologies and Web application architecture. Without that we could not have written this book. We would like to thank our management and colleagues in the IBM Pervasive Computing Division for providing us with that opportunity.

Numerous people have provided in-depth reviews of the book, supported us, or provided us with their invaluable expertise. We are indebted to Thomas Böhme, Cherian Chempolil-Koshy, Sastry Dury, Carsten Günther, Walter Hänel, Fred Hawkes, Alexej Orlopp, Cal Stewart, Michael Wasmund, and Dirk Wittkopp.

About the authors

Jochen Burkhardt

Jochen Burkhardt studied computer science at the Berufsakademie Stuttgart, Germany, where he received a Bachelor of Applied Science degree in 1996. During his studies, he focused on computer networks and programming on the Java platform. The topic of his diploma thesis was the electronics design of a smart-card reader device.

Jochen joined the Smart Card group of the IBM Böblingen Development Laboratory in 1996. He participated in the development of the IBM Multifunction Chipcard operating system and the first implementation of a JavaCard. In 1999, Jochen joined the Pervasive Computing division to work on various projects in the area of automotive and mobile applications.

He likes Techno music, tennis and driving on empty Autobahns.

Horst Henn

Horst Henn received his diploma in computer science and his doctorate in electrical engineering from the University of Stuttgart, Germany, where he taught as an assistant professor from 1970 to 1975, working in the field of digital system design and fault-tolerant semiconductor and super-conductor memory systems. He joined the German IBM Development Laboratory in 1975 developing advanced graphical design software, including the 801 RISC processor design software on an assignment at Thomas J. Watson Research Center, New York. Since then, he has held a couple of managerial positions in advanced technology and system product development, especially in the area of highly reliable distributed system design, e.g. /390 CMOS sysplex, communication subsystem software, and image-processing software for banking applications. He has been engaged in pervasive computing since 1995, when he managed the software development of operating systems for highly secure payment smart cards, access methods, and security software for public key infrastructure. He was engaged in the creation of international standard committees, e.g. G7 Health Card Architecture (DIABCARD), PC/SC, OCF and Java Card. In his current position as Lead Consultant Pervasive

Computing, he works with customers as well as with IBM development and service teams to foster innovative mobile e-business solutions. He is especially interested in the social and human interface aspects of pervasive computing. In the spare time left he likes hiking in the mountains, playing the classical guitar with friends and painting at nice places, especially in France and Italy.

Stefan Hepper

Stefan Hepper received a diploma in computer science from the University of Karlsruhe, Germany in 1995. After graduating, he worked for three years in the Research Center Karlsruhe in the area of medical robotics and component-based software architectures for real-time systems. In 1998, he joined the IBM Böblingen Development Laboratory, where he worked with Java Cards in the areas of security and card management. He was a member of the Java Card Forum and Java Card Management Task Force. After joining the IBM Pervasive Computing division, he was responsible for the UNIX implementation of MQSeries Everyplace, worked on the SyncML reference implementation in the IBM pervasive portal project, and is now working as an architect for synchronization solutions.

Stefan has delivered a number of lectures at international conferences, published papers about distributed software architectures for medical robotics, and held Java Card and Smart Card workshops. His research interests are component-based software architectures, real-time systems, and pervasive infrastructures.

Besides working and being with his family and friends, he likes skiing, motorcycling, and diving.

Klaus Rindtorff

Klaus Rindtorff studied at the University of Dortmund, Germany where he received a diploma in computer science in 1989. He has worked with computers since 1978, and is experienced in the areas of digital electronics, computer graphics, artificial neural networks, and programming languages.

During his university studies, he worked at ISP Software GmbH Dortmund on the implementation of a graphics library for a database system running on the EUMEL operating system. The first contact with IBM was during his diploma thesis about the design of a CMOS chip to accelerate computer ray tracing.

Klaus joined IBM Banking Solutions in 1989 in the Böblingen Development Laboratory, and has since worked on software development projects covering ATMs, document processing, and image recognition using artificial neural networks. During this time, he has received several patents, written a number of articles, and taught computer programming.

From 1994 to 1999 Klaus worked for IBM Global Smart Card Solutions, where he designed and implemented the IBM Open Smart Card Architecture. During his two-year assignment to the USA, he participated as a consultant in many customer projects. He also represented IBM in the Global Chipcard Alliance and in the Smart Card Forum as the chairman of the Interoperability work group.

Since 1999, Klaus has worked as a software architect for IBM Pervasive Computing, where he gathered experience with personal digital assistants, data synchronization, and extending Web applications for mobile devices.

At home he likes to switch the computer keyboard for a piano keyboard and enjoys cooking for his family.

Thomas Schäck

Thomas Schäck is an architect at IBM's Pervasive Computing Division working at the IBM Development Lab in Böblingen, Germany. He started working for IBM in 1996, after obtaining his diploma in computer sciences from the University of Karlsruhe. Since joining IBM, he has worked in Java and C++ development projects centered on the smart card technology. These projects include the OpenCard Framework, which became the standard API for smart-card applications in Java, and work on a smart-card-based digital signature solution. Most recently, Thomas was the architect of a first-of-a-kind Internet payment system prototype for a large German bank, and he is now working as a portal architect in IBM's Pervasive Computing Division. Thomas has published various papers in his field and filed numerous patents. Previous publications include the book *Smart Card Application Development in Java*.

Contributions

This book was written as a team effort and all authors have contributed their specific knowledge and experience to all chapters. Jochen Burkhardt wrote Chapters 6 and 13. Horst Henn authored the introduction to pervasive computing in Chapter 1 and parts of Chapter 2. Stefan Hepper wrote Chapters 4, 7 and 15. Klaus Rindtorff authored Chapters 2, 8 and 14; he also wrote Chapter 3 with Stefan Hepper and Jochen Burkhardt. Thomas Schäck wrote Chapter 5, 9, 10, 11 and 12.

Trademarks

Activ Server
Agenda VR3
ARM
Audrey
BeOS
C35i
CalliGrapher
CJKOS
CodeWarrior
Communicator
Crusoe
DB2 Everyplace
eBookMan
EPOC
Ericsson R380
Excel
ExpressQ
Festival
Fitaly
Graffiti
Handheld Pro
Handspring Visor
HotSpot VM
HP-UX
Ibus//Mobile
IC35
IntelliSync
Internet Explorer
iPAQ
J2ME
J9
Java
Java 2 Platform
Java Enterprise
  Edition
Java Micro Edition
JogDial

KBrowser
KVM
Linux
LongRun
Lotus Notes
M35i
Mac
Microsoft Exchange
MIPS
Mobile Connect
Mosaic
MQ Everyplace
MS Exchange
MS Outlook
MSMQ
Navi Roller
Nokia 7110
Nokia WAP Toolkit
Octave
OpenView
OPL
Oracle Lite DBMS
Palm OS
PdQ
PersonalJava
Photon
Pocket PC
Pocket Word
PowerPC
Psion Series 3
Psion Series 5
QNX Neutrino
Real-time Java
S35i
Sidekick
Solaris
SpeedStep

StrongARM
SwiftMQ
T9
TrueSync
TTS
Unicenter TNG
Unifier
Universal Plug and
  Play
UNIX
UP.Browser
UP.Link
Visual Basic
Visual C++
VisualAge
Micro Edition
Voice Suite
VxWorks
Waba
WabaVM
WebSphere Studio
Windows
Windows CE
Windows ME
Windows NT
Windows32
Word
WorkPad

I TECHNOLOGIES

In this part, we give an introduction to pervasive computing. This part is relevant for everybody who wants to get an overview of pervasive computing – consultants, students, IT architects, or developers. We begin with a brief discussion of the past, present, and our view of the future of pervasive computing, and give a motivation for pervasive computing by showing several typical areas where pervasive computing is introduced in a series of application examples. We give an extensive technology overview, including current human–machine interfaces, devices, operating systems, and standards. We conclude with a topic that is the most important issue to solve: connecting pervasive devices to servers.

1 Past, present, future

Pervasive computing is a new dimension of personal computing that integrates mobile communication, ubiquitous embedded computer systems, consumer electronics, and the power of the Internet. The number of people using pervasive computing devices is approaching one billion, and growing at a two-digit rate. Pervasive computing is based on the combination of key technologies, Web age research, and development methodologies. Microelectronic technology offers small, powerful devices and displays with low energy consumption. Digital communication technology provides higher bandwidth, higher data transfer rates at lower cost, and worldwide roaming. International standardization through standard bodies and industry organizations provides the framework for integration of all components into an interoperable system, including security, service, and billing schemes.

In this chapter we position pervasive computing in the context of key technologies known from the past, and explore its impact on people and businesses as well as on industries and markets. We describe the basic infrastructure, potential services, and examples of state-of-the-art applications, technologies, and standards. Finally we evaluate the future trends and directions.

1.1 The vine and fig tree dream

The driving forces in the evolution of human society have been the longing of human beings for a better life, and the prophets developing and communicating the grand visions. The vision of Micah is a splendid example of a vision created a couple of thousand years ago that is still moving people today:

> And he shall judge among many people, and rebuke strong nations afar off; and they shall beat their swords into plowshares, and their spears into pruning hooks: nation shall not lift up a sword against nation, neither shall they learn war any more.

> *But they shall sit every man under his vine and under his fig tree; and none shall make them afraid: for the mouth of the Lord and hosts hath spoken it.*
>
> Micah 4

We all know that this vision is still a dream for most people on earth. However, our modern society is probably closer to this vision than any society in the past. A long row of inventors from the Stone Age toolmakers to the inventors of computers have been working hard to let the vine and fig tree vision come true. In contrast to ancient times, we need not rely on people to realize this dream for a small, privileged class, but can use machines and equipment to handle our chores. Inventions are spread and adopted much faster than in the past. Inventions like the wheel took thousands of years to travel from the place of invention to a large user community. Very often, inventions were forgotten and had to be reinvented later due to the lack of adequate communication and transport infrastructure. Therefore, highly developed cultures like the Chinese and Roman societies were based on an excellent communication and transport infrastructure. A common language for verbal and written communication independent of time and space was the foundation of these Golden Age cultures. With the combination of common language and excellent transport infrastructure, innovations were communicated and implemented faster and concurrently in many places. Therefore, speed of communication is a very critical success factor for any society.

Many inventors have thought about methods of high-speed communication that do not need requiring transport of physical media. Flag-based communication systems, for example, were already used along the Great Chinese Wall, and along the Mediterranean coastline by the Romans, and are still practiced by sailors today. The Roman system in the Mediterranean was able to send short messages faster than most modern surface-mail systems. However, transmission capacity was very small and use was restricted to government purposes only. These systems, requiring a line of sight between sender and receiver, could only be used when the weather was fine and no rain or fog was cutting off communication. Therefore, these systems never became popular in the rainy and foggy northern countries.

The real breakthrough for high-speed communication was the invention of the first usable telegraph system by Samuel Finley Breese Morse in 1837, using an electrical signal sent over wire. Although Samuel Thomas von Sömmering invented the first electrical telegraphy system in 1809, it was Morse who combined the base electrical technology, a new user interface, and the Morse alphabet into a system that could be used by non-scientists. Now information was transferred lightning quick across continents. In the following years, better user interfaces for data entry, printers for data output, and more comfortable alphabets for data entry, printers for data output, and more comfortable alphabets for data encoding complemented the basic telegraphy system. The popular ASCII alphabet still used in almost every computer today dates back from these early days of telegraphy – one root of our modern internet technology.

1.1.1 The horse does not eat cucumber salad

The dream of 'remote talking' came true when Johann Philipp Reis transmitted the first voice message over wire in 1861. Being a real scientist, he chose the sentence 'Das Pferd frisst keinen Gurkensalat' ('The horse does not eat cucumber salad'), which indicates that he was interested mostly in science and not in commercial use of this new technology. The later invention of the first telephone system with a usable interface by Alexander Graham Bell in 1876 finally opened up a totally new world of communication. Suddenly people were able communicate over long distances from their homes or offices, without complicated conversion of the spoken word into a cryptic sequence of encoded characters. The phone system also conveyed a superior level of trust because people could easily recognize with whom they were talking. Even today, many people prefer doing vital business transactions over the phone instead of using the modern telegraphy machine, a computer. No wonder that the telephone became one of the biggest technology success stories that has changed our society. This is also a stunning example of how important convenient user interfaces are for the widespread acceptance of technology.

However, wire-line telephony systems restricted communication to places where a telephone was installed. Initially, wireless communication was limited to military organizations, emergency units, cab drivers, etc. This was because mobile devices were heavy, required large power supplies and long antennas, and were difficult to use. Mobile phones for private use emerged in the early 1970s. In 1982, Group Special Mobile (GSM, now short for Global System for Mobile communications) was founded to define a technology for mobile phones that would allow roaming across Europe[1]. The first widely used commercial mobile phone system, the Advanced Mobile Phone System (AMPS), was launched in the USA in 1983 using proprietary technology. GSM standardization and development of devices and infrastructure took more time, but in the end created a much larger market.

Major improvements in hardware technology and exploitation of digital technology contributed to create the modern mobile phone systems appearing in the market in the early 1990s. Wireless communication, consumer electronics, and computer technology were merged and created a new environment where people, systems, and computers are integrated in a modern 'vine and fig tree' pervasive computing environment.

1.1.2 The peace dream

Although we have been doing reasonably well in developing technology to make life easier, we did not succeed nearly as well on the implementation of the peace dream. There is only hope that as people communicate with each other, they will realize that the vine and fig tree dream can only come true if the peace dream becomes a reality for mankind. Pervasive computing infrastructure facilitates access to information and modern administration in areas that do not have a traditional wire-based communication infrastructure. Wireless infrastructure can also be implemented faster and with lower investment in the densely populated areas of the world. Thus people living there may also participate in the worldwide exchange of ideas and Internet business that may become a major driving force to let the peace dream come true.

1.2 Pervasive computing

In our time it is not only the law of the market which has its own life and rules over man, but also the development of science and technique.

Erich Fromm, The Sane Society[2]

Personal computing and Internet communication have fundamentally changed our way of working both at offices and at home. Pervasive computing, the next dimension of personal computing, will change and improve not only our work environment but also our daily life and our communication patterns with family, friends, and business partners. Small portable personal assistants combine high-speed, low-power computers, wireless communication, data storage in persistent semiconductor memory and coin-sized disk drives, small colour displays, and video and speech-processing technology. This will give users the freedom not only to communicate efficiently at any place in the world but also to access local information as well as information residing on the Internet at any place and at any time. It is typical for new technologies like the Internet and pervasive computing that they have not been accepted by the majority of people as a prophet would dream of, but are sneaking into society. Only a small number of computer experts, for example, were sending short messages a couple of years ago. Today, children and adults use pagers or their mobile phones daily to send and receive short messages. Digital cameras have begun to replace conventional cameras because they integrate easily with digital media and email. Both technologies create a new business environment and affect the communication style of people.

1.2.1 Pervasive computing scenarios

The personal perception, technology, and business aspects of pervasive computing are described in the following scenarios, with emphasis on technologies that are already available today and have the potential to be widely accepted in the market in the next couple of years.

The automobile

The best way to experience state-of-the-art pervasive computing technology is to drive a modern luxury car. When you are approaching the car, you press a button on your electronic car key to unlock the car, and to adjust the driver seat and rear mirrors to your preferences. When seated, you put your mobile phone in its cradle, and insert your key to unlock the car's electronic system and to switch off the anti-theft system. You enter your destination into the car's navigation system. You dial into your office system by pressing a button on the steering wheel and download some urgent mail to the car communication unit. The system should read the mail to you later while you are on the road.

Finally, you start the engine, and because it is a dark, rainy morning, the lights turn on automatically and the windshield wipers start at low speed. The friendly voice of the navigation system reminds you to turn left at the next traffic light. Now you are on the road, and up to 100 computers in the car make sure that the engine is running smoothly and your ride comfortable. There is some traffic on the road but you feel pretty safe because you know that the car has a computer-controlled traction and brake system that knows about the adverse weather conditions and will adjust the controls accordingly. On the highway, you switch off the navigation system because you want to listen to your urgent email message, which is read by a computerized voice. In the future, the navigation and mail system might coordinate their work, and the manufacturer might invent a pothole detector to make the ride even more comfortable. If the car is involved in an accident, you know that the automatic airbag system will protect you. One day, the automatic emergency call system may alert the carmaker support system via the wireless communication system: in case of a minor accident, it will dispatch a limousine, and in case of a heavy accident it will dispatch an ambulance and provide the emergency doctor with your personal emergency health record.

Although these functions are not available in every car today, the individual technologies already exist and we can expect this pervasive automotive environment to become a standard feature in almost every new car in a few years. The scenario demonstrates some key characteristics of pervasive computing:

- Multiple devices like car key, mobile phone, car audio system, and navigation system are integrated in the system. Devices are used for multiple purposes, e.g. the car key is used to unlock the door, to personalize settings, and to start the engine.

- A large number of different interfaces, such as keys, buttons, displays, touch screen, microphone, loudspeakers, and environmental sensors, are used to build an optimized user interface.

- There is concurrent operation of offline and temporary online systems, e.g. the motor monitoring system is working offline, but can be connected to a service center for diagnosis if required.

- A large number of specialized computer systems are interconnected via local buses and the Internet.

- Short-range (car key) and wide-area (mobile phone) wireless communication are integrated.

- Security elements, e.g. car key, theft protection system, and SIM card in the mobile phone, prevent unauthorized access.

- Personalization of functions adapts the system to the user's preferences, e.g. adjustment of the driver seat and rear mirror. User interfaces are simple, response is fast, and most of the system's complexity is hidden. No PC literacy is required to use and manage the system.

We can expect these types of functions to be integrated into networked operation and to be extended to workplace, home, and mobile environments.

The mobile workplace

An ever-increasing percentage of traditional office workplaces will be transformed into truly mobile workplaces, with portable computers, mobile phones, portable digital assistants (PDAs), printers, and fax machines connected via wireless local area networks and wireless Internet. Totally new forms of organizations will emerge where most people can schedule their work much more flexibly than today. An indication of this ongoing transformation is the growth of mobile workplaces in some of the Western European countries, with yearly growth rates exceeding 30%. This might be a partial solution to avoid the daily traffic jams in large cities, and to overcome the lack of skilled resources in most modern economies by allowing parents to better balance their family and business life.

Mobile workplaces will not be restricted to typical office jobs. Manufacturing companies will use mobile devices to monitor manufacturing processes remotely, to schedule work more efficiently, and to improve communication with employees. Optimization of the supply chains will require a highly efficient, integrated pervasive computing infrastructure.

The retail and distribution industry already relies on isolated pervasive computing devices. Service terminals will become smaller and will interact with customer devices, such as smart cards, mobile phones, paging devices, and PDAs, in order to improve workflow and data integrity. Health and social services will improve information flow and quality of service. The pervasive computing workplace will become a major component of most enterprises in the future.

The massive introduction of mobile workplaces will certainly require new social skills to manage private and business life. People and organizations must learn not only to manage traditional working hours but also to cooperate in a result-oriented business environment where team members are working at different places at different time.

The home

Pervasive computing has arrived at home mainly through mobile phones, PCs, and entertainment devices. Mobile phones have become a major infrastructure of family life in many countries by linking the busy schedules of parents and children. TV sets, video recorders, games consoles, and CD players become integrated into entertainment centres with optional access to the Internet through set-top boxes. New devices that integrate TV, DVD, and games centers, are being introduced to the market. Modern houses feature local area networks (wired or wireless) and appliance buses to control doors, windows, shutters, heating and cooling systems, home appliances, and security systems. Local area networks using data transmission via power lines or wireless technologies will provide the infrastructure to interconnect domestic devices. Through the addition of an Internet connection, the home emerges into a Web-enabled service node for home management, entertainment, security monitoring, and totally new consumer services through a domestic service gateway. Acceptance of all this new technology by users is slow because standards for integration of the different technologies are difficult to establish.

The personal communication environment

Today, people are using multiple devices and services for personal communication, work, and entertainment. Many different devices, such as wire-line phones, mobile phones, pagers, fax machines, PCs, games consoles, digital cameras, music recorders, and video recorders, operate pretty isolated from each other. However, more and more systems are appearing on the market that combine several of these devices, creating new services such as sending a fax from a mobile phone, programming a video recorder from a PC, or controlling the heating system at home via a mobile phone. Typically, these services are not integrated and are provided via a multitude of unrelated channels and service providers. It is difficult for customers to locate a responsible party in case of a problem and to handle multiple service center addresses, personal identification numbers, user names, and passwords. In the pervasive computing environment, personal communication will evolve into an interconnected, cooperative communication landscape with a shared security and access infrastructure. Ultimately, it will work similar to the GSM environment where services are provided by a large number of service providers without forcing the users to change their interface or behaviour. Users will be able to switch off certain communication paths temporarily or route them to different media, for example incoming short messages may be routed to a voice mailbox residing on the PC or on a server. Outgoing email may be converted to voicemail for a user who does not own a PC or does not have access to a PC at the moment. Users or service providers may want to use the lowest-cost communication path to transfer large amounts of data, or may want to be alerted immediately by a short message when a certain event occurs.

The upcoming third generation of mobile devices that uses General Packet Radio Service (GPRS) or Universal Mobile Telecommunications System (UMTS)[5] will support these types of requirements, using packet-switched networks. Multiple quality-of-service options for delay, data rates and error rates are defined. Users will not be disrupted by short distortions on the communication channel but may stay online for a long period of time being charged only for the data actually transferred.

Location-based services

Location-based services exploit the ability of mobile phone systems to determine the position of the device by measuring signal run time from multiple transmitters to a receiver. The satellite-based global positioning system (GPS) may be used to locate the user with an accuracy of less than tens of meters at almost any place on earth. However, buildings, mountains, trees, and heavy rainfall may disrupt GPS signals. GSM operation may still be possible in some environments where GPS does not work, and vice versa. The ability to locate a caller is a strong requirement for handling of emergency calls, because the location of a mobile caller cannot be derived from the telephone extension as in a wire-line phone system. The US government has therefore enforced the introduction of emergency call location services. Caller location identification also enables all kinds of applications linking the Internet to the 'real' world, including roaming between wide area and local area networks. It also raises severe privacy issues when the user location is tracked without explicit user agreement. This problem can be addressed by a user function that allows explicit suppression of location identification, much like suppression of caller identification in GSM mobile phones.

1.2.2 Roaming environment

Advanced users will work with multiple devices, e.g. a multimedia PC for complex information-gathering, e-business, and office tasks; a TV set for entertainment and online shopping; and a Wireless Application Protocol (WAP) phone for mobile communication. Commuters will expect their cars to offer a personalized communication environment, and mobile workers may use a PDA during working hours. Private communication will be mostly through voice complemented, by email and short messages (SMS) (Figure 1.1). Mobile chat, virtual blackboards, auctioning, games, multicast messaging, and collaboration are some of the new communication patterns evolving in the mobile space.

Terrestrial wireless networks, satellite networks, and local area networks in offices, shops, and private homes provide access to the World Wide Web from any place and at any time. Pervasive computing devices will also be engaged in offline peer-to-peer communication or wireless networking. Users not only will roam between different mobile networks but will also use different devices and expect data and functions to be synchronized, hopefully in a totally transparent way, without much user intervention. The new, open environment must guarantee security and privacy in order to be accepted by a large user community. The GSM subscriber identity module (SIM), a secure smart card, provides a trusted

Figure 1.1

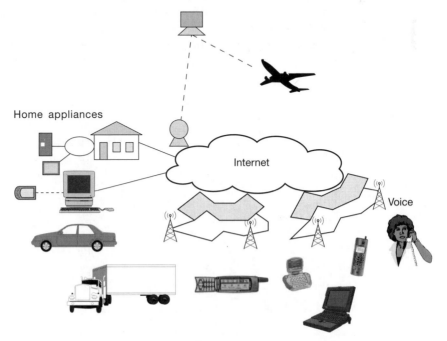

Pervasive communication scenario

computing environment for user identification and secret key storage. The SIM will be extended to enable security functions not only for the mobile service provider but also for other parties like financial institutions and enterprises, to secure their communication with their clients. This type of global security infrastructure is not available in the PC-oriented world today. However, the introduction of public key infrastructure in PC operating systems, secure Web protocols, and the legal endorsement of digital signatures will allow us to build secure systems by merging the Internet and wireless communication into a secure, pervasive computing infrastructure suited for mobile e-business.

1.2.3 Pervasive computing infrastructure

As long as personal devices like organizers and PDAs were isolated from networks, the communication and data exchange with other pervasive computing devices was only possible through proprietary methods within a line of products or from the devices to a PC using special software. In the pervasive world, millions of devices, subscriber identification modules, public land mobile networks (PLMN), public switched telephony networks (PSTN), gateways (e.g. from WAP and voice to Internet Protocol, IP), servers, and applications are interconnected. Last but not least, system management and billing systems must be integrated. Content providers, shops, market places, financial services, and enterprises use this infrastructure to offer their services to their clients (Figure 1.2).

Pervasive portals provide gateways to adapt the pervasive devices to the standard Internet protocols. They also deliver a variety of functions, such as personalization, mobile device management, security, and data

Figure 1.2

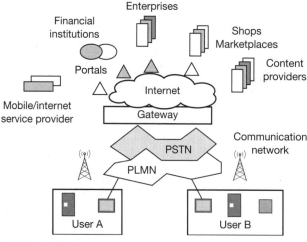

Mobile infrastructure

synchronization. Portals are also able to maintain stable application interfaces between applications and various different devices with rapidly changing features.

In the traditional telecommunications environment, governments restricted the access to the telecommunications market to create secure, integrated, reliable systems. Very often there was only one state-owned organization that serviced the entire country and was very hesitant to introduce new technology. However, this was the only way to ensure inter-operability and guaranteed access for users in the early days of telecommunication. In the new, deregulated communication world, multiple service providers are competing with lower rates and new functions and features based on new technology. However, interoperability and standardization are becoming crucial success factors for the entire industry. Techniques initially developed for the World Wide Web are applied to the communication sector to manage rapid evolution and interoperability. Industry committees are addressing standards issues in order to insure interoperability of their products and services. Nevertheless, standardization is still a rather slow and tedious process. Proprietary, local solutions promise to reduce time to market and to gain a competitive advantage. However, they are very often outperformed in function, performance, and price by standard solutions in a very short period of time due to the competitive environment of open markets and the economy of scale.

Two major technologies representing the two main roads to market are competing for the third generation (3G) of mobile systems.

- *GSM/UMTS* based on the harmonized 3G radio interface. This system is supported by major telecommunication standard organizations and by the Operator Harmonization Group (OHG). It provides worldwide roaming, and a smooth and compatible evolution path from existing GSM to UMTS, and supports WAP.
- *i-mode System* developed by NTT DoCoMo. This is a proprietary 3G system based on a high-speed, packet-switched network and IP. The system was developed in Japan and has now been introduced in Europe and the USA.

Whereas Europe and Asia have adopted the GSM/UMTS standard, mobile communication in the Americas is based mostly on Code Division Multiple Access (CDMA) and Time Division Multiple Access (TDMA) networks, although GSM networks are operational in the densely populated areas in the east and west. However, these networks represent less than 20% of the world market and are migrating to the mobile Internet on various paths. The strength of GSM/UMTS is certainly its support by major standards organizations, suppliers, and the large worldwide user base, whereas the strength of the i-mode system is its maturity, rich set of applications and initial affinity to Internet in respect to protocols and content representation. The i-mode system uses compact Hyper Text Markup Language (cHTML) instead of the Wireless Markup Language (WML) to ease migration from existing Internet applications to mobile applications. This strategy has worked out very well in Japan, where customers are offered a wide variety of services, with especial emphasis on entertainment.

Acceptance of WAP-based Internet services was hampered by the low data-transfer speed and low reliability of first-generation WAP systems. The introduction of high-speed packet-switched support through GPRS and UMTS will provide adequate service for 3G applications.

The evolution of pervasive computing devices with higher computing power and multimode radio-frequency (RF) circuitry will allow support for multiple communication protocols and content representations to accommodate different standards during a transition period.

1.2.4 Personalized services and the virtual pervasive home

The only use of things is to be applied to the service of persons[3]

R. H. Tawney

Pervasive computing is yet another step from the classical supply economy to a customer-driven economy[4]. Basic telephone and Internet services are transformed into highly customized and diversified products and services. Mobile users will expect services that will be easy to use and will deliver results within their expectation window of less than a few seconds. The personal phone directory of mobile phones, which allows calls to be placed much quicker than on a public phone, is an excellent example of an implementation meeting mobile users' expectations. They are not willing to enter large amounts of data using tiny keyboards or pens. They can't look up files or documents when they are using mobile devices. Only very special devices will have an ability to print on paper. Performance and process reliability must be much better than that provided by typical Web applications today. Users will demand highly personalized, easily usable services for browsing, content delivery, and transaction handling with minimum involvement in management of security, devices, and systems.

Therefore, offering typical Web applications on mobile devices is not a viable approach. Information must be condensed, hopefully presented automatically when needed, and adapted to the user's situation and device. Presentation and dialogs must be tailored to the small screen size and the limited time a mobile user is willing to spend. Mobile users also expect to work with their familiar interfaces, user profiles, applications, and data independent of device, location, and time. Users also want to control why, when, and how they are contacted. Flooding mobile users with advertising is certainly not a very good idea, whereas tailored services can create strong relationships between individuals and business.

A special infrastructure element, the 'virtual home', is required to support the following set of functions in a pervasive environment:

- Universal home address for users that is independent of device and location being used. It unifies, for example, phone numbers for voice and fax, addresses for email, messages, and devices.
- Secure system access, privacy (encryption), and endorsement of transactions.
- Personalization of devices, services, and communication channels.
- Server-based vault for personal and financial data, addresses, profiles, bookmarks, service directories (personal information management, payment services, etc.), and administrative data.

Typically, the virtual home will be implemented with a portal server. Users may use different virtual homes for private, business, or financial services. Today, mobile portals implement only part of the key functions or share functions with other systems, e.g. email systems. Without complete and well-managed virtual home functions, pervasive devices are difficult to use and cause major customer dissatisfaction in networked environments. Implementation is hampered not only by lack of standardized user interfaces but also by the lack of well-accepted function-distribution models in the pervasive computing space. These problems are very similar to the problems of the Internet a couple of years ago, and can be resolved by applying the Internet standardization model to the pervasive computing space.

1.3 The pervasive computing market

The pervasive computing market is a typical innovation market. The major driving force for initial growth in Europe and Asia is the basic mobile phone service, which provides high value to the consumer and is easy to use for anybody, whereas the driving force in USA is the extension of Internet services to the mobile space. New complementary products and services are introduced at a rapid pace, and are quickly adopted by industry and consumers. Markets are emerging in different countries with different speed and emphasis on specific products. New innovative products and services can cause major shifts in consumer spending. Therefore, the size and the structure of the market, as well as the growth within the next four to five years, are hard to predict. The number of mobile phone subscribers is probably one of the best indicators of market size and dynamics. At the end of the year 2000, about 600 million subscribers were using mobile phones. This number is estimated to grow to 1.3 billion in 2005 (Figure 1.3).

Figure 1.3

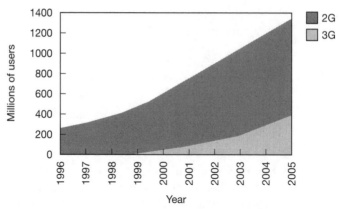

Predicted growth of mobile phone subscribers worldwide
Source: UMTS Forum[5]

In contrast to predictions for other new technologies, mobile phone sales have consistently outperformed most forecasts. The other major pervasive computing market segments are expected to grow at similar rates.

■ *Embedded systems* are typically not visible to the customer, and are delivered to the consumer with other products, such as automobiles, consumer electronics, and appliances.

■ *Consumer electronics* with pervasive computing elements, e.g. digital cameras or video recorders, electronic books, MP3 players/recorders with wireless modems, and direct Internet access.

■ *Hand-held computers* that are typically used as stand-alone devices with optional data transfer from or to a PC or the Internet via built-in modems, mobile phones, pagers, email stations, PDAs, and mobile PCs.

Overall, pervasive computing has grown into a market with a yearly volume of several hundred billion dollars. Growth is fuelled by a combination of new technologies and innovative services. The largest part of the revenue is coming from services rather than products. The mobile service providers have developed a business model supporting rapid change. The majority of devices are not sold but are leased to the customer. Thus, consumers are moving rapidly to state-of-the-art technology independent of the condition of the overall economy.

Mobile phone coverage is approaching 100% in leading mobile countries, such as Finland, Sweden, and Italy, and growing at double-digit rates in other countries. Mobile phone users are already outnumbering the Internet users in Europe and Japan (Figure 1.4).

The ability to access the Internet via a PC seems to influence the pervasive computing market. In Japan, typical users of the i-mode service access the Internet with their mobile phones more often than with PCs.

Figure 1.4

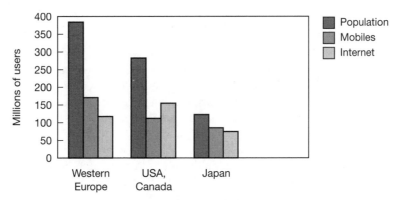

Mobile phone and Internet coverage

Source: UMTS Forum[5]

This is due in part to the high speed and reliability of i-mode's packet-switched third-generation communication system, but also to the limited offerings of PC-based Internet content in Japan – not surprisingly, given the fact that most of the Internet content is presented in English. The i-mode system presents content in Japanese language and is also the first system to offer attractive mobile entertainment services that are highly valued by Japanese customers.

Most Internet users in the USA prefer solutions that combine, for example, a PDA and a PC for Internet access, or offer pocket size email systems that exploit the excellent 'wired' Internet infrastructure and can also be supported by the current mobile infrastructure.

The market in Europe is dominated by GSM phone services that support roaming and seamless GSM service throughout Europe, which is a key requirement for travelling Europeans. Most of the European manufacturers of GSM equipment and terminals have participated in the GSM standards activities and have seized the GSM market.

The WAP Internet access service is not yet widely accepted by European consumers. Volume delivery of WAP-enabled phones began in 2000, and the adaptation rate is rather low (<5%) in most countries.[7] Early WAP services seem to lack attractive applications, and seem to be neither fast nor reliable enough for the busy mobile consumer. Very often, existing HTML-based applications were 'mapped' to WML without considering the very special requirements of mobile users. It can be expected that WAP services will become more popular with the introduction of GPRS packet-switched data service providing higher reliability and bandwidth. However, this must be combined with new and exciting services for professionals and consumers in order to win back disappointed early users. Therefore, voice services are still the major source of revenue for mobile service providers. However, all providers are looking for attractive applications to increase their revenue from value-added services.

1.4 m-Business

Pervasive computing will play a major role in e-business especially in the consumer space and in industries like automotive and transportation. Pervasive devices will be used not only to buy travel-related products and tickets or to exchange messages and email, but will be used in almost every stage of the e-business value chain to provide better and faster service (Figure 1.5).

Pervasive computing will be a key element in attracting new customers and maintaining customer relationships. Some industries, such as banking, have already been hit by the overwhelming demand of customers for timely information and the ability to initiate and check transactions anywhere and at any time. Key enablers for m-business are:

- attractive offerings for the mobile user community;
- easily usable and reliable infrastructure accessible by all parties involved in the business processes;
- security through identification, authentication, privacy, and non-repudiation;
- trusted environment;
- payment system supporting payments from a couple of cents to highly sophisticated high-valued transactions;
- Business models for e-business operations.

Most of the value generated will be indirect and will help to reduce process costs for existing and new business processes. The amount of direct revenue generated by sales to mobile consumers is hard to estimate because the market is in a very early stage and many assumptions must be made in respect to product offerings and user acceptance (Figure 1.6). Development of the m-business market will also depend on the development of overall Internet trade, which still lacks common legal and tax regulations.[6]

A study by the Boston Consulting Group[7] estimates the worldwide m-business market to grow to about $100 billion within the next three years. About 50 billion dollars of this revenue is assumed to flow to the

Figure 1.5

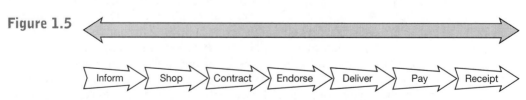

Mobile business interactions along typical value chain

Figure 1.6

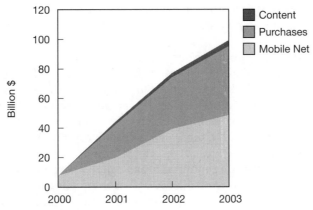

Worldwide m-business forecast

Source: UMTS Forum[5]

mobile service providers. Most purchases are assumed to be of rather low value, e.g. downloading music recordings, images, and games, and will create an estimated revenue of about 50 billion dollars. Only a very small percentage of m-business revenue will flow to content providers because consumers have adopted the Internet model and expect most services to be provided for free.

Revenue predictions at this early stage of m-business are based on early feedback from emerging markets. New product offerings, the quality of m-business support infrastructure, and mobile payment systems will impact heavily on the growth of m-business.

1.5 Conclusions and challenges

Pervasive computing is a new dimension of personal computing enabling communication and Internet services at any place and at any time for most of the population. It will impact our way of life as well as business processes in almost every industry. Pervasive computing is based on easy-to-use interfaces, applications, and the convergence of the following key technologies:

- very-large-scale integration of computer, communication, and consumer electronic circuits;
- wireless communication technology;
- consumer electronics and embedded controllers;
- Internet infrastructure;
- speech technology;

■ standardization, and cooperative Web-age global cooperation and system development.

Pervasive computing has created a highly competitive market worth hundreds of billions of dollars, with two-digit growth rates driven by innovation and customer demand. The majority of the revenue is related to mobile communication services. Value-added services based on the mobile infrastructure represent a significant emerging business opportunity.

Technology and business cooperations are required to shorten time to market and to minimize investments and operational cost. System design and implementation require a broad range of organization, business, engineering, and software skills. Adaptation of solutions to rapidly changing devices, communication protocols, and new standards must be possible without disruption. Adequate security for distribution of sensitive personal data, and execution of transactions in a highly distributed and open environment, must be integrated into the systems.

Therefore, in this book we describe not only pervasive technology, hardware, and software, but also the complete architecture of a pervasive computing system addressing all major areas of design.

1.6 The future

It is difficult to predict future evolution in a rapidly changing environment. However, there is a high probability that the following emerging trends and technologies will have a major impact on the market in the next five to ten years.

Almost every business process involving people will integrate pervasive computing into marketing and delivery channels. Highly personalized services, and the ability to control communication and services via easy-to-use interfaces, are key to gaining acceptance. Mobile communication and the Internet are converging into an overall mobile computing infrastructure with the next generation of the internet (IPv6[8]). Users will be able to connect to the Internet and invoke business functions at any place, much like mobile phone users can place a phone call today. Harmonization of business regulations, payment, and taxation systems, e.g. as addressed by the Global Business Dialogue on Electronic Commerce,[6] is a prerequisite for mobile business roaming. Web workflow architectures like Simple Object Access Protocol (SOAP), Universal Description, Discovery, and Integration (UDDI), and Transaction Authority Markup Language (XAML)[9] will play a key role in assembling flexible service offerings for the mobile space. Multiple user devices will be integrated into a seamless environment with advanced multimedia functions, including TV, on hand-held devices, much like on PCs today. Security and privacy will be guaranteed by extensive use of encryption and public key infrastructure. Most of the new functions will be introduced through new devices and updates to the infrastructure. Pervasive portals servicing millions of concurrent users will demand Web application servers and scalable server infrastructure with high performance and availability. Managing the rapid change in the pervasive computing space will be a major challenge for all participants.

References

1. Prasad, R., Mohr, W. and Konhäuser, W. (eds) (1999) *Third Generation Mobile Communication Systems*. Boston: Artech House.

2. Fromm, E. (1955) *The Sane Society*. Greenwich, CT: Holt, Rinehart & Winston.

3. Tawney, R.E. (1920) *The Acquisitive Society*. New York: Harcourt Brace.

4. Levine, R., Locke, C., Searls. D. and Weinberger, D. (1999) *The Cluetrain Manifesto – The End of Business as Usual*. Cambridge, MA: Perseus Books. http://www.cluetrain.com

5. UMTS Forum. 'Shaping the mobile multimedia future – an extended vision from the UMTS Forum'. http://www.umts-forum.org/reports/report10.pdf

6. Global Business Dialogue on Electronic Commerce. http://www.gbde.org

7. The Boston Consulting Group. 'Despite initial frustration, mobile device users are confident about future'. http://www.bcg.com/

8. IPv6 Forum. http://www.ipv6forum.com

9. Transaction Authority Markup Language. http://www.xaml.org

<table>
<tr><td>**2**</td><td># Application examples</td></tr>
</table>

There are already a lot of different pervasive devices available on the market, ranging from PDAs to WAP phones. Now the question is how to effectively use these devices in business applications. In this chapter, we explore how pervasive computing devices enable exciting new ways of conducting business. We present a series of real-life application examples showing how businesses can benefit from pervasive computing. The examples will give you an overview of what is possible and what is required, and should inspire you to think of tomorrow's applications today.

2.1 Retail

The retail area has seen a long development driven by the quest for faster and cheaper ways to bring goods to the consumer. Today, the consumer can select from large varieties of products, and can just buy them from stores, catalogs, and virtual shopping malls on the Internet.

Mobile devices will further improve processes for the consumers and the retail industry. Mobile computers equipped with barcode readers are used to track products during manufacturing, transportation, and in the supermarket. Smaller devices, better usability, and wireless network access will make them more adequate for the requirements of modern businesses. Standardization of the software-development platforms for these devices will help make them cheaper and ultimately more flexible.

Consumers can currently use their computers, TV sets, or mobile devices to select and order products. Tomorrow's shopping list will reside on a PDA, and may even receive input through other pervasive devices in the household. When completed, the list can be sent to the supermarket, and the purchase is delivered or prepared for pick-up at a time convenient for the consumer. The availability of the orders in electronic format enables faster processing of the data. Finally, data-mining technologies allow a better understanding of the consumer's behaviour and enable direct marketing.

In 1998, Safeway UK and IBM teamed up to deliver a first-of-a-kind personalized remote shopping service.[1, 2] Selected consumers were able to use hand-held devices to build their shopping list from an electronic product catalog. A preselection of products built from their past purchases simplified the creation of the electronic order. Figure 2.1 shows a screenshot of the Safeway application displaying products from one category.

The use of devices fitted with barcode readers enabled consumers to self-scan products at home or in store. The electronic order was then transmitted to the supermarket's server via a modem. Together with updates for the product catalog, the customers received feedback in the form of personalized offers. Once the order was received, the goods were collated and packed ready for collection. An overview of the system architecture is given in Figure 2.2.

Figure 2.1

The Safeway personalized remote shopping service
Picture courtesy of IBM Corp.

Figure 2.2

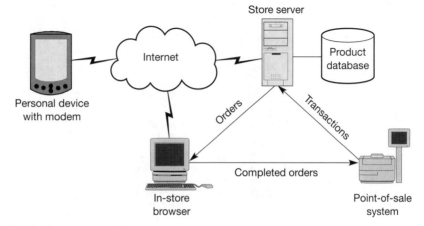

The Safeway scenario

Another example for the use of hand-held devices in retail is the PlanetRx Online shop.[3] PlanetRx specializes in selling drugs online. Products can be listed and ordered from their website. As an additional feature, registered users can access the site from their Palm-connected organizer. The software is installed as an extension of the standard synchronization process, of the PDA. During the synchronization process the data stored on the device is updated, and orders are transmitted back to PlanetRx. Users can reorder products from their shopping list, or order from a weekly specials section. The complete PlanetRx scenario is shown in Figure 2.3.

2.2 Airline check-in and booking

For several years now, airlines have been using the Internet to publish flight schedules, let customers check their frequent-flyer accounts and claim airmiles, and allow travelers to buy tickets directly from the airline instead of booking through a travel agency. Their presence on the Internet establishes a more direct relationship between the customer and the airline. When visiting an airline's website, travelers are likely to see advertisements and special offers, and may book flights that they would not have booked otherwise.

Notably, however, by being present on the Internet, only people who are reasonably computer literate and have access to a PC can be reached. Now airlines are becoming aware of the possibilities that mobile computing offers, and have started developing new applications that enable customers to interact with airline systems via their mobile devices. With the increasing penetration of WAP phones, it will soon be possible to provide many

Figure 2.3

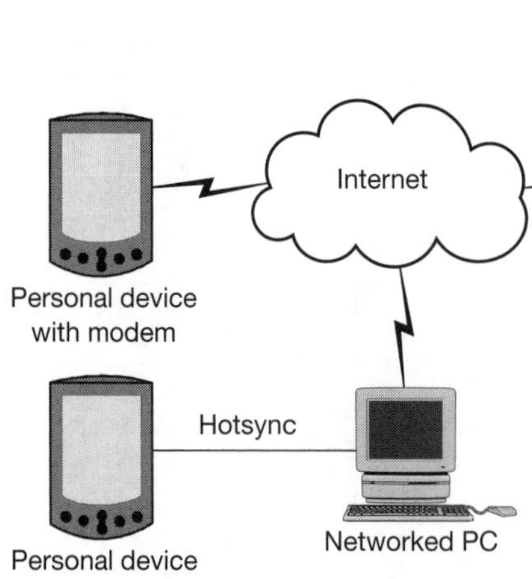

The PlanetRx scenario

travelers with a direct, permanently available connection to airline reservation systems. In the remainder of this section, we present two examples of mobile applications in this area: check-in and booking via WAP phones.

Usually, airlines require passengers to check in about one hour before the departure of the flight. This is so the airline can assign seats to people on the waiting list if other passengers do not show up. Early check-in results in waiting times for passengers, which is especially inconvenient for the most valuable customers of airlines – the business travelers and frequent flyers – who often travel business or first class.

By allowing check-in via WAP phones, airlines can provide increased convenience for their most important clientele. Instead of leaving for the airport early to check in, the traveller can switch on his or her WAP phone, obtain the list of booked flights, and check in for one of them with a single button click.

Although flight booking seems difficult and inconvenient from a WAP phone, it can be implemented in a way that provides good usability to travellers. Personalization can be used to allow users to book a flight with a short sequence of interactions. Many frequent flyers often travel to the same destinations, using the same flights again and again. Thus, using appropriate personalization data for a user, the system can make an intelligent preselection of flights that are of particular interest to the user, so that travellers can select their flights from a small list of relevant options. The data required for personalization might be specified explicitly by the user, or might be obtained from the system by analyzing the previous bookings.

To provide the kind of services described above, WAP phones have to be connected to airline back-end systems via appropriate gateways and WAP-enabled applications. Figure 2.4 shows how access via WAP phones can be added to the already existing access paths to the services of an airline.

Typically, airlines allow customers either to call a customer service representative or to log in to the airline's Web applications using the PC. Some airlines also have systems in place that allow customers to call automatic voice-driven applications. To add WAP access to existing systems, the WAP-enabled applications must be deployed on application servers and must be accessible via WAP gateways in order to be accessible from the customer's WAP phone.

The introduction of WAP technology to provide an additional access path to airline services has several advantages. Customers can effectively and quickly perform tasks such as check-in or reservations anywhere and at any time without waiting until a customer service representative becomes available. In addition, WAP applications can be implemented with little effort, and require little computing capacity. As acceptance of the new access method increases, it also reduces the number of calls to customer service representatives, saving the costs of call centers.

Figure 2.4

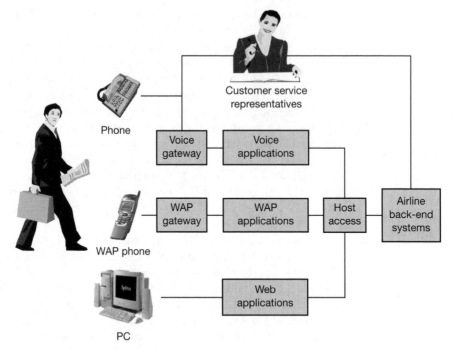

Adding WAP access to airline systems

2.3 Sales force automation

Until now, mobile workers relied on their portable computers in order to access and process data on the road. The availability of faster modems, and even wireless modems, has enabled them to travel and still have access to enterprise data. The complexity of the PC, however, still requires these workers to be trained in using such systems.

The availability of smaller portable devices with a relatively simple interface and the same connectivity provides a new alternative to this scenario. Not only are these devices much easier to use, but they are also much cheaper. This allows an enterprise to give out more devices to more users than before. PDAs enable the mobile professional to use the phone book and calendar while working out of the office, and to stay in contact via email. They are also used to access mission-critical data, such as contracts, technical descriptions, small databases, and graphics anywhere and at any time.

When used with a browser, PDAs can access the Internet, just like the PC. However, the quality of the rendering is limited by the capabilities of the device. Nevertheless, there is great value even in access to dedicated content from the enterprise network, or simple applications such as maps and travel information.

When used with a wireless connection, PDAs enable mobile workers to stay in touch with their company all the time. Work schedules and feedback collected during work can be exchanged with the enterprise network. This can be used to control the delivery of goods, update work assignments, submit orders, and even enter billing information while on the road.

2.4 Healthcare

In healthcare, there is little room for new and complicated devices unless they have an immediate benefit for the patient. Modern medicine already depends on a wide range of computerized devices, sensors, and actors. Clinical professionals have to learn not only about new methods but also about how to use new devices. Nevertheless, many clinical professionals are now using hand-held devices. The users of these devices have to learn new interfaces that are quite different to those of a PC. The new devices also fall behind PCs in terms of screen size and ease of data entry. Also, they get through several batteries when used intensively every day.

Despite all these problems, PDAs have found their way into modern healthcare. Because of their size and mobility, they are able to integrate into fast-paced hospital work as well as into a doctor's daily routine. They have turned out to be tremendously helpful in delivering up-to-the-minute patient data and medical information. Access to laboratory results and surgical reports, as well as ordering processes and physician directory look-up, can be improved by the use of PDAs.[4]

Healthcare applications are probably the most sensitive in respect to security. Integrity of data and privacy must be assured through proper hardware, software and system design. Patients must be identified correctly at all levels of treatment and medical record keeping. Patient and clinical data must be exchangeable and accessible wherever needed, but access must be restricted to professionals with the need to know. International healthcare organizations have standardized almost all data elements and structures required for documentation and data exchange between healthcare institutions, which is an excellent base for real mobile information.

Modern healthcare systems are now using smart cards for patients and professionals.[5,6] Patient cards used for identification and administrative data, e.g. Germany has issued more than 80 million chip cards to the entire population in order to simplify all administration processes. Professional cards are used for authentication of professionals and to control access to critical data and systems. The G8 Health Card specification defines a public-key smart card architecture for an international health professional card to be used by doctors, pharmacists, administrators, nurses, and other healthcare professionals.[7] Doctors and nurses using

PDA-type devices with a smart card reader can access medical records, treatment plans, and administrative data at any time and in any place. Patients can securely transfer critical monitoring data to their doctor. The ability to work offline and to synchronize data securely on the PDA with data on the server is key in the healthcare environment, e.g. in critical areas of hospitals, the use of wireless communication is not allowed to avoid interference with electronic equipment. PDAs are also ideal to assist healthcare professionals to manage their personal work schedules, drug and International Classification of Diseases (ICD) code lists, prescriptions, treatment plans, and other critical information.[8]

The future will bring faster, smaller, and better devices that will lower the acceptance hurdle for use in healthcare environments even further. With integration into hospital communication networks, improved user interfaces, and better data input, the next generation of devices will convince professionals to replace traditional pen and paper by mobile devices. The benefit for all will then be fast and accurate access to patient data through personal mobile devices.

2.5 Tracking

The use of barcodes has revolutionized processes in many industry segments. They enable the fast and accurate identification of goods during transportation. Today they are visible on almost all products. The most common format is the one-dimensional barcode that encodes only a few characters' worth of information and is mostly used for universal product numbers. The two-dimensional bar code format allows several hundred characters of information to be stored, and eventually will even replace stamps.

The future will bring cheaper and smaller radio frequency (RF) tags that can be attached to goods such as labels. In contrast to the passive barcodes that are read optically, they will be read electronically and from larger distances. Figure 2.5 shows an RF tag consisting of a chip and an antenna enclosed in transparent plastic sheet less than a millimeter thick. Being more tolerant to environmental conditions, they will enable the tracking of more goods in more places than before. Advances in integration technology will add limited processing capability to these tags. Tomorrow's overnight parcel services will be able to determine the exact location of a parcel not just because it was registered at some place on its way but because it knows about its destination and even gives feedback in case it is routed wrongly.

An interesting example is tracking luggage in the airline industry. As tags get cheaper, it will become possible to attach to each piece of luggage a small tag that can be detected at certain points on the journey. This will enable airlines to track individual pieces of luggage from check-in to bag-

Figure 2.5

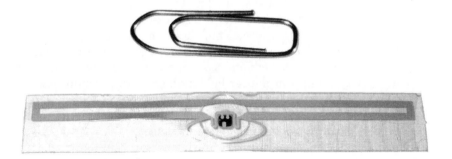

RF tag embedded in a clear plastic strip

gage claim. If any luggage accidentally gets separated from the passenger, the airline can immediately find out the current location of the luggage and arrange reconciliation.

2.6 Car information systems

Car manufacturers are becoming increasingly interested in using pervasive computing technology. A current top-of-the-range car has more than 30 different microprocessors built in, which communicate with each other over a bus. In the future, these processors will be able to not only communicate with each other, but also with the outside world. This will increase the value of the automotive system and allow for completely new services. Many car manufactures have already shown prototypes demonstrating this ability (e.g. General Motors, Daimler-Chrysler, and PSA). Analysts predict that by 2006, nearly 50% of all new cars (and 90% of all luxury vehicles) will have some kind of Internet access capability.

To connect the car with the outside world a gateway is required. The Open Service Gateway Initiative (OSGi) is an industry group that defines and promotes an open standard for networked consumer and business devices connected to the Internet. The first version of OSGi[9] is based on Java and Jini technology, and provides downloading of software, application lifecycle management, gateway security, attached device access, resource management, and remote administration. OSGi is compatible with transport systems such as Bluetooth, HAVi, HomePNA, HomeRF, USB, and WAP. It therefore provides all services needed for connecting cars to the outside world.

Figure 2.6 shows how an OSGi gateway can be integrated into a car information system. The OSGi gateway can receive and send data via a wireless connection to the back-end system. In the car, the gateway is connected to the car bus (e.g. an optical bus). It has access to the car electronics and all car sensors, and can therefore transmit all relevant car data. The back-end system can perform an analysis based on those data and inform the car holder about critical conditions. Over the gateway, the car entertainment system can receive and initiate phone calls, connect to the Internet, and access multimedia information, such as route planning, traffic announcements, and videos.

Another industry initiative with similar goals is the Internet Home Alliance, which was formed in October 2000; members include Cisco Systems, Best Buy, General Motors, Panasonic, and Sun Microsystems. The alliance's goal is to bridge data communications, telecommunications, entertainment distribution, and home-control services within the home and cars. The Internet Home Alliance tries to supplement the OSGi standard.

Connecting cars to the outside world has benefits for car owners and manufactures. Car owners can use new services such as email, Internet access, making phone calls, or automated emergency calls in case of an

Figure 2.6

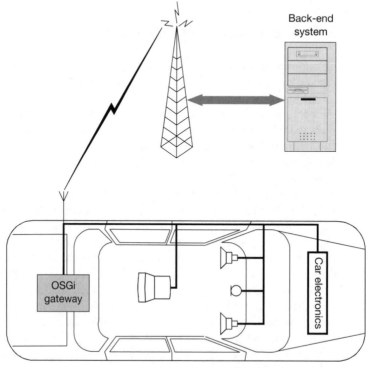

OSGi gateway integrated into a car information system

accident. With connected cars, the car manufactures now have the ability to get real feedback about the quality of their products. They can monitor all critical car data, such as oil temperature, inform the drivers about recalls, download software updates to the car, and more. Repair centers can receive notifications from the car information system about defects, and can order the required parts in advance. When introducing car information systems, special attention must be given to the areas of security, software updates, and management. All three areas are now being studied by the automotive industry, as they present the same problems that must be solved for all pervasive computing devices. Many solutions available for pervasive computing devices such as mobile phones or PDAs can be applied to car information systems and vice versa.

2.7 Email access via WAP and voice

Accessing email and calendars is one of the most attractive applications of mobile devices. Voice mailboxes and SMS provide rudimentary mail services in the GSM environment. However, these services are not integrated with PC email, are limited to rather short messages, and cannot be stored and retrieved like regular email. Many mobile users would like to access their email at any time and at any place. A WAP-enabled mobile phone is well suited to accessing typical email files of a few kilobytes and to sending short responses, but WAP mail services must be tailored to the small bandwidth, small display, and limited key entry capabilities to be really useful. Although WAP phones with larger screens are already offered, small displays will dominate the market for the next years to come. Therefore, users should be able to define classes of mail to be sent to the mobile device. Mail systems like Lotus Notes and Microsoft Outlook support this type of selection through profiles and mail agents. Typically, the selected mail is stored in a folder for further processing. The content of this folder is then used as input to the WAP mail services.

An overview list of the mail should be presented to the user for selection before larger amounts of data are sent to the WAP phone in order to reduce data transfer. The content of the mail must be filtered, e.g. large attachments should be removed, and redundant text such as openings and closures should be condensed. The user should be able to mark mail as read or to delete mail, just as in standard mail systems.

Text-to-speech technology can be used to read email to customers on the move. The amount of speech that can be presented to a user is limited. Therefore, selection and filtering of email must be used to create an email system for voice, much like for WAP. Figure 2.7 shows a typical email system supporting WAP and voice access.

WAP mobile phones access the intranet of the mobile email service provider via a WAP gateway. A mobile email server hosts the application,

Figure 2.7

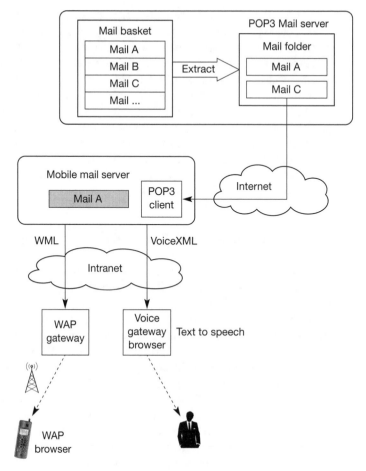

WAP and voice email service

creates WML output, and handles the incoming Hyper Text Transfer Protocol (HTTP) requests. It interfaces with the POP3 mail server where the original email is residing through a POP3 client.

A typical WAP email session involves the following steps:

1. The user accesses a mobile email server using a WAP profile and a start-page URL.
2. The mobile email server verifies whether the user is registered by checking the phone number and/or user identification and mobile password.

3. The user requests email service and provides the POP3 password for access to the POP3 mail server. The mobile email server verifies the address of the server and user identification in the user profile.

4. The server accesses a POP3 mail server on behalf of the user, and extracts the mail files for the user. A mail list is created, converted to WML, and sent to the WAP phone user for selection.

5. The user selects a mail file and sends a display request to the mobile email server.

6. The email server converts the email file to WML and forwards it to the WAP phone for display.

7. The user reads the email with a WAP browser.

8. The user responds with a request for more mail, deletion of mail, or reply.

Much the same steps are required for email access via voice. Users dial in to the voice gateway. Authentication is typically implemented using a customer identification number and a personal identification number, because numbers can easily be entered with a standard phone keypad. Additional checking of the phone number is recommended for mobile phone users. For convenience, the POP3 password will probably also be stored on the mobile email server. VoiceXML data is transmitted to the voice gateway, which hosts a voice browser and a text-to-speech engine for text rendering.

The mobile email server must be a trusted component because it has access to passwords as well as user mail. Enterprises or mobile service providers may install the POP3 server and mobile email server together in their intranet to avoid proliferation of passwords and sensitive mail.

References

1. ACM TechNews (2000). 'Easi-Order'.
   http://www.acm.org/technews/articles/2000-2/0322w.html#item12

2. IBM. 'IBM and Safeway create enjoyable grocery shopping experience'.
   http://www.ibm.com/pvc/industry_solutions/pdf/safeway.pdf

3. PlanetRx.
   http://www-3.ibm.com/pvc/industry_solutions/pdf/planetrx.pdf

4. handheldmed. http://www.handheldmed.com

5. Hartmann, G., Henn, H., Horster, P., Welsch, M. and Witzel, M. (1996) *Security Scheme for Hybrid Opto-Smart-Health-Card*; Proc. Toward an Electronic Patient Record '96, May, 1996.

6. The Slovenia health card system. http://www.zzzs.si/kzz/ang

7. CEN/TC 251/PT37. 'Secure user identification for healthcare – strong authentication using microprocessor cards (SEC-ID/CARDS)'. http://129.142.8.149/ds/it/d21system/12510399.htm

8. Robinson, T. 'Wireless software lets doctors write prescriptions on handhelds'. MicroTimes.com. http://microtimes.com/210/infrobinson210p.html

9. OSGi Service Gateway Specification 1.0 (May, 2000). http://www.osgi.org

3 Device technology

This chapter gives an overview of the rapidly evolving technologies that influence the evolution of mobile devices. The key technologies are presented in three parts. The first part describes the advances in hardware technologies. The second part presents the key software technologies used for the human–machine interaction. The third part gives an introduction to some of the operating systems and Java platforms available for PDAs today. A brief discussion of each technology is given and followed by an outlook onto the future direction.

3.1 Hardware

There is a limit to the size of mobile devices that is imposed by the need to input and output data. The size of the input and output components, such as the keyboard and the liquid crystal display (LCD), influences the total size of a mobile device. While both are integrated into the same package, we cannot expect them to become any smaller than mobile phones are today. Once separated, the advances in integration will deliver even smaller devices. The display may be worn like a wristwatch or a head-mounted display. In the future, alternatives to the keyboard as the main input technology will appear. The devices might not even be visible any more because they will be integrated into the fabric of our clothes or hidden in glasses, pens, or jewellery.

3.1.1 Batteries

The battery technology has developed at a much slower rate than the other technologies presented here. Furthermore, most advances were immediately negated by increased power consumption from faster processors. Until recently, the nickel-cadmium (NiCad) cell was the state of the art of rechargeable batteries. These batteries were heavy and had a tendency to lose capacity through the so-called memory effect. Newer technologies, such as nickel–metal hydride (NiMH), delivered better capacity with less weight and environmentally friendlier components.

Today, lithium ion (Li ion) batteries can be found in all sorts of electronic equipment. Compared with their predecessors, these batteries are lighter and have better energy density, resulting in more power delivered by a battery with the same size. Figure 3.1 shows the various types of battery used for mobile phones.

As a result, the weight of a NiCad battery for a five-year-old mobile phone is often higher than the total weight of a modern mobile phone, including the Li ion battery. While the latter does have a lower capacity, it still offers longer talk time because of the reduced power requirements of modern devices. Table 3.1 gives an estimate of the expected standby and talk time for a mobile phone when used with typical batteries available today. The data is taken from the specification of three batteries of comparable size.

The latest in battery technology is the emergence of lithium polymer cells, which use a gel material for the electrolyte. The batteries are made from a few thin and flexible layers, and do not require a leak-proof casing. This means the batteries can be made in almost any shape or size.

Figure 3.1

NiCad, NiMH, and Li ion batteries for mobile phones (top to bottom)

Table 3.1 **Expected lifetime for NiCad, NiMH, and Li ion batteries**

Chemistry	Standby time (h)	Talk time (m)
NiCad	12–27	85–160
NiMH	16–37	110–210
Li ion	21–50	170–225

3.1.2 Displays

LCDs are already replacing the bulky cathode ray tubes of the past. The advances in manufacturing make them larger and more readable than before, and the dramatic weight, size, and power consumption benefits of LCD technology outweigh their relatively high cost. Today's PDAs usually feature dual-scan (DSTN) displays that control individual display elements via passive matrix addressing. This technology consumes considerably less power than the thin-film transistor (TFT) active matrix technology. This latter technology is more expensive, but is capable of significantly superior display performance and thus is generally used in portable computers.

Better and thinner displays will be available in the future based on the light-emitting organic diode (OLED) or light-emitting polymer (LEP) technologies. OLED technology was invented about 15 years ago; it only recently became commercially attractive when the initial problems with the expected life and efficiency were solved. Instead of crystalline semiconductor material, organic compounds are used. The simplified manufacturing process of smaller structures and a rich selection of organic compounds enable OLEDs to be built in almost any size and colour. This will eventually allow manufacturers to create extremely thin displays that are flexible enough to be bent and shaped as required.

Other new display technologies, such as chip-on-glass (CoG) and liquid-crystal-on-glass (LCoG), integrate the picture elements with transistors on a layer of glass. This allows manufacturing of extremely small displays, with a pixel size of only 10 micrometers. In contrast to regular small displays like those on the back of a camcorder, the microdisplays usually require some form of magnification. They can be found, for example, in projection systems and in head-mounted displays used with wearable computers.

3.1.3 Memory

Memory is becoming cheaper, while the demand from applications is growing. Development is driven in part by smart phones, digital cameras, MP3 players and PDAs. For these mobile devices, the currently available technologies and their associated costs have reached a point where it is now feasible to integrate several megabytes of memory into a mobile device with an acceptable form factor.

On PCs, permanent data can be stored on hard disk drives. For mobile devices, this is often not an option because neither the space nor the power supply is available. Recently, extremely small removable disk drives like the IBM Microdrive shown in Figure 3.2 became available. Their capacity ranges between 340 MB and 1 GB, and is sufficient to store, for example, several hundred pictures when used in a digital camera.

Figure 3.2

The IBM Microdrive with 340 MB capacity

Other devices such as smart phones and PDAs store their operating system code and application data in non-volatile Flash memory and battery-backed random-access memory (RAM) instead. These semiconductor-based technologies require less power and offer faster access than disk drives. The typical capacity of built-in memory in mobile devices ranges from 2 to 16 MB. Expansion slots allow additional memory modules to be plugged into the device, which in turn allow data exchange and replace removable media such as diskettes and CD-ROM for a PC.

If a combination of Flash and low-power Static random-access memory (SRAM) memory is used, only frequently changed data is kept in SRAM. The advantages of SRAM over dynamic random-access memory (DRAM) are a simpler addressing scheme and the lack of refresh cycles. Newer uni-transistor random-access memory (Ut-RAM) tries to combine both technologies on a single die, and so delivers a higher memory capacity on smaller chips with comparably less power required. Another trend is the combination of magnetic and semiconductor memory in the magneto-resistive random access memory (MRAM) and ferroelectric random-access memory FRAM) technologies. The goal is to create a non-volatile memory with a behavior similar to that of static RAM. Because the typical refresh cycles of dynamic RAM are missing, they require very little power. This allows a single type of memory to be used in mobile devices such as PDAs and mobile phones, and replaces the common combinations of volatile and non-volatile memory in use today.

3.1.4 Processors

During the last couple of years, the clock rate of microprocessors and the processing power available from them has increased steadily. Rapid improvements in the CMOS manufacturing process have created ever-smaller structures and delivered higher and higher numbers of transistors per chip. At the same time, the processor core voltage was lowered from the industry standard 3.3 V in 1995 to 1.35 V in 2000. This means lower heat emissions, which in turn paves the way for new improvements like larger on-die caches. This, together with advances in packaging technologies, delivers the modern Central Processing Units (CPUs) found in mobile computers and PDAs today.

Intel's SpeedStep technology

Recent processors include improvements in power management. These processors are capable of changing their internal clock frequencies and core voltage to adapt to changes in power supply. Newer designs are even capable of switching parts of the CPU on or off depending on whether the current calculations require them to be available. One such design is the SpeedStep technology from Intel. While the system is connected to an external power supply, the full clock rate and core voltage are available to the processor, resulting in the maximum performance. When running on batteries, the clock rate and core voltage of the processor are reduced, resulting in significant power savings. The transition between both modes is very fast and completely transparent to the user.

The Crusoe processor

The latest in power-conservation technology is an attempt to reduce the total number of transistors, and to replace most of their functionality by software. The software dynamically translates the original instructions of the operating system and application software into another instruction set for the processor. Through the savings in the number of logic transistors, these processors promise to deliver the same or better performance than traditional CPUs while consuming considerably less power. The Crusoe processor by Transmeta is an example of such a design (Figure 3.3).

The Crusoe processor consists mostly of software. The relatively small processor core is designed as a 128-bit very long instruction word (VLIW) processor capable of executing up to four operations per cycle. The code morphing software on top of that emulates an ×86-compatible processor.

Figure 3.3

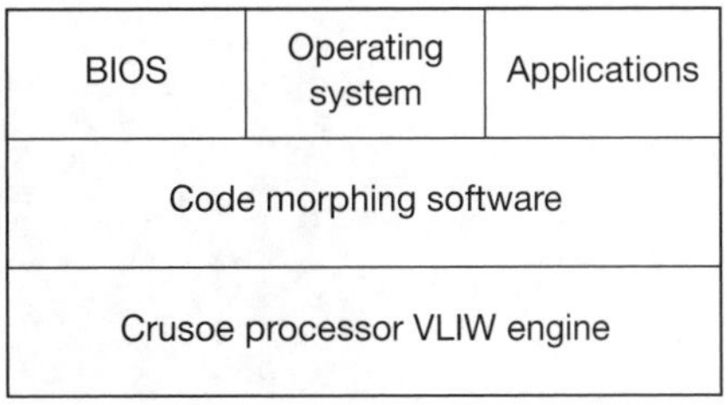

BIOS	Operating system	Applications
Code morphing software		
Crusoe processor VLIW engine		

The Crusoe code morphing software

In theory, this could be any other processor. During the boot cycle, the Crusoe processor loads its software into a section of the main memory. Frequently used code parts are optimized during run-time and kept in a separate cache. A technology called LongRun promises to reduce the power consumption even more by reducing the processor's voltage on the fly when the processor is idle.

The big advantage of this approach is that the Crusoe processor can be used to emulate almost any other processor and uses only a few watts, even with high clock rates. The disadvantage is the high memory requirements of the code morphing software.

3.2 Human–machine interfaces

Like their PC predecessors, many mobile devices also use keyboards and displays to interface with their users. However, these are usually much smaller and specialized for the application and the form factor of particular devices. Phones, for example, tend to have only number keys, plus a few extra keys for the built-in menus. This is because the size of the device is important and because users enter less text than on a PC. Other devices try to limit the number of mechanical keys to an absolute minimum, using them only to trigger the most important applications and for menu navigation. An example is the PDA. Finally, there are devices that have no means of display or keyboard whatsoever. These so-called headless devices are most often used as controllers and interface only to other devices.

3.2.1 Navigation

In order to operate applications in mobile devices, the user navigates through a menu structure, often using special navigation keys. An example is the integrated cursor key that delivers signals for all four directions by pressing or moving it up, down, left, or right.

Figure 3.4

The Navi Roller on a Nokia 7110 phone

Buttons that can be operated with the thumb while holding the device are especially suited for selecting entries from a menu list. These buttons can usually be turned or pressed. For each step in one direction, the menu navigation selects and highlights one of the entries. The entry is selected by pressing the button. To further improve the usability, the buttons can deliver haptic feedback to the user. Examples are the Navi Roller from Nokia (Figure 3.4) and the JogDial from Sony (Figure 3.5). Both are used in current-generation mobile phones to simplify navigation through the built-in applications.

3.2.2 Haptic interfaces

The programmable rotating actuator with haptic feedback is available from VDO.[1] It is basically a rotating control with force-feedback and a push button integrated into one. Sensors detect the position of the knob and an integrated motor produces feedback of torque when rotated. The way in which the motor responds when turning the knob is programmable. Haptic marks define positions of specific feedback force changes. Figure 3.6 shows a mechanical model for the haptic device to illustrate four different feedback characteristics.

When reaching a haptic mark, the user feels a resistance generated by the motor against the turning direction. This force increases until a specific position is reached. When the knob passes that position, the force gets smaller again. This can be used to create the impression of a knob that can be put into a programmable number of positions. It allows a single knob to be used for navigating through a menu structure where each menu choice is represented by one position.

When used in a car, the knob helps the driver to feel the actual selection and to change it without even looking at the control. The programmability of the knob allows to be used it to control several settings with a different number of options through the same interface.

Figure 3.5

The JogDial on a Sony CMD CD5 phone

Figure 3.6

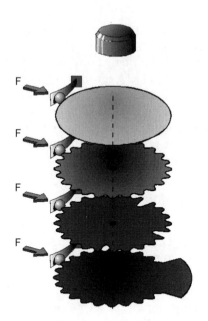

Haptic device model
Courtesy of VDO

3.2.3 Keyboards

Depending on the size of the mobile device, keyboards offer either the full set of keys or a limited set of keys for data input. Adding a full keyboard with a typewriter layout to a mobile device inevitably makes these devices larger. On the other hand, limiting the number of keys will automatically make the operation of the device more complex. Sometimes keyboards cannot be used at all because the form factor of the device simply does not offer the space for it, or the device is used in environmental conditions where a keyboard wouldn't work. Therefore, some devices completely omit keyboards in favour of other input technologies, such as handwriting or voice recognition.

On-screen keyboards

Devices with a reasonably large touch-sensitive display often make a compromise by replacing the mechanical keyboard with a virtual on-screen keyboard. This does not allow touch typing but still offers a convenient method for text entry. Numbers and special characters can be entered after switching into another mode, which alters the keyboard layout accordingly. Figure 3.7 shows the on-screen keyboard of a Palm PDA.

Figure 3.7

The Palm on-screen keyboard

Fitaly

Special keyboard layouts other than the traditional QWERTY typewriter layout may be used to speed up text input. The Fitaly keyboard,[2] for example, arranges the letters based on their individual frequency and the probability of transitions in the English language. The name is derived from the order of letters in one of the top rows of the layout, just as for the QWERTY layout (Figure 3.8). The arrangement of the letters for the Fitaly keyboard is optimized to keep the travel distance of the stylus during text input as short as possible. The letters 'i', 't', 'a', 'l', 'n', 'e', 'd', 'o', 'r', and 's' in the three center rows together with the space bar represent 73% of the keys used for normal English text. Adding the letters 'c', 'h', 'u', and 'm' brings this number to 84%. Remaining keys are never more than two positions away from the central area, and each key is placed near the keys it is most likely to follow in English text.

Figure 3.8

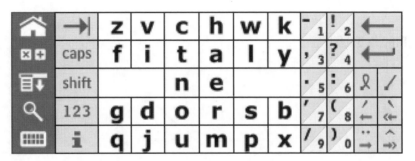

The Fitaly keyboard layout

Courtesy of Fitaly

The Fitaly keyboard can be displayed like an on-screen keyboard (Figure 3.9). On the Palm and many other PDAs, where a separate input area for character recognition exists, it can also be attached to it in the form of a small overlay. This avoids losing precious display space of the application.

The Fitaly keyboard supports all 220 printable characters of the ANSI/ISO Latin-1 character set. Some less frequent characters are available by preceding the character with a special modification symbol. A technique known as sliding can be used to reach accents or umlauts. Instead of lifting the stylus after tapping a character, it is moved out of the character field in one specific direction that is suggested by the direction of the desired accent. This has been naturally extended to also work for diacritical marks (Figure 3.10).

Sliding can also be used to enter a number without changing the keyboard mode. Each of the ten symbols to the right of the main area produces a digit if the stylus is moved out of the field before lifting.

Figure 3.9

The Fitaly on-screen keyboard on a Palm

Figure 3.10

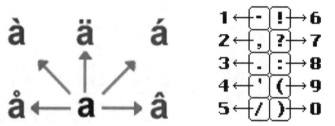

Inputting accented letters and numbers on the Fitaly keyboard

Courtesy of Fitaly

Tegic T9

Several technologies strive to make the best use of a limited keyboard for text input. Perhaps the most popular one is the use of number keys for text input. Each number key is associated with a few letters of the alphabet. To enter words, a sequence of number keys is pressed with short pauses inserted between letters where necessary. To determine the exact letter, the number key has to be pressed several times. For example, the letters 'A', 'B' and 'C' are associated with the '2' key on the number pad of a phone. The '2' key has to be pressed once for 'A', twice for 'B' and three times for 'C'.

The T9 input system from Tegic[3] reduces the number of keystrokes by letting the user press each number key only once and working out later which of the several associated letters was meant. The software does this based on the preceding letters and with the help of linguistic rules derived from a dictionary. Ambiguities, such as the words 'Snow' and 'Pony', both represented by the same key sequence, are be resolved by prompting the user for assistance. This input system is already available on mobile phones and can be used for text-entry on PDAs. Figure 3.11 shows the text-entry process with the T9 keyboard displayed in the memo editor for a Palm device.

Octave

Another approach to enter text without a real or on-screen keyboard is used by Octave from e-acute.[4] Octave maps each letter of the alphabet to one of eight unique strokes. The strokes are based on a common characteristic part of the letters they represent and are located around the tips

Figure 3.11

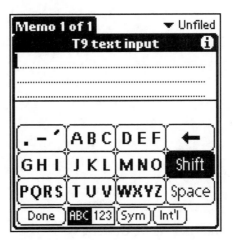

The T9 text input on the Palm

of a star-shaped pattern (Figure 3.12). On devices with a touch-sensitive display, a cut-out template is used to guide movement of the stylus into these eight points, each representing three or four letters of the alphabet.

Four special areas at the top, bottom, and sides outside the star are used to control the text-input process. The lower area, for example, switches into command mode, where special commands are available to insert the current date, change the language dictionary, or add a new word to the dictionary. Simple gestures within the inner area of the star are used to insert spaces or delete the last character.

During text entry, the stylus is moved from one position to the next without lifting it. To end a word, the user simply lifts the stylus from the surface. Word recognition is further augmented by dictionary-based methods. Ambiguities of stroke sequences are resolved by checking the probability of possible interpretations using the built-in dictionary. Once identified, the complete word is offered to the user for acceptance. Figure 3.13 shows the strokes needed to enter the word 'atmosphere'. After only four strokes, the complete word is identified from the dictionary and proposed for acceptance by Octave.

Figure 3.12

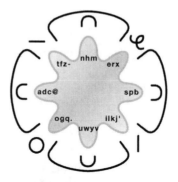

The arrangement of strokes around the Octave star

Courtesy of e-acute

Figure 3.13

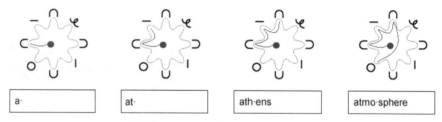

Text entry using Octave

Courtesy of e-acute

The Octave input method can also be used on devices without touch-sensitive displays. In this case, a special button that can be moved into a limited number of positions generates the equivalent of the strokes. Figure 3.14 shows a prototype of a mobile phone with a single button for text entry.

3.2.4 Handwriting recognition

With the availability of sufficient processing power and touch-sensitive displays, handwriting recognition became feasible. The technologies available today differ widely in the amount of processing power and input precision they require. Recognition of cursive handwriting is much more complex than recognition of individually printed letters.

Word recognition

The most expensive approach in terms of computing power attempts to recognize complete handwritten words. This is the most natural way to write for the user, but the most difficult to recognize for a computer. The drawbacks of this approach are that it requires very precise data capture and provides only delayed feedback about the word actually recognized. Figure 3.15 shows a screenshot of text entry with the CalliGrapher[5] software on a Psion Series 5 device.

Figure 3.14

The Octave button on a mobile phone

Courtesy of e-acute

Figure 3.15

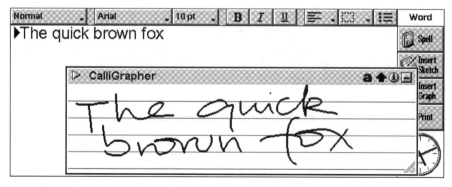

CalliGrapher on a Psion Series 5
Courtesy of Paragraph

Character recognition
Other methods limit the recognition to separated characters, and require the stylus to be lifted between letters. These technologies usually achieve a very high recognition rate but require some cooperation from the user. Usually there is a limited number of ways how an individual letter has to be drawn in order to be recognized by the device. Figure 3.16 shows the Graffiti input method available on Palm OS devices. Letters have to be drawn in a single line exactly as shown, and the stylus has to be lifted after each character.

Some input methods can be trained to the user's writing habits, while others require the user to draw letters in exactly the way the device expects them to. The capability to adapt to an individual writing habit

Figure 3.16

Graffitti help on the Palm

means that several profiles have to be managed if more than one person uses the device. Neither of these technologies can really compete with the keyboard to enter large amounts of text. However, their usability will improve with increasing computing power and memory available in mobile devices.

Localization

Special consideration has to be given to languages that are based not on small alphabets but on a large set of symbols, such as many Asian languages. Dedicated input methods based on standard character sets exist for these languages to allow entering tens of thousands of symbols. These input methods are typically based on the combinations of individual strokes or by using a limited set of phonics to form a single symbol. Figure 3.17 shows the available input methods of CJKOS, an operating system extension that completely adapts Palm OS for the display and input of the Chinese, Japanese, and Korean languages.

3.2.5 Speech recognition

Speech recognition has the advantage of being the most natural input method with only a minimum of requirements in terms of space required to integrate it into mobile devices. However, it is also the most expensive technology in terms of computing power, and the most vulnerable in extreme environments. Recognition of continuous speech is available in computers today, and will certainly become available in mobile devices too. Prototypes are currently available for research, but they still require additional hardware to support the speech processing. Chapter 7 discusses speech-recognition technology in detail.

Perhaps the most obvious devices for the integration of speech recognition are telephones. Some mobile phones already allow the selection of an

Figure 3.17

Input method

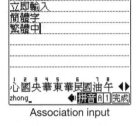
Association input

Phrase input

Input methods available with CJKOS

Courtesy of DYTS

entry from the address book by just speaking the name. In the future, they will be operated entirely by voice, understand complex queries, and may even be able to translate speech into other languages.

The flood of data generated by navigation systems, cell phones, and soon-to-arrive Internet access in cars significantly increases safety risks. Government regulations in some countries already restrict the use of phones in cars. Speech recognition seems to be able to help manage these new information sources and make them usable while driving.

In its simplest form, speech recognition can be reduced to recognition of a very small set of words. This is sufficient to control an application and to enter numeric data. Word recognition is used, for example, to operate devices while driving a car, or to check the status of a bank account via the phone.

Continuous speech recognition requires much larger vocabularies than word recognition, and has to deal with the complexities and ambiguities of the human language. It is available for text entry in PCs today. The same amount of processing power will have to be available in pervasive devices in order to use it there. This can be achieved by faster processors or by special hardware optimized for the recognition process.

3.3 Biometrics

Access to systems providing significant monetary value, confidential information, or critical applications must be secured against unauthorized use. User authentication is therefore a key function in any such system. Classical authentication relies on what you own, what you are, and what you know.

Typically, Internet applications rely on user identifier (UID) and a password. The UID may be in the public knowledge, whereas the password is a secret (what you know) shared by the user and the system administration. Thus, the system can check whether the user is authorized to use the system. However, any person who knows the password can perform user functions. The password can be stolen by watching the user enter their personal identification number (PIN), by capturing data during password transmission, or via access to system administration data. A stolen password is hard to detect because nothing is removed from any system.

GSM mobile phones are protected against unauthorized use through the SIM, a smart card that is issued by the mobile service provider (what you have) and a PIN chosen by the customer (what you know). The PIN is stored and checked in the secure system environment of the SIM and is not transmitted via unreliable media. Intruders must steal the SIM and the PIN in order to act like the authorized user and perform user functions. However, many users prefer not to use a PIN because it is inconvenient, and complicated procedures are required to recover a forgotten PIN and assign a new one.

Biometrics authentication methods rely on what you are. A large number of personal characteristics, such as fingerprint, signature, hand geometry, face recognition, voice recognition, and iris scan, have been proposed. Only methods that work with small sensors, e.g. microphone, fingerprint sensor, or pen entry panels, promise near-term applicability in the pervasive computing space. Therefore, only authentication using fingerprint, speaker verification, or signature verification is discussed in the following section.

Biometrics authentication systems capture the user's characteristics with a sensor, derive characteristic values, and compare this with a known reference. The result of the comparison is either 0, if authentication was not successfully performed, or 1, if authentication was successful. In fingerprint verification, the image system extracts the end and the bifurcation points of finger lines, and uses location and direction as characteristic values for comparison with one or more stored references (Figure 3.18). Generation of reference values and actual values is subject to distortion. The comparison of the data sets is rather complex and introduces additional errors. Therefore, there is always the probability that biometrics authentication will fail, causing major inconvenience to the user. The false accept rate (FAR) is the probability that the system will accept the wrong user. The false reject rate (FRR) is the probability that the system will reject the correct user.

In the case of PIN verification with a SIM card, the FAR for any attempt by an unauthorized user is 0.01%. The system allows for a maximum of three trials before the smart card is shut off, thus the overall FAR for the SIM card system is 0.03%. The FRR is 0 because a correct PIN will always be accepted.

Biometrics authentication systems can be tuned, for example, to achieve a very small FAR. However, this will increase the FRR, and serv-

Figure 3.18

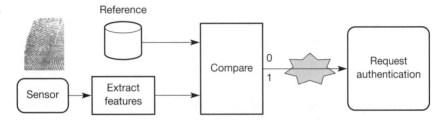

Fingerprint authentication

ice will be denied. Denial of service is acceptable if a reasonable exception path exists. A user of the INS-PASS issued by the US Department of Justice – Immigration and Naturalization Service may ask a security officer for entry if hand geometry or fingerprint authentication is not successful. Service denial for a mobile phone is much more difficult to handle, and will probably not be accepted by customers. In addition to the statistical FRR, every biometrics system has specific systematic problems, e.g. service may be denied if a finger is dirty or injured. Therefore, fingerprint authentication is very much limited to applications where adequate back-up processes in case of service denial are in place.

Another security disadvantage of biometrics systems is their susceptibility to fraud unless the total system is securely encapsulated and communicates with the authentication requestor via a secure channel. The SIM card system uses the smart card for secure storage of the PIN, and uses the keys for secure communication with the service provider. More than one billion smart cards are in use in Europe, and no fraud case involving professionally designed and implemented smart card has been reported. Thus, smart cards will be the security element of choice for pervasive devices. Some devices may use not smart cards but a module on a printed circuit card that serves the very same purpose.

Fingerprint verification will probably be introduced for pervasive computing devices as a convenience item, with a PIN as back-up in case of denial of service. The fingerprint authentication module must communicate with the SIM via a secure channel to maintain system integrity.

Pen-based pervasive computing devices may use signature (or handwriting) verification to secure access to the device. Modern signature-verification systems based on static images can be tailored to a FAR of 0.1% and a FRR of 5%. This level of security is comparable to a PIN-based system and reasonably convenient for the user. However, the system is prone to tampering because none of the system elements are contained in a secure housing.

3.4 Operating systems

The core functionality of every pervasive computing device is determined by its operating system. The major differences of operating systems for pervasive devices from the user's point of view are the human–machine interface, and the speed with which a task can be performed. For pervasive devices, there will likely be no equivalent to the Windows/Intel monopoly in the near future because pervasive devices do have a wide range of usages (from mobile phones to set-top boxes) with very constrained hardware. They will therefore deploy various chip sets (e.g. ARM, MIPS, Motorola, SH3/4, Transmeta) and multiple operating systems (e.g. Palm OS, EPOC, Windows CE).

All operating systems for pervasive devices support the basic operating system concepts, such as processes and file systems, but there are large differences between the various devices. The range is from the absolute minimum required in the Palm OS, to full-blown operating systems like Windows CE. This section will cover the most popular operating systems for the different pervasive computing areas.

Table 3.2 shows that the requirements for an operating system in PDA devices are very different from those for PCs. At the moment, there are two trends visible for pervasive computing operating systems. For personal use, the two major PDA operating systems, Palm OS and Windows CE, are becoming more similar, and can integrate phone functionality in a new device that combines a PDA with a cell phone. For home use, the development is directed towards high-performance multimedia operating systems, such as embedded Linux or BeOS.

Not covered in this chapter is VxWorks, a popular real-time operating system based on a microkernel architecture, which is quite similar to QNX Neutrino.

3.4.1 Palm OS

With a market share of about 80%, Palm OS is by far the most successful operation system for PDAs. PDAs with Palm operating system are available from Palm itself, Handspring, Sony, IBM, and others. The main reason for the success of Palm OS is that it is designed specifically for PDAs, and its easy-to-use approach, known as 'Zen of PDA'. It supplies only a limited number of features, but it optimizes these. This restricted functionality leads to lower memory and CPU usage, which results in longer battery life. The Palm OS is implemented on the 16-bit Motorola DragonBall CPU, which is derived from the 68k line.

At the time of this writing, the actual operating system version was 3.5, which added colour support for 256 colours. Palm OS 4.0 includes enhanced communication support (e.g. Bluetooth support) and 65 536 different colours. This will most likely lead to multimedia PDAs with integrated mobile phones.

Table 3.2	Comparison of PDA and PC use		
		PDA	**PC**
Times turned on per day		High	Low
Time spent per task		Low	High

Core operating system functionality

Palm OS is organized in different horizontal and vertical layers, as shown in (Figure 3.19). To make the vertical layers independent from the underlying hardware, a microkernel encapsulates the hardware-specific functionality. The vertical layers provide application programming interfaces (APIs) for the applications to access the operating system functionality. They are divided into:

- *user interface*, with the graphical input/output (I/O), e.g. buttons, forms, etc.;
- *memory management*, consisting of databases, runtime space, system space, and global variables;
- *system management*, which looks after events, alarms, date and time, strings, etc.;
- *communication layer*, which provides communication over serial I/O, Transmission Control Protocol (TCP)/IP, or Infrared Data Association (IrDA).

Palm OS has the following features:

- *User management*. Since the Palm device is considered to be a personal device, the Palm OS is a single-user operating system.
- *Task management*. Only one application can run at a time, but it is possible to call other applications from the running application. However, internally the Palm OS has the ability to use multitasking.

Figure 3.19

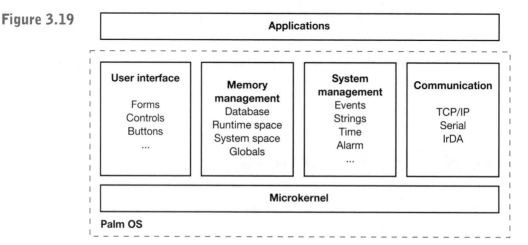

Palm OS architecture

- *Power management*. Palm OS has different operation modes (sleep, doze, running) to save power.

- *OS size*. Palm OS 3.5 is about 1.4 MB (including built-in applications) in size and needs up to 64 kb (including TCP/IP) runtime memory.

- *User interface*. The Palm application starter can be seen on the left side of Figure 3.20, and an example of a Palm application's look-and-feel is shown on the right side of Figure 3.20, with the built-in date book. The major user interface design principles of the Palm OS are: recognize only the Palm handwriting alphabet; one button access to applications; and minimize taps for most-used operations.

- *Memory management*. To keep the operating system small and fast, Palm OS does not separate applications from each other. This has implications for the system stability and security. If one application crashes, then the whole system crashes, so applications must be extremely well tested. It also means that each application can read and alter data contained within other applications.

The memory management divides the available memory into:

- *dynamic heap*: the dynamic heap is execution-based and clears on reset. Its size is between 64 and 256 kb, depending on the total memory size. It is used to store global variables, the stack, and

Figure 3.20

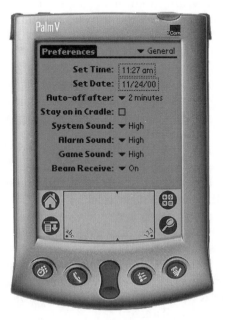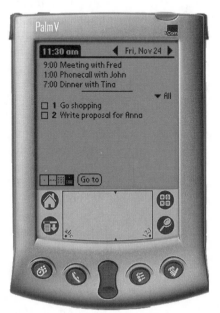

The Palm user interface

dynamically-allocated memory. It provides fast read and write access, but has no ability to protect itself against unauthorized writes;

■ *storage*: this is designed to hold permanent data, such as databases, files, and application code, and is therefore not cleared on reset. The size is limited only by the available physical memory. It provides fast read access and slow write access, and write protection. Internally, all data are stored in databases with transaction support provided by the operating system. This guarantees the integrity of the data even in the event of a system crash.

Software development for Palm OS

Palm supports C and C++ for software development. The C support is quite exhaustive, whereas the C++ support is just at its beginning. Because the Palm OS is written in C, this is currently the best choice for developing performance-critical applications.

The free Palm development environment consists of a software development kit (SDK) based on GNU (GNUs, not UNIX) for Windows, Mac, and Linux. There is also a commercial, integrated development environment available for the Palm: the Metrowerks CodeWarrior. This includes an editor, compiler, debugger, and visual graphical user interface constructor. Unfortunately, the shared library format between CodeWarrior and GNU is not compatible.

Palm supplies a Palm emulator, which emulates the Palm hardware on a PC. This means that Palm programs can be run and debugged on the emulator and then the same program can be downloaded to a real Palm device. Figure 3.21 shows the development cycle for Palm programs. On the PC, the Palm program is edited and then compiled. It can either be run in the Palm emulator on the PC or downloaded to a real Palm (the figure shows the latter). Afterwards, the program can be debugged remotely from PC. When a stable version is reached, this code is the final program. There is no need for any additional compilation steps, as in the EPOC development environment.

Application development in C is simple and fast for the Palm, because there is an extensive system library, and a lot of example programs are available. The support for C++ is minimal at the moment, but will hopefully be improved with the next major release.

Palm applications are synchronous and event-driven. They consist of the main event loop and the event handling. Events can be user interface actions (button pressed, handwriting input, etc.), system notifications (power management, global search, etc.), and application-specific events.

Several virtual machines (VMs) for the Palm are available from third parties, including the KVM (Java 2 Micro Edition) from Sun, the J9 from IBM, and the WabaVM from Wabasoft.

Figure 3.21

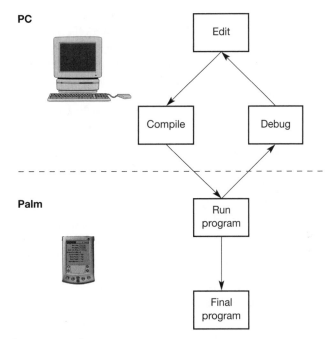

Palm development cycle

The Sun JVM implements the Java 2 Micro Edition standard from Sun, the J9 is performance and real-time optimized, and the WabaVM is targeted for small devices, with a subset of the Java language and Java bytecodes. However, all Java Virtual Mahcines (JVMs) struggle with the very tight resource constraints of the Palm. Because a JVM with class library takes 256–512 kb of storage, and quite a large amount of heap space, they are not very popular at the moment. This will probably change with the next generation of Palm devices, when the minimal memory configuration should be increased. For details about Java on pervasive devices, see Section 3.5.

3.4.2 EPOC

EPOC was originally created by Psion, but is now maintained by an off-spring company called Symbian, which was founded by Psion, Motorola, Panasonic, Ericsson, and Nokia in 1998. The EPOC operating system was designed specifically for phones. There are two versions: EPOC16 for 16-bit processors and EPOC32 for 32-bit processors. The current version of EPOC is Release 5, which is available for NEC V30H (16-bit version) and ARM/StrongARM (32-bit version) processors.

EPOC supports Unicode, which is important for the Asian market. EPOC can display 256 colours.

Core operating system functionality

In contrast to the Palm OS, which consists mainly of one task, EPOC is heavily multitasking. An overview of the EPOC operating system can be seen in Figure 3.22. The base layer provides the fundamental APIs; the middleware layer provides the graphics, data, and other components to support the graphical user interface and applications; EIKON is the system graphical user interface framework; and finally there are the applications.

The EPOC operating system consists of the following features:

- *User management.* Because EPOC devices are considered to be personal devices, EPOC is a single-user operating system.

- *Task management.* The real-time microkernel with low-interrupt and task-switching latency provides multitasking with a pre-emptive, priority-driven scheduler.

- *User interface.* The EPOC user interface supports display, keyboard, and sound. The user interface framework in EPOC is named EIKON and provides all the standard graphical user interface elements, such as buttons, dialogs, and menus. It is also responsible for handling the data and command input. Figure 3.23 shows the EPOC user interface of an Ericsson device with a map application.

- *Memory management.* EPOC has a memory management unit (MMU) concept to provide separate address spaces for each application. The EPOC operating system and development tools also provides a rich set of tools for checking out-of-memory errors and freeing up unused memory. These tools include design patterns, stack clean-up heap failure, and heap-checking tools.

Figure 3.22

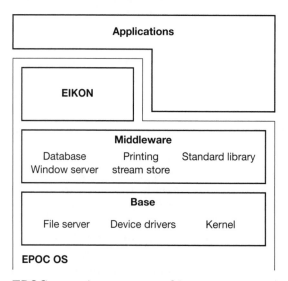

EPOC operating system architecture

Figure 3.23

Ericsson EPOC handheld device

Courtesy of Ericsson

Software Development for EPOC

Programming languages supported by EPOC are C++, Java, and OPL, a proprietary BASIC-like language. C++ is the language of choice for system development and high-performance application programming. There are C++ development environments from GNU, for compiling the device code, and Microsoft Visual C++, for compiling for the emulator, available for EPOC. OPL has a long heritage in Symbian's EPOC and Psion's SIBO software, for rapid application development, and is specific for EPOC. Also included is a runtime environment for Java (JDK 1.1.4 in EPOC Release 5) from Sun with the Abstract Window Toolkit (AWT) graphical user interface classes. Symbian provides a simulator for testing and debugging EPOC programs. The development cycle for EPOC applications is shown in Figure 3.24. The EPOC program is edited on the PC and then compiled for the PC. After that, it can be run in the simulator on the PC and can be debugged. Finally, the program must be cross-compiled for the EPOC device and then loaded onto the EPOC device.

Normally, EPOC applications are developed in C++, because this is the best compromise between performance and development cycle time. OPL is an advanced scripting language that allows for rapid prototyping and is EPOC specific. OPL is an interpreted language and is therefore not suited for programs that require fast execution speed. As can be seen from Figure 3.25, Java is in the middle between C++ and OPL. In contrast to OPL, Java is not proprietary to EPOC, but it can also be used on other platforms.

Figure 3.24

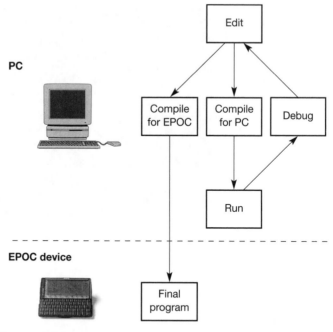

EPOC development cycle

EPOC applications are different from Palm OS applications because EPOC heavily relies on multitasking. Therefore, the application programmer can choose to program either synchronous applications (which would look like Palm OS applications) or asynchronous applications. In the asynchronous case, the application is waiting for messages from other processes (e.g. keyboard) and is not blocking the processor. This results in faster execution of parallel tasks, or power saving if no other task is running.

3.4.3 Windows CE

Windows CE is an embedded operating system developed by Microsoft. Previous versions (1.0 and 2.0) of the Windows CE user interface were similar to the Windows user interface. This meant clicking on about ten pop-up menus with a pen to enter a new date in the date book, which was

Figure 3.25

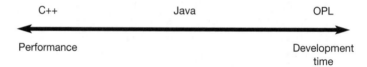

Program performance and development time

far too inconvenient and time-consuming for such a simple, frequently-used task. The current version (3.0, which is used in the Pocket PC) is now better optimized for ease of use. Windows CE is available for 32-bit CPUs such as ×86, SH3/4, ARM/StrongARM, PowerPC, and MIPS.

Windows CE 3.0 offers real-time support, a smart card subsystem for PC/SC compliant readers, is Unicode based, and supports grayscale and color graphics up to 32-bit depth.

Core operating system functionality

Windows CE is a modular operating system that can be configured by the device manufacturer. This is a result of the read-only memory (ROM)-based design of Windows CE, in contrast to more desktop-oriented, disk-based operating systems like Linux or BeOS; it can even be configured at runtime. This allows an operating system with only the essential parts to be created and saves precious space in the device. The different modules are shown in the Figure 3.26.

The kernel provides memory management, task scheduling, and interrupt handling. The graphics/window/event manager (GWE) integrates the user interface functions of graphical output and user input. The object store is the persistent memory of Windows CE and includes files, the registry, and a database. Finally, the communication interfaces include infrared communication via IrDA, TCP/IP, and serial drivers.

Figure 3.26

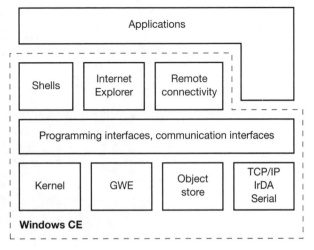

Windows CE architecture

Windows CE offers the following features:

- *User management.* Because Windows CE is designed for PDAs, it supports only one user.
- *Task management.* The task manager supports 32 simultaneous processes and an unlimited number of threads (limited only by the available physical memory).
- *Operating system size.* The Windows CE footprint can be as small as 400 kb for the kernel, up to 3 MB with all modules, and up to 8 MB including Pocket Word and Internet Explorer.
- *User interface.* Windows CE provides menu controls, dialog boxes, and icons, and supports sound. An example of the Windows CE user interface can be seen in Figure 3.27. The desktop shows icons like Word, for a reduced version of Microsoft's text-processing software Word, and the Microsoft media player for playing MP3 music files.
- *Memory management.* A protected virtual memory system that supports up to 32 MB memory per process protects applications against each other. There exists a special heap for the file system, registry, and object store that has a transaction service for ensuring data integrity. The object store can have a size up to 256 MB.

Figure 3.27

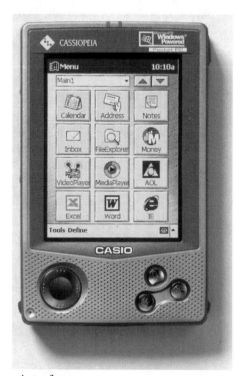

Windows CE user interface
Courtesy of Casio

■ *Security*. Windows CE has support for cryptography with a cryptographic library (Cryptographic Application Programming Interface, CAPI) to securely store information in memory. The kernel-loader authentication program can use public-key signatures to prevent unauthorized applications from running. As an additional feature, it is possible to achieve more security for sensitive data by using the smart card interface of Windows CE. Private data of up to 64 kb can be stored securely and non-volatily on a smart card. Access to the data, however, will be slower because of the electrically erasable and programmable read-only memory (EEPROM) memory used instead of battery-backed RAM.

Software development for Windows CE

Since Windows CE is based on the Win32 API, it offers significant advantages in application software development. It is already known to a lot of developers, and there are professional development tools, such as Visual C++ or Visual Basic, available for this API. It also allows developers to reuse Win32 code from existing PC-based programs. Because Windows CE uses major parts of the Win32 API, the application programming is very similar to that on the PC.

There are JVMs from third parties available for the Windows CE, including the KVM (Java 2 Micro Edition) from Sun, the J9 from IBM, and Waba from Wabasoft.

3.4.4 QNX Neutrino

The first QNX operating system version was available in 1981, and the current QNX Neutrino has now reached the version 2.1. QNX is a real-time operating system consisting of a microkernel surrounded by a collection of optional processes (resource managers) that provide POSIX- and UNIX-compatible system services. Depending on whether resource manager processes are included at runtime, QNX ranges from ROM-based embedded systems up to a full-blown operating system with network support. This microkernel-based architecture is known as universal process model and allows for separation of processes in different address spaces. This is true not only for user processes, but also for the resource manager processes. That means that even if the file system driver or network driver crashes, then the system will still work, which leads to highly reliable and stable systems.

QNX is very well suited for set-top boxes or car devices, but there are also efforts to target the hand-held device space, e.g. to add power management support and a graphical user interface suitable for hand-held devices (Photon). It supports MIPS, Power PC, and ×86 processors.

Core operating system functionality

The core operating system consists of a microkernel that has a size of only 12 kB. This kernel implements four services: interprocess communication (IPC), process scheduling, low-level network communication, and interrupt dispatching. The IPC is based on messages and can be given priorities.

In addition to the core microkernel, there are several resource managers that run as separate processes. Examples include a POSIX-compliant file system and device manager, network services (e.g. TCP/IP), graphical user interface, and power management. This architecture is called universal process model and is shown in Figure 3.28. A small set of core services reside in the kernel, while the remaining code runs in separate processes. This results in an extremely stable and flexible operating system. Malfunction in one part of the operating system (e.g. the device driver) does not cause the whole system to stop. In addition, it allows operating system services to be added or removed at a later date.

QNX Neutrino has the following features:

Figure 3.28

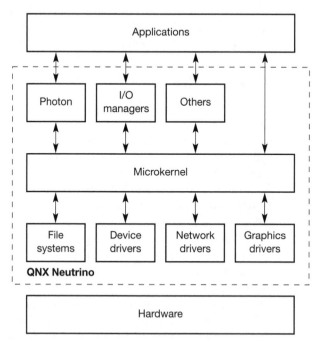

QNX Neutrino architecture

- *User management.* QNX supports only one user.

- *Task management.* QNX supports real multitasking. Through its modular organization, it allows for incremental linking and loading of components, resulting in an on-the-fly operating system configuration.

- *User interface.* X-Window-like concept, based on widgets to implement graphical user interface elements. Consists of a micro-graphical user interface, which can be scaled up or down dynamically.

- *Memory management.* The QNX memory management has an MMU concept for separation of address spaces of applications. The memory protection is used not only for applications, but also for operating system services running in different threads.

- *Additional features.* QNX is POSIX compliant, allowing existing POSIX-compliant code to be reused.

Software development for QNX

The QNX toolkit includes the GNU or Watcom C/C++ compiler, debugger, graphical user interface builder, and PhAB for creating rapid prototypes. In addition, there is a development environment available from Metrowerks.

Since the POSIX standard is C-based, the language of choice for programming fast and compact applications is C. Because most APIs are POSIX-compliant, reusing existing code and developing new code is easy and does not require extensive training. QNX is based heavily on multitasking, so applications should be programmed asynchronously in order to save battery power.

3.4.5 BeOS

BeOS was founded in 1985 with the goal to create a media operating system. Consequently, the current version (5) of BeOS is highly optimized for multimedia applications and is a good candidate for multimedia boxes. It offers multiprocessor support to integrate seamlessly sound and graphic processors, and a 64-bit file system for dealing with the huge amounts of data that modern multimedia applications deal with (e.g. the size of an uncompressed DVD is about 300 GB). BeOS is available for Intel and PowerPC processors.

Figure 3.29 shows how BeOS can be used as an operating system for an Internet personal access device, providing the multimedia foundation that such a device would need.

Figure 3.29

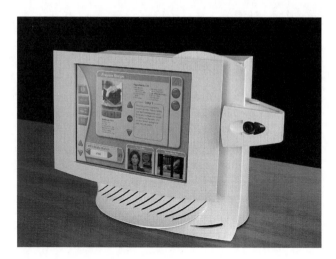

Internet personal access device running BeOS

Courtesy of Be Inc.

Core operating system functionality

To achieve the requirements for real-time multimedia and communication, BeOS features a very-fine-grained multiprocessor support included in its operating system core. The architecture is based on a symmetric multi-processor model, allowing each processor to execute parts of the operating system and give each processor full access to all resources. In addition to that, it supports virtual memory and pre-emptive multitasking.

Another BeOS specialty is the so-called pervasive multithreading. This permits rapid switching between hundreds of small tasks. These tasks can be deployed rapidly on multiple processors, and reassigned when the system's processor load changes.

BeOS has the following features:

■ *User management.* BeOS has multiuser support, just like standard UNIX operating systems.

■ *Task management.* Pre-emptive multitasking with pervasive threads for fast context switching is implemented by BeOS. BeOS also supports and implements symmetric multiprocessing down to the operating system level.

■ *Memory management.* The BeOS memory-management unit provides memory protection between applications and virtual memory support.

■ *Additional features.* BeOS supports a 64-bit file system that allows the user to access up to 18 billion GB, in contrast to 32-bit file systems, which allow up to only 4GB.

Software development for BeOS

For the Intel version, a C/C++ GNU compiler and tools are available; for the PowerPC version, an integrated C/C++ development environment is offered by Metrowerks. BeOS is not well suited for devices with tight memory restrictions, but it does allow the standard Java environment from Sun to be used for software development.

Application development for BeOS is similar to that for a modern multitasking operating system like Linux. BeOS is POSIX-compliant, which makes it easy to reuse code from other POSIX platforms, such as Unix or QNX Neutrino. A rich library supporting multimedia applications offers 2D/3D graphics, OpenGL, and several kinds of media formats (e.g. MPEG, WAV, PNG, TIFF).

3.4.6 Embedded Linux

Embedded Linux is a stripped-down Linux operating system with some special support for pervasive devices. As processors and memory are getting cheaper and more powerful, stripped-down desktop operating systems are become increasingly attractive. For hand-held devices, most of the benefit of Moore's law is put not into performance and larger memory, but in cheaper chips and longer battery life.

Unfortunately, there is currently no standard for embedded Linux. However, there is a group called the Embedded Linux Consortium[6] that promotes embedded Linux systems. At the time of this writing, this consortium consisted of over 80 members. Embedded Linux versions are available for nearly all processors used in high-end embedded systems, including MIPS, ARM, Motorola, and Intel processors.

Core operating system functionality

The operating system functionality is the same as for standard Linux. The following features make Linux so well suited for the embedded market:

- *Configurable kernel.* Linux has a microkernel architecture like the QNX operating system. This allows easy configuration of the operating system core. Services and features can be compiled either into the kernel, or as a loadable module that can be loaded dynamically at runtime. This includes services and functions such as device drivers, file systems, and networking support.

- *Scalability.* Based on the modular kernel concept, Linux can be configured from sizes suitable for a watch up to multiprocessor server systems. Embedded Linux vendors offer configuration tools and utilities for tailoring Linux to the special needs of a specific pervasive device.

■ *Networking*. Because most Linux systems are used as Web servers, the Linux TCP/IP stack is under constant scrutiny for security and optimized for speed. Drivers, utilities, clients, and servers are available for nearly every network function or protocol.

For comparison with the other operating systems described in this chapter, the embedded Linux features are summarized below:

■ *User management*. Embedded Linux offers multiuser support, just like standard Linux operating systems.

■ *Task management*. Pre-emptive multitasking with optional real-time schedulers is implemented. There is also basic support for multiple processors.

■ *Operating system size*. Depending on the configuration, the size of the kernel can range from 200 kB to several megabytes. However, a restriction for embedded devices is the fact that Linux needs quite a lot of runtime memory, typically 2–8 MB.

■ *User interface*. Embedded Linux uses the x-Window system for the user interface. Some embedded Linux vendors provide stripped-down versions to save memory.

■ *Memory management*. The Linux memory management supports MMUs to provide memory protection between applications and virtual memory for paging memory to hard disks.

Software development for embedded Linux

The same software development tools are available for embedded Linux as for a standard Linux system. Available programming languages include C, C++, and Java. Therefore, software development is fairly similar to that for desktop systems. However, the actual Linux devices can be quite different from normal desktop systems, as can be seen in Figure 3.30.

This figure shows an example of what small pervasive devices running embedded Linux can look like today. The watch is designed to communicate wirelessly with PCs, cell phones, and other wireless-enabled devices. It will therefore have the ability to view condensed email messages and receive pager-like messages. Also, personal information management (PIM) functionality, such as calendar, address book, and to-do list, can be accessed. Future enhancements will include a high-resolution display and applications that will allow the watch to be used as an access device for various Internet-based services, such as up-to-the-minute information about weather, traffic conditions, the stock market, sports results, and so on. The technical data of the Linux watch are: ARM7 processor, 8 MB Flash memory, 8 MB DRAM memory, infrared (IR) and RF wireless connectivity, 96 × 112 pixel touch screen, and a roller wheel.

Figure 3.30

Wristwatch running embedded Linux from IBM research
Courtesy of IBM

3.4.7 Summary

Just as pervasive computing devices cover a wide range in terms of size and functionality, so do the operating systems for these devices. The operating systems described above range from the small, lean, and minimalistic Palm OS to the multimedia, multiprocessor-supporting BeOS. This means that there will not be a single dominant operating system in pervasive computing, but rather a variety of them supporting different device categories. Table 3.3 gives an overview of the features of the different operating systems.

The Palm OS is intended for use in PDAs with limited memory and battery power. It is simple to use, with a user interface that is tailored for the special needs of PDAs, power efficient, and easy to program. The major disadvantage of the Palm OS is that there is no security. Every application can read and alter all data, which will become a problem when PDAs are used as personal security devices (PSDs), which will allow access to rooms and be used in e-commerce scenarios.

EPOC was developed for personal organizers and is now gaining market share in the mobile phone market. Its multitasking support is a perfect fit for mobile phones, which need to respond to user inputs and at the same time be able to receive data over the air.

Windows CE 3.0 has special features such as sound support and crypto support. The ability to customize Windows CE for special devices and only include the needed parts of the operating system is very attractive

Table 3.3	Features of the different operating systems

	Palm	EPOC	Windows CE	QNX	BeOS	Embedded Linux
Supported processors	Motorola Dragon Ball	NEC, ARM	×86, SH3/4, ARM, PowerPC, MIPS	×86, PowerPC, MIPS	×86, PowerPC	×86, PowerPC, MIPS, ARM
Operating system structure	Layered	Layered	Modular	Modular	Layered	Modular
Memory protection	No	Yes	Yes	Yes	Yes	Yes
Operating system size	Tiny	Small	Small	Medium	Large	Small–Large
Security	None	Low	High	Medium	High	High
Multi-tasking	No	Yes	Yes	Yes	Yes	Yes
Examples of pervasive devices	PDAs	Mobile phones	Pocket PCs	Car devices, Internet Appliances	Set-top boxes	Set-top boxes

for manufacturers. Like EPOC, Windows CE aims to reach the high-end PDA market, as the supported processors are all 32-bit processors, which need more battery power than the 16-bit Motorola processor of the Palm OS devices.

Neutrino from QNX is very well suited for car devices, as it is a real-time operating system and many car applications have hard, real-time requirements. An additional advantage is the possibility of replacing parts of the operating system while the system is running. This will be the most likely scenario for updating software in cars, with over-the-air connection to the car and the new software transmission modules. Other potential uses of Neutrino are in set-top boxes, Internet appliances (like the 3Com Audrey) and PDAs or pocket PCs, where QNX provides new features such as power saving technology and a Palm-like graphical user interface library.

BeOS is the perfect operating system for set-top boxes and other multimedia devices. As TVs become increasingly intelligent, switch to digital technologies (like MPEG), and interact with other devices (e.g. hi-fi system, room-control computer), the importance of multimedia operating systems will increase.

Embedded Linux is a Linux version configured for a special device. It has all the basic concepts of a standard Linux, including multi-user support, sound, high-end graphics drivers, and many features for ensuring high security. Embedded Linux has the advantage of having the same programming APIs as standard Linux. This means that several programs can run on an embedded Linux device with just a recompile, and developers do not need special training to write applications for this platform.

3.5 Java for pervasive devices

As we have seen already, pervasive devices have a great variety of operating systems. It would therefore be beneficial to have a common programming platform, such as Java. Since the Java Standard Edition requires significant computing resources, and resources are limited in pervasive computing devices, the challenge is to have a small, performing Java implementation for pervasive devices.

This section gives an overview of the different versions of Java, discusses the two relevant Java versions for pervasive devices (Java Micro Edition and Real-time Java), and describes three virtual machines available for pervasive devices (Sun's KVM, Waba, and IBM's VisualAge Micro Edition).

3.5.1 Java

The Java technology was created in 1991 at Sun as a programming tool in a small, closed-door project called the Green Project. The goal of the project was to look for the next wave in computing, which the team thought would be the convergence of consumer devices and computers. For this project, James Gosling created a new language that he called Oak, after the tree outside his window. As the plans for small computing devices were dropped, and the group focused on the Internet, the language was renamed Java and officially announced in 1995.

Because Java has its roots in the small-device area, it is no surprise that after the success of Java on clients with applets and then on servers with Java Enterprise Edition, Java has now finally reached mobile computing devices. The current Java versions are called Java 2 Platform and consist of:

- *Java Micro Edition* (J2ME), which includes different virtual machines, core APIs and market-specific APIs defined in profiles. J2ME has been designed for pervasive computing devices and is explained in more detail below;

- *Java Standard Edition* (J2SE), aimed at the traditional PC. It has a richer set of APIs than J2ME, and is used in VMs that are optimized for performance and security but not size;

■ *Java Enterprise Edition* (J2EE), created by Sun for server systems. It enhances the J2SE with APIs needed for server-based computing, including Java Beans, JSPs, database access, and more. For more details about J2EE see Chapter 10.

Figure 3.31 shows how the different Java versions relate to each other. The base layer consists of the JVMs that execute the Java bytecode. These JVMs range from the Card VM for smart cards, the KVM for pervasive devices, and the standard VM and Client HotSpot VM for desktop computing, up to the HotSpot VM for servers. The HotSpot VM is designed for high-performance applications, and therefore carries out intelligent precompiling of frequently-used code fragments. All VMs comply with the Java programming language definition, but the KVM and the Card VM only support subsets of this definition. On top of this layer are the different core APIs for the various Java editions. The topmost layer consists of the profiles that tailor the Java editions to special environments.

A profile is a collection of Java-based APIs that supplement a configuration to provide capabilities for a specific vertical market or a specific device type. A configuration defines the minimum Java technology libraries and virtual machine capabilities that an application developer or content provider can expect to be available on all devices.

Figure 3.31

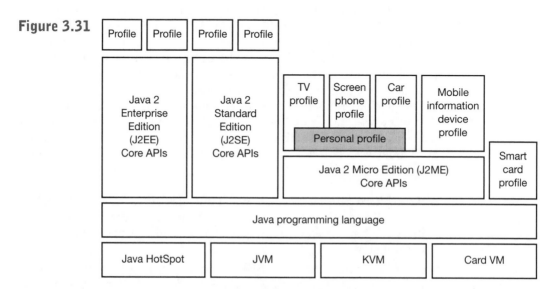

Overview of the Java 2 Platform and the different Profiles

3.5.2 Java 2 Micro Edition

Java 2 Micro Edition is targeted for pervasive computing devices without real-time requirements. Typically these devices are characterized by:

- small amount of available memory (128–512 kB)
- limited energy (battery-operated)
- connected to a network
- restricted graphical display capabilities.

These devices range from smart cards to phones and set-top boxes. To cover this broad range of devices, there are several device configurations and technologies.

As explained above, a configuration defines the minimum Java technology libraries and VM capabilities that we expect to be available on all devices. Based on the Java 2 Micro Edition profile, the following configurations are available:

- *Connected device configuration* (CDC) is based on the PersonalJava technology and has the bytecodes and core APIs of standard Java. It is targeted at devices like screen phones and set-top boxes with more than 512 kB ROM, more than 256 kB RAM, and connection to a network. The main difference to standard Java libraries is the restricted user interface library.
- *Connected, limited device configuration* (CLDC) addresses the geographical user interface, data storage, messaging (e.g. email, SMS), security, and wireless networking for devices with 128–512 kB RAM, such as mobile phones and TV sets. Sun provides a special VM, called KVM, for this configuration that is optimized for memory-constrained environments (see also p. 75).

To enhance the use of Java beyond these two configurations, additional Java2ME technologies are defined:

- *Embedded Java* allows the Java platform to be configured. Unnecessary classes and VM features can be omitted in order to minimize resources and costs for embedded devices. Embedded Java uses the same bytecode as the standard Java edition.
- *Java Card* specifies a subset of Java with a special compressed bytecode format for very small devices, such as smart cards (e.g. SIM cards used in GSM mobile phones, credit cards).
- *Real-time Java* enhances Java with features needed for real-time applications (see Section 3.5.3).

As can be seen, there are many varieties of Java to choose from. This helps reduce the resources needed for the Java implementations running on the different pervasive devices, as the Java functionality can be tailored to the specific needs of the device.

3.5.3 Real-time Java

Standard Java is not suitable for real-time applications, because it does not have a predictable runtime behaviour and does not allow reading and writing directly to the system memory. The use of algorithms can solve some of the shortcomings of the standard JVMs, such as garbage collection that leads to unpredictable execution times in the standard JVM. Others, such as direct access to memory, are not available in standard Java as the Java language definition prohibits this.

A collaboration of companies therefore created the real-time version of Java, Real-Time Specification for Java (RTSJ), which is still in its early phases. The draft specification is available, and a reference implementation will hopefully be available soon. This is the first effort under the formalized Java Community Process (JCP 1.0) for Java enhancements. Companies like Aonix, Cyberonics, IBM, Microware Systems, Nortel Networks, QNX, Rockwell-Collins, and Sun worked together to specify this standard.

Real-time Java will be backward compatible to standard Java, and will include all the features needed to build systems with hard real-time requirements. Here are some of the main features of RTSJ:

- *Predictable execution speed*. Non-predictable execution time, caused by time-slicing scheduling and occasional garbage collection, are the major reasons why standard Java is not very well suited for real-time applications. The first priority in designing RTSJ was to always have a predictable runtime behaviour.

- *Customizable schedulers*. RTSJ introduces the concept of a schedulable object, in addition to tasks and threads. Scheduling can therefore be executed on object level. In addition, RTSJ defines a predictable priority scheduler and allows for easy exchange of a scheduler, e.g. to include a custom scheduler.

- *Advanced memory management*. To support the needs of real-time systems with regard to memory management, RTSJ defines different memory types to allow short- and long-lived objects to exist outside the scope of garbage collection. To achieve this, a new definition of object lifetime is provided, and memory areas such as scoped memory (lifetime defined by syntactic scope), immortal memory (has a scope that is larger than the program and can be used to share data between real-time and non-real-time tasks; similar to shared memory on UNIX systems), and physical memory (see below) are introduced.

■ *Access to physical memory*. Real-time systems often need fast access to sensors or actors that connect the real-time system to the physical world. To accomplish this efficiently, RTSJ has a mechanism for breaking the Java sandbox at defined places to have direct access to the machine memory. This gives Java programs the ability to read or write directly to the memory of sensors or actors.

■ *Object and thread synchronization*. As real-time applications often consist of many threads that must get synchronized at some point in their execution, RTSJ defines synchronized wait-free read and write queues, and monitors for mutual exclusion synchronization, which avoids the priority inversion problem of the standard Java implementation.

■ *Asynchronous event handling*. Many real-time systems are event-driven and therefore make extensive use of asynchronous events such as interrupts. RJTS supports asynchronous events and asynchronous transfer of control to other objects and threads.

With these features, Java is very likely to spread to pervasive computing devices with real-time requirements, for example car appliances.

3.5.4 Java virtual machines for pervasive devices

In this section, we describe some commercially available virtual machines for pervasive devices. First, we will cover Sun's KVM, which implements the J2ME standard. Then the Waba VM is explained, which implements a Java-like technology, but uses native device libraries to achieve smaller and faster programs. Finally, we show a fully integrated development environment for Java on pervasive devices, including a virtual machine, the IBM VisualAge Micro Edition.

Sun's KVM
Between the PersonalJava VM, which deals with devices that have more than 512 kB of memory, and the Java Card VM, which is aimed at smart cards with 32–64 kB memory, there was a gap. Extending the Java Card VM to bigger devices did not make much sense, because the Java Card technology has a restricted bytecode set and a special compressed class file format that prevents dynamic class loading. Since a whole new market of pervasive devices falls into this gap, Sun has filled it with the KVM, expecting devices to have more than 128 kB of memory.
Sun's KVM has the following features:

■ *Full Java VM*. The KVM implements the full JVM specification, unlike the Java Card VM.

- *Small memory footprint.* The KVM was designed with the goal of a minimal footprint, not maximum performance. For example, the KVM on the Palm OS has a footprint of 50–70 kB and needs 128 kB at runtime.

- *16/32-bit CPU.* To be usable for small pervasive devices, the KVM was designed to run on 16-bit processors at 16 MHz. However, it also runs on 32-bit processors.

- *Reference platforms* for the KVM exist for Palm OS, Solaris, and Windows32.

Because the KVM is based on the J2ME configuration, it has some significant differences to J2SE. These deviations are caused by the limited device capabilities. The main deviations are:

- *different UI classes*: the KVM does not provide the AWT or Swing libraries, as most pervasive devices have very limited display capabilities and limited processor power. The KVM therefore uses special native I/O drivers;

- *restricted VM*: to make the VM as small and efficient as possible, the KVM does not implement some of the standard JVM features. Some features are optional, such as floats, multidimensional arrays, and class file verification, and others, such as remote method invocation (RMI), thread grouping, and reflection, are missing completely.

- *subset of J2SE libraries*: to reduce the size of the Java library for memory-constrained devices, only subsets of the J2SE libraries are supported. For example, java.net and java.io are implemented only partially.

A development kit for the KVM, including the KVM source code, is available from Sun. Porting the KVM to a new hardware or operating system is easy. At the moment, the KVM is running on more than 20 platforms, including Nokia and Sony phones, and Motorola devices, and it will soon be available on the EPOC operating system.

Waba

Waba[7] is a programming platform that includes a language, a VM, a class file format, and a set of base classes. However, Waba is designed such that developers can use Java development tools to write Waba programs, and Waba programs can run as Java applets or applications with no native code.

Waba is very similar to Java, but is not compatible with it. Just like Java programs, Waba programs are compiled into interpreted bytecode, and the code can run without any changes on Palm or Windows CE devices containing a Waba VM. The software to build and run Waba programs is licensed under the GNU license, just like Linux. The following is a summary of the description available from the Wabasoft website.

To develop programs in Waba, the Java SDK and the Waba SDK need to be installed on a workstation. The Waba SDK consists of reference documentation, a set of Java classes, and some programs that are used to bundle application classes into a format suitable for small devices. It contains the bridge classes that allow Waba programs to run under Java.

While the syntax and semantics of the Waba language are identical to Java, they are not fully compatible. However, the Java compiler from the Java SDK can be used to compile programs. Before the program can be run on the target device, the bytecodes have to be translated into the bytecodes understood by the Waba VM. A tool called exegen performs the translation, and generates an executable that starts a compiled Waba program.

The Waba foundation classes are different from the foundation classes used for developing a program with the Waba SDK. They interface directly with the VM, and call methods that are native to the device the VM is operating on. The class file format supported by a Waba VM is defined as a subset of the class file format supported by a JVM. The Waba class library is designed to be simple and easy to program. It contains all the basic classes needed to create programs, including I/O, networking, user-interface, and graphics classes. Access to Palm OS and Windows CE databases is possible by using the `Catalog` class. It allows writing single-record blob types to and from a database.

Waba programs are executed by the Waba VM. A Waba program consists of classes and a device operating system-specific launch program. The launch program starts the Waba VM and tells it where the class files for the Waba program are. It also tells the Waba VM how much memory to allocate for the program.

The Waba VM was designed to execute a subset of bytecode instructions defined in the JVM specification. Because the Waba class file format is defined as a subset of the Java class file format, developers can use Java development tools to create class files and bytecode that are compatible with Waba, and execute them under a Waba VM. However, Waba VMs do not support operations related to long and double data types, exceptions, or threads.

Waba VMs can be created that run in very small amounts of memory. For example, the complete Waba VM for the Palm OS platform is around 60 kB (around 30 kB for the executable and 30 kB for the full set of foundation classes). Native functions can be added directly into the Waba VM using the Waba VM source code. The Waba VM contains no Java classes and the `waba.lang` package is not part of the SDK. Nevertheless, developers are able to use the `java.lang` `String`, `StringBuffer` and `Object` classes. When the Waba VM encounters references to the `java.lang` classes, it maps them to their counterparts in the `waba.lang` package.

IBM's VisualAge Micro Edition

The VisualAge Micro Edition J9 VM[8] is the foundation of IBM's embedded systems solution. VisualAge Micro Edition comes with several class library versions, ranging from extremely small to fully featured. These version choices enable developers to minimize resource requirements by choosing the class library support that best fits their device. All the available configurations are subsets of the JDK 1.2 specification. Examples of the class libraries are:

- *jclXtr*: an extremely reduced function library. The library uses 92 kB of ROM/Flash. It contains some APIs from the following packages: java.io, java.lang, java.net, java.util, and java.util.zip.

- *jclCore*: a small library with essential functionality. The library uses 344 kB of ROM/Flash. It contains most APIs from the following packages: java.io, java.lang, java.net, java.util, and java.util.zip.

- *jclGateway*: an extension of jclCore with URL and security functions. The library uses 563 kB of ROM/Flash. In addition to the packages used in jclCore, this package contains java.net.security for permission checking and also the java.lang.Runtime.exec methods.

- *jclMax*: the largest and most feature-rich library. The library uses 2479 kB of ROM/Flash and RAM. It contains most of the APIs from the packages java.io, java.lang, java.lang.ref, java.lang.reflect, java.math, java.net, java.text, java.util, java.util.jar, and java.util.zip. The following security packages are also included: java.security, java.security.acl, java.security.cert, java.security.interfaces, java.security.spec, and com.ibm.oti.security.provider.

VisualAge Micro Edition consists of an integrated development environment that supports JDK 1.2 compatible runtime environments and a set of platform-specific tools (Figure 3.32). The integrated development environment is available for Microsoft Windows and Red Hat Linux. It can be used to debug Java programs locally or remotely. The graphical debugger also supports the well-known operations like setting break points and stepping through the code, and allows viewing of the values of variables. It also allows the source code to be modified on the fly, but this feature is not supported on every target platform.

Supported target platforms are Windows, Linux, and many embedded environments, including Palm OS, Neutrino, embedded Linux and Windows CE. This enables, for example, the development of Java classes for the Palm OS platform with a Windows or Linux PC, and also allows running or debugging the software on the device immediately. In this debugging scenario, the J9 virtual machine running on the Palm device is connected to the PC via TCP/IP (Figure 3.33).

Figure 3.32

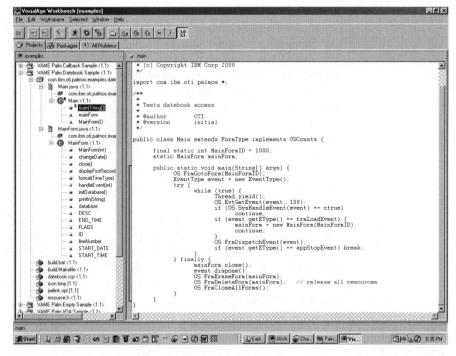

VisualAge integrated development environment

VisualAge Micro Edition supports code versioning and includes a repository server for team working. Also included is a smart linker, which creates a special prelinked class file archive where all unused methods are removed. This space optimization becomes all the more important, the less memory the target device offers. For including Java application in the device ROMs, ROM-able class archives can also be created.

Figure 3.33

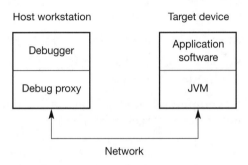

Remote debugging connection

Comparison

The three VMS described here represent different approaches and therefore have different advantages and disadvantages. Table 3.4 gives an overview of the features of different VMs.

The Sun KVM is the reference implementation for the connected limited device configuration (CLDC) configuration and is available on many platforms. A disadvantage of this more generic approach is that the execution speed is slow and the VM needs large libraries, as the native libraries of the device are not used.

Waba is an open-source project that tries to overcome these drawbacks by having a compressed bytecode format and by using the native libraries. The Waba VM must therefore be rewritten for each new operating system.

The J9 from IBM follows a similar path, but is aimed at the professional market. It therefore delivers libraries that are compliant with the Java standards. It is also integrated in a visual development environment with remote debugging ability. In contrast to the KVM and the Waba VM, the source code of the J9 is not available; the J9 is not available free of charge, but bundled with the Java VisualAge Micro Edition development environment from IBM.

Table 3.4	Comparison of VMs for pervasive devices		
	KVM	**Waba**	**J9**
Platforms	Palm, Windows CE, EPOC, Linux, Windows, Solaris	Palm, Windows CE	Palm, Windows CE, Neutrino, Linux, Windows
Performance	Low	High	High
Memory use	High	Low	Low
Libraries	Device-independent	Device-dependent	Device-dependent
Standards	Java2ME		Java, Java2ME
Source code available	Under Sun license	Open source	No
Development environment	Standard Java tools with KVM running on development platform	Standard Java tools with Waba VM running on development platform	Integrated development environment with remote debugging ability

3.6 Outlook

At present, the size and shape of a mobile device is dictated largely by its display and keyboard. However, the future will bring better, thinner displays based on the LEP or OLED technologies available. These will help to create displays flexible enough to be bent and shaped as required. This technology, together with Li polymer batteries and processors that require less power, will eventually enable manufacturer to design mobile devices that demonstrate hitherto unknown degrees of compactness in an almost unlimited number of form factors.

As pervasive computing is going to give us 'any time, anywhere' access to information and services, we need to acknowledge that people will carry their access devices 'all the time, everywhere'. These future access devices must not only meet the functional requirements but must also begin to accommodate our aesthetic, social, and emotional lives. Already, the PDA and mobile phone have started to take on the user's personality with fashionable accessories. With shrinking technology and increasing competition for pocket space, the concept of wearables has been explored. Instead of creating additional devices to wear, why not start by enhancing the things we already wear, like jewellery?

3.6.1 Digital jewellery

The technology shown in Figures 3.34 and 3.35 was created by the design laboratory within IBM Almaden Research's User Science and Experience Research (USER) group. Their research in digital jewellery explores the technological, aesthetic, social, and emotional needs with pervasive devices.

Figure 3.34

Watch and bracelet that contain the means to display data from a separate mobile device

Courtesy of IBM Corp.

Figure 3.35

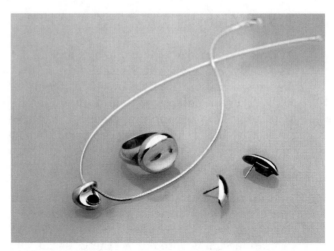

Ring containing a pointing device that may be used to interact with applications; necklace containing a microphone for voice interaction; and earings containing speakers for possible telephony applications

Courtesy of IBM Corp.

Prototypes range from conceptual models, to functional, non-wireless mock-ups, to fully wireless devices. While full realization of digital jewellery awaits further development of wireless and power technologies, the physical models coupled with meaningful scenarios can depict an understandable vision of how digital jewellery could contribute to the seamless integration of technology into everyday life.

The bracelet and watch shown in Figure 3.34 contain the means to display data from a separate mobile device carried by the user. Data transmission from that device will be wireless, e.g. using Bluetooth technology. A pointing device integrated into the ring shown in Figure 3.35 may be used to interact with applications. The necklace and earrings contain a microphone and speakers used for voice interaction and possibly telephony applications.

References

1. VDO. http://www.vdo.de

2. Textware Solutions. http://www.fitaly.com

3. T9. http://www.tegic.com

4. e-acute. http://www.e-acute.fr

5. Atelier. http://www.ateliersoftware.com

6. Embedded Linux Consortium. http://www.embedded-linux.org

7. Wabasoft http://www.wabasoft.com

8. OTI. http://www.embedded.oti.com

Further reading

1. Edwards, L. (1999) *Programming Psion Computers*, EMCC Software Limited.

2. Tanenbaum, A.S. and Woodhull, A.S. (1997) *Operating Systems: Design and Implementation*; Englewood Cliffs, NJ: Prentice Hall.

3. Murray, J. (1998) *Inside Microsoft Windows CE*. Microsoft Press.

4. http://www.qnx.com

5. http://www.be.com

6. http://www.research.ibm.com/WearableComputing

7. Tasker, M. *et al.* (2000) *Professional Symbian Programming – Mobile Solutions on the EPOC Platform*. Wrox Press.

8. http://www.linuxdevices.com

4 Device connectivity

Pervasive computing devices do not develop their full potential unless they are connected to applications and services through the Internet. This chapter covers protocols for device-to-device and device-to-server interactions that are relevant in the pervasive computing domain, including wireless protocols, mobile phone technologies, Bluetooth, the Mobile IP, synchronization protocols such as SyncML, and transaction protocols and protocols enabling distributed services, such as Jini. In addition to those protocols, we investigate further algorithms and protocols that address security issues. Because system and device management will become a big challenge to support millions of devices, the last section will discuss device management in the pervasive space.

4.1 Protocols

Standardized protocols are basic prerequisites for meaningful use of pervasive computing devices. Most devices are not very powerful or useful when used stand-alone. They need to exchange data with other devices, for example via wireless protocols.

Wireless protocols will support IP in the near future, making Mobile IP (a specially tailored IP for the needs of mobile devices) very important. We introduce this protocol below and explain its relation to the IPv6 protocol.

Another important topic is the consistency of databases and their data (e.g. calendar entries) between a server and various pervasive computing devices. This problem is solved with synchronization (also called replication). The major protocols supporting this concept are discussed below.

As connected pervasive devices form a distributed network, distributed services and architectures such as Jini are gaining interest in the pervasive computing domain and are explained in this chapter.

To ensure the delivery of the data in an environment, where the device can be switched off or the connection can break down at any time, message and transaction protocols are used to maintain integrity. These protocols are explained in the section on message- and transaction-based protocols.

Today, the main focus is on connection protocols such as WAP and Bluetooth. The first step of a large-scale deployment is to get the devices connected. Soon, these protocols will be established, then data-related protocols will become more important. They will help to ensure security and guaranteed delivery of messages expected by device users. Only when this infrastructure is in place will e-commerce using mobile devices have a substantial basis.

4.1.1 Wireless protocols

Wireless protocols are the natural communication choices for small hand-held devices such as PDAs and mobile phones. By definition, no cables are required in order to communicate with other devices.

Several wireless protocols already exist, and most are evolving rapidly. This section offers an overview of WAP and discusses Object Exchange (OBEX), IrDA, Bluetooth, and mobile phone technologies. The 802.11B protocol, a wireless local area network (LAN) protocol with high band-width (11 Mbps), will not be covered here. It is more suited for wireless connection of laptops to a LAN, than for pervasive computing devices. However, it may be used in a hybrid solution, where the pervasive device can make use of 802.11 inside an office and UTMS while outside.

WAP/WML

WAP is a technology designed to provide mobile terminal (i.e. mobile phones) users with rapid and efficient access to the Internet. WAP was conceived by Ericsson, Nokia, Motorola, and Openwave Systems, and is now driven by the WAP Forum industry association with over 200 members. WAP integrates telephony services with browser technology, and enables easy-to-use interactive Internet access from mobile handsets. Typical WAP applications include over-the-air e-commerce transactions, online banking, information provisioning, and messaging.

The WAP protocol is similar to HTTP, a high-level Internet communication protocol. WAP has been optimized, not only for use on the narrow-band radio channels of second-generation digital wireless systems, but also for the limited display capabilities of today's mobile terminals. The wireless equivalent of HTML is WML, which defines a textual format and a compressed binary format (WBXML). Unfortunately, there is currently no end-to-end security available in WAP, but this will change in the future through a working group that has been set up to solve this issue.

WAP is still a very young standard, and at the moment there are discussions under way as to whether WML can be integrated into Extensible Hyper Text Markup Language (XHTML) to unify HTML and WML. Mobile access to the Internet will increase with new phone technologies and more user-friendly devices (e.g. PDA devices with an integrated phone). Therefore, WAP will become enormously important in the near future; for this reason, we have dedicated a whole chapter to WAP (see Chapter 6).

OBEX

OBEX was originally defined for IrDA as IrOBEX, but it is independent from the underlying transport protocol. With the creation of the Bluetooth standard, OBEX has become the high-level protocol to use in order to be independent of the underlying transport protocol. OBEX was created to wrap an IrDA communication as completely as possible, thereby dramatically simplifying the development of communication-enabled applications. It has pull and push commands for bidirectional communication (unlike HTTP, which has only pull) and consists of two models:

- *The session model* structures the dialog between two devices. It uses a binary packet-based client/server request/response model.
- *The object model* carries information about the objects being sent, as well as containing the objects themselves. The object consists of a sequence of headers. A header is an entity that describes some aspect of the object, such as the name, length, descriptive text, or the object body itself. The headers can be parsed, similar in concept to the headers in HTTP.

OBEX also specifies an authentication method with a challenge/response scheme, but does not specify an encryption scheme. The two transport layers of choice for OBEX are IrDA and Bluetooth. Both have their advantages and disadvantages and therefore complement each other.

Bluetooth

Bluetooth is on RF specification for short-range data exchange. It is named after Herald I. Bluetooth, 910–85, who was the king of Denmark and first unified the country. Bluetooth was founded by Ericsson, IBM, Intel, Nokia, and Toshiba, and now has more than 1300 members. Bluetooth has the following characteristics:[1]

- *Frequency band*. Bluetooth operates in the 2.45-GHz industrial–scientific–medical (ISM) band.
- *Security*. There are several security mechanisms defined by the Bluetooth specification, such as authentication based on private keys and encryption.
- *Transmitting capabilities*. Bluetooth is omnidirectional and has a range up to 10 m. It supports isochronous and asynchronous transmitting services.
- *Bandwidth*. Bluetooth is capable of providing a data transfer rate up to 1 Mbps.

- *Speech*. There is support for three digital speech channels simultaneously.

- *Cost*. Bluetooth is still relatively expensive, with an expected price of $5–10 per Bluetooth module.

Bluetooth is the protocol of choice to connect two or more devices that are not in direct line of sight to each other. For example, a digital camera can send pictures to a hard disk that is in a nearby briefcase. Figure 4.1 shows a headset for a mobile phone connected via Bluetooth to the mobile phone in the user's pocket.

Because the user of a Bluetooth device has very limited capabilities to control who can talk to the device (by turning it on or off), there must be some mechanism in place to protect the device. Bluetooth offers different security modes, including authentication based on private keys and encryption, to solve this problem.

IrDA

The IrDA specifies several infrared communication standards, but the important ones for pervasive computing devices are IrDA-Data and Infrared Mobile Communications (IrMC).[2,3]

Figure 4.1

Bluetooth headset
Courtesy of the Bluetooth organization

IrDA has the following characteristics:

- *Frequency band*. Infrared light is used as the physical transport medium.
- *Security*. Unlike Bluetooth, IrDA has no security concept, but relies on higher-level protocol security.
- *Transmitting capabilities*. Because IrDA is based on infrared light, it consists of point-to-point connections with a narrow angle (30-degree cone) between sender and receiver. IrDA is designed for short-distance communication (0–30 cm).
- *Bandwidth*. IrDA supports data rates up to 4 Mbps, with 16 Mbps under development.
- *Speech*. There is support for only one digital speech channel.
- *Cost*. IrDA senders and receivers are mass-produced, therefore they are very cheap ($1–2).

IrDA is perfectly suited for high-speed data connections (e.g. connecting a device to a wired network). To initiate a data exchange, it requires a device to be in direct line of sight to the other IrDA device (e.g. to exchange virtual business cards).

4.1.2 Mobile phone technologies

The low-level communication protocols of mobile phones are radio-based and suited for long-distance communication (up to about 100 km). However, the technologies used today have a very limited bandwidth, meaning that data exchange rates are very slow. This will change with the third-generation protocols, like UMTS. Table 4.1 provides an overview of the different mobile phone communication protocols and their properties.

The sections that follow explain cellular systems, and the foundation of the mobile phone technology, and then discuss the different mobile phone system generations in more detail.

Cellular systems for mobile communication

Digital mobile communication systems use electromagnetic waves at frequencies around 1 GHz. Small antennae in the range of a couple of centimeters can be used to send and receive signals from a mobile station (mobile phone). However, the reach of mobile stations is rather limited due to power constraints and high damping of signals in the gigahertz range. Therefore, transmitters (senders or base stations) must be placed on a grid at relatively small distances to cover an entire area. Every transmitter covers a cell, which may vary in size from a couple of hundred meters in a city to tens of kilometers in rural areas. Every cell can handle

Table 4.1	**Overview of different generations of mobile phone communications**			
	1G	**2G**	**2+G**	**3G**
Protocol	AMPS, C-Net	GSM, TDMA, CDMA	GPRS, HSCSD, EDGE	UMTS, W-CDMA
Technology	Analog, circuit-switched	Digital, circuit-switched	Digital, circuit- or packet-switched	Digital, packet-switched
Speech quality	Poor	High	High	High
Bandwidth	Low	Low	Medium	High
Security	None	Depending on protocol, low to high	High	High

multiple channels. The limited reach of transmitters is certainly a disadvantage if mobile services must be delivered to a large area because many transmitters are required. However, the limited reach of senders allows reuse of scarce frequency bands between distant transmitters. Thus, a large number of mobile stations can be serviced.

Figure 4.2 shows that there might be dark spots where no mobile service is capable, even when senders are placed with care. Location and size of black spots may vary with weather conditions and mobile device characteristics. Frequently, the high investments for a complete coverage cannot be justified in rural areas, thus in many cases, mobile services are restricted to densely populated areas or the main commuter corridors. Mobile service providers typically publish maps where serviced areas are indicated. However, buildings and other objects may disrupt the signal.[4] Therefore, applications based on mobile systems must be designed to allow for non-availability of service or disruption of services. Typically this is achieved through a combination of online and offline operation.

Mobile stations are normally receiving signals from more than one station. Typically the station connects to the transmitter with the strongest signal. A moving station, e.g. a mobile phone in a car, may travel from one cell to another. The GSM system has been designed to allow movement of stations at a speed up to 150 km/h. Multiple base stations typically receive the signal of a transmitter. Signal delay is indicative for the distance between the transmitter and the mobile station. The station can be located through triangulation with accuracy of 30–150 m by combining

Figure 4.2

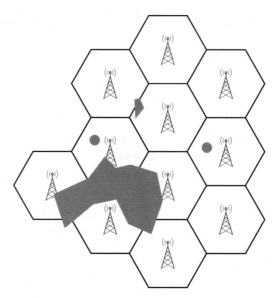

Cellular phone array

the information from three stations (this can also be achieved with two stations and a combination of angle of arrival (AOA) and time difference of arrival (TDOA) measurements). This allows the location of the mobile station to be detected, e.g. in case of an emergency call or to offer location-based services. Because such informative is sensitive and user-related, many countries have laws to prevent unauthorized use of these data (e.g. the Wireless Communications and Public Safety Act of 1999 in the USA).

First-Generation mobile systems

Usable wireless systems first came to market in the 1970s. In Germany the B-Net, which needed heavy transmitters and receivers, was successful as a car phone system, and in northern European countries the Nordic Mobile Telephone (NMT) system was launched. The successor of the B-Net, the C-Net, was in use in Germany until the end of 2000. In 1983, AMPS started the wireless phone market in North American countries.

All first-generation (1G) systems are analog, circuit-switched systems. Circuit-switched means that there is a dedicated point-to-point connection between the two ends of the call. As the systems were analog-based, they had poor speech quality and a low bandwidth for services like fax or data transmissions. Some analog systems are still in use (e.g. AMPS throughout the Americas), primarily because there is near 100% coverage for them. Analog systems have no built-in security for data transmission or user authentication.

Second-generation mobile systems

The second-generation (2G) mobile phone communication systems are digital, circuit-switched systems. The switch from analog to digital technology improved the speech quality enormously, and allowed for some additional services, such as encryption of the signal, authentication of the user, authorization, anonymity, and the ability to send short, alphanumeric messages. However, due to the circuit-switching technology, data transmission rates were still low (9.6–14.4 kbit/s).

Because there were a lot of incompatible analog mobile phone standards in Europe, the European Union in 1982 decided to develop a common standard, Groupe Spécial Mobile (GSM). GSM was finally standardized in 1991 and renamed Global System for Mobile communications. It works at 900 MHz, offers full international roaming, automatic location services, signal encryption, user authentication and authorization, anonymity, SMS, fax, and data service. SMS is becoming the most popular service of GSM, with about 12 billion SMS messages sent per month worldwide (data from October 2000). The GSM-900 standard is adopted worldwide in over 160 countries, and is the most popular mobile phone system, with more than 400 million users worldwide (including GSM-1800 and GSM-1900 at year end 2000). This results in a market share of about 60%, followed by the analog AMPS with a share of about 20%. To get a higher user density per cell in cities, GSM-1800 was developed. This works like GSM-900, but in the 1800-MHz frequency band, and offers better speech quality.

The USA also switched to digital systems, but largely stayed with their 850-MHz frequency range from AMPS. Because there were no standardization movements as in Europe, the result was three incompatible systems: the old analog AMPS, and the new digital TDMA and CDMA systems. In contrast to GSM, TDMA and CDMA do not support encryption, authentication, or SMS. With the user density in big cities becoming a problem, CDMA and TDMA switched to 1900 MHz. There is now a US GSM version in place operating in the same 1900-MHz frequency band, therefore called GSM-1900. The reason for all these different frequencies is the lack of standardization. UMTS will be the first telephone standard that also defines worldwide valid frequencies.

Table 4.2 shows the development of the wireless phone market. The first three rows show the most popular digital systems: the GSM system has by far the most subscribers. The figure also displays the trend towards digital systems, as the number of digital system subscribers has grown by more than 25% in six months, and the number of analog system users has declined by 10% in the same time.

Two-and-a-half-generation mobile systems

Between the 2G and 3G mobile phone systems lies an intermediate step, generation 2+G. In contrast to a generation 3G system, a generation 2+G

Table 4.2	**Worldwide wireless phone subscribers (millions)**

	April 2000	October 2000
GSM	304	397
CDMA	62	76
US TDMA	44	56
Total digital	457	579
Total analog	83	75
Total wireless	540	654

Source: EMC World Cellular Database

system requires only minor hardware and software changes by the phone companies. In Europe, 2+G systems like GPRS and High-speed Circuit-Switched Data (HSCSD) are already in operation. However, users need new mobile phones in order to use these services.

The easiest way to achieve a higher bandwidth than GSM is by aggregating multiple GSM channels, for example in the HSCSD technology. In HSDSC, multiple basic traffic channels are bundled to achieve data rates of up to 57.6 kbps. Different numbers of channels can be assigned to upstream or downstream data transmission. HSCSD can provide a fixed bit rate in transparent mode, or a variable bit rate in non-transparent mode. The advantage of HSCSD is that it is still compatible with GSM technology and therefore requires no major changes or investments by the service provides. Static assignment of channels is not well suited for the typical requirements of Internet applications, where a small burst of data is sent from the client to the server, followed by a large burst of data as response. Therefore, most GSM-based systems will not implement HSCSD, but will move directly on to the next generation of packet-oriented data transmission.

GPRS has been standardized by the European Telecommunications Standardization Institute (ETSI) as part of the GSM Phase 2+ development. It gives GPRS providers a smooth transition to the third-generation (3G) networks, as network architecture, services, and business models are similar. It represents the first implementation of packet switching within GSM. Rather than sending a continuous stream of data over a permanent connection, as in circuit-switched systems, packet switching utilizes the network only when there are data to be sent. This results in a more efficient use of the network, as one physical connection can be shared. The transmission rates range from 20 kbps to 171 kbps. The drawback of packet switching is that there is no guaranteed bandwidth, which can be important for live video streams. However, technologies are available, such as ATM, where guaranteed bandwidth can be reserved even with packet-switched networks.

By breaking the transmitted data into packets instead of sending them as a continuous stream, mobile devices remain connected 'virtually' to the server, using airtime only when data are actually being sent. GPRS thereby optimizes airtime use (and possibly associated connection costs) as well as power consumption. This will simplify access to the Internet, making it cheaper and therefore more attractive.

The packet-based GPRS protocol is ideally suited for burst-data applications, such as email or Internet access, and also enables virtually permanent connections to data sources, allowing information to arrive automatically rather than being sought (push model instead of a pull model). Another benefit of the packed-based approach is that being connected to the Mobile Internet does not interfere with receiving a phone call, because the data session may be suspended while the call is answered. Furthermore, it enables broadcast, multicast, or unicast message services that cannot be achieved using standard circuit-switched networks.

Third-generation mobile systems

3G mobile phone systems will bring packet switching and high data rates in the range of several Mbps. This will be a breakthrough for mobile computing, making high data rates and full Internet access using the standard Internet TCP/IP protocol possible for pervasive devices. It will also support bandwidth-hungry multimedia applications, such as full-motion video and video conferencing.

Requiring new hardware for transmission, it will be some time before the 3G networks offer good coverage. 3G networks are expected to be in operation in Japan by 2001, in Europe and Asia/Pacific by 2002, and in the USA by 2003–4.

The UMTS is part of IMT-2000, the 3G wireless services specification of the International Telecommunication Union (ITU). The UMTS Forum was established to focus on spectrum availability, licensing issues and long-term market surveys for third 3G. The UMTS frequencies in the USA are still used by TV stations that have contracts running until 2003–4 with an option to extend it. There are discussions and negotiations about how to make UMTS happen as soon as possible. It is expected that worldwide coverage will be achieved by the year 2005.

UMTS is based on wide-band CDMA (W-CDMA), which was originated by Japan's NTT DoCoMo and is now adopted for 3G use by ETSI. In addition to speech and data, W-CDMA also supports high-speed multimedia services, such as video films, video conferencing, and Internet access, and offers data throughput up to 2 Mbps. Table 4.3 shows how the data transmission rate influences the availability of offered services. For reference, the wired-line ISDN is inserted.

Table 4.3 Delivery time of different services for different phone technologies

Service	ISDN	2G (GSM)	2+G (GPRS)	3G (UMTS)
Email file (10 kB)	1 s	8 s	0.7 s	0.04 s
Web page (9 kB)	1 s	9 s	0.8 s	0.04 s
Text file (40 kB)	5 s	33 s	3 s	0.2 s
Large report (2 MB)	2 min	28 min	2 min	7 s
Video clip (4 MB)	4 min	48 min	4 min	14 s
TV Quality Movie (6 GB)	104 h	1100 h	52 h	~5 h

Source: UMTS Forum (2000) Report 11

Since the patent issues about CDMA seem to be resolved, W-CDMA will soon get a wide availability because the GSM community, which supplies the dominant technology today, supports it. Among the supporters of W-CDMA are NTT DoCoMo, Ericsson, Nokia, and Qualcomm. UMTS and W-CDMA are important for future mobile devices because they offer the high data rates needed for accessing the Internet via mobile devices.

4.1.3 Mobile Internet Protocol

As soon as high-speed mobile connection is available, the next step is to use this connection from a mobile device to access the Internet. This section explains the standard IP and the Mobile Internet Protocol (Mobile IP). Finally, the new Internet Protocol v6 and its effects on the Mobile IP are discussed.

Standard Internet Protocol and mobile devices
At the moment, the standard protocol used in the Internet is IP version 4 (IPv4). IPv4 defines nodes that have a unique and fixed address consisting of a quadruplet. The Internet addressing scheme is similar to that of the telephone. In a telephone network, the addressing scheme consists of a number for the country, a number for the city, and then a number for the individual telephone connection. IP addressing also has a prefix that determines the subnet the address is part of. This prefix can be followed by a group and subgroup prefix before the address number for the individual device.

The messages that are sent through the Internet are called packages. They incorporate the sender's address and port number, and the recipient's address and port number. A scenario for sending a package over IP can be seen in Figure 4.3.

Figure 4.3

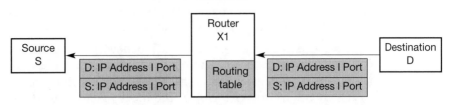

Sending a package using the standard IP

The delivery of packages via intermediate hosts is called routing. The routers take the destination address, mask out the low-order bits, and then look up the resulting network address in their routing table. Thus, the IP address typically carries with it information that specifies where it belongs in the IP topology. The routing table contains the next routing host for each network address, and tells the routing host to which host the received package has to be forwarded. There can be many routing hosts between the sender and the receiver of a package.

IPv4 was designed for PCs that do not move around, and it works quite well for this purpose. When using IP with mobile devices, the problem is maintaining an existing transport layer connection with the device. Preferably the device should keep its IP address and port number fixed. As the mobile device moves, it reaches new points of attachment with a different IP address range. The device can now get a new IP address from this point of attachment, but then the connection to its old address will be broken. Mobile IP, provides a way to solve this problem and how to enable mobile devices to communicate over IPv4.

Mobile Internet Protocol

The Mobile IP was created to overcome the problems of IPv4 for mobile devices. In 1996, the Mobile IP working group submitted an IPv4 Mobile Host Protocol to the Internet Engineering Steering Committee (IESC).

To overcome the address problems of IPv4 for mobile nodes (devices) as described above, Mobile IP uses two IP addresses: a fixed home address and a care-of address that changes at each new point of attachment. The home address is attached to a home agent, so whenever the mobile node is not attached to the home network, it gets all the packages intended for the mobile node and forwards them to the mobile node's current point of attachment.

For establishing a connection to a mobile node, the following steps must be performed:

- *Discover the care-of address.* The Mobile IP discovery is built on top of a standard protocol, the router advertisement. The router advertisements already existing in the IP standard are extended to carry information about the care-of addresses. This enables the routers to update their routing tables.

- *Register the care-of address.* Whenever the mobile node moves, it registers its new care-of address with its home agent. The mobile node needs to authenticate itself to the home agent to prevent unauthorized nodes from registering at the home agent. The authentication is performed with a digital signature.

- *Tunnel the care-of address.* The home agent modifies the received packages so that the care-of address appears as the destination IP address. This is called redirection or tunnelling. When a packet arrives at the care-of address, the reverse transformation is applied. This results in a packet that once again has the mobile node's home address as the destination IP address. Figure 4.4 shows this tunnelling process for the request. As the sender address is unchanged, the reply from the mobile node goes directly to the sender, not via the home agent. This results in asymmetric routing – triangle routing – and can cause routing inefficiencies.

Mobile IP is still an ongoing effort and under discussion. One of the open points is the firewall concept. Firewalls block incoming packages that do not meet specific criteria. One of these criteria is that no incoming packet can have an internal IP address as source. But with the Mobile IP protocol, this is exactly the case if a mobile node outside its home network wants to send a packet to its home network.

Changes to Internet Protocol Version 6

IPv6 will include many features for mobility support that are currently missing in IPv4. IPv6 features relevant for Mobile IP are stateless address autoconfiguration and neighbor discovery. With these two features, a mobile node can create or obtain a topologically correct care-of address for the current point of attachment, without the need for a foreign agent to provide the mobile node with such address.

A big difference between IPv4 and IPv6 is that IPv6 expects all nodes to implement strong encryption and authentication features. Therefore,

Figure 4.4

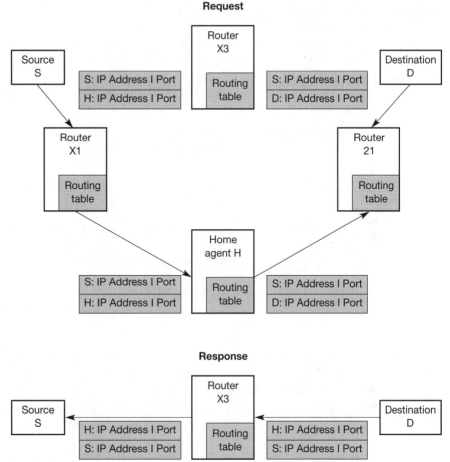

Sending a package via Mobile IP

Mobile IP for IPv6 can use the IPv6 security features, and need not provide its own security mechanism.

Although IPv6 will support mobility to a greater degree than IPv4, it will still need Mobile IP to make mobility transparent to applications and higher-level protocols such as TCP. Therefore, the Mobile IP working group will submit an IPv6 Mobile IP protocol to the IESG for standardization.

4.1.4 Synchronization and replication protocols

Synchronization, also called replication in the database area, keeps data consistent between different devices. An example of synchronization is having an electronic calendar on the PC and on the PDA. Changes in the

Table 4.4   Different synchronization solutions

	Clients	Server	Used for
AvantGo	Palm OS, Windows CE	AvantGo Server	Retrieving content channels (e.g. Web pages)
Mobile Connect	Palm OS, Windows CE, EPOC	Lotus Notes, MS Exchange, RDBS	PIM applications, databases
IntelliSync	Palm OS, Windows CE	Lotus Notes, MS Outlook, etc.	PIM applications
TrueSync	Mobile phones (Ericsson, Motorola, Nokia), Palm OS, Windows CE	Lotus Notes, MS Outlook, Sidekick, etc.	PIM applications

PC calendar should be reflected in the PDA calendar, and vice versa. Another scenario is software update. When a lot of devices are out in the field, there comes a time when it is necessary to update parts of the software in these devices. Synchronization can be used to efficiently update only the required parts of the software and take account of the dependencies (e.g. library versions).

At the moment there are many synchronization products available for different devices and different needs. Some of them are listed in Table 4.4 (AvantGo is from AvantGo Inc., Mobile Connect is an IBM product, IntelliSync is provided by Puma Technologies, and TrueSync is from Starfish Technologies).

Unfortunately, all solutions have different synchronization protocols, and it is therefore not easy to synchronize two clients with the same software to the same server (e.g. a PDA and a mobile phone). The goal of the SyncML standard is to solve this problem. SyncML is explained in more detail below.

Synchronization principles

To synchronize data, such as calendar entries or address books, between several pervasive computing devices, there are two strategies: device – server synchronization; and device–device synchronization. As can be seen in Figure 4.5, this can result in complex scenarios, where different device clients can even synchronize with different servers. When performing device-to-device synchronization, one device needs to act as a server. To handle out-of-sync situations, a special protocol is needed.

Synchronization protocols typically consist of the following steps:

1. *Presynchronization*. To prepare the actual synchronization, some action must be taken before this can happen. These actions fall into the following groups: authentication, authorization, and determination of device capabilities. Authentication ensures that the server is who it claims to be, and that the client is who it claims to be. Authorization checks whether the client is allowed to perform the requested action (e.g. delete, update, or create new entries). Finally, the server determines the device capabilities (e.g. maximum buffer size) to optimize the data flow to the device.

2. *Synchronization*. This is the part in which the synchronization data are exchanged. Between two synchronization partners, all local IDs of data entries are mapped to global IDs known to both partners. Every partner therefore has a mapping table to map local to global IDs. Only the updated, new, or deleted entries are exchanged. If both partners

Figure 4.5

One client – one server sync

Multiple clients – one server sync

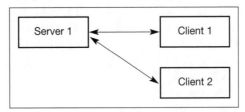

Multiple clients – multiple servers sync

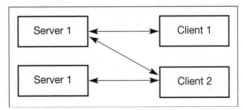

Various synchronization scenarios

update the same data entry, there will be a conflict. This update conflict can be resolved in different ways: attempt to merge the updates, duplicate the entries, let one entry win over the other, or do nothing and report the conflict so that the user can solve it.

3. *Post-synchronization*. At this point all the clean-up tasks are performed, such as updating the mapping tables and reporting unresolved conflicts.

In the following section, we present an example of a synchronization protocol, SyncML.

SyncML

In late 1999, Ericsson, IBM, Lotus, Motorola, Nokia, Palm, Psion, and Starfish founded the SyncML initiative. After the official launch in February 2000, the initiative consists of more than 600 organizations supporting the SyncML standard (as of May 2001).

The vision of the SyncML members is to enable ubiquitous data access from any device to any networked data. To achieve this goal, SyncML released documents describing the protocol and transport bindings, source code of a reference implementation (called SyncML Framework), and source code to demonstrate the use of SyncML.

In contrast to the Microsoft Mobile Information Server, which tries to synchronize only Microsoft Office data to different client devices, SyncML supports standard formats for PIM (xCard and xCalendar) and for database synchronization (XRelational).

The SyncML protocol is based on Extensible Markup Language (XML) and is independent of the transport protocol. HTTP, OBEX, and Wireless Transaction Protocol (WTP) are defined as transport bindings for a SyncML-compliant device. Each synchronization message is an XML document, which is sent. The recipient can identify the format of the message by the MIME type of that message, e.g. clear-text XML or binary XML (WBXML).

A typical SyncML system is shown in Figure 4.6. Application A (e.g. Palm Calendar) is sending synchronization data via its client sync engine to the SyncML Framework. The SyncML Framework translates the API calls (e.g. Update, Create) and the data into a valid SyncML document and sends it to the server. On the server side, the SyncML Framework receives the document, parses it, and then sends the command and data to the server sync engine, which then talks to application B (e.g. Lotus Notes Calendar).

The SyncML Framework is available for Windows, Linux, Palm OS, and EPOC. It aims to give device manufactures a jump-start in integrating SyncML into their devices, as it gives the Sync Engine an API for easy use, handling all the XML encoding and the transport protocol-related

Figure 4.6

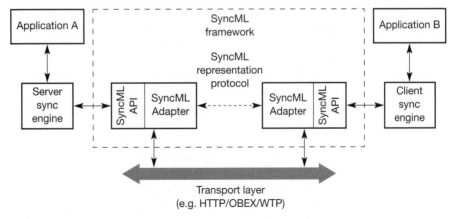

SyncML Framework

issues. SyncML-compliant devices and synchronization products are now available from Nokia, Ericsson, and Motorola.

4.1.5 Distributed services

Many pervasive computing scenarios consist of networked components that build a distributed system, like mobile phones or PDAs with wireless connectivity. With this distribution and connectivity new challenges arise. Not only are distributed and networked systems gradually becoming more difficult to build than stand-alone systems, but also the complexity is growing exponentially with the number of interacting systems. In addition, networks are not reliable, secure, static, or deterministic. There are not only gradual differences to stand-alone systems, but completely different architectures are required to deal with these issues. For example, the non-deterministic behaviour of a network leads to the problem of deciding whether a component has failed, or whether it is just very slow in processing the request. Distributed services must take all this into account and find a solution for these problems.

While pervasive computing devices get wireless connectivity to build a distributed system, distributed services will become increasingly important. Two examples for distributed infrastructures are presented below: Sun's Jini and Microsoft's Universal Plug and Play.

Jini

Jini, defined by Sun Microsystems, provides a technology for distributed Java software systems.[5] Jini was originally designed for software and hardware, and was targeted for the small office/home office market with a focus on instantaneous networking. However, Jini has developed far beyond the use of consumer devices that can be plugged into a network, just as appliances are plugged into a power supply. Jini is now used in the enterprise space, where it provides a service-oriented infrastructure, self-healing networks, and federation of services for an easy legacy system integration.

Jini requires that all participants have a Java VM running on their system. This is a more restricted approach than, for example, that of CORBA or DCOM, where data types of different languages are mapped. However, this approach has the advantage that there is no problem with primitive data types (e.g. the number of bytes for an integer value in C depends on the hardware platform). Because all systems require the Java VM, it is also easy to distribute data as well as code. Downloading code has one drawback: it is difficult to ensure that the downloaded code has the same quality as the code already running on that device and does not make the device unusable.

The main weakness of Jini is that currently it is not secure. Jini uses the Java RMI architecture, which still needs some improvement in security. In addition, Jini needs services for authentication and authorization. Hopefully this will be included in a future version of Jini.

As mentioned, Jini uses Java RMI as a communication layer between the different Jini participants. Some very useful services to enable spontaneous, self-healing distributed systems are built on top of RMI. They are based on five key concepts:

- *Discovery:* the service that finds other members in the Jini community and joins them, enabling spontaneous networking capability.

- *Look-up:* a directory that understands the Java-type hierarchy. This means that a look-up search is not simply a text string search, but is based on the object type and even considers the inheritance hierarchy.

- *Leasing:* ensures that the Jini network is stable and self-healing. Resources or services are only leased, meaning they have an expiry time stamp. After that time, they must be requested again and it would become obvious if the service or the providing server was no longer available.

- *Remote events:* allow Jini services to send notification to participants in a Jini community.

- *Transactions*: similar to database transactions. They allow a program to perform a series of computations and reach a consistent state after either all steps are completed successfully, or none of them has been completed. The transactions solve part of the problem of the non-deterministic network behavior mentioned before.

A typical Jini scenario is shown in Figures 4.7 and 4.8. The service consumer first contacts the look-up service and requests a service, e.g. printing (the request in Figure 4.7). The look-up service searches its list

Figure 4.7

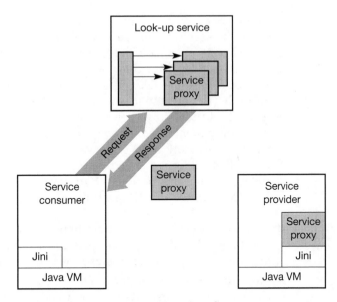

Jini scenario for accessing a remote service: first step

of registered services and returns the code to talk to the requested service (proxy service), e.g. printer driver for a specific printer (the response in Figure 4.8).

Figure 4.8

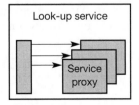

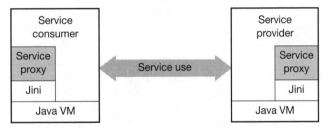

Jini scenario for accessing a remote service: second step

The service consumer can now execute this piece of Java code and therefore use the service of the service provider directly, e.g. send objects to the printer driver, which translates them into the printer protocol (the service use in Figure 4.8). After the look-up service provides the code to talk to the requested service provider, it is no longer involved. This prohibits communication bottlenecks that would occur if the look-up service received all requests first to forward them to the appropriate service provider.

As already mentioned, a prerequisite for Jini is the Java RMI functionality. Unfortunately, a lot of pervasive computing devices do not support Java or RMI yet, and are therefore not able to participate in the Jini community. To solve this problem, Sun developed a proxy concept called Jini Surrogate Architecture. This architecture consist of two parts:

- *Surrogate host:* a full Java 2 system with Jini support. In addition, it knows how to talk to its clients (e.g. WAP, X10, OSGi, USB). It offers discovery services and can store the proxy code for the client.
- *Surrogate client:* the first kind of client does not have a JVM and therefore cannot execute the proxy code. This means that the host must execute the proxy code. The other kind of client has a limited JVM, which allows the proxy code to be executed, but does not have the RMI capability (e.g. J2ME KVM). Executing the proxy code on the client takes workload from the server without requiring the client to implement the RMI package.

Jini allows spontaneous networking and is very attractive for pervasive computing devices that are not attached permanently to a specific network. An example of using Jini in the pervasive computing space is the OSGi, which is used in automotive systems (see Chapter 2).

Universal Plug and Play

Universal Plug and Play (UPnP) was created by Microsoft and currently has a lot of supporters (Compaq, Hewlett-Packard, IBM, Intel, Matsushita, Mitsubishi, Siemens, Sony, and others). It has the same goals as Jini: to provide spontaneous networking and device interoperability. However, UPnP chooses a different approach. Instead of building the distributed infrastructure service on Java, UPnP uses HTTP and XML, which are both open standards. As a consequence, UPnP can distribute data but not code over the network. This can be an advantage (more secure) or a disadvantage (less functionality).

UPnP allows for zero-configuration networking and relies heavily on the Dynamic Host Configuration Protocol (DHCP) for devices in order to dynamically join a network. DHCP is used for retrieving an IP address and to get the DNS server location. It also relies on Auto IP, an enhancement to DHCP to claim IP addresses in the absence of DHCP servers that is based on generating randomly an address in a reserved address space.

UPnP does not depend on a specific transport protocol, and it can be used with wireless transport protocols. It does not define any security protocols and therefore relies on the protocols used below UPnP or the security mechanism implemented by applications using UPnP.

The services offered by UPnP are very similar to those offered by Jini. Instead of using a programming language like Java to implement these services, UPnP builds on XML standards, such as the Simple Service Discovery Protocol (SSDP) for service discovery, the General Event Notification Architecture (GENA) for events, and SOAP for remote procedure calls. These services are explained in more detail below.

- *IP addressing*. A device that will join an UPnP network must get an IP address. This can be achieved by two different methods in UPnP. The first is to use DHCP, meaning the device must have a DHCP client. The device sends out a request to be answered by a DHCP server. If no DHCP server answers the request in a reasonable time, then the device uses Auto IP to generate an IP address from a set of reserved IP addresses.
- *Discovery*. The discovery mechanism allows devices to advertise their services to control points, and to use new control points to search for devices of interest. The messages sent in both cases are XML documents based on the SSDP protocol.
- *Description*. After a device has announced itself to a control point, it needs to tell the control point what kind of service it is offering. This is called a description in UPnP and is represented by an XML document that the control point requests from the device.
- *Control*. After the control point has the description of the device and therefore knows the provided services, it can send requests to the device. UPnP calls these requests 'control messages'. They are represented by XML documents based on the SOAP standard, which allows remote function calls.
- *Events*. Control points can subscribe to events on devices. Whenever an event occurs, the device will send a notification to all subscribed control points. The mechanism for subscribing and sending the events is taken from the GENA protocol, that also uses XML documents for communication between event generator and event receiver.
- *Presentation*. Devices can specify a presentation URL under which the device can be configured remotely via a browser.

A UPnP scenario can be seen in Figures 4.9 and 4.10. The device (client) uses DHCP to get an IP address from the DHCP server (Figure 4.9). After it has received a valid IP address, it can participate in the UPnP network. Therefore, it starts the discovery mechanism that is

Figure 4.9

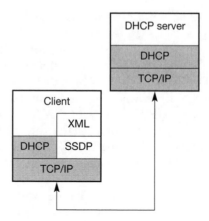

UPnP scenario using DHCP: first step

based on SSDP and advertises its services via an XML document to a listening control point (Figure 4.10).

Now the control point knows the device name, a universal device ID and a URL where it can get the device description. The next step for the control point is to request the device description. The device sends back an XML document containing vendor-specific data, the offered services, a control URL, an event URL, and a URL for presentation (e.g. when a device consists of several subdevices). After that, the control point is able to use the services of that device.

Figure 4.10

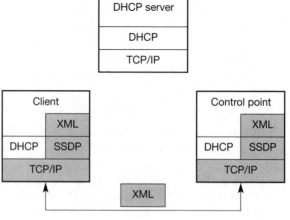

UPnP scenario using DHCP: second step

As UPnP requires mainly IP and XML, it does not need much space on a device and is therefore well suited for pervasive devices. The example given on the UPnP website is a digital camera using UPnP to offer remote-control services.

4.1.6 Message- and transaction-based protocols

Message- and transaction-based protocols ensure delivery and atomic operations in the pervasive computing space, where communication breakdowns, or devices being switched on and off while attempting to transmit data, are likely scenarios. This becomes extremely important for e-commerce applications. If something is bought over the Net via a mobile device, it is essential that the order is received, but only once.

The following sections explain the different technologies available, and then give an overview of available products.

Messaging and transaction technology

Guaranteed message delivery and atomic operations are two different technologies. Nevertheless, it does make sense to put both in the same section, as normally we would want ensured delivery for atomic operations. Databases on mobile devices therefore often use messaging systems as their transport layer.

One issue that is slowing down the fast spreading of message systems and transactional databases is the lack of standards. The solution to this problem can possibly be achieved on a higher level using SOAP. SOAP provides a mechanism for exchanging structured and typed information between peers in a decentralized, distributed environment using XML. SOAP is a new proposal to the ITEF and is supported by many companies.[6] For more information about SOAP see Chapter 9.

Message queuing solves the problem of assured delivery of a message. This is achieved via a queuing system, where the application puts the message in the queue and the queuing system ensures the delivery.

Queuing systems also allow asynchronous delivery of messages. This is of interest for devices that are not always connected to a network (e.g. PDAs). As soon as there is a connection to the network, the queuing system delivers the message to the recipient. It can be specified how long the message may wait in the queue before it becomes obsolete (e.g. ordering stock).

Figure 4.11 shows some typical messaging scenarios. Complete topologies can be built with queues. Besides the trivial one-to-one queues, the configuration can include distributing one message to several queues (e.g. sending to multiple devices), or collecting messages from different queues into one queue (e.g. forwarding email from different accounts to one device).

Transactional databases are the natural choice for grouping messages into an atomic block (also called transaction). Transactions are important

Figure 4.11

One-to-one queues

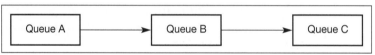

One-to-many queues

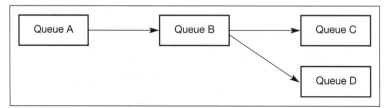

Many-to-one queues

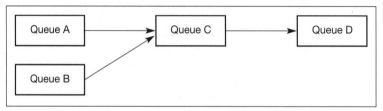

Messaging scenarios

in the e-commerce area to ensure either that no action is performed or that all actions are performed (e.g. one action could be a payment and the other an order).

Transactional databases are very common on server systems, but not many pervasive computing devices have a built-in transactional database with rollback and standard SQL as query language. This is because until recently databases were very big and needed a lot of runtime memory. This is changing now, and more and more database vendors are providing smaller versions that are suitable for pervasive computing devices, interoperating with the databases on the host side. Therefore, transactional databases with an SQL interface will soon be integrated into pervasive computing devices.

Messaging and transaction products
While there are several messaging systems available on the server side, e.g. the free SwiftMQ, which is based on Java Message Services, there are not many products that implement message or transaction support for small devices. The major products are ExpressQ from Broadbeam

Corporation (formerly Nettech Systems), MQ Series Everyplace (MQe) from IBM, Microsoft's MSMQ, and iBus//Mobile from SoftWired. Table 4.5 shows the various message queuing systems and their availability for client operating systems. The footprint of the major products is between 64 and 150 kB.

The situation for databases is similar to that of the message queuing systems. Currently, few relational databases support more than one client device platform. Table 4.6 details the most popular two: IBM's DB2 Everyplace (DB2e) and Oracle's Oracle Lite.

Both databases also have support for database synchronization between pervasive computing client devices and servers.

4.2 Security

In this section, we give an introduction to security in pervasive computing, focusing on the server-side aspects of pervasive computing applications. We start with an overview of the basic security concepts, including identification, authentication, authorization, transaction authorization, and non-repudiation, and give an outline of how they can be implemented. Then we give an overview of the most relevant cryptographic algorithms that are commonly used to realize these concepts as a

Table 4.5	Message queuing systems			
	Palm OS	**Windows CE**	**EPOC**	**Embedded Linux**
ExpressQ	✓	✓		
MQe	✓	✓	✓	
MSMQ		✓		
iBus/Mobile	✓	✓	✓	✓

Table 4.6	Relational databases for pervasive computing devices	
	Supported platforms	**Database footprint**
DB2e	EPOC, Linux, embedded Linux, Neutrino, Palm OS, Windows CE	150 KB
Oracle Lite	EPOC32, Palm OS, Windows CE	50–750 KB (depending on configuration)

basis for secure pervasive computing applications. We present standard cryptographic protocols for authentication and secure transmission of data, and give some examples of how these protocols are used in pervasive computing applications.

4.2.1 Security concepts

Before discussing security of pervasive computing applications, it is important to understand the basic security concepts. Below, we explain briefly the concepts of identification, authentication, authorization, and non-repudiation that will be used in the remainder of this chapter.

Identification

There are various methods for identifying users accessing a server using pervasive computing devices. The most universal method is using a user identification that the user has to enter or that is stored in the device. Another method that may be employed if the user has a mobile phone is using the telephone number. If the user has a certificate, the certificate's unique identifier can be used. Because the user may access a server using different identifiers, depending on the device used, these identifiers have to be mapped to canonical user IDs.

Authentication

Authentication means proving that somebody actually is who he or she says they are. Authentication may be performed in various ways, depending on the capabilities of the device used, resulting in different levels of assurance of the user's identity. The most universal authentication method is authentication by user identification and password. After a secure connection between the client and the server has been established, for example using Secure Sockets Layer (SSL) from a PC or Wireless transport layer security (WTLS) from a WAP phone, the application prompts the user for the identification and a password using an appropriate form. The user identification and the password, or a hash of the password, are transmitted to the server and verified to authenticate or reject the user.

A more secure method that may be used with PCs, or soon with WAP phones with a wireless identification module (WIM), is authentication using a smart card. The importance of smart cards is increasing, especially in Europe and Asia, as they are used as SIMs in all GSM phones, and more and more smart-card-based payment systems and public-key infrastructures (PKIs) emerge. Here, an authentication protocol is executed between the smart card on the client side and the authentication software on the server side, e.g. by an applet or a browser itself. Usually, the server gives a random challenge to the client, who provides it to the smart card and requests a signature over the card identification and the challenge. Often, a password provided by the user has to be given to the smart card before a signature can be obtained to ensure that someone who finds or steals the card cannot abuse it. Finally, the card identification with the signature is sent back to the server for verification (Figure 4.12).

Authorization

A common authorization scheme is to define principals and associate permissions that these principals posses. Permissions can be used to invoke particular methods of particular objects. Such schemes are appropriate when there is only one sort of client and one sort of authentication protocol that may be used by these clients. Because pervasive computing applications may be accessible from various clients using different authentication methods, authorization to perform an action may depend not only on the principal, but also on the device and authentication method he or she currently uses. Table 4.7 gives an example.

User A has a PC and a WAP phone. A can access his or her account information and transfer money from the PC after authenticating themselves using a smart card. Access to the account information from the PC is also possible after authentication with user identification and password. From the WAP phone, the user can only view the account information after authentication with user identification and password. User B has only a normal telephone, thus there is no entry besides the voice entries, which specify that user identification and password are required for this user to view account information or transfer money. User C has a PDA and can view account information and transfer money authenticated by user identification and password.

Figure 4.12

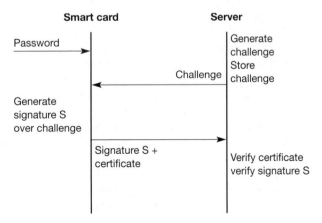

Example of an authentication protocol

Table 4.7   **Examples of authorization**

User/role	Device	Authentication mechanism	Permissions (application/function)
User A	PC	Smart card 1024-bit signature	Home banking/ view account
	PC	Smart card 1024-bit signature	Home banking/ transfer amount
	PC	User ID/password	Home banking/ view account
	WAP phone	User ID/Password	Home Banking/ view account
User B	Voice	User ID/password	Home banking/ view account
	Voice	User ID/password	Home banking/ transfer amount
User C	PDA	User ID/password	Home banking/ view account
	PDA	User ID/password	Home banking/ transfer amount

Transaction authorization

Some applications allow users to initiate transactions that are very sensitive, e.g. money transfers in home-banking applications or placing orders in brokerage applications. To achieve an appropriate level of security for these transactions, the user usually has to authorize each individual transaction. The technical means for transaction authorization must assure that only the legitimate user is able to authorize transactions. Two commonly used solutions for this problem are digital signatures endorsed by a password and transaction authorization numbers (TANs).

Digital signatures endorsed by a password

To enable transaction authorization through digital signatures endorsed by a password, the user is equipped with a token that has the ability to store securely a key, and to generate digital signatures using that key. The token has to be set up in a way that allows generation of a signature only if the user provided a password before. When a user initiates a sensitive transaction, the server requests the user to generate a digital signature over a challenge and the transaction data using the token. The user enters the password for the token and the token generates the required signature. The signature is passed to the server, which checks it and executes the transaction only if the signature is correct. Thus, authorizing a transaction is only possible if one possesses the token and knows the password for the token. A person who steals the token will not be able to use it because he or she will not know the required password.

Transaction authorization numbers

TANs are secret numbers delivered to the legitimate user in blocks. The organization that sends the TANs to the user makes sure that the users are aware of the importance of the TANs: the user may have to acknowledge formally that they have received a TAN block, and they may have to sign a statement that they will keep the TAN block secret and never reveal it to anyone else. When a user initiates a sensitive transaction, the server requests the user to enter the next valid TAN (each TAN may be used only once). The user enters the TAN and it is sent to the server. The server checks whether the TAN matches the number it expected. Only if this is the case does it execute the transaction.

Non-repudiation

Non-repudiation means that a user cannot falsely deny later that he or she authorized a transaction. To ensure non-repudiation, transaction authorization must result in data – like a digital signature, for example – that can be used later to prove that the transaction was authorized by the user.

4.2.2 Device security

The security of pervasive computing devices varies considerably. Some devices are considered very secure and are even used for financial transactions while others provide only a very low level of security. The security of a particular device depends on many parameters. Several devices run unchangeable software, while others allow loading arbitrary software – potentially Trojan horses – into the device. A number of devices have no memory protection and thus do not isolate data of an application from other applications, which potentially might be dangerous. Some devices can only support signatures and encryption with small key lengths that are not considered secure, while others have enough computing power to support key lengths that provide a very high level of security. A few devices have secure hardware modules built in to store private keys, while others only have one memory shared between applications.

When implementing distributed pervasive computing applications that need to be secure, it is very important to be aware of the level of security that the client devices support.

WAP phones

Many WAP phones allow secure sessions to WAP gateways or WAP servers to be established, although at the time of writing WAP phones offer RSA encryption and signatures up to only 768 bits. It is expected, however, that with the introduction of WIMs, WAP phones will support keys lengths of up to 1024 bits.

Currently, there are also issues regarding end-to-end security. The WAP gateways of the telecommunication companies required for connecting WAP phones to application servers terminate the secure WTLS connection to the device at the telecommunication company and establish an SSL connection to the application server. As a work-around, WAP phones that can be configured manually can be set up to connect directly with a WAP gateway within the application provider's secure domain, but this is very inconvenient for users. The solution to this problem will be a redirection scheme that allows the application server to redirect a WAP phone that originally connects via a telecommunication company's WAP gateway to reconnect via a trusted gateway instead; in the long term, a Transport Layer Security (TLS) subset may be used instead of WTLS.

Another security issue is the over-the-air configuration capability of some WAP phones. Intended to allow telecommunication companies to change the configuration of phones in the field if required, this feature can potentially be misused by attackers. One possible attack is to send a configuration message to a phone that changes the WAP gateway to which the phone connects to a malicious one. When the user selects the WAP services after the change, the user's phone connects to the malicious gateway, which may display wrong information and obtain user IDs and passwords from the user.

For more details about WAP and WAP security, see Chapter 6.

PDAs

Many PDAs allow downloading and installing of arbitrary software, and thus are prone to Trojan horse attacks. PDAs that have no memory protection to isolate applications from each other are especially vulnerable, because a Trojan horse can easily access data owned by other applications.

As many PDAs do not have a powerful processor in favour of battery life, they support only relatively small key sizes for encryption of session keys and digital signatures.

4.2.3 Server-side security

Pervasive computing brings new requirements to server security. If an application provider needs to support only PC clients, things are quite easy. An applications provider can set up an outer and an inner firewall, place central access control in the 'demilitarized zone', and deploy the Web applications behind the inner firewall, as shown in Figure 4.13

Figure 4.13

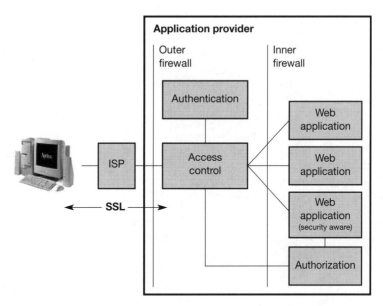

Set-up for a secure Web application

End-to-end security from the PC to the application provider's domain can easily be achieved by using the SSL protocol. After the user's PC has signed on to the ISP, the ISP acts as a pass-through for the messages exchanged between the client PC and the application provider's servers. For client authentication, form-based authentication, HTTP basic authentication, or SSL client authentication can be used. Most Web applications found in the Internet today use form-based authentication.

Additionally, to enable applications to be used from pervasive computing devices such as WAP phones, PDAs, and voice-only phones, appropriate gateways are required. If the application provider – as well as the users of the applications – trusts the gateway providers (e.g. a mobile service provider who operates a WAP gateway), the infrastructure required at the application provider's site is similar to the previous case (see Figure 4.14). Access control and authentication, however, must now be able to handle different kinds of client devices and their markup languages (e.g. when form-based authentication is used to authenticate users), and four different versions of the login form may be required: an HTML form for PC clients, a WML form for WAP clients, a VoiceXML form for voice-only phones connecting via a voice gateway, and a very simple HTML form for PDAs.

This set-up does not provide end-to-end security. In the gateways, all data exchanged between the different devices and the application provider temporarily needs to exist in the clear so that it can be converted.

Figure 4.14

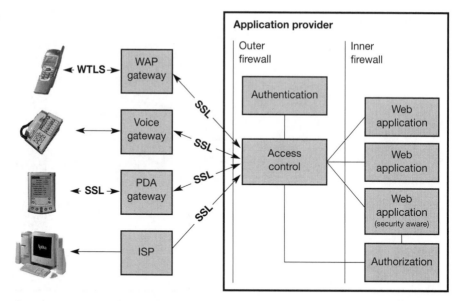

A pervasive Web application using external gateways

Certificate-based client authentication supported by some devices cannot be exploited this way. For example, a WTLS connection initiated from a WAP phone is terminated at the WAP gateway, thus the application provider will get the SSL certificate of the WAP gateway, but not the original WAP certificate provided by the client itself.

If an application provider wants to have end-to-end security, and to be able to obtain client certificates, it has to operate its own gateways, as shown in Figure 4.15. In this case, the devices connect directly to the appropriate gateways at the application provider's site.

A user with a WAP phone either dials in directly, connecting to the application provider's WAP gateway, or dials into and connects via a third-party WAP gateway and then is redirected to the local WAP gateway by the access control component. In each case, an end-to-end secure connection can be established between the WAP phone and the WAP gateway before data begin to flow.

A user with a voice phone dials in directly to the application provider's voice gateway. Over the connection between the phone and the gateway, voice is transmitted in clear. The security of communication depends on the security of the phone lines.

PDA users can dial in directly to the application provider's PDA gateway. The connection between the PDA and the PDA gateway can be secured using SSL as well as the connection between the PDA gateway and the access control server.

Figure 4.15

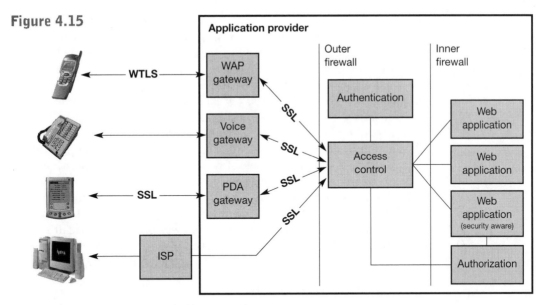

A pervasive Web application using own gateways

4.2.4 Cryptographic algorithms

In this section, we give an overview of the most relevant cryptographic algorithms. There are two important classes of cryptographic algorithms that we want to present – symmetric algorithms and asymmetric algorithms. While symmetric algorithms use the same key for encryption and decryption of data, asymmetric algorithms use two keys – what one key encrypts, the other one decrypts. We aim to give only a basic understanding of cryptographic algorithms. For more comprehensive and detailed information, see Schneier's book *Applied Cryptography*.[7]

Symmetric cryptographic algorithms
Symmetric cryptographic algorithms are fast and can be used to encrypt and decrypt large amounts of data. However, the fact that the same key has to be used for encryption and decryption causes a problem when symmetric algorithms are to be used to ensure privacy of communication – the key itself has to be securely transmitted up front. For information on algorithms not described here or for more details, refer to *Applied Cryptography*.[7]

Data Encryption Standard
The Data Encryption Standard (DES) was developed to protect computer and communications data, initiated by the National Bureau of Standards (NBS) and the National Institute of Standards and Technology (NIST) in 1972. The first request for proposals was issued in 1973, but none of the

submissions met the requirements. A second request was issued in 1974; this time, the NBS received a promising proposal from IBM, which became DES. The DES algorithm is a block cipher, i.e. an algorithm that divides the data to be encrypted into blocks and operates on one block at a time. DES uses a block size of 64 bits and a key size of 56 bits. DES keys are actually represented by 64 bits, but the least significant bit of each byte is used for parity checking only and ignored by the algorithm. The fundamental building block of DES is a substitution followed by a permutation, called a round. DES has 16 rounds, i.e. 16 substitutions and permutations are applied to each 64-bit block of data. Because of its repetitive nature, DES can be implemented easily in hardware. The key size of 56 bits used in the DES algorithm is quite small. Given today's powerful computers, the DES algorithm offers only mediocre security. At RSA '99, a DES challenge was announced where the 56-bit key was broken by special hardware in less than 24 h, although more than the average of 50% of the key space had to be searched by a network of many cooperating computers.

Triple Data Encryption Standard
Triple DES is based on DES but uses 112-bit keys. The key is divided into two 56-bit keys, K_1 and K_2. The data to be encrypted are encrypted under K_1, decrypted under K_2, then encrypted again under K_1. This is also known as the encrypt–decrypt–encrypt (EDE) mode. To decrypt, the cipher is decrypted using K_1, encrypted using K_2, and decrypted using K_1 again. Triple DES offers a very high level of security. Brute force attacks, which are possible against DES, are not feasible against Triple DES because the key space to be searched grows exponentially with the size of the key, i.e. finding a 112 bit key by exhaustive search takes 2^{56} times longer than finding a 56-bit key.

The Advanced Encryption Standard
The Advanced Encryption Standard (AES) will be the successor of the DES. Several algorithms have been proposed for the new standard. Of five finalists, NIST chose Rijndael as the proposed algorithm. Rijndael is a block cipher with a variable block length and key length. It allows the use of keys with a length of 128, 192, or 256 bits to encrypt blocks with a length of 128, 192, or 256 bits. All nine combinations of key length and block length are possible. It is possible to extend both block length and key length to multiples of 32 bits. Rijndael can be implemented very efficiently on a wide range of processors and in hardware.

Public-key algorithms
The basic idea that led to public-key algorithms was that keys could come in pairs of an encryption and a decryption key, and that it could be impossible to compute one key given the other. This concept was invented by Whitfield Diffie and Martin Hellman,[8] and independently by Ralph Merkle.[9]

Since then, many public-key algorithms have been proposed, many of them insecure or impractical. All public-key algorithms are very slow compared with secret-key algorithms. The well-known RSA algorithm, for example, takes about 1000 times longer than DES when implemented in hardware, and 100 times longer in software, to encrypt the same amount of data. However, public-key algorithms have a large advantage when used for ensuring privacy of communication: they use different keys for encryption and decryption. The private key may be known only to its owner and must be kept secret. It may be used for generation of digital signatures or for decrypting private information encrypted under the public key. The public key may be used for verifying digital signatures or for encrypting information. It does not need to be kept secret because it is infeasible to compute the private key from a given public key. Thus, receivers or signers of messages can post their public keys to a directory, where anybody who wants to send a message can look them up. Each entity in the network needs to store only its own private key, and a public directory can store the public keys of all entities, which is practical even in large networks.

RSA

Ron Rivest, Adi Shamir, and Leonard Adleman invented the RSA algorithm.[10,11] It is based on the difficulty of factoring the product of two large prime numbers. RSA uses key pairs, where the public key consists of a modulus m and a public exponent e, and the private key consists of the same modulus m and a private exponent d. The two keys are generated from two randomly chosen large prime numbers, p and q. To assure maximum security, the lengths of these numbers should be equal. The box below shows the computation of the numbers needed. As the problem of

| **RSA in detail** | The modulus m is computed as the product of the two primes $m = pq$ |

The modulus m is computed as the product of the two primes $m = pq$

Next, an encryption key e is chosen so that e and $(p - 1)(q - 1)$ are relatively prime.

The decryption key d is chosen so that $ed = 1 \pmod{(p - 1)(q - 1)}$ or $d = e^{-1} \bmod ((p - 1)(q - 1))$

Let x be the plain text with the same size as the modulus and y the cipher text.

Then the formulas for encryption and decryption are as follows:

$y = x^e \bmod m$

$x = y^d \bmod m$

More details on the mathematical background of the RSA algorithm can be found in Cormen et al.[12]

factoring two large prime numbers is very hard to solve, it is infeasible to compute the private key from the public key if the primes multiplied to obtain the modulus are big enough. Today's smart cards usually offer key sizes between 512 and 1024 bits. A modulus size of 512 bits is not considered secure. A modulus size of 1024 bits is considered to offer a reasonable level of security for applications such as digital signatures and encryption for documents.

Digital Signature Algorithm

NIST proposed the Digital Signature Algorithm (DSA) in 1991 for use in the Digital Signature Standard (DSS). The security of the algorithm relies on the difficulty of computing discrete logarithms in a modulus whose length defines the key size. The algorithm was designed by the NSA, which along with the proposed key size of only 512 bits led to criticism regarding its security. In 1994, the standard was issued with a variable key length from 512 to 1024 bits. For more information and the mathematics behind the algorithm, see Cormen *et al*. (1989).[12]

Elliptic curves

Elliptic curves were first proposed for use in public-key cryptosystems in 1985.[13,14] Algorithms using elliptic curves are faster than RSA or DSA, and require smaller key sizes for the same level of security. Elliptic curves over the finite field $GF(2^n)$ are especially interesting, because they allow for efficient implementations. The advantages of elliptic curves make them good candidates for use on small pervasive computing devices, because the computations can be conducted without powerful processors.

4.3 Device management

With millions, or soon even billions, of phones and PDAs in use, system and device management is becoming a major problem. Approximately eight million PDA units are in use at the time of writing, and 38 million are expected by 2003. The numbers for mobile phones are even more impressive: between 2003 and 2005, the number of phones deployed worldwide will exceed 1 billion. By 2004, 70% of new cellular phones and 80% of new PDAs will offer some form of access to the Internet. Meta Group predicts that by 2003, 40% of corporate users will be using wireless devices. And these numbers don't even include the future devices that will all be connected, such as cars and home appliances.

This section explains the major challenges of device management, discusses an example of device management – software distribution – and describes some approaches for solving the device-management task.

4.3.1 Device management challenges

Incorporating pervasive devices into existing business models presents some serious challenges:

- tracking the device location;
- device–user relationship (is the device used by only one user, or by several users?);
- version control of devices and software that are out in the field;
- software updates of existing devices;
- installation of new software on existing devices;
- providing secure access to device information.

Ignoring these issues will result in increasing costs as the number of devices per user is increasing. A study by Gartner Group shows that the average cost per hand-held device is approximately $2700 per device per year (including technical support, asset tracking, and synchronization).

Therefore, getting out millions or billions of connected devices is not enough. There needs to be a device-management system in place to deal with the various issues involved.

4.3.2 Software distribution

Software distribution deals with the problem of getting new software, or updates of existing software, to the devices that are out in the field. To accomplish this, a device-management system must take the following issues into account:

- *Hardware capabilities*. When downloading new software to a device, you need to know a few things about the device hardware, including processor type, available memory, and any other hardware features needed to select the appropriate software version to download (e.g. display or connectivity capabilities).
- *Hardware version management*. As pervasive computing devices are replaced in very short cycles, a device management needs to keep track of the different hardware versions to select the corresponding version of the software for downloading.
- *Software version management*. Software is changing even more rapidly than hardware. Therefore, software version management is a must for a device-management system. The software that needs to be managed includes not only application software, but also the operating system. The management system must keep track of all installed software versions on one specific device. Only when this information is available

is it possible to decide whether new software or an updated version of existing software will run without problems on this specific device.

- *Library management.* Libraries are used by different programs and therefore need special attention. The device-management system needs to know not only which libraries and versions are installed on the device, but also the version of a library needed for each program version. This can result in situations in which different versions of the same library are on one device, as different programs on the device may need different versions of that library. The device-management system should also be able to detect when a library is no longer needed on a device and can therefore be deleted.

- *Devices are not always connected.* As mobile devices are not always connected to the network, device-management systems need to keep track of devices that have already received the new or updated software, and devices that still need to get it.

- *Insecure connections.* As many wireless connections are insecure, the distributed software and data need to be protected (e.g. with encryption).

- *Unstable connections.* Connections to mobile devices can break, either for technical reasons, or because the user switches off the device. Software distribution therefore needs to take this into account and provide mechanisms for detecting incompletely transferred software and retransmiting missing parts.

- *Operating system updates.* Operating system updates are a very sensitive task, as we do not want to have a situation in which the device does not work any more after the update. This means that there must be a mechanism in place to ensure that the device is still operational after the update. Common methods to achieve this are a rollback mechanism, in which the update fails to get back to the original operating system version, or to update only modules rather than the complete operating system.

As this list shows, software distribution for mobile devices is a complex task and requires a lot of preparation by the provider of the software distribution service.

4.3.3 Approaches

There is no single solution to solve all the issues mentioned above. We need to combine several different technologies for solving the software distribution problem for pervasive devices. One basic prerequisite to achieve device management is that the devices can be separated clearly from each other (e.g. with a unique identifier). Some techniques to solve the software download problem include:

- *Hardware capabilities*. There are standards for retrieving hardware device capabilities. The most popular for pervasive computing devices is the CC/PP standard (see Chapter 6). Unfortunately, there are no pervasive computing devices available at the time of writing that implement this standard. This should change in the near future, allowing for a standardized method to retrieve the hardware capabilities.

- *Hardware and software version management*. The device-management system needs to store in a database all hardware and software versions out in the field, and all allowed combinations of hardware and software.

- *Library management*. The device-management system must also keep track of all library versions and maintain a list correlating different software versions with the corresponding library version. In addition, it must have a list for each device, in which all libraries on that device with their versions are stored. The library management should be able to detect when a library is no longer needed on a device, and initiate deletion of that library to reuse the memory on the device.

- *Devices are not always connected/unstable connections*. As devices are not always connected, and connections are unstable, the management system needs to keep track of all devices and their installed software. To achieve reliable software distribution, it can utilize transaction protocols and use rollback techniques on the device to get back to a consistent state after an unsuccessful software install.

- *Insecure connections*. Using standard authentication and encryption methods on the application layer, the device management can ensure a secure communication over insecure transport protocols.

- *Operating system updates*. Operating system updates can be achieved securely when using modular operating systems, where parts of the operating system can be exchanged at runtime.

When building a device-management system, the server side as well as the pervasive computing devices need to be included in the system design. A solution for a device management system can be seen in Figure 4.16. In this solution, the data management in the server layer is solved with databases or IT management systems, such as Hewlett-Packard's OpenView, Tivoli from IBM, or Unicenter TNG from Computer Associates. The gateway layer consists of a device gateway per device category with a synchronization engine. Finally, the devices in the device layer have a corresponding synchronization client to talk to their gateway. Synchronization can easily solve a lot of the software update problems

Figure 4.16

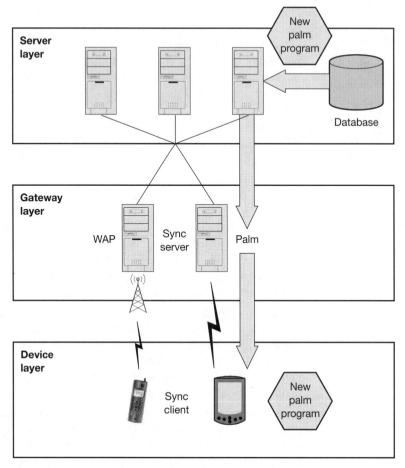

Device-management system example showing the installation of a new program on a Palm Pilot

4.3.4 Summary

Device management is a big problem for service providers or business units that support pervasive computing devices. If there is no efficient device-management system in place, this can dramatically increase the total cost of ownership of pervasive computing devices.

As shown in the example of software distribution, a device-management system will face a lot of challenges; it therefore needs to be designed well and to be in place before the number of devices in the field becomes unmanageable.

References

1. Bluetooth 'The Bluetooth Specification'.
   http://www.bluetooth.com/developer/specification/specification.asp

2. Megowan, P., Suvak, D. and Kogan, D. (1999) 'IrDA Object Exchange Protocol IrOBEX V1.2'.
   http://www.irda.org/standards/specifications.asp

3. Stossel, J. (ed.)(1999) 'Infrared Data Association Specifications for Ir Mobile Communications (IrMC) V1.1'.
   http://www.irda.org/standards/specifications.asp

4. Andreson, J.B., Rappaport, T.S. and Yoshida, S. 'Propagation Measurements and Models for Wireless Communications Channels,
   http://www.cs.berkeley.edu/~gribble/cs2947_wireless/summaries/propagation.html

5. Edwards, W.K. (1999) *Core Jini*. Engelwood Cliffs, NJ: Prentice Hall.

6. Perkins, C. (1998) *Mobile IP: Design Principals and Practice*. Reading, MA: Addision-Wesley Longman.

7. Schneier, B. (1996) *Applied Cryptography*. New York: J. Wiley & Sons.

8. Diffie, W. and Hellmann, M.E. (1976) 'Multiuser cryptographic techniques' in *Proceedings of AFIPS National Computer Conference, 1976*, 109–112.

9. Merkle, R.C. (1978) 'Secure communication over insecure channels', *Communications of the ACM*, 21(4), 294–299.

10. Rivest, R.L., Shamir, A. and Adleman, L.M. (1979) 'A method for obtaining digital signatures and public-key cryptosystems', *Communications of the ACM*, 21, (2), 120–126.

11. Rivest, R.L., Shamir, A. and Adleman, L.M. (1979) 'On digital signatures and public-key cryptosystems', MIT Laboratory for Computer Science technical report, MIT/LCS/TR-212.

12. Cormen, T.H., Leiserson, C.E. and Rivest, R.L. (1989) *Introduction to Algorithms*. Cambridge, MA: MIT Press.

13. Koblitz, N. (1989) 'Elliptic curve cryptosystems', *Mathematics of Computation*, 48 (177), 203–209.

14. Miller, V.S. (1986) 'Use of elliptic curves in cryptography', Advances in Cryptology, *Crypto '85 Proceedings*. Springer-Verlag, 417–426.

Further reading

1. Sun Microsystems (1999). Java Server Pages Specification Version 1.1
   http://java.sun.com/products/jsp/download.html

2. Akerley, J., Hashim M., Koutsoumbos, A. and Maffione, A. (1999)
   *Developing an e-Business Application for the IBM WebSphere
   Application Server*. IBM Redbooks. http://www.redbooks.ibm.com

3. Schiller, J. (2000) *Mobile Communications*. London: Addison-Wesley.

4. Hansmann, U., Merk, L, Nicklous, M.S. and Stober, T. (2001) *Pervasive
   Computing Handbook*. New York: Springer.

5. Wireless Internet Today (June 2000) 'Wireless Application Protocol'.
   http://www.wapforum.org/what/whitepapers.htm

6. Microsoft (2000) *Universal Plug and Play Device Architecture* V1.0.

5 Web application concepts

In this chapter we explain how PCs can be connected to Web applications through the Internet. Although some concepts and technologies described here can be considered classical and are well known, we will revisit them briefly. In this way, they can serve as references to compare with the newer concepts and technologies presented in subsequent chapters.

We give an overview of the history of the World Wide Web (WWW), as well as the relevant concepts, protocols, and standards for communication between Web clients and servers via the Internet. One special topic we cover here is transcoding, the transformation of content to device-specific markup.

We discuss Web application security issues, and present possible solutions ranging from usage of the standard HTTPS protocol to client authentication schemes for the Internet. As well as the typical client authentication methods supported by today's browsers, we also discuss the use of smart cards for secure user authentication.

5.1 History of the World Wide Web

Although the Internet existed long before the WWW, it became popular only when a convenient, graphical way to access it became available through the WWW, and Web browsers were developed to access its information. The history of the WWW began at the European Center for Nuclear Research (CERN). CERN runs several particle accelerators across Europe, and employs large teams carrying out research in physics. The teams typically have members from various European countries who have to share a constantly changing set of documents, drawings, blueprints, etc. The researchers were originally connected via the Internet, but had no convenient way to publish information in order to share it with researchers in other locations. To allow for effective collaboration between these teams, CERN physicist Tim Berners-Lee in March 1989 made the initial proposal for a web of linked documents. A text-based prototype was operational one year later and was presented at the Hypertext '91 conference in San Antonio, Texas. The first browser with a graphical user interface, Mosaic, was developed at the National Center for

Supercomputing Applications (NCSA) and was released in February 1993. It was so popular that Marc Andreessen left the NCSA and formed a company named Netscape Communications Corporation, with the goal of developing Web software for clients and servers. They went public in 1995 with a market value of $1.5 billion.

In 1994, CERN and Massachusetts Institute of Technology (MIT). founded the World Wide Web Consortium (W3C) to develop the Web further, standardize protocols, and reach interoperability. Since 1994, hundreds of universities and companies have joined the consortium. The consortium's documents, and information on its activities, are available on its website.[1]

After the WWW had established itself as the most popular way of accessing information via the Internet, Microsoft entered the arena with its Internet Explorer. Since then, Microsoft and Netscape have fought for dominance in the browser business in the so-called browser war, frequently coming up with new versions that have additional features. Not surprisingly, Microsoft was able to capture a significant part of the market share quickly by bundling its browser with their operating systems at no additional cost.

5.2 World Wide Web architecture

The WWW allows access to linked documents spread across an enormous number of machines connected to the Internet. From the user's perspective, the Web consists of a large number of documents that can be displayed with Web browsers. These documents can be connected to other documents by hyperlinks that establish connections to these other documents, no matter where they are located. When displaying a hyperlink, a browser marks it usually by underlining it or displaying it in a different colour. When the user clicks on a hyperlink, the browser follows the link by requesting the referred document from the referred server.

From the server's perspective, the Web is a network of millions of potential clients. Each website has one or more servers that make documents accessible to clients. When receiving a request from a client, a server retrieves the requested document from hard disk or memory, or dynamically from an application server, and sends it back with the response to that request.

The protocol used between the Web clients and Web servers is HTTP, shown in Figure 5.1.

HTTP is a simple, stateless protocol. The browser sends an HTTP request that specifies the document to be returned. To serve the request, the Web server reads the requested documents and sends it back in an HTTP response. If the document is not available, it sends back an error message. Note that usually, messages are not exchanged directly between

Figure 5.1

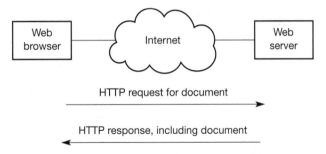

Principles of communication between a browser and a server

the client and the server. In real-life scenarios, several proxies and fire-walls might be involved in the communication, as shown in Figure 5.2.

Often, the machine in which the Web browser runs does not have a direct connection to the Internet, but accesses the Internet via a proxy and one or more firewalls. Also, many servers do not have a direct Internet connection. They may be located behind one or more firewalls and a proxy for authentication of clients or caching. Websites that have to handle a large number of hits often take advantage of a network dis-patcher for load balancing between several Web server instances.

Although HTTP does not have restrictions on the types of documents that may be transmitted, most documents on the WWW use HTML, which was developed specifically for the Web.

Figure 5.2

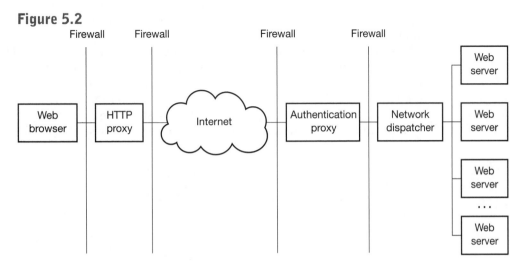

Real-life example of communication between a client and a server

5.3 Protocols

In this section we give a brief overview of the most important protocols in the Internet, as shown in the protocol stack depicted in Figure 5.3. We'll start with a brief introduction to the network layer and transport layer protocols TCP/IP, followed by information on the security protocols SSL and TLS and the application layer protocol HTTP.

5.3.1 TCP/IP

The Internet has two main transport layer protocols: the connection-oriented TCP and the connectionless user datagram protocol (UDP). We focus on TCP here, as it is the basis of HTTP, which we will discuss in subsequent sections. TCP provides a reliable end-to-end byte stream over an unreliable internetwork. As internetworks consist of different parts that may have very different bandwidths, topologies, packet sizes, and other parameters, TCP was designed to dynamically adapt to these differences and tolerate many kinds of failures.

5.3.2 SSL and TLS

SSL is a protocol for secure connections via the Internet on top of TCP/IP. It was originally developed by Netscape. Over time, it evolved through several versions to SSL 3.0, supported by today's software, and finally into TLS, the successor of SSL standardized in the Internet Engineering Task Force (IETF). This section will discuss TLS 1.0.[2] The primary goal of TLS is to provide privacy and data integrity of messages exchanged between two communicating parties over an untrusted network, like the Internet. In addition, TLS also allows for mutual authentication of the communicating parties.

The TLS protocol consists of several layers. The lowest layer is the TLS Record Protocol, which assures privacy and reliability of connections and is used for encapsulating higher-level protocols, such as the TLS Handshake Protocol. This protocol provides connection security, which ensures that a peer's identity can be authenticated using public-key cryptography, and that the negotiation of a shared secret is secure and reliable.

Figure 5.3

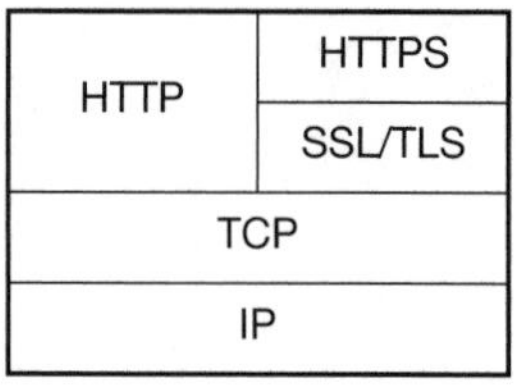

HTTP	HTTPS
	SSL/TLS
TCP	
IP	

Protocol stack

When TLS is used to secure client–server communications, in most cases the handshake protocol only conducts server authentication. During the handshake protocol, the server transmits its certificates to the client. The client validates the server certificates and extracts the public key from one of the certificates. This key is used to encrypt the session key for further communications. TLS allows for optional client authentication. During the handshake protocol, the server can send a certificate request that requires the client to send its certificate and a certificate verify message to the server. The server can authenticate the client by validating the obtained certificate and using the public key from that certificate to verify the client's signature contained in the certificate verify message.

5.3.3 HTTP

HTTP is a generic, stateless application level protocol.[3] HTTP can be used for many tasks beyond its original use for transmitting hypertext. Examples of other tasks are use as name servers, in distributed object management systems, and in service-oriented architectures as a basis for the SOAP protocol (see Chapter 9). HTTP supports typing and negotiation of data representations, such that systems can be implemented independently of the data they transfer. HTTP defines requests that are sent from user agents to servers and responses that are sent from servers back to user agents.

Requests
HTTP requests include a request line, headers, and, optionally, a message body, e.g. data to be stored or processed at the server. The request line includes a method, a uniform resource identifier (URI) identifying the resource on which to apply the request, and the HTTP version as shown in Example 5.1.

Example 5.1 **The request line**

```
GET http://www.w3.org/pub/WWW/TheProject.html HTTP/1.1
```

HTTP defines eight methods:

- *GET* is used to retrieve the file identified by the request URI.
- *POST* requests that the server accepts the data enclosed in the request as a new subordinate of the resource specified by the request URI. It is intended to be used for functions such as annotation of existing resources, posting messages to bulletin boards, and providing data such as the result of submitting a form.

- *HEAD* allows a user agent to obtain a resource's header without the message body.

- *PUT* requests to store data enclosed in the request under the request URI.

- *DELETE* requests that the server delete the resource identified by the request URI.

- *OPTIONS* is used in requests for information about the communication options available on the request response chain identified by the request's URI.

- *TRACE* can be used to invoke a remote loop-back of the request message. It allows a client to see what is being received at the server's side and to trace the request chain between client and server by examining the Via header fields.

- *CONNECT* is reserved by the specification for use with proxies that can dynamically switch to being a tunnel.

To allow clients to pass additional information about requests or the clients itself, an HTTP request can contain request header fields, e.g. `Accept`, `Accept-Charset`, `Accept-Encoding`, `Accept-Language`, `Authorization`, `Expect`, `From`, `Host`, `Proxy-Authorization`, `Range`, `Referrer`, or `User-Agent`. The `Accept` and `User-Agent` fields are especially important with regard to pervasive computing, as they can be used by a server to determine the client capabilities and deliver content in an appropriate form.

HTTP requests may optionally include a message body. The presence of a message body in a request is signalled by the inclusion of `Content-Length` and `Transfer-Encoding` header fields.

Responses

For each incoming request, the servers send back a response that consists of a status line and optionally a message body, e.g. a Web page or data returned by a Web application. The status line consists of the HTTP version, a status code, and its associated textual phrase. The first digit of the status code defines the response's class:

- *1xx – informational:* the request was received and is being processed.

- *2xx – success:* the action was received, understood, and accepted. The code for success is 200 (OK).

- *3xx – redirection:* further action is required in order to complete the request.

- *4xx – client error:* the request contains bad syntax or cannot be fulfilled. Some examples of client errors are 401 (Unauthorized), 403 (Forbidden), 404 (Not Found), and 405 (Method Not Allowed).

- *5xx – server error:* the server failed to fulfill an apparently valid request. Some examples of server errors are 500 (Internal Server Error) and 503 (Service Unavailable).

5.3.4 HTTPS

HTTPS means using the HTTP protocol over a secure connection instead of a plain transport connection (see Figure 5.3). Current practice is to layer HTTP over SSL, distinguishing secured traffic from insecure traffic by using port 443 instead of port 80. In the future, HTTP will be layered over TLS similarly, as described in RFC 2818 released by the IETF.

5.4 Transcoding

There are many situations in which existing Web applications have to be enabled for pervasive computing devices. It is the expectation that any type of information or service that can be accessed with a Web browser should also be accessible to ever-new waves of diverse pervasive devices. Obviously, content and use need to be adapted to the requirements and constraints of these devices to optimize the user experience – a need that was not been foreseen when the initial application was deployed. One approach for this is transcoding.

Transcoding means transforming certain input formats to different output formats, e.g. transforming content from one markup language to another, transforming images with a high resolution to a low resolution representation, or repaginating a large page into several smaller pages. Transcoders are typically capable of dealing with any kind of input, and are able to generate any kind of output. However, transcoding works best if the input is structured data, for example XML, and becomes very tedious and error prone when markup that is intended for presentation has to be screen-scraped and transformed into other types of markup.

Technically speaking, transcoding performs post-processing of content generated by a Web server in one of two places: in an HTTP proxy that intercepts the HTTP data stream to apply transcoding as required, or within the application server itself. If the Web server produces structured data rather than presentation markup, this black-box approach allows for a clean separation of data as generated by the Web server and presentation generated by transcoding (Figure 5.4)

These methods both have advantages and disadvantages. Deployment of the transcoder in the application server itself allows for use of SSL encryption, transparency for clients, and selective transcoding of particular content subsets, which are not possible when a transcoder is set-up as an HTTP proxy. On the other hand, the HTTP proxy set-up can be used with

Figure 5.4

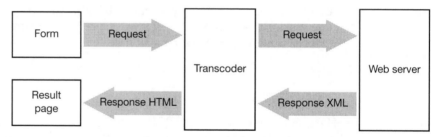

A transcoder intercepting communication between a client and a Web server

any Web server, while deployment of transcoding within the application server might easily lead to dependencies on particular implementation details of the application server.

The general concept of transcoding does not limit the markup languages of both input and output to any particular set of languages. However, transcoder implementations typically provide built-in support for HTML and XML, while other formats will often require custom code. The decision as to which transformation should be applied to the input content can be based on the type of markup language of the input, the device type and its particular constraints, additional HTTP header fields, network constraints, user preferences, and organizational access policies. Some of this information is provided as part of every HTTP request; the rest is based on configuration of the transcoder.

For HTML input, transcoders are usually capable of dropping or replacing information from the HTML input, e.g. dropping, downsizing, or dithering embedded images, replacing them with a link for separate download, or replacing tables with ordered lists. This is useful if the user agent that requested the HTML document is capable of displaying only a certain subset of the HTML level that the document was authored for. Creating output in other markup languages, e.g. WML, that will contain only a certain information subset from HTML input is usually not possible through a straightforward transformation. To achieve this, decisions must be made by the transcoder regarding which document elements to transform into output and which elements to drop. Some transcoders provide a set of APIs that help in writing code to specify which parts of data in an HTML documents are relevant and how to create output in another markup language. As HTML is focused on presentation rather than structured data, these data need to be extracted from the HTML document through page-specific code, which is tied to one Web page at one point of time – if the Web page changes, the custom code to transcode this page might also have to be changed.

On the other hand, XML input contains tagged data that can be parsed and searched for data elements using XML parsers. Thus, transcoders do not need to provide any particular functionality to handle XML documents, but rather provide capabilities to select, load, and execute Extensible Stylesheet Language (XSL) stylesheets (see Chapter 9) based on device and user agent types. This is the most flexible approach in that it works for any XML instance, and allows for any kind of transformation that can be performed with the XSL-T programming language. XML is the preferable input format for transcoding.

5.4.1 Transcoding v. device-specific content generation

To a certain degree, transcoding allows existing applications to be used with new devices, whereas device-specific content generation using JSPs is something that has to be implemented as a part of an application itself.

Device-specific content generation is the method of choice when an application is implemented from scratch, or when at least access is available to the back-end system or database on which an existing application relies. Compared with transcoding, this method provides superior performance and scalability, and even allows implementation of different dialog flows optimized for individual devices.

Transcoding can be used to enable an existing application that may not be modified for pervasive computing, or for processing data provided by content syndicators. However, existing applications often do not deliver desirable XML input to the transcoder, so screen-scraping code that is specific to a page at one point of time has to be written. Transcoding to various combinations of screen sizes, markup languages, and information subsets is possible in a generic way, e.g. by application of stylesheets, only when applications provide output in structured data formats that allow for effective post-processing, such as XML.

A good example for transcoding is rendering of information in a portal for different devices. Now that many content syndicators provide news, weather, stock quotes, and other information in XML formats, portals can integrate those data with the respective look and feel for each device simply by supplying different stylesheets for transcoding.

5.5 Client authentication via the Internet

While early Internet applications did not need know user identities, today's e-business applications need to know the identity of users in order to be able to perform business transactions. The required level of assurance of the user's identity depends on the security requirements of Web applications. For non-sensitive Web applications, such as portals, email services etc., simple authentication mechanisms are usually sufficient to indicate the user's identity. Sensitive applications providing high-value transactions on the other side require real proof of user identities. In the following sections we present user-authentication methods for the

Internet, listed in increasing level of security and assurance of the user's identity. We explain smart-card-based authentication, the method that provides the highest level of security, in particular detail.

5.5.1 Basic and digest access authentication

Basic authentication is a simple authentication protocol that has been defined as an extension of the HTTP 1.1 protocol in RFC 2617.[4] Origin servers as well as proxies can use basic authentication to authenticate Web clients.

When a Web client requests a protected resource on an origin server, the origin server returns an error message with the error code 401 (Unauthorized) and one or more challenges to the client, as shown in Example 5.2.

Example 5.2   **The origin server's error message**

```
WWW-Authenticate: Basic realm='sample'
```

The client prompts the user for credentials and resends the original request with an additional Authorization header field. To perform basic authorization, the client sends the user identification and password, sepa-

Example 5.3   **Basic authorization**

```
Authorization: Basic QWxhZGRpbjpvcGVuIHNlc2FtZQ==
```

rated by a single colon as a base64 encoded string, as shown in Example 5.3.

Similarly, when a client requests a resource that is protected by a proxy, the proxy returns an error message with the error code 407 (Proxy Authentication Required) and one or more challenges. The client resends the original request, including an additional Proxy-Authorization field. Figure 5.5 shows the messages exchanged during the authentication protocol.

When using basic authentication, the user identification as well as the password are transmitted in base64-encoded clear text. As a result, an attacker may eavesdrop on the communication to obtain passwords that could be used for later access to the protected resources.

To overcome this obvious weakness, the digest access authentication scheme was developed. Clients receive a nonce as a challenge from the

Figure 5.5

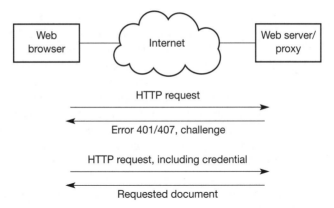

Basic authentication

server and send back a message digest over the username, the password, the given nonce value, the HTTP method, and the requested URI. By default, the MD5 algorithm is used to compute the message digest. As only a digest is transmitted over the communication line, and a nonce is included in computation of the digest, it is not possible to obtain the user's password by eavesdropping on the communication or to perform a successful replay attack. This protocol still does not provide the security of Kerberos or client-side private-key systems. It is vulnerable to man-in-the-middle attacks, unless communication between the client and server is secured by encryption.

5.5.2 Form-based authentication

When using basic or digest access authentication, the window displayed by the browser to obtain the required credentials from the user disturbs the user interface flow of a Web application. To avoid this, many applications use form-based authentication in order to give a better-looking interface.

Instead of a simple error message, the server or proxy sends a page with a form that prompts the user to enter their credentials, usually user identification and password. When the user enters the data and presses the form's submit button, the credentials are posted to the server, where they are verified. If this is successful, the user is allowed to access the protected resources. Similarly to basic authentication, form-based authentication is insecure unless communication is protected by encryption.

5.5.3 SSL/TLS client authentication with client certificates

SSL/TLS authentication using client certificates and private keys on the client side provides a higher level of security than the previously described mechanisms. As public-key cryptography is employed, no secret authentication credentials need to be stored on the server. The server needs only a public key and a directory of registered users.

To authenticate a user, the server sends a random challenge to the client. The client has to sign the challenge using a private key, and sends back the signature together with its client certificate. The server validates the certificate, extracts the public key from the certificate, and uses it to verify the signature over the random challenge. If the signature is valid, then the client may access the protected resources. This method can be considered secure against eavesdropping and stealing of information from the server, but it is prone to Trojan horse attacks that aim to obtain the private key stored on the client.

5.5.4 Authentication using smart cards

As the Internet is used increasingly as a platform for e-business transactions, security becomes a primary issue for Web applications. Many Web applications are too sensitive to be secured appropriately using software-only security mechanisms like the ones described above. To provide a sufficient level of protection for these applications, smart cards can be used to securely authenticate users, and to secure individual transactions through digital signatures. Smart cards are credit-card-sized tokens with a tamper-resistant chip that typically includes a microprocessor, and a small amount of RAM and EEPROM storage. For communication, smart cards use contacts, a contactless communication unit, or a combination of both. Applications cannot simply read or write data on a smart card; they need to communicate with the smart card through application protocol data units (APDUs). When the smart card receives a request APDU, it processes it and replies with a response APDU.

In this section, we explain how smart cards can be integrated with Web applications, and show how secure authentication via the Internet can be achieved using either asymmetric or symmetric cryptographic algorithms on smart cards. We give an overview of the predominant smart card types, and present two important interfaces for smart card applications: PC/SC and the OpenCard Framework (OCF).

Application integration
There are various ways to implement authentication using a smart card; we describe two of these in more detail. One way is to integrate the smart card into the standard TLS/SSL protocol; the other is to use custom pairs of authentication applets and servlets.

TLS/SSL client authentication using a smart card
A smart card can be used for client authentication within the TLS/SSL pro-

tocol by making it accessible to the browser through an appropriate interface, e.g. PKCS#11 for Netscape Communicator or CAPI for Microsoft Internet Explorer. To enable all entities involved in a business application, the users have to be equipped with a smart card, a smart card reader, and software to enable their browser to access the smart card via the reader, i.e. an appropriate CAPI or PKCS#11 provider. The servers hosting the application must be set up to perform TLS/SSL client authentication, and must be connected to an appropriate public-key infrastructure. Only special smart cards that support exactly the cryptographic operations required for TLS/SSL client authentication can be used.

Smart-card-based authentication using an applet and a servlet
Frequently, smart cards are used that do not provide the functions needed for client authentication according to the TLS/SSL protocol. Examples are low-cost smart cards that support only symmetric cryptographic algorithms and thus are not able to perform the public-key algorithms to generate the required digital signatures. In these cases, an authentication protocol based on the capabilities of a particular smart card has to be implemented. A very simple and convenient way to do so is to implement an authentication applet/servlet pair.

Public- v. secret-key-based authentication
In recent years, smart card technology has advanced quickly. It has now reached a state where smart cards integrate easily into public-key infrastructures. Many of today's smart cards provide memory of up to 32 KB to store keys, certificates and information and they have crypto-coprocessors that allow them to generate digital signatures using RSA or DSA algorithms with key lengths of up to 1024 bits or even 2048 bits. However, many applications still use low-cost smart cards that support only symmetric cryptographic algorithms.

Authentication using public-key smart cards
Figure 5.6 shows how smart cards that support public-key cryptography can be used to perform authentication through a challenge–response protocol. The server gives a random challenge to the smart card. The smart card uses its private key to generate a digital signature over the challenge. The digital signature and the certificate associated with the smart card's private key are sent to the server. The server verifies the certificate and then uses the public key contained in the certificate to verify the signature.

Authentication using non-public-key smart cards
Figure 5.7 shows how authentication can be performed using smart cards that do not support public-key cryptography. The server gives a random challenge to the smart card and requests a signature over a card ID and the challenge. Often, a password provided by the user has to be given to the smart card before a signature can be obtained, to ensure that someone

Figure 5.6

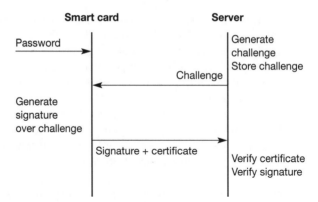

Authentication protocol for public-key smart cards

who steals or finds the card cannot abuse it. The smart card uses a card individual key to generate a message authentication code (MAC) over the card ID, the challenge is obtained from the server, and the ID and the MAC are sent back to the server. The server uses the card ID to derive the card individual key from a master key, and uses that card individual key to verify the MAC sent from the card.

Types of smart card

In recent years, a number makes and types of smart cards have come to market. We can identify three major categories: simple file-system-oriented smart cards without public-key capability, advanced file-system smart cards with public-key capability, and programmable smart cards, such as JavaCards and Windows-powered smart cards.

Figure 5.7

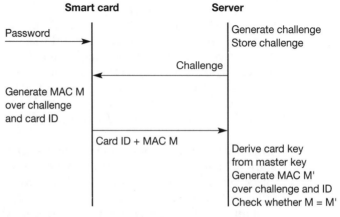

Authentication protocol for non-public-key smart cards

Simple file-system smart cards

File system smart cards provide a file system whereby reading and writing of files can be protected by various methods. These cards support only symmetric cryptographic algorithms, such as DES or Triple DES. To use a simple file-system smart card for authentication, a file containing the card ID can be created on the card, and the access conditions for that file can be set so that it can be read with a MAC after a challenge has been provided. This allows a protocol like that shown in Figure 5.7 to be run.

File-system cards with public-key cryptography

File-system cards with public-key cryptography support can store private keys and associated certificates. Key pairs are usually created in the card, and the private key never leaves the card. The private key is used internally only, for generating digital signatures or decrypting session keys or small amounts of data. To use file-system cards with public-key support for authentication, a private key and an associated certificate must be present in the card. This allows a protocol like that shown in Figure 5.6 to be run.

JavaCard

Smart cards that conform to the JavaCard specification[5] can host several applets. Applets are applications that reside on the card and offer an APDU interface to off-card applications. The JavaCard allows off-card applications to select an applet on the card by specifying the applet's application ID. After that, they can send a sequence of APDUs to the selected applet. Applets are implemented using a subset of the Java programming language, relying on Java libraries tailored for use in smart cards. For more information on the JavaCard architecture and JavaCard programming, see Chen (2000).[6] To use a JavaCard for authentication, the card must contain an applet that exposes an appropriate APDU interface to the external world, e.g. a command that can be parameterized with a challenge, returning a digital signature over the challenge and a command to obtain certificates stored in the card. This functionality allows the kind of protocol shown in Figure 5.6 to be run.

Windows-powered smart cards

The Windows-powered smart card allows implementation of custom commands. It is possible to implement commands that use functions from the card's internal crypto library to provide a function for generating digital signatures. Storing and reading of certificates is possible by default. This functionality also allows for PKI authentication protocols as shown in Figure 5.6.

Smart card APIs

In this section, we present two APIs for smart card applications: the PC/SC interface for native applications running on the Microsoft

Windows operating systems and the OpenCard Framework for Java applications and applets. The need for these standard interfaces came from a variety of different smart-card readers and smart cards, all of which were delivered with their own access software with no common API. As a result, smart-card applications had to include code that was dependent on the API of a particular smart-card reader manufacturer. Because of this, it was hard to migrate applications to other readers or allow for use of different readers. Below, we explain how the PC/SC and OpenCard Framework APIs have solved these problems to allow for smart-card reader and smart-card interoperability.

PC/SC

PC/SC is the standard interface for native smart-card-aware applications on Windows operating systems. The interface is included in Windows ME, Windows 2000 and future Windows versions. It has been defined by the PC/SC workgroup, which included Apple, Bull, Gemplus, Hewlett Packard, IBM, Infineon, Intel, Microsoft, Schlumberger, Sun Microsystems, and Toshiba. The workgroup's mission was to promote a standard specification to ensure that smart cards, smart-card readers, and computers made by different manufacturers worked together, and to facilitate the development of smart-card applications for PCs and other computing platforms. One specific goal was to specify common PC programming interfaces and control mechanisms. In December 1997, the PC/SC Workgroup released the PC/SC Specification 1.0,[7] defining the architecture and key interfaces for using smart cards from applications on PCs. Figure 5.8 shows an overview of the PC/SC architecture.

Smart cards (*ICCs* in PC/SC terminology) are accessed by applications on the PC via a smart-card reader (*IFD* peripheral devices in PC/SC terminology). There may be many smart-card readers per system, e.g. those connected via serial line, those integrated in the keyboard, and PC-card-based smart-card readers. Associated with each smart-card reader is an IFD handler, which is usually implemented as a device driver that provides a standard interface as defined in Part 3 of the PC/SC specification.

The ICC resource manager provides system-level service. It manages smart-card readers and inserted smart cards, controls shared access to these devices, and supports transaction management primitives.

The service providers provide applications with a high-level interface mapped to specific smart-cards. The PC/SC specification defines common interfaces for services, such as authentication, file access, and cryptography, and defines how to define extensions for domain-specific requirements.

Applications written to the PC/SC architecture typically make use of the resource manager and specific service providers, e.g. by waiting for card insertion, obtaining a service provider for the inserted smart card from the resource manager, using the service provider to have the smart card perform certain functions, and finally freeing the resources to allow other applications to use the card thereafter.

Figure 5.8

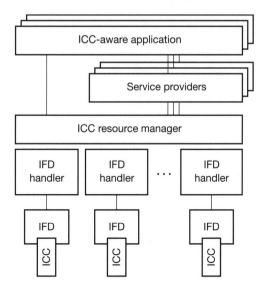

PC/SC architecture overview

The OpenCard Framework

The OCF has become the standard interface for smart-card applications written in Java. In 1997, IBM, Sun, Netscape and others founded the OpenCard Consortium to establish the OCF as a de facto standard for accessing smart cards from Java. In 2000, the OpenCard Consortium released OCF Version 1.2 and OpenCard for Embedded Devices 1.2.

OCF allows smart card applications to be implemented in Java independent of the card terminal used to access the smart card and independent of the smart card used (Figure 5.9).

To achieve independence from particular card terminals, the Consortium defined a card terminal interface with functions required to access a smart card, e.g. resetting the card, getting the answer to reset, sending an application protocol data unit to the card, and getting the response. There are OpenCard card terminal drivers for virtually all PC smart-card readers on the market. A pure java card terminal can be implemented, or the reader can be accessed via a generic PC/SC card terminal for OpenCard that provides a bridge to the PC/SC card terminal interface.

To achieve independence from particular cards, card services are used. Card-service interfaces can be defined for particular sets of smart-card functions. Two interfaces that are defined in the OCF itself are the File Access Interface and the Signature Interface. The File Access Interface allows files on a smart card to be accessed. The Signature interface allows digital signatures to be generated. Once a card service interface has been defined, various card service implementations that implement the interface can be developed for different cards.

Figure 5.9

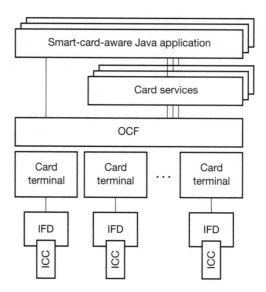

The OCF

The main role of the OCF is on the client side of Web applications, running in a Java applet. The most advantageous way to deploy the OCF in such an application is to install the OCF and the required card-terminal classes locally on the client, adding the OpenCard JAR (Java Archive) files and executables to the browser's paths. The card services to be used should be packaged with the applet JAR file that is deployed on the application server, so that they can be updated easily without changing client installations.

The OCF is available from the OCF website.[8] The website also provides documentation, user guides, links to papers and books about the OCF, and the latest news and announcements from the OpenCard Consortium. For comprehensive information on developing smart-card applications in Java, see Hansmann *et al*. (2000).[9]

References

1. World Wide Web Consortium: http://www.w3.org

2. Dierks, T. and Allen, C. (1999) 'The TLS Protocol Version 1.0'. IETF. http://www.ietf.org/rfc/rfc2246.txt

3. Fielding, R., Gettys, J.C., Mogul, J.C., Frystyk, H., Masinter, L., Leach, P., Berners-Lee, T. (1999) 'Hypertext Transfer Protocol – HTTP/1.1'. IETF. http://www.ietf.org/rfc/rfc2616.txt

4. Franks, J., Hallam-Baker, P., Hostetler, J., Lawrence, S., Leach, P., Luotonen, A. and Stewart, L. (1999). 'HTTP Authentication: Basic and Digest Access Authentication'. IETF. http://www.ietf.org/rfc/rfc2671.txt

5. Sun Microsystems (2000) 'Java Card™ 2.1.1 Platform Specifications'. http://java.sun.com/products/javacard/#documentation.

6. Chen, Zhiqun (2000) *Java Card™ Technology for Smart Cards: Architecture and Programmer's Guide*. Addison-Wesley.

7. PC/SC Workgroup (1999) 'PC/SC Specification 1.0'. http://www.pcscworkgroup.com/

8. OpenCard Framework. http://www.opencard.org

9. Hansmann, U., Nicklous, M., Schäck, T. and Seliger, F. (2000) *Smart Card Application Development Using Java*. Berlin: Springer.

Further reading

1. Tanenbaum, A.S. (1996) *Computer Networks*. Upper Saddle River: Prentice Hall.

6 WAP and beyond

WAP has become a synonym for new, wireless Internet services. This chapter describes the basics of WAP e-business implementation, device characteristics, protocol stack, security issues, products, and tools currently available on the market.

6.1 Introduction

Mobile communication services provide limited data rates and lower reliability compared with switched-line networks. Compared with modern desktop computers, mobile devices provide only a constrained application environment tailored to small, low weight devices with low-energy consumption, powered by small, rechargeable batteries. Mobile users demand devices that are easy to use and are adapted to the mobile environment. The standard PC methods to access and manage Internet applications cannot be mapped to the mobile environment because too many user interactions and lengthy data transfers would cause customer dissatisfaction.

Therefore, mobile equipment manufacturers founded the Wireless Application Protocol Forum (WAP Forum) in 1997 to define an architecture that extends the Internet technology for mobile devices. Founding members were Ericsson, Motorola, Nokia, and Openwave Systems, (formerly known as Phone.com, formerly known as Unwired Planet). Today, the WAP Forum comprises over 200 members ranging from network operators over mobile device suppliers to content developers and many IT companies.

The WAP architecture defines an optimized protocol stack for communication over wireless lines, an application environment for mobile phone applications, a content description language, and a miniature browser interface. The ability to work with a wide variety of devices is a key feature of the WAP architecture. The mobile user interfaces are typically limited:

- *Small display*. A standard mobile phone display has a size of 96×65 pixels. A PDA display is slightly larger at 160×160 pixels, but today's desktop PCs feature screen sizes of 1024×768 pixels and larger.

- *Restricted input capability.* Mobile phones offer a keyboard with 12 keys for data input, which makes entering text a time-consuming process, e.g. entering the character 'z' requires four keystrokes. Dictionary-assisted input methods such as T9 or Octave help to make entering text more convenient. The pen-based character input of PDAs allows trained users to enter data faster, but it does not match the capabilities of a full-size PC keyboard.

- *Limited memory and processing power.* A typical mobile phone has 8–32 MB of RAM and a 16-bit digital signal processor CPU running at about 10–20 MHz, while desktop computers come with 128 MB of RAM and 1-GHz processors.

- *Low-speed network connections with high latency.* Today, a typical GSM channel for WAP in Europe offers 9.6 kbps compared with 56 kbps of an analog PC modem or even 768 kbps with asymmetric digital subscriber line (ADSL).

These limitations have influenced the architecture at various levels. The replacement of HTML pages (typical 10 kB) with highly condensed WML pages, called cards, reduces the overhead of content presentation and reflects the limited display capabilities of mobile devices. A compact binary encoding of the data stream minimizes the data flow between device and server. The protocol and the browser are designed to run on very small, embedded systems with subsecond response time.

Within a short time, the WAP architecture has grown into a complex specification with many overlaps with the global Internet architecture. Some of the basic assumptions, such as limited data rate and client processing power, are no longer valid for the high end of mobile devices. Therefore, many solution providers, but also device and equipment manufacturers, favor a rapid merging of WAP and Internet technology into a mobile Internet architecture. However, WAP technology is reasonably mature, is supported by major industry players, and will exploit the improved speed of GPRS and UMTS systems. Therefore, the WAP architecture and systems built on this foundation will play a major role in the pervasive computing industry and will be embraced by the global mobile Internet architecture.

6.2 Components of the WAP architecture

The WAP architecture is similar to the Open System Interconnect (OSI) Reference Model defined by the International Organization for Standardization (ISO). The layered model describes how information flows from a Web application to the physical interface of the mobile device up to an application residing on a mobile phone. Each layer performs only one specific network function, e.g. provides transactional services. Each layer is independent and can be implemented without affecting the other layers. A typical WAP application uses only functions of the application layer, which itself uses the layers beneath it. Figure 6.1 illustrates the layers of the WAP architecture of a mobile phone.

6.2.1 Bearers

A bearer is the low-level transport mechanism for network messages. The WAP protocol stack is designed to operate with a variety of bearer services, with emphasis on low-speed mobile communication channels. One bearer service, for example, is an HSCSD connection with a minimum of 9.6 kbps. Short messages can also be used as a bearer for WAP, but speed is limited. GPRS and UMTS will also enable faster, packet-switched bearer services for WAP applications.

Packet-switched bearer services are much better suited than circuit-switched services for mobile devices because they can provide reliable services in an inherent, unreliable mobile environment. They also support the typical 'on demand' requests of mobile users better and faster than circuit-switched bearer services. Major mobile networks have been GPRS-enabled since the beginning of 2001. The gating factor for service introduction will probably be the billing model and billing system to support packet-switched operation on a large scale unless flat-fee models are introduced.

Figure 6.1

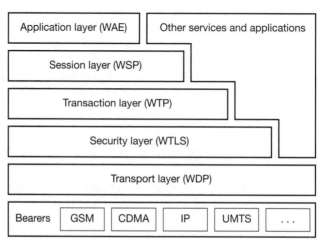

WAP architecture (client)

6.2.2 Transport layer – Wireless Datagram Protocol

The Wireless Datagram Protocol (WDP)[1] operates above the bearer services and provides a connectionless unreliable datagram service similar to UDP, transporting data from a sender to a receiver. The WDP layer provides the upper layers (security, transaction, and session) with a uniform interface to operate independently of the underlying bearer services. WDP offers simultaneous communication from the upper layers to the bearer services.

Errors during transmission at the WDP layer can be communicated via the Wireless Control Message Protocol (WCMP), similar to the Internet Control Message Protocol in the IP world. A typical WCMP message would be 'receiver cannot be reached'. The WCMP interface also provides an independent control channel for diagnostics and administration.

6.2.3 Wireless Transport Layer Security

WTLS[2] specifies a framework for secure connections, using some protocol elements from the Internet TLS protocol. WTLS offers base cryptographic services for WAP applications that can, for example, be used for transferring sensitive data between the device and a server. WTLS provides data integrity, privacy, and client and server authentication.

Before data exchange, a WTLS session has to be established by performing an initial key exchange and negotiation of the cryptographic algorithm to use (see Chapter 4). WTLS gives several options for key exchange, including RSA, Diffie-Hellman (DH) key exchange, or elliptic curve cryptography (ECC). Privacy of communication can be secured using the Data Encryption Standard (DES) or the International Data Encryption Algorithm (IDEA).

6.2.4 Wireless Transaction Protocol

WTP[3] provides a reliable data-transport mechanism. WTP in a WAP stack can be considered the equivalent of the TCP layer in the IP stack, but it is optimized for low bandwidth. WTP offers three classes of transaction services:

- *class 0* provides unreliable one-way messages without confirmation of messages, e.g. single request within an existing wireless connection;
- *class 1* provides reliable one-way message without result messages, e.g. push services like SMS, where no response is expected;
- *class 2* provides reliable two-way request–response messages, e.g. every request is answered with a response, like a confirmation or the result of a query.

6.2.5 Wireless session protocol

The Wireless Session Protocol (WSP)[4] provides connection-oriented services based on WTP and connectionless services based on WTLS or WDP. It supports HTTP 1.1 functionality and semantics in a binary-encoded format to minimize data transfer to the mobile phone.

One of WSP's prime features is to hold a shared state between the client and the WAP gateway (see WAP Infrastructure, below). To provide this feature in an HTTP environment, the WAP gateway typically maps the WSP states to cookies stored in the gateway. Thus, the WAP gateway emulates the preferred solution used by HTTP servers.

6.2.6 Wireless Application Environment

The Wireless Application Environment (WAE)[5] combines Web and mobile phone technologies. It provides a network-neutral application environment and permits a high degree of device independence by using the WAP protocol stack.

The WAE contains a microbrowser that is capable of displaying WML pages and executing WMLScript, a scripting language similar to JavaScript. The microbrowser also includes an additional wireless telephony application interface (WTAI) with telephony functions allowing call control, network text messaging, and offering a phone book interface.

6.3 WAP infrastructure

In order to run a WAP application, a complex infrastructure consisting of a mobile client, a public land mobile network such as GSM, a public switched telephony network such as ISDN, a WAP gateway, an IP network, and a WAP application server is required. Additionally, there may be system components such as WAP portals, proxy servers, routers, and firewalls. Several service providers will be engaged in providing the actual service providing to consumers requiring sophisticated service-level and billing agreements. The WAP-specific parts of this chain are described below.

The programming model of the WWW defines a direct connection between the client and the application server, as shown in Figure 6.2. More detailed information about the Web programming model can be found in Chapter 5.

WAP introduces an additional component between the client and the application server: the WAP gateway (see Figure 6.3). The WAP gateway performs two main tasks:

- *Protocol conversion*. The WAP gateway is a protocol intermediary between the client and the server. The communication between the client and the WAP gateway is performed with WAP protocols, and the communication between the WAP gateway and the server is based on HTTP protocols.

■ *Content encoding.* Data transferred between the client and the WAP gateway are binary encoded in order to minimize data transfer.

All requests from the phone are sent to the WAP gateway. The WAP gateway decodes the binary messages from WSP, transforms them to HTTP, and sends them to the selected application server. The host name or IP address of the application server is part of the URL given in the

Figure 6.2

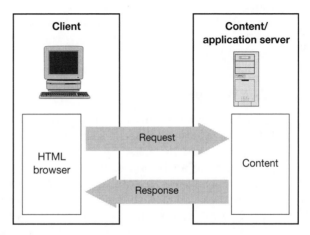

The WWW programming model

Figure 6.3

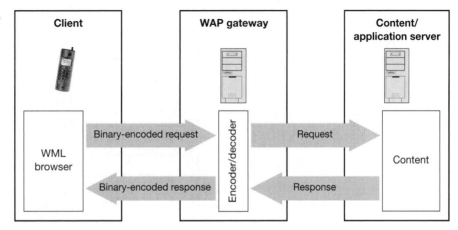

The WAP programming model

request from the phone. The application server prepares the response and sends it to the WAP gateway, where it is encoded in the gateway and forwarded to the phone.

Figure 6.4 illustrates the protocol stacks inside a WAP gateway and the flow of a request and response pair through the stacks.

This path through the protocol stacks in combination with the conversion from WML to binary WML is computing intensive. Therefore, the hardware running the WAP gateways should be very powerful in order to avoid long delays.

The devices participating in a WAP communication and the associated protocol stacks are shown in Figure 6.5. In this scenario, the mobile phone is connected via the point-to-point protocol (PPP) to a dial-in router of a telecommunication provider. The dial-in router sends all requests from the mobile phone to the WAP gateway. The WAP gateway receives the incoming WAP requests and forwards them to the server via the HTTP protocol.

6.3.1 WAP profile

A WAP browser requires a set of parameters to build a connection to an Internet application like the scenario shown in Figure 6.5. These parameters are stored in a WAP profile on the mobile client, much like the parameters of an IP connection are stored in a browser profile on a PC. The number of profiles that can be stored in a mobile phone is limited to three or five – some mobile phones have been delivered to customers even with a single fixed profile. Frequently, users do not switch their profiles at all, so they are restricted to one WAP gateway of their service provider.

Figure 6.4

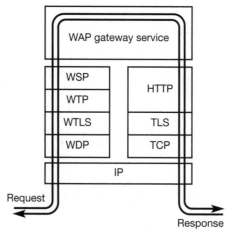

The WAP gateway protocol stack

Figure 6.5

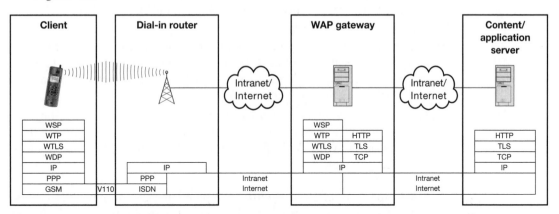

Sample WAP infrastructure

The WAP profile contains the following elements:

- *Homepage*. The URL address of the Internet start page (format *http://x.yy.z.xyz/homepagexyz.wml*).
- *Connection Type*. Defines the communication protocol between the mobile phone and the dial-in router as either continuous (switched line) or temporary (packet switched).
- *Connection Security*. Set to either ON or OFF. A WTLS session is established between the mobile phone and the WAP gateway when the setting is ON.
- *Bearer*. Defines the bearer service used for data transfer. When 'SMS' is selected, the server number and service number must be supplied. The data-transfer mode, e.g. HSCSD, is used in GSM systems and the following parameters must be specified.
- *Dial-up number*. Extension of dial-in server to which the WAP gateway is attached.
- *IP Address*. The IP address of the WAP gateway
- *Authentication type*. Defines whether a security certificate is to be used for client authentication. Setting is 'normal' or 'secure' with certificate. Certificates can be requested from a service provider.
- *Data call type*. Defines the signalling between the mobile phone and the dial-in server. Analog signalling is generally slower than ISDN signalling, but it is required in some countries where access only via analog lines is possible.

- *Data call speed*. Defines the communication speed between the phone and the network; usually 9600 or 14400 Baud (higher rates are expected in the future).

- *User name*. A generic or dedicated user name. Access to the network and the WAP gateway of an Internet provider or a corporation will require positive user identification through a user-specific name and user authentication through a password.

- *Password*. Secret password for access to the network to which the WAP gateway is attached. User name and password are used only for network access with WAP phones and/or PCs, and are not passed on to the WAP gateway.

Most mobile phone users will have problems in entering all of these parameters correctly. A single faulty character in the profile will disable the WAP service. Problem determination is complex because no automatic diagnosis tools can be used before a connection with the WAP gateway is established. Therefore, some mobile phone manufacturers support over-the-air provisioning (OTP) – the setting of profiles via SMS. The user requests a profile by sending a specific SMS message to the service provider. Then, the profile is sent in a response message and must be activated by the user.

The use of WAP profiles was designed according to the PC browser model. However, the introduction of the WAP gateway in the communication path between the client and the Internet application server has caused some infrastructure problems. Companies may choose to install a private WAP gateway, in order to overcome the inherent security problems, but they must force all users to install a special profile for access. This may work for employees, but may not work for customers who are not willing to switch profiles whenever they want to access a specific service.

WAP portals offered by mobile service providers, industry associations, or Internet providers may provide a partial solution to this problem that is typical of any non-IP-based access, such as WAP and voice. In addition to the basic connectivity, portals also provide personalization, customization services, and security frameworks for their customers, and a public key infrastructure for content providers. The WAP forum is addressing some of these problem areas with an extension of the WAP security architecture, but it will take several years before the new functions are implemented in the majority of mobile phones. Therefore, WAP system designs will exploit various schemes used in the IP world to secure the communication between client and application provider.

6.4 WAP security issues

Overall, WAP provides a couple of advanced security features that are not available in the IP environment. Over-the-air communication privacy is ensured by encryption, and mobile subscriber ISDN numbers are not exposed. The GSM SIM provides good identification and authentication. Typical IP infrastructures do not use this type of security at the client side. However, the introduction of a WAP gateway in the information flow between client and server creates potential security leaks unless the WAP gateway is operated in a secure environment and trusted by all participants.

Some security issues have been identified within the current WAP architecture:

■ *End-to-end security*. The current WTLS architecture does not support end-to-end security. The communication link between the mobile device and the WAP gateway is secure, as is the link from the WAP gateway to the server. However, all messages that go from the mobile device to the server or vice versa are decrypted by the WAP gateway, and then encrypted again for transmission to the server. This means all messages are available in clear text within the WAP gateway. As a result, the user and the application provider must trust the operator of the WAP gateway.

■ *Missing secure authentication*. To allow for highly secure authentication to servers, generation of digital signatures must be performed in tamper resistant devices, such as smart cards, which are not part of the current WAP specification. To overcome this issue, the WAP Forum proposed a WAP identification module (WIM) specification. WIM is a device for storing private keys and performing user authentication in a WTLS session set-up. In mobile phones, SIMs with extended functionality may be used as WIMs.

■ *Unauthenticated OTP*. Many mobile phones can be configured remotely using OTP. When configuration data are received via the OTP mechanism, the originator cannot be authenticated via a cryptographic mechanism. This means that a user has no proof of the origin of the message and may end up accepting malicious configuration messages accidentally.

■ *Missing public key infrastructure*. The WAP Forum proposed a WAP Public Key Infrastructure (WPKI). WPKI is a specification of client and WAP gateway certificate requests based on PKCS#7. This allows the exchange of public keys in a defined manner.

6.4.1 WAP session security

Missing end-to-end security is one of the major problems of the current WAP architecture. The lack of such security requires the user and the application provider to trust the operator of the WAP gateway, since the operator has the ability to intercept all messages in clear. Figure 6.6 illustrates the secure parts of the connection.

A WTLS session exists between the client and the WAP gateway, and an SSL or TLS session exists between the WAP gateway and the server. When the client sends an encrypted message to the server, the WAP gateway decrypts the message, encrypts it according to SSL/TLS, and forwards it to the server. This means that each message exchanged between the client and the server exists at least temporarily in clear text on the WAP gateway. Obviously, the same is true for the response sent back by the server. For example, in a banking application, all data, such as account information and PIN/TAN codes, exchanged between the user and the bank are exposed at the WAP gateway. Unless the bank operates its own WAP gateway, the gateway operator will be a telecommunication company, which is unlikely to be trusted by a bank. As a result, some banks have already set up their own WAP gateways to be able to achieve an appropriate level of security for their applications. The downside of this approach, however, is that customers need to add a configuration to their phones that enables them to access directly the bank's WAP gateway instead of going through the preconfigured gateway of the telecommunication company.

The WAP Forum proposed two approaches to resolve this issue. One approach is to create a subset of the TLS protocol that is appropriate for use with small mobile devices (Figure 6.7). This would enable end-to-end security without decrypting and re-encrypting the messages in the WAP gateway, which would also remove load from the WAP gateway.

The other approach is to redirect sessions that require secure communication from the WAP gateway, installed at the mobile service provider location, to a trusted gateway, e.g. a WAP gateway installed at the bank itself (Figure 6.8). To do so, the server sends a redirection message to the

Figure 6.6

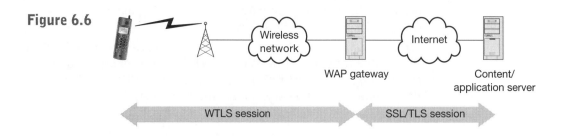

WAP session security

Figure 6.7

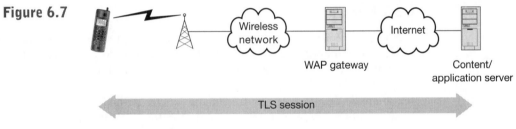

TLS end-to-end security

Figure 6.8

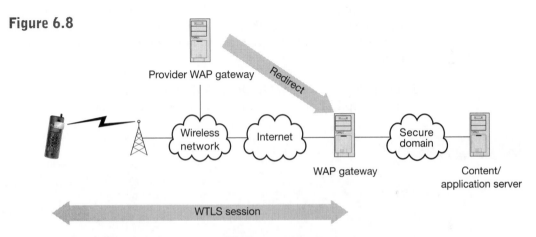

Redirection to a secure WAP gateway

mobile device in order to cause the subsequent requests to the server to be sent through the secure WAP gateway. However, a redirection message is required from the banking application, which increases the response time for the transaction.

6.5 Wireless Markup Language

HTML and JavaScript are designed for desktop computers, and are far too complex for today's mobile devices. Several subsets of HTML have been defined to accommodate less powerful devices than PCs. However, none of these proposals has the kind of broad support from the industry that WML[6] and WMLScript[7] defined by the WAP Forum for mobile devices have received.

6.5.1 Markup

WML is an XML-based markup language designed especially for small devices. Compared with HTML, WML introduces new features suited for use with mobile devices but lacks many of HTML's features:

- An application can transmit multiple pages (called cards) simultaneously in a single transmission unit called a deck.
- WML has the concept of events, e.g. a timer can executes tasks such as displaying a new page after a certain period of time.
- WML can preserve the content of variables between different WML pages (cards). This means that WML, unlike HTML, is not stateless. For example, a variable that is used in one card can be shared with another card because variables are not cleared when a new card is loaded.

Example 6.1 shows a WML deck. A deck is the unit that is transferred from the application or content server to the mobile device.

Example 6.1   **A WML deck**

```
<?xml version="1.0"?>
<!DOCTYPE wml PUBLIC "-//WAPFORUM//DTD WML 1.1//EN"
"http://www.wapforum.org/DTD/wml_1.1.xml">

<wml>
 <card id="card1" title="Sample">
  <p>
   Hello World!
  </p>
 </card>
</wml>
```

In WML, a single page is called a card. Cards and decks are defined in WML to reduce client/server interaction and therefore to reduce the response time for user interactions. Figure 6.9 shows the result of the example above.

6.5.2 WMLScript

WML contains the scripting language WMLScript for performing simple tasks on the mobile device, such as validating user input. WMLScript is derived from ECMAScript, which itself is derived from JavaScript.

Figure 6.9

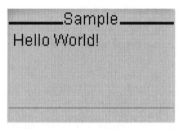

The result of entering the WML Script in Example 6.1

Variables in WML are type less. They can hold a null value or any sequence of characters.

WMLScript Version 1.3 contains the following standard libraries:[8]

- The Lang library provides base functions for WMLScript, such as `min`, `max`, and `random`.
- The optional Float library contains floating-point functions, such as `floor`, `round`, and `pow`.
- The String library contains string-manipulation functions, such as `subString` and `length`.
- The URL library provides functions for handling absolute and relative URLs.
- The WMLBrowser library provides functions for manipulating the associated WML context, such as loading a new page or updating the display. It also contains functions such as `setVar` to set the value of a WML variable.
- The Dialogs library contains user interface functions to prompt for input or confirming an action.

Specific implementations of WMLScript may contain more libraries than required by the WAP standard. These libraries may contain crypto functions, phone book access, or dialling services.

Example

The WMLScript shown as Examples 6.2 and 6.3 is an example of a simple temperature converter. The user enters a temperature and selects the target measurement unit (degrees Celsius or degrees Fahrenheit). The example consists of two parts – a WML deck containing the markup, and the WMLScript containing the program code used for converting the temperature. The markup code displays an entry field for temperature input and two links for measurement unit selection. After entering the temperature and selecting a link, the function `convert` in the WMLScript code is executed. The function sets the variable `conversion` of the WML deck and redraws the complete card that now contains the conversion result. Because the screens of mobile phones are typically quite small, short names are often used, such as 'Temp Converter' for the title of the deck.

Example 6.2 | **Temperature converter WML deck**

```
<?xml version="1.0"?>
<!DOCTYPE wml PUBLIC "-//WAPFORUM//DTD WML 1.1//EN"
"http://www.wapforum.org/DTD/wml_1.1.xml">
<wml>
 <card id="card1" title="Temp Converter"
 newcontext="true">
 <p>
   <!-- input field -->
   Temp: <input format="N*M" name="temperature"
    title="Temperature:"/>
   <!-- result -->
   <br/> = $(conversion)
   <br/>

   <!-- trigger conversion -->
   to <a href="temperature.wmls#convert('conversion',
   'CELSIUS',$(temperature))">&#176;C</a> or
   <a href="temperature.wmls#convert('conversion',
   'FAHRENHEIT',$(temperature))">&#176;F</a>
   </p>
 </card>
</wml>
```

Example 6.3 | **Temperature converter WMLScript code**

```
/*
*@param varName - the variable to store the results
*@param to - the target measurement system
*@param temperature - the temperature
*@return a string containing the converted temperature
 */
extern function convert(varName,to,temperature)
{
 // define variables
```

continued

```
var returnString = "ERROR";
var result;

// conversion code
if (to == "CELSIUS")
{
  result = (5/9) * (temperature - 32);
  returnString = String.toString(result);
  returnString = String.format("%.1f ", returnString);
}
else if (to == "FAHRENHEIT")
{
  result = (9/5) * temperature + 32;
  returnString = String.toString(result);
  returnString = String.format("%.0f ", returnString);
}
// set result variable in browser and refresh the
browser
WMLBrowser.setVar(varName,returnString);
WMLBrowser.refresh();
}
```

Figure 6.10 shows the conversion result from 20°C to 68°F on a mobile phone.

Figure 6.10

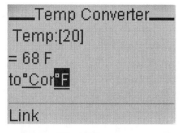

Result of the temperature conversion shown in Examples 6.2 and 6.3

6.5.3 Binary-encoded formats

As mentioned earlier, the messages exchanged between the WAP gateway and the mobile devices are binary encoded to reduce the number of bytes transferred. Both WML decks and WMLScripts are encoded. A mobile device usually accepts images only in the wireless bitmap (WBMP) format. Unlike regular bitmaps, wireless bitmaps contain no header information and are compressed for transmission efficiency.

As an example, the encoding of the deck shown in Example 6.1 reduces the size from 210 bytes for the WML source to 44 bytes for the binary WML (WBXML) data. The conversion result is shown in Example 6.4.

Example 6.4 | **Example 6.1 converted to WBXML**

```
Hexadecimal                            ASCII
01046A007FE75503636172643100360       ..j...U.card1.6.
53616D706C65000160032048656C6C6F      Sample..`. Hello
20576F726C64212000010101              World! ....
```

The limited memory of WAP devices also restricts the size of binary WML decks that can be sent to the mobile phone. It is the responsibility of the server application to limit the amount of data according to the capabilities of the respective device. Typical values for the maximum deck size range from 1400 to 2048 bytes. Because the server application doesn't know the exact size of the binary-encoded WML deck in advance, it can only estimate the size based on the source WML deck. This is a problem for news applications and other applications sending large amounts of text to the mobile device that have to be paginated. Pagination is sometimes also referred to as deck fragmentation.

6.5.4 Usability

One of the most important things when creating a WAP application is to reduce the information to the essential parts. One reason for this is the relatively small size of a mobile device screen compared with a desktop browser. The application developer needs to check whether the user interface of the application fits into the mobile device screen. Figure 6.11 illustrates Examples 6.2 and 6.3 with a heading that is too large to display.

Figure 6.11

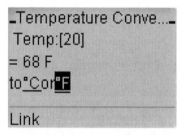

The heading from Examples 6.2 and 6.3, which is too large to display

In Examples 6.2 and 6.3, the measurement units are also abbreviated to make the output of the converter fit into a single screen without scrolling.

Another important part is the use of entry field and links. Figure 6.12 illustrates the actions the user has to perform in order to convert a temperature from 20°C to 68°F.

The code shown in Example 6.5 implements the same functionality but uses a `choice` element and a `go` element instead of two simple links.

Figure 6.13 shows the result of the code shown in Example 6.5

This example demonstrates that even small differences in the implementation can involve much more user interaction and make the application less attractive to the user. Because of the limitations imposed by the user interfaces of mobile devices, usability is an even more important topic than for applications for PC-based browsers.

Figure 6.12

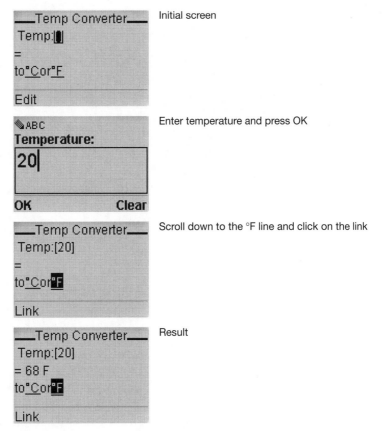

Converting a temperature from 20°C to 68°F

Example 6.5 | **Using the** choice **and** go **elements instead of two simple links**

```
<?xml version="1.0"?>
<!DOCTYPE wml PUBLIC "-//WAPFORUM//DTD WML 1.1//EN"
"http://www.wapforum.org/DTD/wml_1.1.xml">
<wml>
 <card id="card1" title="Temp Converter"
  newcontext="true">
  <p>
   Temp:
   <input format="N*M" name="temperature"
  title="Temperature:"/>
   <br/>
   = $(conversion:noesc)
   <br/>
   to: <select name="target" value="CELSIUS"
  title="Target Unit">
    <option value="CELSIUS">Celsius</option>
    <option value="FAHRENHEIT">Fahrenheit</option>
    </select>
   <do type="accept" label="Calculate">
    <go
  href="temperature.wmls#convert('conversion',$(target),$(
  temperature))"/>
    </do>
   </p>
  </card>
</wml>
```

Figure 6.13

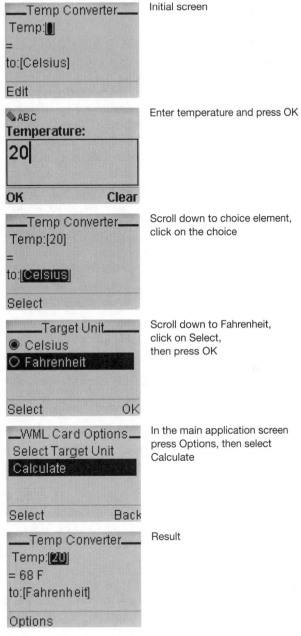

Initial screen

Enter temperature and press OK

Scroll down to choice element, click on the choice

Scroll down to Fahrenheit, click on Select, then press OK

In the main application screen press Options, then select Calculate

Result

The results of the code shown in Example 6.5

6.6 WAP push

WAP push is a service that allows information to be sent to a mobile device without previous user interaction.

The WAP programming model introduced above describes a set-up in which all interaction is triggered from the client. The client sends a request to the server and gets a response for each request. This is called 'pull technology'. In contrast is 'push technology', in which data are sent to the client that do not form an answer to an explicit request. Examples of a push message are the result of a tennis game, or stock quotes that are sent to the mobile device from a news agency.

A push operation is triggered from a push initiator by sending a push message to the push proxy gateway using the Push Access Protocol (PAP).[9] This is used to deliver content with standard Internet technology to a push proxy gateway (PPG).[10] The PPG delivers the message to the mobile device using the push over-the-air protocol. Depending on the capabilities of the PPG, a notification about the outcome of the push operation is sent to the push initiator. The set-up of a push operation is shown in Figure 6.14.

6.6.1 Push Access Protocol

PAP carries an XML-formatted document over the Internet. PAP uses, but is not limited to, HTTP as a transport mechanism. PAP offers the following services:

- *Push submission* sends a message to a mobile device.
- A *confirmation notification* is sent to the push initiator when the push message is delivered to the mobile device, or when a delivery failure occurs.
- A *push cancellation* is sent from the push initiator to the PPG when a previously submitted push submission should be cancelled.
- A *status query* response contains the status of a push submission.

Figure 6.14

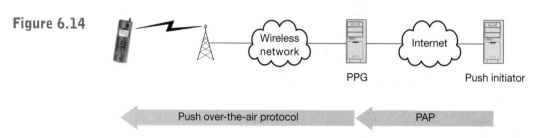

Push message flow

- A *client capabilities query* request returns the capabilities of a mobile device.

6.6.2 The push over-the-air protocol

The push over-the-air (OTA[11]) protocol is a protocol layer for transmitting push messages over the WSP. It is the part of the push framework that is responsible for exchanging content between the user agent and the PPG.

6.7 Products

The market for mobile phones is basically split into two segments. The low-end segment provides basic voice and SMS services. Emphasis is on ease of use, innovative design, and small device size. The high-end segment ranges from basic WAP devices to wireless PDAs. WAP gateways are developed by mobile equipment providers and IT infrastructure providers exploiting their investments in IP protocol stacks. In this section, we describe a selection of mobile phones, WAP gateways, and WAP simulator tools that are available on the market today.

6.7.1 WAP phones

The number of WAP phone models is increasing steadily, and prices are falling. In this section we present some of the most common phones in use today. It can be accepted that WAP will become a standard feature for all GSM mobile phones.

Nokia 7110
The Nokia 7110 (Figure 6.15) was one of the first WAP phones available, and most applications have been developed and tested with this phone. It is a dual-band (GSM 900 and GSM 1800) phone, and supports data rates of up to 14.4 kbps. It has a display with 96×65 pixels, which is the equivalent of four lines with 25 characters each. The maximum deck size is just over 1400 bytes.

The Nokia 7110 supports five configuration profiles. The built-in microbrowser ignores all emphasis tags (`big`, `small`, `em`, `strong`, `b`, `i`, `u`). Tables are supported, but every cell appears in a new line.

The Siemens 35 series
The current Siemens 35 series consists of three GSM mobile phones (Figure 6.16) and an organizer (Figure 6.17).

Figure 6.15

Nokia 7110

Courtesy of Nokia

Figure 6.16

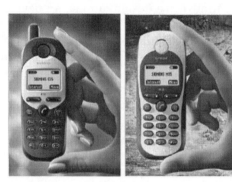

The Siemens 35 series phones

Courtesy of Siemens

Figure 6.17

Siemens IC35 Organizer

Courtesy of Siemens

The C35i is designed for consumers. The M35i is designed for outdoor use, featuring a five-line display and reminder list. The S35i is designed for business use. The features of the phone are an IrDA link, a seven-line display, a calendar, voice dialling, and an organizer with calendar, appointments, and alarm list.

All phones are dual band (GSM 1800 and GSM 1900) and use the UP.Browser WAP 1.1 browser from Openwave Systems. The WAP browser supports suppression of the head and status lines by pressing the #key several times. This increases the number of lines available for WAP browsing (up to seven lines with the S35i phone and up to five lines with the C35i and M35i phones). All Siemens phones provide five configuration profiles. The deck size limit of all Siemens 35 series devices is 2 kB.

The Siemens Unifier (IC35) basically is a PDA with an integrated WAP 1.1 browser. The IC35 connects to a mobile phone via the IrDA interface or a serial cable. The IC35 supports three configuration profiles.

The IC35 offers the following applications: appointment calendar, address book, task list, text editor, pocket calculator, euro converter, and telephone manager. It has an IrDA interface as well as a serial interface, offers a slot for multimedia cards, and has a smart card slot.

One of the most interesting applications for the Unifier is mobile banking. The additional smart card slot allows automatic starting of the banking application and connection set-up as soon as a banking smart card is inserted.

Ericsson R380

The Ericsson R380 (Figure 6.18) is a mobile phone with an integrated organizer. It is a dual-band (GSM 900 and GSM 1800) phone, and supports data rates up to 9.6 KBps. Its touch screen has a size of 360 × 120 pixels, and supports pen input. The R320 2.0 WAP browser supports WAP 1.1.

The integrated organizer is based on the EPOC operating system and features typical PDA applications, including address book, calendar, notepad, and support for synchronization with PC applications.

Figure 6.18

The Ericsson R380
Courtesy of Ericsson

6.7.2 WAP gateways

Wireless service providers or Internet providers offer Internet access with mobile phones through WAP gateways. Enterprises or banks may also install WAP gateways in order to prevent exposure of private data to other parties. For example, a bank may prefer to operate their own WAP gateway to lower the risk of somebody listening to the communication between the customer's mobile phone and the application server of the bank. Enterprises may install their own WAP gateways in their intranets because the security policy may not allow traffic from the wireless operator's network into the company's intranet. Typically, access to a WAP gateway requires a specific configuration profile, including dial-in number, protocol settings, optional user identification and password, WAP gateway IP address, and home page URL, much like the profile used for Internet access. However, mobile phones limit the number of profiles that can be stored and managed. Customers may also not be willing to switch profiles. Therefore, the number of WAP gateways easily accessible by a customer is rather limited.

WAP gateways are available from several sources, including an open-source implementation named Kandel. In this section we describe products from Nokia and Openwave Systems to give two examples.

Nokia Activ Server

The Nokia Activ Server 2.0[12] consists of a WAP gateway, a Web server for static content, and a servlet engine. It is a Java application available for Windows NT/2000, HP-UX, and Sun Solaris. The following plug-ins, shown in Figure 6.19, are available for the Activ Server:

Figure 6.19

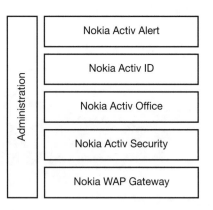

The Nokia Activ Server components

- *Nokia Activ Security* is a plug-in for the Nokia Activ Server offering WAP 1.1 compliant server authentication and data encryption. Activ Security is available with 56-bit and 128-bit key-length encryption. It supports SSL connections from the WAP server to the Web applications. The Security Pack is available for the same platforms as the Nokia Activ Server.

- *Nokia Activ ID* is a plug-in that enables personalized WAP applications based on the MSISDN (telephone) number recognition.

- *Nokia Activ Office* is a plug-in for PIM applications. It offers WAP email connectors for POP3, IMAP4, Lotus Notes, and Microsoft Exchange (via IMAP4) mail servers. The plug-in also supports replicating notifications of calendar entries to the mobile phones.

- *Nokia Activ Alert* provides an API for WAP push applications. It allows notifications or information to be sent to the mobile phone.

Openwave Systems WAP gateway

The WAP gateway from Openwave Systems[13] is called UP.Link server (Figure 6.20). It consists of the UP.Link WAP gateway, the UP.Link WAP enhanced services, and the UP.Admin administration interface. The UP.Link WAP gateway provides the protocol translation, security, activity tracking, and administration tools needed to implement a wireless Internet solution. It supports multiple air-link standards, including CDMA, cellular digital packet data (CDPD), GSM, integrated digital enchanced network (iDEN), personal digital cellular (PDC), personal

Figure 6.20

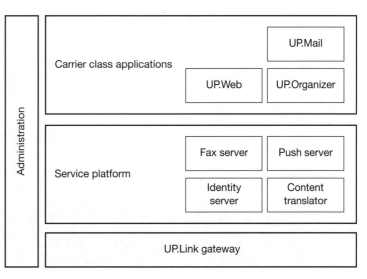

The UP.Link server components

handyphone system (PHS), and TDMA. Packet, circuit and SMS bearers are supported. The UP.Link enhanced services features a content translator, a push server, a fax server, and an identity server. The UP.Link administration component provides a Web-based administration system for the UP.Link server.

6.7.3 WAP simulator tools

Simulator tools are used as a substitute for real WAP phones while developing WAP applications. Simulators typically display an image of the real phone and provide the same functionalities. They also offer debugging features, like the ability to decode binary WML deck content back to source code, or a tool for examination of the device cache. However, simulators may not represent all specific features of an actual WAP browser implementation, and may not emulate the behavior of a specific communication network. Therefore, applications must also be tested on real devices in real-life environment.

WAP simulator tools are available from many vendors. In this section, we describe the Nokia WAP Toolkit 2.0 as an example.

The Nokia WAP Toolkit 2.0
The Nokia WAP Toolkit (Figure 6.21) is an environment for creating and testing WML and WMLScript applications. It runs in Windows as a Java

Figure 6.21

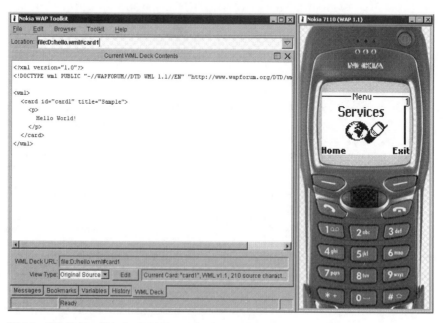

Nokia WAP Toolkit in 7110 emulation mode

application. It includes a graphics editor for WBMP images, and allows GIF and JPEG images to be converted to WBMP. The Nokia WAP Toolkit has two simulation modes:

- The generic WAP phone emulation supports WAP 1.2 functionality, including WML, WMLScript, and WAP push services.
- The Nokia 7110 emulation mode is an exact simulation of the Nokia 7110 mobile phone.

6.8 i-Mode

i-Mode is an Internet service for mobile devices that is currently available in Japan, and will be available in the future in the USA and Europe. A typical device is shown in Figure 6.22. It is well accepted, with several million subscribers. It allows users to browse specially formatted websites and to receive email using their mobile phones. 3G i-mode phones are offering a display size of about 24 × 10 characters. i-mode uses a packet-switched bearer service with 9.6 kbps that allows for permanent connections. The monthly fee depends on the number of packets exchanged.

A phone is tied to a service provider; changing a service provider requires a new phone to be purchased. The i-mode gateway is always installed at the provider's site. Mail is stored at the server or in the phone, depending on the service provider business model. The size of each mail is limited to a certain size, e.g. 500 characters. Longer mails are truncated.

Figure 6.22

i-Mode device

The devices on the market today allow Internet pages to be displayed in the S-JIS character set with GIF images; some phones even allow animated GIF. The number of supported HTML tags is different for each different device type. Simple devices support the following HTML 1.0 tags: `<!-- -->`, `<A>`, `<BASE>`, `<BLOCKQUOTE>`, `<BODY>`, `<BR>`, `<CENTER>`, `<DIR>`, `<DD>`, `<DIV>`, `<FORM>`, `<HEAD>`, `<H>`, `<HR>`, `<HTML>`, `<IMG>`, `<INPUT>`, `<LI>`, `<MENU>`, `<OL>`, `<OPTION>`, `<P>`, `<PLAINTEXT>`, `<PRE>`, `<SELECT>`, `<TEXTAREA>`,`<TITLE>`, and `<UL>`.

New i-mode phones support SSL end-to-end security without client certificates. Root certificates of the well-known trust centers are stored in the phones. The user can disable these certificates partially or completely.

A Java Micro Edition VM (CLDC, see Chapter 3) is also integrated in new phone models. Java applications must implement a specific base class defined by the VM, because Java applets or AWT are not included in the class library. The functions of the VM are very limited, for example only one application can be executed at one time, and access to the phonebook is disabled due to security reasons.

i-mode phones do not support cookies, which means a special cookie proxy is necessary to support complex Web applications.

6.9 Outlook

The third generation of mobile devices offers increased bandwidth and more processing power than the second-generation devices. This brings standard Internet technologies, such as the TCP/IP stack and a subset of HTML, into the reach of mobile phones, which might limit the use of WML language and the WAP stack to low-end devices. Since the standard Internet protocols are designed for wire-line networks, there is a need to extend the functionality to wireless devices. The W3C develops technologies to merge wireless and wire-line technology to a single, extendable basis.

Below, we present two examples of these technologies: Composite Capability/Preference Profiles (CC/PP) and XHTML.

6.9.1 Composite Capability/Preference Profile

An ever-increasing number of different smart devices will appear in the future. Thus, the adaptation of content to display capabilities and data rate will be of utmost importance. User preferences, like language selection, also have to be considered. The PP[14] enables devices to provide capability profiles to gateways or servers for adapting content to the device and the user preferences. A CC/PP profile contains the hardware and software configuration as well as the user settings. Example 6.6 shows the CC/PP profile for a smart phone.

Example 6.6 | **CC/PP PROFILE OF A SMART PHONE**

```xml
<?xml version="1.0"?>
<rdf:RDF
 xmlns:rdf="http://www.w3.org/1999/02/22-rdf-syntax-ns#"
 xmlns:prf="http://www.w3.org/TR/WD-profile-vocabulary#">

<rdf:Description about="HardwarePlatform">
 <prf:Defaults
  Vendor="XY Company"
  Model="0815"
  Type="Smart Phone"
  ScreenSize="160x160x8"
  CPU="PPC 166 MHz"
  Memory="2MB"
 />
 <prf:Modifications
  Memory="8MB" />
</rdf:Description>

<rdf:Description about="SoftwarePlatform">
 <prf:Defaults
  OS="XY Phone OS"
  XHTMLVersion="1.0"
  Color="yes"
  Images="yes"
 />
</rdf:Description>

<rdf:Description about="UserPreferences">
 <prf:Defaults
  Language="EN"
 />
 <prf:Modifications
  Language="DE"
 />
</rdf:Description>
</rdf:RDF>
```

Figure 6.23 illustrates an example configuration for an imaginary smart phone. Instead of the typical 2 MB from the standard configuration, the smart phone in this example is equipped with 8 MB of memory.

The profile is encoded in the XML/RDF format. Resource Description Framework (RDF[15]) is a mechanism to exchange metadata between applications in a machine-readable form. RDF is defined by the W3C.

6.8.2 Extensible Hypertext Markup Language

XHTML[16] is the XML-based successor of HTML 4.0. HTML and XHTML are recommendations for the Internet community defined by the W3C. XHTML allows mobile phone manufacturers to design a language that fits their needs based on HTML, the standard publishing language of the WWW. XHTML is a family of document-type definitions (DTDs) providing a subset or an extension of HTML 4.0, depending on the device and where it is used. XHTML requires documents to be well-formed XML. This means that some guidelines have to be followed. For example:

- element and attribute names must be in lower case because XML is case sensitive, e.g. `<html>`, `</body>`;
- end tags are required for all elements, e.g. `<p>Hello World</p>`;
- quotes are required for attribute values, e.g. `<hr size="5" />`.

Example 6.7 shows an example of XHTML.

Figure 6.23

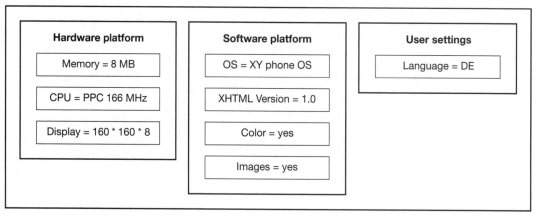

Example CC/PP configuration

Example 6.7 **Example of XHTML**

```
<?xml version="1.0"?>
<html xmlns="http://www.w3.org/1999/xhtml" xml:lang="en"
lang="en">
  <head>
   <title>Sample</title>
  </head>
  <body>
   <p>Hello World!</p>
  </body>
</html>
```

The W3C has defined a special XHTML subset for pervasive devices named XHTML Basic. XHTML Basic is a DTD tailored for desktop, TV, and mobile phones that is still rich enough to be used for simple content authoring. New document types can be defined by extending XHTML Basic in such a way that XHTML Basic documents are in the set of valid documents of the new document type.

XHTML Basic is designed for appliances like mobile phones, television sets, PDAs, vending machines, pagers, car navigation systems, mobile game machines, digital book readers, and smart watches.

References

1. WAP Forum (April 1998) 'Wireless Datagram Protocol Specification'. http://www.wapforum.org/what/technical.htm

2. WAP Forum (April 1998) 'Wireless Transport Layer Security Protocol'. http://www.wapforum.org/what/technical.htm

3. WAP Forum (April 1998) 'Wireless Transaction Protocol Specification'. http://www.wapforum.org/what/technical.htm

4. WAP Forum (April 1998) 'Wireless Session Protocol'. http://www.wapforum.org/what/technical.htm

5. WAP Forum (April 1998) 'Wireless Application Environment Specification'. http://www.wapforum.org/what/technical.htm

6. WAP Forum (April 1998) 'Wireless Markup Language Specification'. http://www.wapforum.org/what/technical.htm

7. WAP Forum (April 1998) 'Wireless Markup Language Script'. http://www.wapforum.org/what/technical.htm

8. WAP Forum (April 1998) 'Wireless Markup Language Script Standard Libraries'. http://www.wapforum.org/what/technical.htm

9. WAP Forum (November 1999) 'WAP Push Access Protocol Specification'. http://www.wapforum.org/what/technical.htm

10. WAP Forum (November 1999) 'WAP Push Proxy Gateway Specification'. http://www.wapforum.org/what/technical.htm

11. WAP Forum (November 1999) 'WAP Push OTA Specification'. http://www.wapforum.org/what/technical.htm

12. Nokia Developer Forum. http://www.forum.nokia.com

13. Openwave Systems. http://www.openwave.com/

14. W3C (July 1999) 'Composite Capability/Preference Profile (CC/PP)'. http://www.w3.org/Mobile/CCPP/

15. W3C (March 2000) 'Resource Description Framework (RDF)'. http://www.w3.org/RDF/

16. W3C (January 2000) 'XHTML™ 1.0: The Extensible Hypertext Markup Language'. http://www.w3.org/TR/xhtml1/

Further reading

1. WAP Forum (April 1998) 'Wireless Application Protocol Architecture Specification'. http://www.wapforum.org/what/technical.htm

2. WAP Forum (April 1998) 'Wireless Telephony Application Specification'. http://www.wapforum.org/what/technical.htm

7 Voice technology

Automated speech recognition enables computers to convert spoken language to text. Speech is the natural communication method for humans, and therefore is a very convenient user interface for applications. At the same time, speech recognition is a difficult task for computers. Although speech recognition has been researched since the 1950s, commercial continuous speech-recognition systems with an acceptable recognition rate became available only a few years ago.

Within the next five years or so, pervasive devices will have enough memory and processing power to use speech recognition as a user interface method. This will have dramatic impact, especially on the consumer market. Today, the user interface of most video cassette recorders (VCRs) and mobile phones is so complex that the average user utilizes only a small part of the devices' features, because they do not know, or do not remember, how to use all the available features. This will change with voice-based user interfaces, because it will be a simple task for the user to tell the device what they want it to do.

Speech recognition may also start a new era in the pervasive computing space. Mobile phones have now reached a form factor where they can get no smaller because of the space needed for the keyboard and the display. Devices will become unusable if the size of the displays and keyboards is reduced further. With speech recognition, these devices will shrink even more, and could even be integrated into watches, jewellery, or clothing.

In this chapter, we will cover the basics of speech recognition. We will describe two important standards in the area of voice-based user interfaces: VoiceXML, a markup language for speech, and Java Speech, a Java API that provides speech capability to Java applications. Typical speech applications, such as speech recognition on the PC, speech recognition over a telephone line, and text-to-speech translation, will then be covered. Finally, we take a closer look at speech recognition in pervasive computing, and at security when using speech as user interface method.

7.1 Basics of speech recognition

Speech recognition is a wide, complex field, and it is beyond the scope of this book to cover it in depth. However, we will give a short overview of the problems of speech recognition, and the approaches and techniques used to solve them.

7.1.1 Speech-recognition techniques

Just as written language has letters as units, speech recognition can be based on phonemes or words. The speech signal is transformed into frequency space representation for further processing. Only vowels generate resonance frequencies in the speech signal; consonants are produced by turbulent airflow in the human speech system, and therefore show up as noise in the frequency space of the speech signal. These resonance frequencies, or Eigenfrequencies, are called formants. From formants, the speech-recognition system can derive phonemes via signal analysis, using pattern-recognition algorithms.[1,2]

Figure 7.1 gives an overview of a continuous speech-recognition system. The system receives the digitized speech signal as input, and transforms it into the frequency space (e.g. by applying a Fourier transformation). The

Figure 7.1

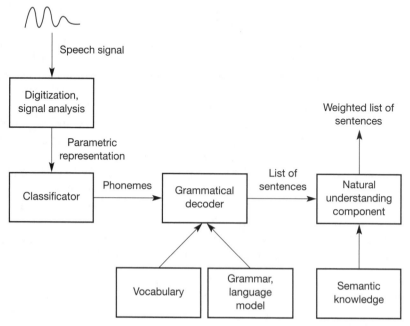

Overview of a continuous speech-recognition system

following signal analysis calculates a feature vector representing the spectral distribution of the speech signal for a given time frame. This parametric representation of the speech signal is given to the classificator. The classificator uses pattern-recognition heuristics to generate phonemes out of the spectral vector (e.g. with techniques called segmentation and labelling). The grammatical decoder uses the vocabulary and grammar rules or language models (e.g. bi- or trigrams) to construct a list of possible sentences for the received phoneme sequence. A grammar or language model can reduce the number of possibilities by magnitudes, as not all words in a vocabulary are allowed at all places within a sentence. Finally, the natural understanding component takes this list and sorts out the most probable words based on semantic knowledge.

The recognition rate measures the accuracy of speech-recognition systems when analyzing speech. A word-recognition rate of 90% means that on average, one out of ten words is recognized wrongly.

7.1.2 Challenges of speech recognition

As mentioned above, a lot of research has been carried out since the 1950s to achieve speech-recognition systems with recognition rates that are acceptable for everyday use. These systems are still not available for the generic case of speaker-independent and task-independent speech recognition. This is due to the fact that speech recognition has some serious challenges.

The recognition accuracy is constrained by the following problems:

- *Isolated, connected, and continuous speech*. Isolated word recognition is one of the simpler problems, because isolated words are clearly separated and distinguished from each other. Continuous speech recognition, however, is very difficult because the word boundary for a spoken word is not defined clearly, poor articulation of words creates ambiguities, and stronger coarticulation (simultaneously produced adjacent vowels and consonants) causes problems. The worst case is spontaneous continuous speech, because the spoken sentences often are grammatically incorrect and may contain hesitations or press noises such as 'hmmm'. In connected word recognition, it is difficult to recognize the word boundaries, but there are no fill words as in continuous speech.

- *Vocabulary size*. The recognition accuracy depends on the vocabulary size. The vocabulary size varies inversely with the speech-recognition accuracy and efficiency, as more words introduce more ambiguities and require more time to process.

- *Speaker dependent/speaker independent*. Speech-recognition systems trained and used by a single speaker perform much better than systems dealing with different speakers. This is due to the fact that a system used by only one speaker can be trained quickly and efficiently for that particular speaker.

■ *Task and language constraints*. Speech recognition can be much simplified if the system uses limited grammar and dictionaries. For example, an airline information system can restrict its grammar to, say, 1000 possible combinations of words. Since this increases the recognition speed and accuracy dramatically, almost all speaker-independent speech-recognition systems with a word-recognition rate higher than 70% are using this technique.

■ *Environmental noise*. Environmental noise can have a large impact on the recognition rate. Critical environments for speech-recognition systems are offices, public places, cars, trains, factories, etc. However, speech-recognition systems can be adapted through training and filtering to special environmental noise. In-car speech-recognition systems, for example, are using these techniques.

■ *Channel quality*. The quality of the speech channel depends mainly on the microphone. Different microphones produce different speech signals. If the channel uses a digital line, such as GSM or UMTS, the digital processing of these channels also has an effect on the recognition rate. For more information about GSM and UMTS, see Chapter 4.

■ *Line and digitization noise*. Regular analog lines may introduce systematic distortions, e.g. echoes during overseas calls, or damping of high frequencies. Digitization and short interrupts on digital lines (e.g. GSM, UMTS) also create systematic distortions.

■ *Vocabulary ambiguity*. Words like 'show' and 'snow' sound similar, and it can be difficult for speech-recognition systems to recognize the correct word. Humans use context information to solve this problem. For example, it is easy for humans to decide that the sentence must be 'show me your house' and not 'snow me your house', but for a computer this is a complex task.

With so many problems to solve, speech-recognition systems that have a recognition rate of 99% for continuous speech, are speaker independent, and support a large, context-free vocabulary are far in the future. Nevertheless, speech-recognition do systems exist that achieve word recognition rates of over 95%, with a vocabulary of more then 60 000 words, after training by the speaker, for example from IBM or Lernout & Hauspie. However, even a rate of 95% still means that every twentieth word is recognized wrongly and must be corrected manually. With continuous improvements of hardware support and speech-recognition algorithms, speech recognition will increase usability and will be applied in new areas.

7.2 Voice standards

When using speech recognition in the computing world, there are two important standards to consider. The first is VoiceXML, which can be used in a Web environment together with a voice browser to make the Web application accessible through the telephone. The second is the Java Speech API, which enables Java programs to use speech as the user interface method.

7.2.1 VoiceXML

VoiceXML is a markup language for speech that is based on XML and enables Web applications for voice-accessed devices. Version 1.0 was developed by AT&T, IBM, Lucent Technologies, and Motorola, and has been submitted to the W3C for standardization.

The VoiceXML 1.0 specification provides a high-level programming interface to speech and telephony applications.[3] VoiceXML standardization has the following goals:

- To simplify creation and delivery of Web-based, personalized, interactive voice–response services.
- To enable phone and voice access to integrated call-center databases, information, and services on websites and company intranets.
- To enable new voice-capable devices and appliances.

A VoiceXML application is a collection of dialogs, which are equivalent to WML or HTML pages. The two basic dialog types are `forms`, which are used for presenting and gathering information, and `menus`, which offer the choices to the user. An example of a VoiceXML file is given in Example 7.1.

In Example 7.1, the user hears an introduction ("Welcome ...") and then a menu, where he or she can chose one option. If the system recognizes one of the keywords 'Menu', 'Order', or 'Exit', it processes the corresponding JSP or VoiceXML page. The recognition rate at this stage will be pretty good because the system must choose from a small list of only three keywords, which all sound quite different. To get even better recognition rates, a grammar can be specified with `<grammar ...>` (see the next section for how to specify speech grammars). VoiceXML allows a standard reply for unrecognized voice input to be defined. In Example 7.1, this is done with two levels: the first responds with the short text "Please say Menu, Order or Exit", whereas after the second unrecognized input the long version is used. For more VoiceXML examples, see Chapter 15.

Example 7.1 **Example of VoiceXML**

```xml
<?xml version="1.0"?>
<vxml version="1.0">
 <form>
   <block>
    Welcome to Uncle Enzo's Pizza Service.
    <goto next="#main" />
   </block>
 </form>
 <menu id="main" scope="document">
  <prompt>Main Menu: <enumerate/></prompt>
  <choice next="/PCVShop/Shop/VoiceMenu.jsp">Menu
   </choice>
    <choice next="/PVCShop/Shop/VoiceOrder.jsp
     ">Order</choice>
  <choice next="/PVCShop/Shop/Exit.vxml ">Exit</choice>
  <prompt timeout="4s">What do you like to do? </prompt>
  <grammar src="/PVCShop/Shop/VoiceMenu.gram"/>
  <catch event="nomatch noinput help" count="1">
   Please say Menu, Order or Exit.
  </catch>
  <catch event="nomatch noinput help" count="2">
   Uncle Enzo's Pizza ordering service allows you to
order via the telephone. Say Menu to hear the menu, say
Order to create an order, say Exit or hang up to cancel.
   </catch>
  </menu>
</vxml>
```

7.2.2 Java Speech API

To use speech recognition and text-to-speech transformation from Java programs in a consistent manner, Sun, Apple, AT&T, Dragon Systems, IBM, Novell, Philips, and Texas Instruments developed the Java Speech API.[4] The API supports two core speech technologies: speech recognition and speech synthesis (text-to-speech).

The Java Speech API separates the speech-recognition and text-to-speech engines from the application. This allows for an easy exchange of the underlying speech engine without changing the application. The application can use the new engine and benefit from better recognition rates. It also allows building applications to be built in which customers can chose their preferred speech engine.

Some implementations of the Java Speech API are IBM's Speech for Java, Lernout & Hauspie's TTS, and Festival, developed at the University of Edinburgh.

Components of the Java Speech API

The Java Speech API consists of the following packages:

- *javax.speech* defines an abstract software representation of a speech engine. A speech engine can deal with either speech input or speech output. Therefore, speech recognizers and text-to-speech systems are both examples of speech engines. Speaker-verification systems and speaker-identification systems are also speech engines, but they are not currently supported through the Java Speech API.
- *javax.speech.synthesis* defines the API for text-to-speech engines. It is possible to customize the text-to-speech engine via the Java Speech Markup Language (JSML) API. JSML provides cross-platform control of speech synthesizers.
- *javax.speech.recognition* defines the API for speech-recognition engines. It allows for grammar-based speech recognition, and is a finite state machine. The grammar has to be in the Java Speech Grammar Format (JSGF), which provides cross-platform control of the speech recognizers.

Example 7.2 pronounces the string 'Hello World' in English. It uses the simple `speakPlainText` method to generate the speech output. In addition to `speakPlainText`, the Java Speech API provides a much more flexible method for generating speech output: `speak`. This requires input in the JSML.

Example 7.3 shows how to recognize "Hello World". Grammar in the JSGF is needed. The trivial grammar shown has a single public rule called `<sentence>` that defines what a user may say. Valid sentences with this grammar are `hello world`, `hi there`, or `hello computer`.

The Java program for our example could look like the code shown in Example 7.4.

The main method sets up the speech recognizer, assigns the grammar, and adds the `HelloWorld` class as listener. As `HelloWorld` is subclassed from `ResultAdapter`, the method resultAccepted is called from the speech recognition engine, if a spoken sentence matches the given grammar. The implementation of our `resultAccepted` method gets the best recognition match for the spoken text with `r.getBestTokens` and prints the recognized words to the standard output stream.

Example 7.2   **Text-to-speech using the Java Speech API**

```java
import java.util.Locale;
import javax.speech.*;
import javax.speech.synthesis.*;
public class HelloWorld {
 public static void main(String args[]) {
  try {
    // Create a synthesizer for English
    Synthesizer s = Central.createSynthesizer(
      new SynthesizerModeDesc(Locale.ENGLISH));
    // Start the synthesizer
    s.allocate();
    s.resume();
    // Speak "Hello world"
    s.speakPlainText("Hello world", null);
    // Wait until speech output is finished
    s.waitEngineState(Synthesizer.QUEUE_EMPTY);
    // Close the synthesizer
    s.deallocate();
   } catch (Exception e) {
    e.printStackTrace();
   }
  }
 }
```

Example 7.3   **Java Speech Grammar**

```
grammar javax.speech.demo;
public <sentence> = hello world | hi there | hello
computer;
```

Example 7.4 **Speech recognition**

```java
import java.io.FileReader;
import java.util.Locale;
import javax.speech.*;
import javax.speech.recognition.*;
public class HelloWorld extends ResultAdapter {
 static Recognizer recog;
 // Receives RESULT_ACCEPTED event: prints it, clean up,
    and exits
 public void resultAccepted(ResultEvent e) {
    Result r = (Result)(e.getSource());
    ResultToken tokens[] = r.getBestTokens();
    for (int i = 0; i < tokens.length; i++)
      System.out.print(tokens[i].getSpokenText() + " ");
    System.out.println();
    // Finish
    recog.deallocate();
    System.exit(0);
 }
 // main
 public static void main(String args[]) {
  try {
    // Create a recognizer that supports English.
    recog = Central.createRecognizer(new
      EngineModeDesc(Locale.ENGLISH));
    // Start recognizer
    recog.allocate();
    // Load the grammar from file, and enable it
    FileReader r = new FileReader(args[0]);
    RuleGrammar grammar = recog.loadJSGF(r);
    grammar.setEnabled(true);
    // Add the listener to receive the results
    recog.addResultListener(new HelloWorld());
    recog.commitChanges();
    // Request focus and start listening
    recog.requestFocus();
    recog.resume();
    } catch (Exception e) {
    e.printStackTrace();
    }
  }
}
```

7.3 Speech applications

Speech technologies are applied mainly in the following areas: desktop speech recognition for speech dictation, telephone speech recognition for transaction and information access services (e.g. flight information systems), text-to-speech transformation to access text documents via the phone (e.g. listen to email via a mobile phone), and embedded speech recognition. Embedded speech recognition is covered in Section 7.4; the other areas are explained in more detail below.

7.3.1 Desktop speech recognition

Speech recognition became popular with the advent of speech-recognition programs for the desktop computer. It augmented the traditional graphical user interface. Typical uses are:

- *to execute commands via speech,* to access features that otherwise would need several mouse clicks (e.g. "Make selected text bold");
- *to provide audible prompts,* e.g. "Do you want to replace the existing file?", which can then be answered by the user with either "Yes" or "No". This helps to avoid distracting the user from the current task;
- *speech dictation:* speech dictation systems are available from various vendors, and experienced users can achieve typing rates exceeding 100 words per minute with an accuracy of over 95%. These systems are very popular for professionals with high dictation demands, such as lawyers, and for disabled people.

7.3.2 Telephone speech recognition

Telephone speech recognition requires more sophisticated speech signal preprocessing than a desktop-based speech-recognition system. This is because telephone lines have a very limited frequency band and different channel characteristics (high noise levels, microphones, transmission characteristics of wireless phones), which results in loss of voice information. In addition, telephone lines can have short drop-outs, especially when the call is made via a mobile phone. The speech-recognition system must therefore be designed specifically for telephone use.

Telephone speech recognition enables companies to automate their call centers and provide their customers with access to information and resources. It helps enterprises to provide a 24-hours-a-day, seven-days-a-week service to their customers at reasonable cost, because most questions can be answered by a computer with a speech-recognition system and access to a database containing frequently asked questions.

The first step is to use speech recognition to provide a more natural and efficient interface than touch-tone systems can for processes such as accessing information, voice mail, menu selection, and entering numbers. These systems are now becoming available in cinemas, hotels, and airports.

The next step is the introduction of interactive telephone speech systems that are capable of answering questions like 'Please tell me all Delta flights leaving before 10 pm to New York.'

7.3.3 Text-to-speech

Text-to-speech, also called speech synthesis, is a technique to generate speech output from text input. This is an important technology for telephone systems and pervasive computing, as it allows access to documents such as email from standard phones or mobile phones. For example, Internet portals such as Yahoo[5] already offer the possibility to access email, news, and weather over the phone.

The first generation of text-to-speech systems used formants synthesizers to generate the speech signal. This restricted naturalness and intelligibility, and were therefore sometimes difficult to understand. This is due to the fact that the computer synthesizes phonemes or diphones (from the middle of one phoneme to the middle of the next phoneme).

The second generation of text-to-speech systems used pre-recorded syllables, which were combined to make full words. These needed much more memory than first-generation systems, but generated a much more natural-sounding speech output.

The current, third generation uses a corpus-based approach with units of flexible length, such as pre-recoded syllables, words, and sentences. With the help of prosody generation, these systems are able to generate speech output that is almost undistinguishable from a human speaker.

7.4 Speech and pervasive computing

Because the mobile phone is the most common mobile device, speech is an important channel for systems supporting these devices. This support can be implemented in two different ways. One approach is to stick with the standard phone system (mobile or conventional) and use a voice gateway on the other side of the phone line to process the speech input. Another approach is to process the speech input directly on the device, known as embedded speech recognition. Both scenarios are explained in more detail below.

7.4.1 Voice gateways

A voice gateway allows access to a computer system via speech input and output. Figure 7.2 shows the architecture of such a system. The architecture looks very similar to that of a WAP gateway (see Chapter 6). The voice gateway includes a speech recognition and text-to-speech engine for voice input and output. Keys entered by the user, e.g. to make a selection during text-to-speech sessions, are transmitted via multifrequency coding (MFC) and recognized very reliably. The voice gateway is driven by VoiceXML documents, and uses a voice browser to process these documents. The VoiceXML documents can be static, or they can be generated dynamically using a server-side scripting technology such as JSP. In addition to the VoiceXML documents that describe the application flow, voice grammars can be used to achieve a higher recognition rate, and prerecorded voice files containing frequently spoken words or sentences (e.g. 'Thank you') can be used to achieve a more natural text-to-speech output.

The voice gateway architecture has the advantage that virtually billions of phones, conventional and mobile, can use this method to access information on the Web or on the back-end system. Typical applications are transaction-based systems or information systems for the transport and entertainment industries. In addition, personal information can be accessed via phone by people that are not using a PC, or do not have access to a PC while on the road.

7.4.2 Embedded speech recognition

Several companies are working on pervasive devices with integrated speech-recognition capabilities. For example, many high-end mobile phones have keyword-spotting speech recognition: the user says the name of the person that they wants to talk to, and the phone then looks up the number in the built-in address book and dials the number.

Figure 7.2

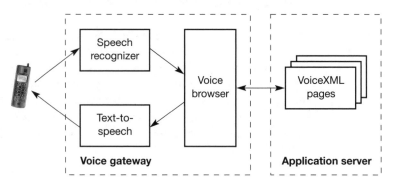

Voice gateway architecture

The combination of a PDA with speech recognition and an intelligent agent can support queries like 'Please tell me the weather forecast for L.A. for tomorrow.' The PDA would then connect to the Internet, retrieve the information, and come back with an answer, such as 'The weather in L.A. tomorrow is rain with scattered showers.' This will bring a new level of usability and acceptance to pervasive computing devices. Speech recognition for PDAs is already showing on the horizon, as IBM and Lernout & Hauspie have already shown working speech-enabled PDA prototypes.

As a concrete example of a pervasive computing device using speech input and output, we will discuss the IBM personal speech assistant (PSA) prototype. This consists of a speech coprocessor and a Palm-compatible PDA loaded with the Voice Suite Palm applications. The PSA allows spoken access to the standard Palm applications. An application can define a vocabulary of up to 500 words to be recognized by the PSA, but five or ten words are normally sufficient for most tasks. In addition, an application may define keywords that the PSA responds to.

Figure 7.3 shows the PSA with the PSA Speech Suite running. As can be seen in the display, all common Palm tasks can be accessed via voice. Additional functions are also available, including reading news, translating speech, or recording speech. The hardware supporting the speech recognition ability is embedded in a thin sleeve. Figure 7.3 shows the PSA sleeve piggybacked to a run-of-the-mill WorkPad c2, the IBM version of

Figure 7.3

IBM's PSA together with an IBM WorkPad c2
Courtesy of IBM Corp.

the Palm III. The sleeve contains a 133-MHz PowerPC processor, 4 MB of flash memory, a loudspeaker, a microphone, and a battery. The additional processor is needed because the 16-MHz/16-bit Palm processor is not able to perform the computing-intensive speech-recognition process. However, one can easily imagine that in the near future, powerful and sufficiently cheap processors with low power consumption will be available to provide PDAs with built-in speech-recognition capabilities. Today's high-end PDAs, such as the Compaq iPAQ,[6] already have the processing power and the memory capacity required for embedded speech-recognition. Therefore, downloadable speech-recognition programs will soon be available for these devices, which will be a first step towards built-in speech recognition for pervasive devices.

7.5 Security

Speech applications are much more popular for applications such as phone banking than for PC applications, although speech systems typically do not allow for user authentication or encryption. People seem to trust an unknown voice more than an unknown system that sends an email. However, speech application providers must be concerned about security. Mobile phone systems such as GSM can provide user authentication through the SIM, which is typically protected by a PIN. Thus, mobile phones offer much better authentication than wired-line phones without a SIM card.

Speaker verification (see also Chapter 3) can authenticate a user based on a short voice string. The combination of SIM authentication, speaker verification, and a back-up solution with a manually entered PIN or password provides adequate security for a large number of voice applications.

Voice encryption is today restricted to top secret areas in government and industry. Mobile phone technology could provide this feature easily if there was a demand for this type of security for private communication

References

1. Jelinek, F. (1999) *Statistical Methods for Speech Recognition*. Cambridge, MA: MIT Press.

2. Waibel, A. and Lee, K. (eds) (1990) *Readings in Speech Recognition*. San Mateo, CA: Morgan Kaufmann.

3. W3C (May 2000) 'Voice eXtensible Markup Language (VoiceXML™) version 1.0'. http://www.w3.org/TR/2000/NOTE-voicexml-20000505/

4. 'Java Speech API White Paper'.
   http://java.sun.com/marketing/collateral/speech.html

5. Yahoo Internet Portal. http://www.my.yahoo.com

6. Compaq. 'iPAC Pocket PC'.
   http://www.compaq.com/products/handhelds/pocketpc/

7. Günther, C., Klehr, M., Kunzmann, S. and Ross, T. (2000) 'Building voice enabled Internet portals based on VoiceXML'. Proceedings of ESSV 2000: 11, Konferenz 'Elektronische Sprachsignalverarbeitung', Cottbus, 2000.

8 Personal digital assistants

We are currently on the edge of an explosion of mobile devices with hitherto unprecedented connectivity and processing power. These devices replace traditional tools, such as pen and paper, the address book, and the calendar, and integrate them into a single, convenient, mobile package. What makes mobile devices so attractive is not so much the fact that they deliver new functions, but that they mimic well-known processes, combine their data, and make the data available everywhere and at any time. This chapter takes a brief look at the history of PDAs, than discusses the types of devices and their connectivity characteristics. Finally, the available standards and typical software components for PDAs are explained.

8.1 History

The PDA is not just a small desktop computer. In contrast to the PC, the focus is on the application, rather than trying to be a general-purpose computing device. All PDAs available today come with a set of built-in applications. These are usually PIM applications, such as a calendar, a notepad, an address book, and a to-do list. On top of these applications, many PDAs offer additional applications, such as spreadsheets, games, calculators, and a clock.

The first-generation PDAs available during the mid-1980s were also called organizers. They were mostly calculators with a database, and offered only a few simple functions, such as a calendar and a phone book. They had to compete with their real-life paper-based equivalents, which was not easy because the latter were convenient, often smaller, and did not require batteries.

The breakthrough for the second generation came around 1993, with the availability of smaller, more powerful devices, with better displays and text input technologies. A main factor for success was the improved connectivity of the PDA. Instead of the user having to enter each phone number, address, or appointment via a tiny keyboard, or printing it letter by letter using a stylus, these PDAs could be connected to the PC. This enabled users to enter large amounts of data at the PC, from where it was sent to the PDA, and allowed the PDAs to exchange data with other applications. It also solved the problem of losing the data when the battery run out by introducing a convenient back-up facility.

It cannot be ignored that another considerable success factor was the appeal the PDAs had on the technology-savvy users always willing to pay a premium for the latest gadgets. It is no surprise that these devices were often seen in company with mobile phones.

The next improvement was the appearance of small, keyboard-less and programmable PDAs around 1995. The tiny keyboards of early organizers proved too large to be integrated into a device that was meant to fit into a shirt pocket. A stylus and a touch-sensitive screen replaced them. The simplicity of the user interface and the power-saving features incorporated into the dedicated operating systems of these devices were the main factors for success.

While being inherently programmable from the beginning, it was not until operating systems that allow loading of additional applications became available that a truly simple software-development environment existed. This programmability is typically exploited not by the user but by third-party application providers. New applications can now be created and added to all PDAs at any time, giving the user the ultimate decision as to which applications will be available on the PDA. The result is a truly personal assistant.

8.2 Device categories

Over time, two categories of PDA have emerged. The first is a descendant of the organizer, with a tiny keyboard and a relatively large display in a clamshell-like package. These devices usually feature a rich set of connectors and often offer expansion slots. The operating system and user interface is similar to that of PCs. Examples include the Psion Series 3

PDA from Ericsson
Courtesy of Ericsson

and 5, and the Windows CE Handheld Pro devices. New devices have appeared that are halfway between a PDA and a mobile PC, but obviously these can hardly be carried in a shirt pocket. Figure 8.1 shows a Psion Series 5-compatible device from Ericsson.

The second category is the palm-sized devices that have no keyboard but have a touch-sensitive display, stylus-based operation, and handwriting-recognition-based text-input method. They usually weigh little more than 100 g, and are small enough to be carried around easily. In order to keep these devices small, designers had to remove or limit some features, such as connectors and expansion slots. Examples for devices from this category are the Palm, the IBM WorkPad (Figure 8.2), the Handspring Visor devices, and the PocketPC.

Another type of PDA in this category is the portable multimedia reader and the content player device. Similar to PDAs, these devices are designed for reading or listening to books in electronic format. The text can be downloaded to the device, and is rendered on a display typically larger than that of a PDA. Otherwise these devices generally feature the same functionalities (calendar, address book, to-do list) and synchronize their data with a PC. With sufficient processing power, these device even allow you to listen to audio books or to play MP3-encoded music. An example for such a device is the Franklin eBookMan,[1] shown in Figure 8.3. These devices are likely to evolve into a category of their own, but their acceptance will depend significantly on the availability of a sufficient number of titles and a competitive pricing compared with traditional media. This, requires the pending copyright and piracy problems for the distribution of digital media to be solved first.

Figure 8.2

The IBM WorkPad c3
Courtesy of IBM Deutschland GmbH

Figure 8.3

The Franklin eBookMan
Courtesy of Franklin

8.3 Personal digital assistant operating systems

A mobile device consists of hardware, an operating system, and applications. In contrast to the PC, the manufacturer of the device sometimes delivers all three. Currently, a fierce competition is taking place to set the standard for the operating system used on mobile, and especially wireless, devices. The three main contenders to set the standard for wireless operating systems are:

- *Microsoft*, with Windows CE;
- *Palm Computing*, with its Palm operating system;
- *Symbian*, with its EPOC operating system.

In the following sections, we will describe these operating systems briefly. See Chapter 3 for more details about the operating system characteristics and the development environments available for these devices.

8.3.1 Windows CE

Microsoft's Windows CE comes in several form factors for the mobile market:

- *Pocket PC:*[2] hand-held devices without a keyboard that are pen-driven;
- *Handheld PCs:* clamshell-sized, with a tiny keyboard;

■ *Handheld PC Professional:* smaller than a laptop computer, but larger than a Handheld PC.

The operating system is also available for non-mobile applications, such as video game consoles and set-top digital television boxes. On some platforms, cut-down versions of standard Microsoft software packages, such as Word and Excel, are bundled with the operating system.

8.3.2 Palm OS

Originally part of US Robotics, Palm Computing[3] was first subsumed into 3Com and then subsequently spun off from its parent into an independent company. By mid-2000, seven million Palm devices had been sold, giving Palm about three-quarters of the global hand-held computing market. So far, all devices manufactured by Palm are hand-held, stylus-operated devices with a touch-screen, and support handwriting recognition.

Palm is proactively licensing its Palm OS operating system, and working together with partners such as Handspring (for the Handspring Visor), IBM (for the WorkPad PC companion), Qualcomm (for the PdQ smart phone), and Symbol (for a barcode-enabled Palm device).

8.3.3 EPOC

In mid-1998, Nokia, Ericsson, Motorola, and Psion Software teamed up to form a company called Symbian[4] with the aim of developing the software and hardware standards for the next generation of wireless devices. The result of this effort is the EPOC operating system, originally developed by Psion. Since then, industry leaders such as Sony, Sun, Philips, and NTT DoCoMo have joined the Symbian alliance and licensed EPOC.

Symbian plans to evolve EPOC technology and publish two reference designs. The first is intended for PDAs and digital handsets. The second will be an entirely new design for tablet-like devices with stylus operation, handwriting recognition, and integrated wireless communications.

8.3.4 Alternative operating systems

Competition to these three main contenders will come from other operating systems, such as BeOS, QNX Neutrino, and embedded Linux. See Chapter 3 for a discussion of operating systems for pervasive devices. An example for a PDA with an embedded Linux operating system is the Agenda VR3, announced by Agenda Computing.[5] The device shown in Figure 8.4 uses an embedded Linux operating system, is capable of connecting to the Internet, and features a preloaded set of PIM applications. The Agenda VR3 is the first ever PDA built from the ground up on

Figure 8.4

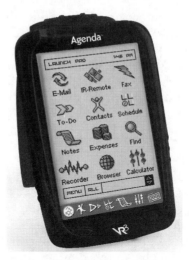

The Agenda VR3 PDA
Courtesy of Agenda Computing

Agenda Linux, a Linux embedded operating system that is completely open source. The VR3 combines a fast 66-MHz MIPS processor, substantial RAM, and a robustly versatile operating system to create a PDA that can tackle even the most complex of tasks.

8.4 Device characteristics

A number of characteristics distinguish PDAs from PCs. Because of the way they are used, PDAs utilize different technologies than PCs, which in turn has significant consequences for software developers that will be discussed below.

In general, it is correct to say that almost everything is smaller on a PDA than on a PC. There is a smaller screen, a smaller keyboard (or none at all), less memory, less processing power, and less power. The technologies used for these components often differ significantly from those known from the PC.

8.4.1 Memory

The typical storage technology found in mobile devices is a form of non-volatile memory. ROM or Flash memory is used to store the operating system code and other less frequently changed information. Application data are typically held in battery-backed RAM, or in some cases EEPROM. Memory extensions are available through additional non-volatile memory or from the addition of magnetic storage. Extremely small hard disks are available today that offer up to 1GB of storage. Developed for use in consumer goods such as cameras and media players, these disks are also available for mobile devices. Being mechanical, they are usable only in appropriate environmental conditions and where sufficient battery power is available for read/write access.

8.4.2 Databases

All operating systems of mobile devices offer some form of internal database to store application data. Only a few copy the traditional file model from the PC because it becomes less applicable in the context of mobile devices. Updates to information stored in a database often require in-place modification and have to be processed immediately. There is little room for buffering any data before performing the update because the device may be switched on or off at any time. The integrity of databases must be guaranteed or the device may cease to function completely.

The API to access the internal databases is often based on a random-access file model, or sometimes on a more abstract record-based model. For performance reasons, most APIs offer more or less immediate data access to the programmer. When trying to achieve data integrity, reading the data is not usually a problem, but storage technologies often require special handling when writing to memory. Therefore updates are generally carried out only for chunks of memory through special routines provided by the operating system.

8.5 Software components

To be useful, a PDA needs more than just an operating system and applications. It also requires connectivity and synchronization in order to process data and exchange them with other devices.

8.5.1 Applications

A typical PDA comes with a suite of built-in applications. These usually include phone and address book, calendar, to-do lists, notepad, calculator, alarm clock, email, data synchronization, and games. Other applications that can be found on PDAs include browsers, world-time clock, file manager, spreadsheets, financial applications, media players, and drawing utilities. Common to all applications is a carefully designed user interface that is intuitive and at the same time makes optimal use of the limited display space. Figure 8.5 shows the calendar application on a Palm device. The user can switch to any day of the week by tapping one of the push-buttons at the top (1), or to another view (day, week, month) with the

Figure 8.5

The calendar application on a Palm

push-buttons at the bottom of the display (2). To add a new calendar entry, or to change an existing one, the relevant line is selected with the stylus and text is entered (3). Frequently used actions can be triggered through command buttons (4). Entries that have an alarm (3) or a note (5) associated with them are marked with symbols. The design makes optimal use of the display space and minimizes the number of actions required to perform an operation.

There is already a huge selection of applications available for download from the Internet for all PDA types in use today. With the availability of electronic document formats, a rich selection of documents ranging from simple references to complete books became accessible for reading on PDAs.

8.5.2 Connectivity

PDAs usually communicate with the PC through a special docking station, also called a cradle, which is connected to the PC via a cable. This connection is used mostly for back-up purposes and to load applications and data onto the device. Current PDAs also feature an infrared communication port that can be used to exchange data with a PC, other PDAs, or mobile phones.

Future devices are likely to replace infrared connections with some form of low-cost wireless communication feature, such as Bluetooth, in order to communicate with other devices. The advantage of this is that it does not require a cable, nor does the device have to be in direct line of sight with the device it is communicating with. When used together with a Bluetooth-enabled mobile phone, the PDA can get wireless network access without requiring the user to handle two devices at the same time. In fact, the mobile phone may reside in a briefcase or pocket, while the PDA utilizes the phone's network connection.

In the future, the PDA and the mobile phone are likely to merge into a single class of mobile devices. We will see more advanced mobile phones running the same operating system and offering the same functionality as PDAs. We will also see PDAs with added wireless connectivity but not necessarily usable as a phone. The preferences of the user, and the availability of the appropriate display and battery technologies, will decide about the direction of this evolution. Figure 8.6 shows a device from Ericsson that combines a PDA with a mobile phone in a single unit.

8.5.3 Synchronization

With the exchange of data comes the need for synchronization. What if a phone number was added or modified on the PDA but not on the PC? The next time the PDA is connected to the PC, the new data must be copied, and the relevant entry in the database needs to be updated. The complexity of synchronization regards the question of what to do if data were modified or deleted on the other side. Synchronization software handles these situations and updates the databases following some simple precedence rules.

The built-in applications of a PDA synchronize their data with a PC or server that operates as a back-up medium and allows the exchange of data with other applications. New applications loaded into the device are not necessarily part of this standard procedure but require similar mechanisms. Usually there is a way to extend the device-specific synchronization process and integrate new applications. This requires additional software on the PC or server side in order to understand the application-specific data and make them available for exchange with other applications. See Chapter 4 for more details about synchronization.

Figure 8.6

Ericsson Platform
Courtesy of Ericsson

8.5.4 Device management

When devices are not owned privately but are, for example, used by mobile workers within a company, there is a need for device management. A typical company will require some control over the devices used by its employees. Internet service providers (ISPs) offering network access via mobile devices, also face the challenge of managing thousands or even millions of them. This becomes especially evident when the typical user group of the mobile device is no longer the Internet-savvy user who also owns a PC, but the novice who wants to access the available services without wanting to know how it all works.

Managing devices means automatically configuring newly deployed devices, or at least assisting the user in doing so. Downloading new applications or updates to existing software on the device will become necessary, and will have to be controlled carefully to guarantee permanent availability of service. The latter quickly turns into a challenge when users are neither willing nor able to manage the devices themselves, and the mobility allows only sporadic remote access to them. Further details about device management can be found in Chapter 4.

8.6 Standards

Standards are critical to all applications that depend on the access and exchange of information from many different sources. They are especially important for pervasive devices because many of them use new technologies that still require widely accepted standards to develop.

8.6.1 Electronic document formats

Several electronic document standards already compete to be the predominant standard for mobile device platforms. The well-known standards from the PC turned out to be either not portable or too slow in adapting to the requirements of the PDA. These requirements include smaller displays, new operating systems, and conservative use of the available memory.

The available applications that support these standards usually consist of a reader application on the PDA and a set of tools for the workstation. The PDA application is used to display the relevant document format and allows the electronic documents to be read and searched. Workstation tools on the PC include authoring and conversion applications. The authoring tools allow new documents to be generated, and often support some simple HTML-like markup in order to apply text styles such as bold or italics The conversion tools are used to convert text from one of the prominent PC document formats to the format understood by the reader application.

Almost all formats available on PDAs today rely on fast and efficient compression of text data. Most of them offer bookmarks and hyperlinks to enhance the manageability of large texts. Some also add features of a database, such as indexing, fast navigation, and searching. The electronic document standard will become especially important with the advent of electronic books and the capability of PDAs to serve as a platform for them.

8.6.2 Synchronization protocols

Data synchronization for PDAs will become as important as storage media compatibility was for the PC. There is limited use for the freedom to carry and access personal data everywhere if the data cannot be exchanged with others. The exchange of data, however, will be based not on a specific storage medium such as a floppy disk, but on a dedicated protocol for information exchange and data synchronization.

A networked device exchanges data with a server using the HTTP protocol. When communicating with other devices in its vicinity, it will probably use a cable, an infrared beam connection, or another low-cost wireless communication, such as Bluetooth. All of these require a protocol for data exchange and some common data format. In order to update the appointment list from the server, or to exchange a virtual business card with another device, the two must be able to understand and physically connect with each other.

PDAs usually come with some PC-based software that allows for backup and data synchronization using a proprietary protocol. Data synchronization with a server is not supported, so there is little need for an open standard.

However, data synchronization with a server is no longer limited to a single device, so there is demand for a common protocol and data format. The Mobile Application Link[6] (MAL) is such a communication protocol. First defined as a proprietary standard, it was soon released as open source. MAL defines a common API available on the mobile device, the workstation, and the server. In the meantime, the open-source development has been stopped.

SyncML[7] is a synchronization standard that enables all devices and applications to synchronize data between devices and with a server over any kind of network. The SyncML initiative was founded by Ericsson, IBM, Lotus, Motorola, Nokia, Palm, Psion, and Starfish Software. Meanwhile, more than 300 companies support this new industry initiative to develop and promote a single, common data-synchronization protocol.

The SyncML protocol can be used between individual devices, as well as between a device and a server. The protocol is capable of dealing with the special challenges of wireless synchronization, such as the relatively low reliability of connections and the high network latencies. The data format of SyncML is based on XML and has been designed with the requirements of mobile devices in mind. SyncML uses the compact WBXML encoding defined for WAP in order to minimize the use of bandwidth. See Chapter 6 for more information about WAP.

8.6.3 Database formats

All applications on a PDA need to store some data, and must have an application-specific format defined for it. Some of that may be useful information for more than just one application, for example email addresses that are stored by the address book and used by the mail application. For some data managed by the built-in applications of the device, there are APIs defined by the operating system to access them. Other applications, such as those developed by third parties, often do not offer such an interface. Here, the need for a common access method arises.

PDA operating systems currently do not protect the data of one application against access by another. Therefore the only obstacle for an application developer is the knowledge of the data format used to store the particular information. If an application is designed to allow other applications to access its data, it needs to use a documented data format. If it is also meant to exchange those data with other devices, this format must not rely on any operating-system-specific database format.

Using a simple record-oriented format, such as comma-separated values (CSV), allows applications to easily access and share data. However, there are many limitations, including the manageability of the data and the performance impacts of this simple format. More advanced database formats have been defined and are available across the PDA platforms. Similar to the electronic document standards, most of them are available as a combination of device and workstation applications. A database viewer on the device allows data to be searched and modified. A set of authoring and conversion tools allows the generation of new databases, as well as importing data from other sources. When combined with a forms processor or an application generator, they support the development of simple datacentric applications. These database standards allow the exchange of data between devices, but still lack an interface to share data on the device itself.

Structured Query Language (SQL) is a well-known and widely accepted standard interface for relational databases. Consequently, this interface is now available on PDAs as well. IBM's DB2 Everywhere[8] is available on most PDA platforms and provides a local data store with the logical appearance of a relational database. Applications can share data and access them using a common API that supports execution of SQL statements. DB2 Everywhere is a tiny database that requires about 100 KB of memory on the device, so there are limitations such as the available SQL subset. Synchronization software with specific plug-ins allows the relational database to be synchronized with any Open Database Connectivity (ODBC) data source.

Example 8.1 shows the code for inserting a new record into the memo database in Palm OS. New memory segments have to be locked by the code before copying data to it. The Palm OS Database Manager functions beginning with the prefix Dm handle the insertion into the database.

| Example 8.1 | **Inserting a record into a Palm OS database** |

```
/** Create a new record in the memo database
 @param dbP database pointer
 @param item database record
 @return zero if successful, errorcode if not
 */
Err MemoNewRecord(DmOpenRef dbP, MemoItemPtr item)
{

  Err result;
  ULong offset;
  VoidHand recordH;
  MemoDBRecordPtr recordP,nilP=0;

  // allocate a chunk in the database for the new record
  recordH = (Handle)DmNewHandle(dbP,
  (ULong)StrLen(item->note));
  if (recordH == NULL) return dmErrMemError;

  // pack the the data into the new record
  recordP = MemHandleLock(recordH);
  offset = (ULong)&nilP->note;
  DmStrCopy(recordP, offset, item->note);
  MemPtrUnlock(recordP);

  // insert the record into the database
  result = DmAttachRecord(dbP, index, recordH, 0);
  if (result) MemHandleFree(recordH);
  return result;
}
```

Example 8.2 demonstrates how to insert a new record into a DB2e database using the SQL library functions. The new record is inserted as a string into the column text of the database table memos.

Example 8.2 **Inserting a record into a database using DB2e**

```
/** insert a new record into 'memos'
 @param hdbc the database handle
 @param string the text to insert
 @return a DB2e return code
*/
SQLRETURN Db2eInsertRecord(SQLHDBC hdbc, char *string)
{
SQLHSTMT hstmt;
SQLRETURN rc;
long length;

SQLAllocStmt(hdbc, &hstmt);
SQLBindParameter(hstmt, 1, SQL_PARAM_INPUT,
                    SQL_C_CHAR, SQL_VARCHAR, 0, 0,
                    string, StrLen(string), &length);
rc = SQLExecDirect(hstmt,
"INSERT INTO memos (text) VALUES(?)", SQL_NTS);
if (rc != SQL_SUCCESS) diagnostics(sqlBuffer);
SQLFreeStmt(hstmt, SQL_DROP);
return rc;
}
```

8.7 Mobile applications

An ideal application for a mobile device consists of loosely coupled tasks that can be exposed to mobile users selectively, depending on a given mobile user's context. A mobile user's context can be described as the user's location, the device type, connectivity, resource situation, and the user profile.

With the exception of simple stand-alone applications, all mobile applications will have a need to connect to a server over the network. This is either for replication of application data from the server to the device, or from the device to the server, or in both directions.

8.7.1 Mobile application characteristics

Typically, a mobile application possesses the following properties:

- *Disconnected or intermittently connected operation*. Users must be able to use a mobile application while not online. Information about changes of data replicated to the device is queued until the next network access, and must then be processed during synchronization with the server.
- *Context awareness*. A mobile application presents itself differently to different users based on their context, which is made up of attributes such as user's role, device used, location, and time of day, i.e., it must infer the purpose of access, and present itself accordingly.
- *Device and network adaptation*. The application must adapt to different device form factors, and different network characteristics. Many mobile devices have limited resources, including battery power, display size, communication bandwidth, memory and processing power. The application must respect these limitations and make appropriate use of the network connection.
- *Local collaboration*. A mobile application should collaborate with local resources and other on-device applications. This includes sharing data and services between applications on the same device or other reachable devices in the vicinity.

8.7.2 Connection types

Mobile devices show different connection profiles that influence the design and implementation of a mobile application, and that become especially evident when accessing information from the Web. They can be categorized into:

- *online connected devices*, typically with an integrated wireless connection to the network. A browser loads and displays Web pages on demand, and the user can navigate through the Web interactively. Caching of Web pages is used only for performance optimization;
- *intermittently connected devices* e.g. through a modem, will typically use hoarding. The user can configure the pages (often defined through channels) to be cached, and can define whether other pages available via links on these pages should also be cached. Limited forms processing is still possible by queuing requests for transmission during the next connection;
- *offline devices* do not have a network connection. They are connected to a host (e.g. a PC via cable or infrared beam connection) for back-up and data synchronization. If the host has a network connection, data

from the Web can be replicated to the device during this process. Hoarding (or caching) is used to keep a local copy of the data accessible for applications.

8.7.3 Mobile application classification

The need to exchange data, and the availability of network access, are major design factors. Depending on the communication characteristics and the connection type of a device we can classify mobile applications into three categories: browser-based, native, and hybrid.

Browser-based applications
The browser-based application model is the simplest, if it is applicable. It is suitable for applications intended primarily for information browsing with limited query capability and simple form submissions. Applications such as portfolio tracking, requesting stock quotes, and city weather forecasts fit this category well. Some of the advanced browsers come with scripting, and local queue- and cache-management capabilities. With JavaScript, simple computations such as user input validation or the total sum of an order can be performed locally. However, scripting capability alone is inadequate for exploiting device functions, and for collaborating with other local applications. Caching and queuing enable disconnected operations. In general, this model does not take full advantage of on-device functionality. It requires a back-end connection for simple tasks such as information aggregation (combining information entered on two different forms). Furthermore, there is little or no support for data management or for incremental activities, such as building a product order over several sessions. If connectivity is assured, the back end may provide these capabilities.

Native applications
The native application model offers the highest potential to exploit local device functions and form factors. The most sophisticated user interfaces are possible with this model. Large amounts of data, for example historical shopping data, can be presented efficiently. Caching data on the device enables disconnected or intermittently connected operations. Tasks such as information aggregation and intelligent presentation of data are relatively easy to implement. On the negative side, this model requires separate and intensive development efforts for each new device. Further, deploying new versions of mobile applications to users presents a significant system-management challenge. This model is suitable for applications that manage large amounts of data locally, or have complex use models, or need to support an incremental mode, and operate in either disconnected or intermittently connected mode.

Hybrid application

The hybrid application model aims to incorporate the best aspects of both browser-based and native application models. A browser is used to render the user interface. Scripting functionality is used for user input validation, and limited on-device computations. Native function invocation capability is used to manage data locally, and to exploit device-specific capabilities. The usefulness of the hybrid model can be improved significantly if the application controls the user interface, including navigation, and if browser menus and features are hidden from the end user.

8.7.4 Device adaptation

In order to support multiple device types, a Web application has to identify the actual device being used when generating the appropriate response data. Usually this is achieved by checking the user-agent string sent as a part of each HTTP request. While this differentiation is acceptable for most applications in use today, it has some significant shortcomings. Mobile phones supporting the WAP standard are already available with different screen sizes, and in the future more devices with even more different capabilities will become available. The actual markup and the layout of content available from the Internet cannot be based on the user-agent information alone. Standards such as CC/PP will be required to assist in the device adaptation of information. See Chapter 6 for more information about CC/PP.

8.8 Personal digital assistant browsers

When accessing the WWW with a PC, HTML is the lingua franca for all browsers. However, because of the device characteristics of PDAs, dedicated markup languages have been introduced for them. The disadvantage of having so many markup formats is that all content available from the Internet has to be accessible in a specific format suitable for rendering on a mobile device. Hopefully, the availability of XHTML will replace all of them with a single markup language again. See Chapter 6 for more details about XHTML.

There are currently three different types of browsers available for mobile devices:

■ *HTML markup*. Full support of the HTML standard is typically not feasible on relatively small devices such as PDAs. Most browsers falling into this category limit the supported HTML tag set. Problems often exist with the support for images, frames, and scripting. Because websites are usually created with the capabilities of PC-based browsers in mind, the presentation of these sites on PDAs is generally unsatisfying.

- *Dedicated markup.* Instead of HTML, these browsers support another markup format optimized for small devices. This can be WML, compact HTML, or other device-specific formats. The usual gateway may be omitted, and the plain textual markup is parsed on the device itself. Due to the relatively simple format, this is feasible even for PDAs with limited memory. The results are good, but the number of available sites is still very small.

- *Markup conversion.* Browsers in this category connect the user through a custom gateway server that can filter out unnecessary HTML coding and convert the markup and images into a device-specific format. These browsers usually achieve excellent results, but they use a proprietary markup. Most client software is available free of charge but works only with the respective gateway server.

8.8.1 Browser examples

The following examples from the rich selection of PDA-based browsers are not just scaled-down versions of a PC browser. The AvantGo[9] and the KBrowser[10] are both available on many platforms, support bookmarks and graphics, and attempt to optimize the presentation of information for PDAs.

AvantGo

The AvantGo browser is a graphical Web browser that runs through a custom proxy server (gateway) to filter out unnecessary HTML coding and convert images. Pages are downloaded from the Internet to the PDA during synchronization. They are stored and can be accessed offline. If the PDA is connected to the network using a modem, online browsing is possible as well. Figure 8.7 demonstrates how an actual HTML page is

Figure 8.7

An HTML page converted for a PDA

displayed on the Palm after conversion by the gateway. Figure 8.8 shows another version with improved navigation and dedicated markup for PDAs available from the same website.

KBrowser

The KBrowser from 4thpass is a cross-platform graphical WML microbrowser that provides access to WAP-based services. It supports WML 1.1 with WMLScript and the WBMP image format. Figures 8.9 and 8.10 illustrate how the KBrowser renders pages with WML markup. These figures also demonstrate the browser's capability to render tables and images.

Figure 8.8

The PDA version of the page shown in Figure 8.7

Figure 8.9

A WML page displayed by the KBrowser

Figure 8.10

Another WML page displayed by the KBrowser

A large number of sites on the Internet already support WML, and the number keeps growing.

Open-source browsers

It almost looks like the browser war we witnessed for the PC is recurring for the PDA platforms. While the result may differ from the scenario we now have for the PC platform, the lack of widely accepted standards will help to proliferate browser-based applications on PDAs.

There are many new initiatives and open-source projects in progress that are attempting to create the necessary parts for a complete WAP infrastructure: the WAP stack, the WML browser, and the WAP gateway.[11] Browsers are under development in many programming, languages, and for many different platforms. 5NINE, for example, a developer of Wireless Data Infrastructure technology for Linux, has recently announced the launch of WMLBrowser.org,[12] an open-source development project for creating a WML browser to work with all types of Linux environments. The WML browser will be a full-featured WAP client with support for secure and insecure connection-oriented and connectionless modes. Its scalable architecture is aimed at making it ideal for all sorts of devices through graphical user interface toolkit abstraction, and support for various transport technologies, including Bluetooth, IPv4, IPv6, and others.

References

1. Franklin eBookMan. http://www.franklin.com/ebookman/

2. Microsoft Pocket PC.
   http://www.microsoft.com/mobile/pocketPC/default.asp

3. Palm. http://www.palm.com

4. Symbian. http://www.symbian.com

5. Agenda Computing. http://www.agendacomputing.com

6. Mobile Application Link. http://www.mobilelink.org

7. SyncML. http://www.syncml.org

8. IBM DB2 Everywhere.
   http://www.ibm.com/software/data/db2/everyplace/

9. AvantGo. http://www.avantgo.com/frontdoor/index.html/

10. 4thpass KBrowser. http://www.4thpass.com/kbrowser/index.html

11. Openwap.org. http://www.openwap.org

12. WML browser.org. http://www.wmlbrowser.org

Conclusion

In this part of the book, we have given an introduction to technologies and relevant standards for pervasive computing. The advances in technology will make available smaller devices and displays with lower energy consumption. Better communication technology will provide them with higher bandwidth at lower cost. Finally, ongoing standardization of software and hardware components will improve their usability, and will help to exploit them in a large scale. Together, this will create new types of devices for new applications scenarios. They will not replace PCs but will likely reduce the number of PCs and reduce the frequence of PC Internet access, because a larger group of users will accept these new, smaller devices that are easier to use and better suited for their intended purpose.

II ARCHITECTURES

In this part, we will present an end-to-end architecture for pervasive computing applications that support different kinds of devices and communication protocols. We explain how applications adhering to this architecture can be implemented, elaborating on the implementation of the application server and integration of WAP phones, classical telephones via voice gateways, PDAs, and PCs. As a continuous example, we use the Uncle Enzo's Web shop application that allows goods to be ordered and paid for over the Internet. Later, we extend this to allow logon and viewing of the previous transactions through the different devices. This part is especially interesting for IT architects, consultants, and developers who face the challenge of implementing pervasive computing solutions.

9 | Server-side programming in Java

In this chapter, we give an overview of the concepts and technologies that we consider the most important in the development of Web applications in general, and pervasive computing Web applications in particular. We start with an overview of the Java 2 Enterprise Edition (J2EE) architecture, followed by a more detailed description of some key technologies, including Java servlets, EJBs, and Java Server Pages (JSPs). Given the importance of XML, we dedicate a major part of this chapter to this technology. We present technologies for building Web services that are based on XML, including the SOAP and UDDI. We conclude with an overview of the model–view–controller pattern, and its use in development of Web applications.

9.1 Java 2 Enterprise Edition: overview

As e-business becomes more and more important across industries, companies must be able to develop and deploy custom applications that provide unique business services to their customers and increase productivity of their employees in very short development cycles. At the same time, these business applications need to be portable to assure long-term viability. They have to scale from initial pilots to highly available company-wide services that can be used by thousands of clients at the same time. Multi-tier applications that include clients, application servers, and database and transaction servers are required, to connect the existing IT infrastructure of companies to an intranet and the Internet. However, such applications are difficult to architect, and they require a variety of skill sets and many different resources to be integrated with Internet technology. As experience shows, integration of such applications can take a significant amount of overall development time.

The Java technology has proven consistently to decrease the effort required to develop a system as well as the time from start to launch. It is available on a multitude of different platforms, ranging from PCs to mainframes, and provides the same set of standard APIs on all of these systems. The unified J2EE standard wraps existing resources, such as naming services, messaging services, and database and transaction systems that are required by multi-tier applications with a unified, component-based application model to enable components, tools, systems, and applications for solving enterprise requirements. While Sun Microsystems invented Java, J2EE represents a joint effort of various leaders in enterprise software development, including middleware and tool vendors, database-management system providers, application vendors, component developers, and operating system vendors. J2EE simplifies enterprise applications by allowing them to be based on standardized, modular components, and by providing a complete set of services to those components.

Reusable and exchangeable J2EE components provide choices for company developers and IT organizations. The J2EE platform enables them to assemble their applications from a combination of standard components and their own custom components. For example, an e-commerce site for an Internet shop can be built using off-the-shelf EJB components for shopping cart behaviors, modified EJB components for specific customer services, and custom layouts using JSPs that create a special look and feel for the site. This approach results in shorter development time, and better quality and maintainability. It also allows for portability across a range of platforms.

9.1.1 J2EE architecture

J2EE includes many features of the Java 2 Platform, Standard Edition, such as cross-platform portability, the Java Database Connectivity (JDBC) API for database access, common object request broker technology (CORBA) technology for interaction with existing enterprise resources, and a security model that protects data in Internet applications. J2EE also adds support for EJBs, the Java servlet API, JSP, messaging, and XML technology.

J2EE handles many details of application behavior automatically, and does not require complex programming on the application level. Many complexities inherent in enterprise applications are handled by the J2EE platform. Resource pooling, transaction management, and lifecycle management are built into J2EE, and are available to applications and components. Thus, application and component developers can focus on specifics such as user interfaces and business logic rather than solving general problems.

The J2EE platform provides choices for graphical user interfaces across a company's intranet or on the WWW. Clients can run on desktops, laptops, PDAs, cell phones, and other devices. Pure client-side user interfaces can use standard HTML, WML, VoiceXML, or other markup languages and Java applets. Support for simple markup languages enables the use of a broad range of clients, including small devices. Additionally, the J2EE platform allows a Java plug-in to be downloaded to add applet support where required by Web browsers, and it supports stand-alone Java application clients.

For server-side deployment of dynamic content, the J2EE platform provides both the servlet API and JSPs. The servlet API allows the implementation of server-side application functions that can use the entire Java API. JSPs enable dynamic generation of all kinds of markup through server-side scripting.

The J2EE application model (Figure 9.1) divides enterprise applications into components, containers, and connectors. Application developers implement components, while system vendors implement containers and connectors to hide complexity and promote portability. Containers mediate between clients and components, providing services transparently to both. Connectors define a portable service API to plug into existing products, promoting flexibility by enabling various implementations of specific services.

The J2EE application model encapsulates different layers of functionality in specific types of components. Business logic is encapsulated in EJBs. Client-side presentation is presented through HTML Web pages, through Web pages containing applets, through pages generated dynamically using Java servlets or JSPs, or through stand-alone Java applications. Components communicate transparently using standards such as HTML, XML, HTTP, SSL, RMI, Internet Inter-Orb Protocol (IIOP), and others. J2EE comprises the following technologies:

Figure 9.1

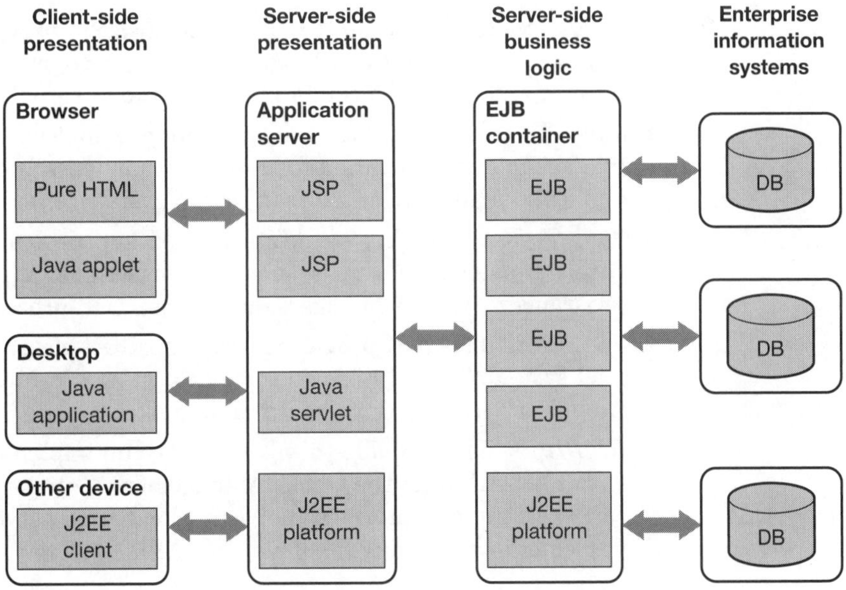

Client-side presentation	Server-side presentation	Server-side business logic	Enterprise information systems
Browser	**Application server**	**EJB container**	
Pure HTML	JSP	EJB	DB
Java applet	JSP	EJB	
Desktop		EJB	DB
Java application	Java servlet	EJB	
Other device			DB
J2EE client	J2EE platform	J2EE platform	

J2EE application model

- *EJBs*. The EJB specification defines an API that allows cross-platform, component-based application components to be created, deployed, and managed.

- *JSPs*. The JSP technology allows dynamic Web content to be created using markup templates with embedded scripting elements. It also enables rapid development of Web-based applications that are server and platform independent.

- *Java servlets*. The Java servlet API provides a simple, consistent mechanism for extending the functionality of a Web server through application modules implemented in Java.

- *Connector*. The J2EE connector architecture allows the J2EE platform to be connected to heterogeneous enterprise information systems.

- *Java Naming and Directory Interface (JNDI)*. This provides uniform connectivity from the Java platform to information assets. It allows implementation of Java applications that uniformly access multiple naming and directory services.

- *Interface Definition Language (IDL)*. This provides interoperability with CORBA to allow for heterogeneous computing. Java IDL includes an IDL-to-Java compiler and a lightweight object request broker (ORB) that supports IIOP.

- *JDBC*. This provides uniform interface to a wide range of relational databases, and provides a common base on which higher-level tools and interfaces can be built.

- *Java Message Service (JMS)*. This specification provides a standard Java API for company messaging services, such as reliable queuing, publish and subscribe communication, and push/pull technologies.

- *Java Transaction API (JTA)*. This defines a high-level transaction management specification for resource managers and transactional applications in distributed transaction systems.

- *Java Transaction Service (JTS)*. This API ensures interoperability with transaction resources, such as transactional application programs, resource managers, and transaction-processing monitors.

- *Java Mail*. This API provides a set of abstract classes that models a mail system. The API provides a platform- and protocol-independent framework to build Java-based mail applications.

- *RMI-IIOP*. This provides developers with an implementation of the Java RMI API over the Object Management Group's IIOP. Developers can write remote interfaces between clients and servers, and implement them using the Java RMI APIs.

9.2 Servlets

Servlets are Web components that generate dynamic content. They are platform-independent Java classes that are compiled into platform-independent Java byte code. They can be loaded dynamically into, and executed by any, Web server that provides a servlet container as specified in the Java servlet specification.[1] Servlet containers are available on virtually any platform, ranging from PCs to UNIX servers, and even mainframes.

Clients can access servlets via a request–response paradigm based on the behavior of the HTTP that is implemented by the servlet container. When receiving a request that targets a servlet, the Web server forwards it to the responsible servlet container. The servlet container determines the servlet to be invoked based on its internal configuration, dynamically loads that servlet if required, and finally calls it with objects that represent the request and the response. The servlet handles the request, e.g. by invoking application logic on the same server or a third tier, and generating content representing the result. Finally, it sends back the response with the result via the servlet container and the Web server.

9.2.1 Basic servlet methods

All servlets have to implement several methods that are defined in the `Servlet` interface. The most important of these methods are `init`, `service`, and `destroy`. The `init` method is responsible for initializing a servlet and obtaining resources that a servlet needs throughout its entire lifetime, e.g. database connections, connections to back-end systems, and connections to directories. Servlet containers call this method when they load a servlet.

The `service` method is responsible for handling all incoming requests. For each incoming request targeted at a particular servlet, the servlet container calls this method with an object representing the incoming request and an object representing the response to be created as arguments.

The `destroy` method is responsible for freeing up all resources that have been allocated in the `init` method. Servlet containers call this method before unloading a servlet.

9.2.2 HTTP servlets

As the communication protocol used between clients and servlet containers is usually HTTP, the Servlet API provides classes to support the application in analyzing incoming HTTP requests and constructing valid outgoing HTTP requests. The most relevant classes are `HttpServlet`, `HttpServletRequest`, and `HttpServletResponse`.

The class `HttpServlet` is a base class from which developers can derive their own servlets. It adds additional methods that are automatically called by its implementation of the `service` method to aid developers in processing HTTP-based requests. According to the different HTTP request types, these methods are named `doGet`, `doPost`, `doPut`, `doDelete`, `doHead`, `doOptions`, and `doTrace`. Typically, a servlet developer will define only `doGet` and `doPost`. The other methods are not usually required for web applications. The methods listed above are called with an `HttpServletRequest` and an `HttpServletResponse` object as arguments.

The `HTTPServletRequest` object represents the incoming HTTP request. It allows information contained in the request to be accessed, such as parameters, headers, cookies, SSL attributes, and preferred language settings of the client. Data contained in the request can be read from an input stream. An `HTTPServletRequest` object can also be used to create a session with the client that originated the request.

The `HTTPServletResponse` object encapsulates all information to be returned to the client, either by HTTP headers or the message body of the client. It allows headers to be set in the response and response data to be written to the output stream, controls buffering, and provides convenience methods for redirecting the client or sending errors if necessary.

Often, the dialog between a client and a server requires a session that spans multiple request/response pairs. To support developers in implementing sessions, the Servlet API provides the `HTTPSession` interface. A servlet can create a session to a client by invoking the method `getSession` with the argument `true` on an `HTTPServletRequest` object. The `HTTPSession` interface provides methods for setting the maximum session timeout, associating objects with the session, and disassociating objects from the session. Servlet containers may implement this interface using different mechanisms for session tracking, e.g. URL rewriting or cookies.

Example 9.1 shows an HTTP servlet that for each incoming request returns a response with information about the particular request, including remote user, address and host from which the request originated, request headers and parameters, cookies, and attributes, rendered in HTML markup.

9.3 Enterprise Java Beans

The EJB architecture is the standard component architecture for building distributed object-oriented business applications in the Java programming language. It allows applications to be built by combining components that have been developed using tools from different vendors. It makes application development easier as developers do not have to understand details about transaction and state management, multi-

| Example 9.1 | Simple HTTP servlet |

```java
import java.io.*;
import java.util.*;
import java.security.cert.*;
import javax.servlet.*;
import javax.servlet.http.*;

public class HttpServletExample extends HttpServlet {

  public void doGet (HttpServletRequest req,
    HttpServletResponse res)
  throws ServletException, IOException {
    PrintWriter out;

    res.setContentType("text/html");
    out = res.getWriter ();

    out.println("<HTML><HEAD><TITLE>Snoop" +
      "Servlet</TITLE></HEAD>"
      + "<BODY BGCOLOR=\"#FFFFEE\">");

    out.println("<H1>HTTP Servlet Example - " +
      "Request/Client Information</H1>");
    out.println("<H2>Request source:</H2>");
    out.println("Remote user is " + req.getRemoteUser() +
      "<BR>");
    out.println("Remote address is " +
      req.getRemoteAddr() + "<BR>");
    out.println("Remote host is " + req.getRemoteHost() +
      "<BR>");
    Enumeration e = req.getHeaderNames();
    if (e.hasMoreElements()) {
      out.println("<H2>Request headers:</H2>");
      out.println("<TABLE Border=\"2\" WIDTH=\"65%\"
        BGCOLOR=\"#DDDDFF\">");
      while (e.hasMoreElements()) {
        String name = (String)e.nextElement();
        out.println("<TR><TD>" + name + "</TD><TD>" +
          req.getHeader(name) + "</TD></TR>");
      }
      out.println("</TABLE><BR><BR>");
    }
```

▶

continued

```
      e = req.getParameterNames();
      if (e.hasMoreElements()) {
        out.println("<H2>Servlet parameters (Single Value" +
          "style):</H2>");
        out.println("<TABLE Border=\"2\" WIDTH=\"65%\"" +
          "BGCOLOR=\"#DDDDFF\">");
        while (e.hasMoreElements()) {
          String name = (String)e.nextElement();
          out.println("<TR><TD>" + name + "</TD><TD>" +
            req.getParameter(name) + "</TD></TR>");

        }
      out.println("</TABLE><BR><BR>");
      }

    Cookie[] cookies = req.getCookies();
    if (cookies != null && cookies.length > 0) {
      out.println("<H2>Client cookies</H2>");
        out.println("<TABLE Border=\"2\" WIDTH=\"65%\" "
      + BGCOLOR=\"#DDDDFF\">");
      for (int i=0; i<cookies.length; i++) {
        out.println("<TR><TD>" + cookies[i].getName() +
          "</TD><TD>" + cookies[i].getValue() +
          "</TD></TR>");
      }
      out.println("</TABLE><BR><BR>");
    }
    e = req.getAttributeNames();
    if (e.hasMoreElements()) {
      out.println("<H2>Request attributes:</H2>");
      out.println("<TABLE Border=\"2\" WIDTH=\"65%\" " +
        "BGCOLOR=\"#DDDDFF\">");
      while (e.hasMoreElements()) {
        String name = (String)e.nextElement();
        out.println("<TR><TD>" + name + "</TD><TD>" +
          req.getAttribute(name) + "</TD></TR>");
      }
      out.println("</TABLE><BR><BR>");
    }
    out.println("</BODY></HTML>");
  }
}
```

threading, connection pooling, etc. The EJB architecture addresses the development, deployment, and runtime aspects of a company application's lifecycle. Once an EJB has been developed, it can be deployed on any application server that provides a container conforming to the EJB specification.[2]

EJB technology gives developers the ability to model the full range of objects that are useful in the company by defining two distinct types of EJB components: session beans and entity beans. Session beans represent behaviors associated with client sessions, for example a purchase transaction on an e-commerce site. Entity beans represent collections of data – such as rows in a relational database – and encapsulate operations on the data they represent. Entity beans are intended to be persistent, living as long as the data they are associated with exist.

9.3.1 Roles of Enterprise Java Beans

The EJB specification defines different roles for the parties involved in creation of Web applications:

- *The EJB provider* is the producer of enterprise beans, who generates an EJB-jar file that contains one or more EJBs. The bean provider is responsible for the Java classes that implement the enterprise beans business methods, the definition of the bean's remote and home interfaces, and the bean's deployment descriptor. The expertise of the bean provider typically lies within the application domain. For transactions, concurrency, security, and distribution, the bean provider can rely on the EJB container.

- *The application assembler* combines beans into larger units. It takes EJB-jar files produced by a bean provider and generates EJB-jar files that contain EJBs along with application assembly instructions and potentially other types of application components, e.g. JSPs.

- *The deployer* takes EJB-jar files provided by bean providers and/or application assemblers and deploys the contained beans in a specific operational environment that contains a specific EJB server and container.

- *The server/container provider* provides the environment in which EJBs can be deployed and run. Conceptually, these might be different entities, but in reality they are often identical, as most servers include a container.

- *The persistence manager provider* is responsible for the persistence of Entity Beans installed in an EJB container. It provides tools that are used at deployment time to generate the code that connects EJBs to data in databases or existing applications.

- *The system administrator* is responsible for the administration of the enterprise's IT infrastructure, which includes the EJB server and container.

The EJB architecture is intended for distributed transaction-oriented enterprise applications based on enterprise beans as components. An enterprise bean typically contains business logic that operates on the company's data. Instances of enterprise beans are created and managed during runtime by a container. Services information, such as transaction and security attributes, are separate from the enterprise bean class to allow the services information to be managed by tools during application assembly and deployment. The container in which the bean is deployed mediates client access to the enterprise beans. If an enterprise bean uses only services as defined in the EJB specification, it can be deployed in any EJB-compliant container. Enterprise beans have associated client views that are unaffected by the container and server in which the bean is deployed to ensure that both the enterprise beans and their clients can be used in multiple environments without changes or recompilation.

9.3.2 Enterprise Java Bean contracts

To define the responsibilities of the involved components, the EJB specifications defines several contracts:

- *The Client-view contract* between a client and a container provides a uniform development model for applications using enterprise beans. It is 'remotable', so both local and remote programs can access an enterprise bean using the same view. The client view includes the home interface and the remote interface. The home interface, which is specified by the bean provider, defines the methods to be used by clients to create, remove and find EJB objects. The remote interface, which is also specified by the bean provider, defines the methods that can be called by clients.
- *The component contract* between an enterprise bean and its container specifies the requirements to the enterprise bean and the container to make them work together.
- *The EJB-jar file contract* defines a standard format for packaging enterprise beans with their declarative information, which can be processed by application assembly and deployment tools. It is a contract between the bean provider and the application assembler, as well as between the application assembler and deployer. EJB-jar files include Java class files for enterprise beans, their remote and home interfaces, and an XML deployment descriptor.

9.3.3 Types of Enterprise Java Bean

EJB architecture differentiates three types of enterprise beans:

- *Session beans* typically execute on behalf of a single client. They can be transaction-aware and can update shared data in an underlying database, but they do not directly represent shared data. Session beans are relatively short-lived and are removed when the EJB container crashes. EJB containers provide a scalable runtime environment to execute a large number of session objects concurrently. Session beans may be stateful or stateless.

- *Entity beans* provide object views of shared data in a database, allowing shared access from multiple clients. Entity beans live as long as the data in the database that they represent. The entity bean and its remote reference survive EJB container crashes.

- *Message-driven beans* execute on receipt of a single client message. They can be transaction-aware and can update shared data in an underlying database, but they do not directly represent data in a database. Message-driven beans are relatively short-lived and are stateless. They are removed when the server crashes and restarts.

9.4 Java Server Pages

JSP technology allows applications that contain dynamic Web content, such as HTML, XHTML, XML, WML, VoiceXML and Dynamic Hypertext Markup Language (DHTML), to be built. A JSP page is a document that describes how to process a request to create a response, combining template data with dynamic actions leveraging the Java platform. The features that can be used in JSPs are standard directives and actions, scriptlets, and expressions.

9.4.1 Java Server Pages execution

JSPs are executed in a JSP container installed on a Web server. The container forwards requests from a client to JSPs, and responses generated by JSPs back to the client. The underlying semantics of JSPs are based on Java servlets. A JSP describes how to create a response from a given request, optionally using or creating other objects in the process. A JSP container must support HTTP. Other protocols may be supported as well. The default request and response objects therefore have the type `HttpServletRequest` and `HttpServletResponse`, respectively. The first time a JSP container receives a request for a particular JSP, the container loads the JSP template and compiles it into a JSP servlet (Figure 9.2). Once this has been done, all further requests are passed directly to the JSP Servlet, i.e. the flow depicted by dotted arrows in Figure 9.2 is omitted.

Figure 9.2

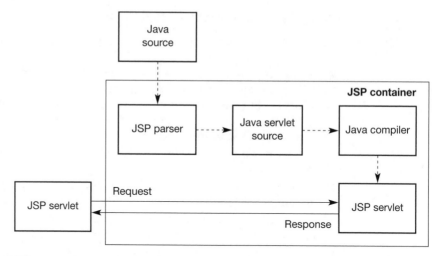

JSP processing

9.4.2 Access to application data

During their execution, JSPs can create and/or access Java objects. There are several scopes for objects used in a JSP:

- *Page scope*. The objects with page scope are accessible only within the page in which the objects were created. References to objects with page scope are held in the *page context* object.
- *Request scope*. The objects with request scope are accessible within pages or servlets processing the same request in which they were created. If the request is forwarded to a resource in the same runtime environment, the objects with request scope are still reachable. References to objects in this scope are held in the *request* object.
- *Session scope*. The objects with session scope are accessible from pages that process requests that belong to the same session in which they were created. References to objects in this scope are held in the *session* object.
- *Application scope*. The objects with application scope are accessible from pages that process requests that are in the same application in which they were created. References to objects with application scope are stored in the *application* object associated with activation of a page.

9.4.3 Java Server Page elements

JSPs may contain the following elements:

- *Fixed template data* are used to describe the pieces that are used verbatim either in the response or as input to actions, for example HTML, WML, or XML markup.
- *Directives* (Example 9.2) provide global information that is independent of specific requests received by a JSP. For example, a directive may specify the scripting language to be used in the JSP, or the content type to be set for the response.
- *Actions* follow the syntax of XML elements, having either a start tag, a body tag and an end tag, or an empty tag (Example 9.3).

Example 9.2 **JSP directive syntax**

```
<% @ directive ... %>
```

Example 9.3 **JSP action syntax**

```
<xyztag attr1="attribute value" ... > body </xyztag>
or
<xyztag attr1="attribute value" ... />
```

Example 9.4 shows a simple JSP that accesses a bean holding consumer data to print out the first and last name of a consumer. The first JSP tag with the label `jsp:useBean` makes a bean of the type

Example 9.4 **A simple JSP**

```
<HTML>
  ...
  <BODY>
    <jsp:useBean id="consumerBean"
      class="sample.ConsumerBean"
                scope="request"/>
    Welcome, Mr./Mrs. <%=consumerBean.getFirstName()%>
    <%=consumerBean.getLastName()%>
    ...
  </BODY>
</HTML>
```

sample.ConsumerBean available to scriptlets and actions within the page. The JSP will expect the bean to be provided in the request under the name consumerBean. In the body of the page, there are two expressions that use this reference to get the first and last name of the consumer.

As mentioned above, JSPs are compiled into servlets before they are invoked. The resulting servlet contains code that writes the markup contained in the JSP to the output stream. Wherever there is a bean tag to access data or a scriptlet in the JSP, the appropriate Java code is inserted into the generated servlet (Example 9.5).

Example 9.5 **Servlet code generated from a JSP**

```
...
out.println("<HTML>");
out.println("<BODY>");
...
out.println("Welcome, Mr./Mrs. " +
consumerBean.getFirstName());
out.println(consumerBean.getLastName());
...
out.println("</BODY>");
out.println("</HTML>");
...
```

Programmers using JSPs should be aware that JSPs are intended for use as views rather than for containing application logic. Although it is possible to place virtually any Java code in JSPs, programmers should restrict themselves to using Java scriptlets only where absolutely necessary, and use the JSP tags wherever possible. Placing Java code in JSPs prevents a clear separation of application logic from presentation; it is preferable to use the model–view–controller pattern instead, in which a controller is responsible for invoking the application logic and calls JSPs as views, providing any required data encapsulated in beans.

9.5 Extensible Markup Language

XML describes data objects called XML documents, and partially specifies the behaviour of computer programs that process these documents. XML is an application profile of Standard Generalized Markup Language (SGML). XML was designed to be easily usable over the Internet, to be human-legible, and to support a large variety of applications that process and create XML documents.

Unlike HTML, XML allows for clear separation between data representation and presentation in the form of markup. Data can be represented in XML documents that can be parsed and processed easily by applications in order to extract relevant parts of the contained information. This is of particular advantage in pervasive computing applications, where the same data often have to be rendered to different presentation formats for various kinds of devices.

Data are represented in XML documents that have a structure formally described through DTDs or XML schema definitions (XSD). To read XML documents, and to provide access to their structure and content, applications use XML processors. The XML specification describes the required behavior of XML processors in terms of how to parse XML data and how to provide the information to applications.

One option for processing XML documents is to use XSL style sheets that render the data contained in an XML document in a particular presentation markup language. Another option to process XML documents programmatically is to use document object models (DOMs) or simple API for XML (SAX) parsers.

9.5.1 Extensible Markup Language syntax

XML documents consist of entities that can contain either parsed or unparsed data. Parsed data consist of characters, partially forming character data, and partially forming markup that describes the document's storage layout and logical structure. An XML document is well formed if it contains exactly one root, taken as a whole it meets all the well-formedness constraints specified in the XML specification, and each of the parsed entities that is referenced within the document is well formed according to the XML specification. Example 9.6 shows a well-formed XML document.

Example 9.6   **XML document**

```
<?xml version="1.0"?>
<pizzas>
 <pizza lowfat="no">
   <name>Salami</name>
   <description>Topped with salami and
     cheese.</description>
   <price>5.99</price>
 </pizza>
</pizzas>
```

XML allows custom XML vocabularies to be defined to describe particular data structures. Software for a pizza shop might use a pizza element for describing pizzas, for example. By using compatible XML formats to describe their data, applications can easily interoperate with each other by exchanging XML-encoded messages.

9.5.2 Extensible Markup Language namespaces

As XML's main goal is interoperability, and everyone is free to create their own XML vocabularies, XML would not work if different developers chose the same element names to represent conceptually distinct entities. To prevent potential naming conflicts, XML provides the concept of namespaces.

XML namespaces provide a context for XML document elements allowing elements to particular implementation semantics to be resolved. In our pizza example, the price element on one system might represent the sales price to be paid by customers, but on another system it might represent the purchase price that the store has to pay. Example 9.7 illustrates how namespaces help to resolve any potential ambiguity.

Example 9.7   **XML namespace**

```
<?xml version="1.0"?>
<pizzas xmlns:sales="http://pizza.org/shop/prices"
        xmlns:purchase="http://pizza.org/customer/prices">
  <pizza lowfat="no">
    <name>Pizza Salami</name>
    <description>Topped with salami and
      cheese.</description>
    <purchase:price>0.99</price>
    <sales:price>2.99</price>
  </pizza>
</pizzas>
```

9.5.3 Document type definitions

As we described above, XML provides a flexible syntax for describing well-formed documents. Because of this flexibility, an XML document may contain problems on the application level, even though it is well formed. Example 9.8 shows such a case.

Example 9.8 **A well-formed, but invalid XML document**

```xml
<?xml version="1.0"?>
<pizzas>
  <pizza lowfat="no">
    <pizza lowfat="no">
      <name>Pizza Salami</name>
      <description>Topped with salami and
        cheese.</description>
      <price>5.99</price>
    <price>3.99</price>
  </pizza>
 </pizza>
</pizzas>
```

Obviously, the document is well formed, but there is a `pizza` element within another `pizza` element, and the inner `pizza` element contains two price tags instead of one. Although there is nothing inherently wrong with this XML document, it would probably confuse applications that expect no nested `pizza` elements and only one price per element. To detect such problems while parsing XML documents, a standard mechanism for validating an XML document against certain predefined rules is required.

The DTD language was invented specifically for defining validation rules for SGML documents. It allows the specification of grammars that define allowable tags and the attributes or other tags they may contain. Since XML is a simplified subset of SGML, DTDs can also be used to define XML validation rules. An XML processor can use a DTD at runtime to validate a given XML file against the predefined XML schema.

DTDs define which elements are required in an XML document, which elements are optional, how many occurrences of a given element are allowed, etc. They also describe the relationship between elements and how attributes relate to different elements. Example 9.9 shows the DTD for the XML document shown in Example 9.8.

Example 9.9 **DTD for the XML document in Example 9.8**

```
<!ELEMENT pizzas (pizza)*>
<!ELEMENT pizza (name, description, price)>
<!ATTLIST pizza lowfat CDATA #IMPLIED>
<!ELEMENT name (#PCDATA)>
<!ELEMENT description (#PCDATA)>
<!ELEMENT price (#PCDATA)>
```

This document states that the `pizzas` element may contain many `pizza` elements. Each `pizza` element must contain a `lowfat` attribute and three subelements, all of type `#PCData` (parsed character data). Documents that conform to this document type definition would then add the following document type declaration:

```
<!DOCTYPE pizzas SYSTEM "pizza.dtd">
```

The XML document type declaration contains or points to markup declarations providing a DTD, in this case `pizza.dtd`. The document type declaration can point to an external subset containing markup declarations, or contain the markup declarations directly in an internal subset, or it can do both. The DTD for a document consists of both subsets taken together. An XML document is valid if it has an associated document type declaration, and if the document complies with the constraints expressed in it.

9.5.4 Extensible Markup Language processors

To work with XML data, programmers need to be able to process XML files from their applications. The W3C defines the term 'XML processor' as a software module capable of reading XML documents and providing access to their content and structure. One of the main advantages of adopting XML as the universal standard for describing data is that many interoperable XML processors provide the functionality to accomplish this goal. With a standard XML processor, applications can programmatically read XML documents and access any element name, body, or attribute within these documents.

Document object model
The DOM is a standard for programmatically accessing the structure and data contained in an XML document. The W3C has approved the DOM level. The DOM is based on an in-memory tree representation of the XML document. When an XML file is loaded into the XML processor, it must build an in-memory tree that correctly represents the document. The DOM also defines the programmatic interface (including the names of the methods and properties) that should be used to programmatically traverse an XML tree and manipulate the elements, values, and attributes.

Example 9.10 reads an XML document from a given URI and counts the number of occurrences of a given prefix in the XML document by recursively traversing the tree.

Example 9.10

Example of DOM

```java
package domexample;

import org.w3c.dom.Document;
import org.w3c.dom.Node;
import org.w3c.dom.NodeList;

import com.ibm.xml.parsers.DOMParser;

/**
 * This sample program counts the occurrences of a
 * given prefix in an XML document using DOM.
 */
public class DOMOccurrenceCount {

 public static int count(Node node, String prefix) {
  int occurrences = 0;
  if (node != null) {
   switch (node.getNodeType()) {
    case Node.DOCUMENT_NODE:
     occurrences += count(((Document)
       node).getDocumentElement(), prefix);
     break;

    case Node.ELEMENT_NODE:
      NodeList element_children = node.getChildNodes();
      if (element_children != null) {
       int len = element_children.getLength();
       for (int i = 0; i < len; i++) {
        occurrences += count(element_children.item(i),
          prefix);
       }
      }
      break;

    case Node.ENTITY_REFERENCE_NODE:
     NodeList entity_ref_children =
       node.getChildNodes();
     if (entity_ref_children != null) {
      int len = entity_ref_children.getLength();
      for (int i = 0; i < len; i++) {
```

▶

continued

```
        occurrences += count(entity_ref_children.item(i),
          prefix);
      }
    }
    break;

  case Node.TEXT_NODE:
    if (node.getNodeValue().startsWith(prefix)) {
     occurrences++;
    }
    break;
   }
  }
 return occurrences;
}

public static void main(String argv[]) {
 try {
  long before = System.currentTimeMillis();

  DOMParser parser = new DOMParser();
  parser.parse(argv[0]);
  Document document = parser.getDocument();
  int occurrences = count(document, argv[1]);

  long elapsedTime = System.currentTimeMillis() -
    before;

  System.out.println(occurrences + " occurrences of '" +
  argv[1] + "'");
    System.out.println("(Processing time: " +
  elapsedTime + ")");
  } catch (Exception e) {
    e.printStackTrace();
  }
 }
}
```

Simple application programming interface for Extensible Markup Language
One of the major downsides to the DOM standard is the overhead of loading an entire XML document into memory. This can become very problematic, especially for large data files processed on servers that have to process large numbers of requests in parallel. When transmitting large amounts of XML data through the Internet, it is inefficient to receive the entire file before beginning to process it. As XML developers realized these disadvantages, they began to define an alternative specification: Simple API for XML (SAX).

SAX is a very simple XML API that allows developers to take advantage of event-driven XML parsing. Unlike the DOM specification, SAX does not require the entire XML file to be loaded into memory. As soon as the XML processor finishes reading an XML element, it calls custom event handlers to process the element and its associated data. This is advantageous for use in small devices with restricted memory, as well as for scalable XML processing on servers.

Example 9.11 shows how a SAX parser can be used to count the occurrences of a given word in an XML document.

Example 9.11	**Example of SAX**

```java
package saxexample;

import org.xml.sax.HandlerBase;
import org.xml.sax.Parser;
import org.xml.sax.helpers.ParserFactory;


/**
 * This sample program counts the occurrences of a
given prefix in an
 * XML document using SAX.
 */
public class SAXOccurrenceCount extends HandlerBase {
  private int occurrences_ = 0;
  private String prefix_ = null;

  public SAXOccurrenceCount(String prefix) {
    prefix_ = prefix;
    occurrences_ = 0;
  }

public void characters(char ch[], int start, int length)
{
    if (prefix_.equals(String.valueOf(ch, start, length)))
```

▶

continued

```
{
    occurrences_++;
  }
}

public int getNumOccurrences() {
  return occurrences_;
}

public static void main(String argv[]) {
  try {
    long before = System.currentTimeMillis();

    SAXOccurrenceCount counter = new
      SAXOccurrenceCount(argv[1]);
    Parser
    parser=ParserFactory.makeParser(
    "com.ibm.xml.parsers.
    SAXParser");
    parser.setDocumentHandler(counter);
    parser.setErrorHandler(counter);
    parser.parse(argv[0]);

    long elapsedTime = System.currentTimeMillis() -
      before;

    System.out.println(counter.getNumOccurrences()+
              " occurrences of '" + argv[1] + "'");
    System.out.println("(Processing time: " + elapsedTime
      + ")");
  } catch (Exception e) {
    e.printStackTrace();
  }
}
}
```

The main method creates a SAXOccurrenceCount object and a Parser object, and registers the counter object with the SAX parser for handling document events. Whenever the parser generates a document event, it calls the appropriate method of the counter. As we want to count occurrences of a given prefix in the XML document text, we only overwrite the method characters that the parser invokes when it encounters text fields.

9.5.5 Extensible Stylesheet Language

When using the standard DOM API to process XML data, it becomes tedious to extract specific pieces of data from large documents or to transform certain parts of an XML document into another format such as HTML.

Let us assume that we need to find all of the low-fat pizza price elements. In order to do this with the standard DOM API, code is needed that traverses the entire tree looking for those specific elements that match the criteria (in this case, price elements that are within `pizza` elements where the attribute `lowfat` equals `yes`). In another example, assume you wish to transform all pizza elements and their associated data into a simple HTML table for the user to interact with. Using the standard DOM API, you must manually traverse the tree and create the output string containing the HTML table.

In order to simplify and standardize these tasks, the W3C introduced a specification for XML transformations called Extensible Stylesheet Language (XSL) and a simple query language referred to as XPath.

XPath

XPath defines a syntax to select a set of nodes in an XML tree. The selection is relative to the current node that the pattern is applied to. The simplest pattern is an element name; it selects all the child elements of the current node with that element name. For example, the pattern pizza selects all the `pizza` child elements of the current node.

The XPath syntax is complete. It allows you to identify the context of a given element within a document (e.g. `price` elements that live within pizza elements). It also provides powerful filtering syntax to help identify specific nodes that match a given criteria (e.g. where `lowfat=yes`). To find all the low-fat pizza price elements within a `pizzas` element, you would use the following pattern string:

```
/pizzas/pizza[@lowfat="yes"]/price
```

When a pattern is applied to a given node, it simply returns a list of nodes that match the given pattern. This simplifies development because there is no longer a need to explicitly write code to traverse a DOM tree in order to find a particular piece of data.

Extensible Stylesheet Language stylesheets

XSL simplifies one of the most common XML tasks: transforming nodes from one XML format into another. The need for this originated on the Web as developers wanted to take their XML data and transform them into HTML to be displayed in browsers. XSL also is very useful for defining transformations from a given XML format to another distinct XML format. If an XML document does not use the exact XML vocabulary that a system expects, it can perform an XSL transformation to convert the XML file to the desired vocabulary.

An XSL file contains a list of declarative templates that define the transformation rules. Each template defines exactly how to transform a given node from the source document to a node (or some other type of data) in the output document. XSL Patterns within a template allow the portions of the document to which the template applies to be defined. The XML file in Example 9.12 can be transformed using the XSL stylesheet shown below Example 9.13.

Example 9.12   **XML file**

```
<?xml version="1.0"?>
<pizzas>
<pizza lowfat="no">
  <name>Pizza Salami</name>
  <description>Topped with salami and
    cheese.</description>
  <price>5.99</price>
 </pizza>
</pizzas>
```

Example 9.13   **XSL style sheet**

```
<?xml version="1.0"?>
<xsl:stylesheet xmlns:xsl="http://www.w3.org/TR/WD-xsl">
 <xsl:template match="/">
 <HTML>
  <BODY>
  <H1>Pizzas</H1>
  <OL>
  <xsl:for-each select="pizzas[@lowfat="no"]">
   <LI><xsl:value-of select="name"/>, <xsl:value-of
     select="price"/>,
   <xsl:value-of select="description"/></LI>
  </xsl:for-each>
  </OL>
  </BODY>
 </HTML>
 </xsl:template>
</xsl:stylesheet>
```

The result would be the HTML file shown in Example 9.14.

Example 9.14 **Resulting HTML markup**

```
<HTML>
 <BODY>
  <H1>Pizzas</H1>
  <OL>
   <LI>Salami, $5.99, Topped with salami and cheese.</LI>
  </OL>
 </BODY>
</HTML>
```

Notice how XSL Patterns are utilized within the match and select attributes of the different XSL elements to identify a set of elements. The text within the `<xsl:template>` tags defines the transformation rule for that set of nodes. It is interesting that XSL uses a standard XML vocabulary to define the transformation process.

The output of the examples above rendered in an HTML browser would look like this:

Pizzas
1. Salami, $5.99, Topped with salami and cheese.

9.5.6 Extensible Markup Language Signatures

XML Signatures provide integrity, message authentication, and signer-authentication services for data of any type. Signed data may be located within the XML that includes the signature, or elsewhere. XML Signatures can be applied to any digital content (data object), including XML, in one or more resources. Enveloped or enveloping signatures are generated over data within the same XML document as the signature; detached signatures are generated over data external to the signature element. The XML Signature is a method of associating a key with referenced data.

In Example 9.15 the mandatory SignedInfo element is the information that is actually signed. The validation process consists of two mandatory steps: validation of the signature over SignedInfo and validation of each Reference digest within SignedInfo. The CanonicalizationMethod is the algorithm used to canonicalize the SignedInfo element before calculating a digest for signing. The SignatureMethod is the algorithm that is used to generate the SignatureValue from the canonicalized SignedInfo. It combines a digest algorithm and a key-dependent algorithm and possibly other

| **Example 9.15** | **XML Signature** |

```
<Signature Id="SampleSignature"
xmlns="http://www.w3.org/2000/09/xmldsig#">
 <SignedInfo>
  <CanonicalizationMethod
   Algorithm="http://www.w3.org/TR/2000/CR-xml-c14n-
    20001026"/>
  <SignatureMethod
   Algorithm="http://www.w3.org/2000/09/xmldsig#dsa-sha1"/>
  <Reference URI="http://www.w3.org/TR/2000/REC-xhtml1-
    20000126/">
  <Transforms>
   <Transform Algorithm="http://www.w3.org/TR/2000/CR-
     xml-c14n-20001026"/>
  </Transforms>
  <DigestMethod
   Algorithm="http://www.w3.org/2000/09/xmldsig#sha1"/>
  <DigestValue>j6lwx3rvEPO0vKtMup4NbeVu8nk=</DigestValue>
  </Reference>
 </SignedInfo>
 <SignatureValue>MC0CFFrVLtRlk=...</SignatureValue>
 <KeyInfo>
  <KeyValue>
   <DSAKeyValue>
    <P>...</P><Q>...</Q><G>...</G><Y>...</Y>
   </DSAKeyValue>
  </KeyValue>
 </KeyInfo>
</Signature>
```

algorithms, such as padding, e.g. RSA-SHA1. The algorithm names are signed to avoid substituting weaker algorithms.

Each Reference element contains the digest method and resulting digest value calculated over the identified data object. A data object is signed by computing its digest value and a signature over that value. The signature is later checked via reference and signature validation.

KeyInfo indicates the key for validating the signature. KeyInfo is optional as the signer may not wish to reveal key information, or the information may already be known within the application's context. If the signer wishes to bind the keying information to the signature, a reference can identify and include the KeyInfo as part of the signature.

9.5.7 Extensible Markup Language-related technologies and vocabularies

The technologies presented above represent the core XML technologies. In this section, we briefly present some related XML technologies and vocabularies that are gaining popularity. Many of these technologies are currently evolving within various W3C working groups.

Mathematical Markup Language

Mathematical Markup Language (MathML) is an XML application for describing mathematical notation and capturing its structure and content. The goal of MathML is to enable mathematics to be served, received, and processed on the Web, just as HTML has enabled this functionality for text.

Extensible Hyper Text Markup Language

Today's HTML files are usually not well-formed XML documents, for example it is common to have begin tags without a subsequent end tag. This makes it difficult, if not impossible, to process HTML using standard XML tools. XHTML documents are well-formed XML documents that work in conjunction with XML processors. This also makes it much easier for pervasive computing clients, such as phones and PDAs, to process: XHTML has a more regular structure, and is easier to parse than HTML, which has many tags that need no end tag. A special subset of HTML for pervasive devices has been defined by Baker *et al.*[3]

Synchronized Multimedia Integration Language

Synchronized Multimedia Integration Language (SMIL) is an XML-based language for describing multimedia presentations. SMIL allows a set of independent multimedia objects to be integrated into a synchronized multimedia presentation.

Vector Markup Language

Vector Markup Language (VML) is an application of VML that defines a format for the encoding of vector information, together with additional markup to describe how that information may be rendered on the screen. VML supports the markup of vector graphic information in the same way that HTML supports the markup of textual information.

Channel Definition Format

Channel Definition Format (CDF) permits Web publishers to offer frequently updated channels, from any Web server for automatic delivery to receiver programs on PCs or other devices.

SyncML

SyncML is an XML format that defines messages to be used in the SyncML synchronization protocol to synchronize data between clients and servers. More information on SyncML can be found in Chapter 4.

9.6 Web services

The concept of Web services has been developed to allow business applications to communicate and cooperate via the Internet. It implies a paradigm shift compared with the way the Internet works today. While current applications that interact with other applications via the Internet have to know their peers a priori, and need to be pointed to these peers by humans, the concepts and the technology that we describe in the remainder of this section allow applications to find Web services and to bind to these services automatically without human interaction (Figure 9.3).

For example, one company may call another company's Web service to send a purchase order directly to its order system service via an Internet connection. Other examples are an enterprise portal that calls a search service to search for websites on a particular topic, or a dictionary on a PDA that calls a dictionary service when it is asked for a word that is not known in its local repository.

Web services following this concept allow objects to be distributed across websites where clients can access them via the Internet. Global service registries are used to promote and discover distributed services. A client that needs a particular kind of service can make a query to the global service registry to find services that suit its needs. The client can select one of the services, bind to that service, and use it for a certain period of time. As service discovery and selection can be performed without human interaction, services can be switched very quickly, even on a per-request basis. Automated service discovery also allows robust networks of services to be established. If multiple Web services exist that provide identical functions, a client can easily switch to a back-up system when the currently used service fails.

Figure 9.3

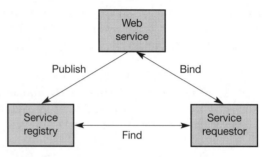

Web services: publish, find, bind

The most important standards in this area are SOAP, the associated Web Services Description Language (WSDL) for communication between Web services, and UDDI for registration and discovery of Web services. Microsoft and IBM initiated SOAP and UDDI, and now a large number of major companies support these initiatives.

9.6.1 Universal Description, Discovery, and Integration

The UDDI[4] initiative has the goal to establish Web-based registries that make available information about businesses or other entities and their technical interfaces. UDDI provides a specification for distributed Web-based information registries of Web services, as well as a publicly accessible set of implementations of the UDDI specification. The UDDI specifications define how to publish and discover information about Web services.

The term 'Web service' in the context of UDDI describes business functionality that a company exposes in order to allow other companies or software programs to use the service, usually through an Internet connection. The existence of the service alone, however, is not very helpful. Clients that want to use the service need a standard way of discovering services that match their needs and use of these services.

One approach that is used today is contacting the provider of the service and asking for information about the cost, terms, and conditions of use, and the technical interfaces to a service. Often, this information is also available on websites, but there is currently no standard format for the service descriptions that allow automatic finding of suitable services.

UDDI provides a distributed registry of businesses and their service descriptions based on a common XML format that can be processed automatically. The information provided in a UDDI business registration consists of three parts:

- *White Pages* include address, contacts, and known identifiers. They provide information about the identity of a business.
- *Yellow Pages* give information on what kind of services a business provides. They include industrial categorizations based on standards taxonomies.
- *Green Pages* describe how business services work. They provide the technical information required for using the service, i.e. references to specifications for Web services as well as support for pointers to file- and URL-based discovery mechanisms.

The UDDI project includes the shared operation of a business registry on the WWW. Multiple operator sites run this distributed registry that can be used by any business that wants to make its information available, or by anyone who wants to find information. Companies can use the UDDI business directory at a business level to find companies in a given industry that provide a given type of service, or to check whether a given partner has particular service interfaces. Programs and programmers use the UDDI business registry to find information on services. Applications need the information from the directory to bind to and use business services, while programmers need the UDDI information to implement systems that are compatible with advertised services or to describe their own services to allow others to call them.

The UDDI interface allows users to find businesses on the Web, and to discover what technical interfaces these businesses provide. Often, these businesses will have interfaces based on SOAP.

9.6.2 Web Services Description Language

As communications protocols and message formats for use on the Web are being standardized, it becomes necessary to have a means for describing the communications between clients and services in a formal way. To address this need, WSDL defines an XML grammar for describing network services as a set of endpoints that are operating on messages that contain either document-oriented or procedure-oriented information.

WSDL describes operations and messages abstractly, and binds them to concrete network protocols and message formats to define ports. It allows the combination of related ports into services. WSDL uses the following elements in the definition of network services:

- *Types:* a container for DTDs using a type system (such as XSD).
- *Message:* an abstract, typed definition of the data being communicated.
- *Operation:* an abstract description of an action supported by the service.
- *Port type:* an abstract set of operations supported by one or more endpoints.
- *Binding:* a concrete protocol and data format specification for a particular port type.
- *Port:* a single endpoint defined as a combination of a binding and a network address.
- *Service:* a collection of related endpoints.

WSDL is extensible to allow description of endpoints and their messages for different message formats or network protocols. Since a single type system grammar is not sufficient to describe all message formats present and future, WSDL does not introduce its own type definition language but allows the use of other type definition languages via extensibility. In addition, WSDL defines a common binding mechanism. This is used to attach specific protocols, data formats, or structures to abstract messages, operations, or endpoints, and allows the reuse of abstract definitions. In addition to the service definition framework, WSDL defines specific binding extensions for SOAP 1.1, HTTP GET/POST, and MIME. These language extensions are layered on top of the core service definition framework. It is possible to use other binding extensions with WSDL as well.

Example 9.16 shows the WSDL definition of a simple service providing pizza prices. The service supports a single operation called GetPizzaPrice, which is deployed using the SOAP 1.1 protocol over HTTP. The Web service receives a pizza name as a string, and returns the price as a float.

Example 9.16 | **Description of a SOAP Web service**

```xml
<?xml version="1.0" encoding="UTF-8"?>
<definitions name="PizzaPriceService"
  targetNamespace=http://www.PizzaPriceService.wsdl.
  com/wrapperedService
 xmlns=http://schemas.xmlsoap.org/wsdl/
  xmlns:piz=http://www.PizzaPriceService.wsdl.com/wrappere
  dService
 xmlns:soap=http://schemas.xmlsoap.org/wsdl/soap/
 xmlns:xsd="http://www.w3.org/1999/XMLSchema">

<message name="IngetPriceRequest">
  <part name="meth1_inType1" type="xsd:string"/>
</message>

<message name="OutgetPriceResponse">
  <part name="meth1_outType" type="xsd:float"/>
</message>

<portType name="PizzaPriceService">
  <operation name="getPrice">
    <input message="IngetPriceRequest"/>
    <output message="OutgetPriceResponse"/>
  </operation>
</portType>

<binding name="PizzaPriceServiceBinding"
type="PizzaPriceService">
  <soap:binding style="rpc"
```

▶

```
continued        transport="http://schemas.xmlsoap.org/soap/http"/>

                 <operation name="getPrice">
                  <soap:operation soapAction="urn:PizzaPriceService"/>
                  <input>
                    <soap:body
                    encodingStyle=http://schemas.xmlsoap.
                    org/soap/encoding/namespace="urn:PizzaPriceService"
                    use="encoded"/>
                  </input>
                  <output>
                    <soap:body
                   encodingStyle=http://schemas.xmlsoap.org/soap/
                        encoding/ namespace="urn:PizzaPriceService"
                        use="encoded"/>
                  </output>
                 </operation>
                </binding>

                <service name="PizzaPriceService">
                 <documentation>Pizza Price Service</documentation>
                 <port binding="PizzaPriceServiceBinding"
                       name="PizzaPriceServicePort">
                  <soap:address
               location="http://localhost:8080/soap/servlet/rpcrouter"/>
                 </port>
                </service>
               </definitions>
```

At the beginning of Example 9.16 some types are defined for later use: PizzaPriceRequest and PizzaPriceResponse. These types are then used to define the messages GetPizzaPriceInput and GetPizzaPriceOutput. The next part defines a port type named PizzaPricePortType, which provides an operation named GetPizzaPrice that receives a GetPizzaPriceInput message and returns a GetPizzaPriceOutput message. In the next part of the document, the PizzaPricePortType is bound to the SOAP protocol through the binding named PizzaPriceSoapBinding. Finally, the service for getting pizza prices named PizzaPriceService is defined using the previously defined binding and port type.

9.6.3 Simple Object Access Protocol

SOAP[5] provides a simple mechanism for exchanging information via the Internet. It is a lightweight, XML-based protocol for exchanging structured and typed information between peers in a distributed, decentralized environment. A major design goal was simplicity and extensibility. Thus, there are many features from traditional distributed object systems and messaging systems that are not in the core SOAP specification, e.g. distributed garbage collection, batching of messages, objects-by-reference, or activation.

SOAP does not define application semantics such as a programming model or implementation specific semantics. Rather, it defines a simple mechanism for expressing application semantics by providing a modular packaging model and encoding mechanisms for encoding data within modules. Thus, it can be used in a broad range of computing system, from messaging systems to RPC. SOAP consists of the following parts:

- *The SOAP envelope* defines a framework for the definition of messages. It allows specifying what is in a message, who should process it, and whether it is optional or mandatory.
- *The SOAP encoding rules* define a serialization mechanism for exchanging instances of application-defined data types.
- *The SOAP remote procedure call (RPC) representation* defines conventions that can be used to represent remote procedure calls and responses as SOAP messages.

Although these parts are described together in the SOAP specification, they are functionally orthogonal. To promote simplicity through modularity, the envelope and the encoding rules are defined in different namespaces. In addition to the SOAP envelope, encoding rules and RPC conventions, SOAP defines protocol bindings that describe how to carry SOAP messages in HTTP messages, either with or without the HTTP extension framework.

Example 9.17 shows a simple SOAP message that requests the price for a certain type of pizza at an imaginary pizza service.

9.6.4 Creating and using Web services

To create a Web service, the following steps are required:

1. A developer implements the code that implements the Web service's function. In the pizza example, the function would be to return the price for a given pizza as a float. As SOAP is language independent, it is possible to use different programming languages alternatively, e.g. Java, C#, Visual Basic, C++, etc. It is also possible to enable existing code to be used via SOAP.

Example 9.17	A SOAP message

```
POST /PizzaPrice HTTP/1.1
     Host: example.com
     Content-Type: text/xml; charset="utf-8"
     Content-Length: nnnn
     SOAPAction: "http://example.com/GetLastPizzaPrice"

     <SOAP-ENV:Envelope
           xmlns:SOAP-
     ENV=
     http://schemas.xmlsoap.org/soap/envelope/
        SOAP- ENV:encodingStyle=
        "http://schemas.xmlsoap.org/soap/
           encoding/">
     <SOAP-ENV:Body>
        <m:GetPizzaPrice xmlns:m="Some-URI">
           <pizzaName>Pizza Salami</pizzaName>
        </m:GetPizzaPrice>
     </SOAP-ENV:Body>
   </SOAP-ENV:Envelope>
```

2. The next step is to create a WSDL service description and code for wrapping the function implemented by the developer, so that it can be invoked from the Internet via SOAP. This will usually, be done by using appropriate generator tools, rather than writing the service description and the SOAP wrapper by hand. Such tools exist for Java, C#, and Visual Basic, for example.

3. After implementing the functional code of the Web service, and generating the wrapper code that enables it to be invoked using SOAP, both components are deployed on an application server. At this point, the Web service is already operational, but it cannot be discovered yet.

4. To allow clients to discover and bind to the new Web service, it has to be registered with the global UDDI directory by using a tool to provide information for the White, Yellow, and Green Pages, as described in Section 9.6.1. One part of the information that is published in this process is the WSDL description generated in step one.

Once a company has deployed a Web service and published it to the UDDI directory, other companies can use the service. This requires the following steps:

1. A company discovers a service using a browsing tool to search the UDDI directory and obtains the service entry. The entry contains White, Yellow, and Green Pages information, including contacts, business information, and references to technical specifications of the service, respectively.

2. The company uses the business information obtained from the Yellow Pages to establish a relationship with the provider of the service. This may require signing contracts or just accepting certain terms and conditions.

3. The developers of the company use the technical information to create a client that uses the service. This task can be done partially by tools, as the WSDL description of a Web service contains enough information to automatically generate proxy code using appropriate tools.

9.7 Model–view–controller pattern

The simplest way to implement Web applications generating dynamic content is to use JSPs that receive a request, invoke application logic to perform the required operations on the server side, and finally create and return an appropriate response (Figure 9.4). This concept is appropriate only for very simple applications. It is too inflexible for real-life Web applications, and it does not provide appropriate separation of responsibilities between Java programmers and Web designers.

The Model–view–controller (MVC) pattern (Figure 9.5) offers much more flexibility and provides a clear separation of responsibilities. The controller receives all incoming requests and controls their execution. The model is responsible for application data and transactions that can be associated with it; it encapsulates the business logic. A view is responsible for displaying data. To execute a request, the controller accesses the model and displays views as required.

To avoid passing model references to the view, we combine the MVC pattern with the command pattern. Commands encapsulate access to the model and act as result containers that can be passed to views. A command in this context is implemented as a bean that has a certain number of input properties, an execute method, and a certain number of output properties. The controller initializes the command bean by providing the

Figure 9.4

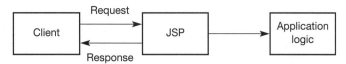

A Web application using direct invocation of JSPs

Figure 9.5

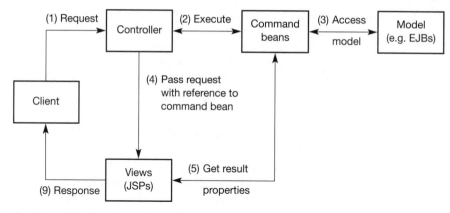

A web application based on the MVC

required input properties, calls the execute method to let the command perform its function, and passes the command bean to a view that then extracts and displays information from the output properties.

For Java Web applications, the controller is usually implemented as a servlet or a component invoked by a servlet, receives incoming requests, and determines which commands should be invoked to handle the request. Upon execution, the commands perform the appropriate actions on the model, which can be stateful, and in turn may invoke appropriate application logic encapsulated in EJB. Depending on the result of command execution, the controller finally calls the appropriate JSP to generate the response for the client, or an error page if the model returned an error. As a result of successful execution, the commands contain result data that can be obtained by JSPs via appropriate get methods.

9.8 Conclusion

In this chapter, we have described technologies for building Web applications in Java. We have covered servlets, EJBs, JSPs, and the XML technology in some detail, and introduced the MVC and command patterns. In the next chapter, we will present an architecture for pervasive computing applications that employs some of these technologies to support multiple different devices on the same application.

References

1. Sun Microsystems (1999) 'Java Servlet Specification 2.2'. Sun Microsystems.

2. Sun Microsystems, (2000) 'Enterprise Java Beans Specification 2.0.' Sun Microsystems.

3. Baker, M., Ishikawa, M., Matsui, S., Stark, P., Wugofski, T. and Yamakami, T. (2000) 'XHTML™ Basic'. http://www.w3.org/TR/xhtml-basic/

4. UDDI.org (2000) 'UDDI Technical Whitepaper'. http://www.uddi.org

5. Box, D., Ehnebuske, D., Kakivaya, G., Layman, A., Mendelsohn, N., Frystyk Nielsen, H., Thatte, S. and Winer, D. (2000) 'Simple Object Access Protocol (SOAP) 1.1'. http://www.w3.org/TR/SOAP/

Further reading

1. Gamma, E., Helm, R., Johnson, R. and Vlissides, J.(1995) *Design Patterns*. Reading, MA: Addison-Wesley.

2. Sun Microsystems (1999) 'Java Server Pages Specification 1.1'. Sun Microsystems.

3. Sun Microsystems, (2000) 'Java 2 Platform Enterprise Edition Specification 1.4'. Sun Microsystems.

4. Bray, T., Paoli, J., Sperberg-McQueen, C.M. and Maler, E. (2000) 'Extensible Markup Language (XML) 1.0 (Second Edition)'. http://www.w3.org/TR/REC-xml

5. Eastlake, D., Reagle, J., Solo, D., Bartel, M., Boyer, J., Fox, B. and Simon, E. (2000) 'XML-Signature Syntax and Processing'. W3C Candidate Recommendation. http://www.w3.org/TR/xmldsig-core/

6. Christensen, E., Curbera, F., Meredith, G., and Weerawarana, S. (2000) 'Web Services Description Language (WSDL) 1.0'. http://www.w3.org/TR/wsoll

10 Pervasive Web application architecture

In this chapter, we propose an architecture for pervasive computing applications that support multiple devices, such as PCs, WAP phones, PDAs, and voice-only phones enabled to access Web servers through voice gateways. The architecture addresses the special problems associated with pervasive computing, including diversity of devices, markup languages, and authentication methods. In particular, we show how pervasive computing applications based on this architecture can be secured.

10.1 Background

The problems that application programmers initially faced when implementing Web applications with browser access from PCs have, to a large degree, been resolved. Various technologies are available that allow application programmers to create transactional Web applications in a straightforward manner, supported by a large number of tools.

With the advent of pervasive computing, application programmers now face many new challenges. Users have many different devices that look and behave in very different ways. Examples of several kinds of pervasive computing devices were presented in the first part of this book, including WAP phones, PDAs, and voice-recognition devices. These devices provide different user interfaces, use different markup languages, use different communication protocols, and have different ways of authenticating themselves to servers. Ideally, Web applications that support pervasive computing should adapt to whatever device their users are using. Obviously, applications must provide content in a form that is appropriate for the user's particular device – WML for WAP phones, VoiceXML for voice interaction via a voice browser, HTML for PCs, and so on.

However, solely targeting the application's output to devices is not sufficient in most cases. If device capabilities differ significantly, the entire interaction between the user and the Web application has to be tailored to the device's capabilities to provide a good user experience. A good example for this is access to a Web application from a PC versus access to the same Web application from a WAP phone. As the PC has a large screen, it is appropriate to present a substantial amount of information per screen, and it is possible to have many entry fields in a single form with extensive selections. A typical dialog between the PC user and the Web application consists of just a few screens. When the user accesses the same application from a WAP phone, only a small amount of information can be displayed on a single screen, and only a handful of entry fields may be contained in a form; both input and output have to be reduced to an absolute minimum. Wherever possible, applications should employ personalization to avoid unnecessary data input or at least provide good suggestions, e.g. using history-based profiles or estimated likelihood. A typical dialog between a WAP user and the Web application consists of more screens than the equivalent dialog with a PC user; at the same time, the amount of data that has to be entered by the user has to be minimized.

As a consequence, architectures for pervasive computing applications must not only allow for filtering of unnecessary information, and for output targeted to different devices, but must also be flexible enough to accommodate different flows of interaction depending on the user's device.

Another challenge that is posed by pervasive computing is increased scalability and performance requirements. Given the ever-increasing numbers of mobile phone owners, and the concurrent increasing number of mobile phones, the number of potential clients for a pervasive computing Web application is several factors larger than for classical Web applications. In addition, the frequency of users accessing the application from mobile phones will be higher than that of PC users, as the phone is always available. Thus, pervasive computing Web applications need to scale to larger numbers of users than classical PC-only Web applications. However, high scalability alone is not enough – as users typically access pervasive computing applications to 'look something up quickly' or 'just order something', they expect short response times, resulting in a requirement for high performance.

10.2 Scalability and availability

Given the ever-growing number of pervasive computing devices, scalability of pervasive computing applications is a very important issue. Large telecommunication companies expect millions of users to subscribe for some applications, for example.

Availability is of particular importance in the pervasive computing environment. Unlike PC users, most users of pervasive computing devices and applications will neither understand nor accept comments like 'server currently down for maintenance' – if a service is not available when they need it, they will assume that it does not work, and will stop using the application or switch to another service provider.

Both issues can be resolved by system topologies that employ parallelism and redundancy to guarantee scalability and availability. An example of such a topology is shown in Figure 10.1.

Figure 10.1

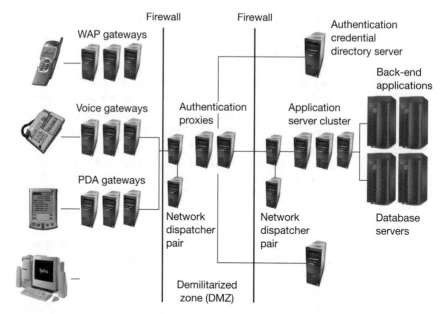

A scalable topology for pervasive computing Web applications

Scalability and availability can be achieved by running multiple instances of every component that might become a bottleneck. Typically, the gateways perform tasks that require significant computing power. WAP gateways, for example, may have to execute the WTLS protocol in the direction of the clients, and the SSL protocol in the direction of the servers, for many parallel sessions, requiring computation-intensive decryption and encryption of data. Voice gateways use voice-recognition engines and thus require even more computing power. A scalable system will use a cluster of gateways for each device type, to which additional machines can be added as required.

From the various gateways, a potentially large number of requests flow to the servers that host pervasive computing Web applications. Typically, a network dispatcher is used to route incoming requests to the appropriate servers, balancing the load between them. To support efficient handling of HTTPS, the dispatchers support a mode in which requests originating from a particular client are always sent to the same server to avoid repeating SSL handshakes. To assure high availability, pairs of network dispatchers can be used, in which one is active and a back-up monitors the heartbeat of the active dispatcher to take over if a failure occurs.

To allow for central authentication, authorization, and enforcement of access policies, authentication proxies are used, located in the demilitarized zone between two firewalls, so that all incoming requests can flow to application servers only via the authentication proxies. They check each incoming request to see whether the client from which it originates is already known, and whether it is allowed to access the desired target function of the Web application according to a centrally defined policy. To do so, it needs access to the credentials required for authentication and to the policies for authorization. If a request from a new client arrives, the authentication proxy performs client authentication before letting any request pass through to the application servers. An authentication proxy may consume significant computing power, e.g. when SSL server authentication has to be performed for a large number of sessions. Thus, a cluster of authentication proxies is required for larger systems.

Requests initiated by authenticated clients flow from the authentication proxies to the application servers behind the inner firewall. The application code and the presentation functions that make up the Web application front end is running on these servers. Here, the requests coming from the clients are received and processed. To implement a scalable Web application, a cluster of application servers is usually used to which additional machines can be added when the load increases.

Typically, the front end of a Web application interacts with a back end that hosts persistent data and/or legacy systems.

10.3 Development of pervasive computing Web applications

To implement Web applications, four major kinds of role are typically required in a development team: business logic designers, user interface designers, application programmers, and experts for existing legacy database and transaction systems.

Business logic designers define the functions to be performed and the application flow. User interface designers are responsible for application design, defining the look and feel of the Web application, designing user interaction, and guaranteeing good usability. Web designers work with technologies such as HTML and JSPs, mostly using high-level visual tools. Application developers are responsible for implementing the application logic and connectivity to database and transaction systems in the back end. Java developers work with technologies such as servlets, EJBs, LDAP, JDBC, etc.

In teams developing pervasive computing applications, an additional role is usually needed – the pervasive computing specialist, who knows about the capabilities of devices and the infrastructure required to support pervasive computing applications, such as WAP gateways, voice gateways and gateways for PDAs. These people are the experts in technologies such as WML and VoiceXML, which normally cannot be handled well by traditional Web designers.

10.4 Pervasive application architecture

As we pointed out in Chapter 9, the model–view–controller (MVC) pattern is a good choice when implementing Web applications. We presented the standard mapping of the pattern to servlets, JSPs, and EJBs, where the controller is implemented as a servlet, the model implemented as a set of EJBs, and the views as JSPs.

Pervasive computing applications, however, add an additional level of complexity. As devices are very different from each other, we cannot assume that one controller will fit all device classes. In the MVC pattern, the controller encapsulates the dialog flow of an application. This flow will be different for different classes of devices, such as WAP phones, voice-only phones, PCs, or PDAs. Thus, we need different controllers for different classes of devices. To support multiple controllers, we restrict the servlet's role to that of a simple dispatcher that invokes the appropriate controller depending on the type of device being used.

To avoid duplication of code for invocation of model functions between controllers, we employ the command pattern.[1] In our case, a command is a bean with input and output properties. An invoker of a command sets the input properties for the command and then executes the command. After the command has been executed, the result can be obtained by getting the command's output properties. Instead of invoking model functions directly, the controllers create and execute commands that encapsulate the code for model invocation.

To invoke a view JSP, the controller puts the executed command into the request object or the session object associated with the request depending on the desired lifetime. As commands are beans, their output properties can easily be accessed and displayed within JSP, as shown in Figure 10.2.

10.4.1 Securing pervasive computing applications

Like traditional Web applications, Web applications supporting pervasive devices have to be secured by appropriate encryption, authentication, and authorization mechanisms. The secure pervasive access architecture presented here is designed to process client requests on the application server in a secure and efficient way. It addresses user identification, authentication, and authorization of invocation of application logic depending on configurable security policies. Figure 10.3 shows an example in which the a user accesses a function of a particular Web application from a WAP phone.

All incoming requests originate from the device connectivity infrastructure. This infrastructure may include different kinds of gateway that convert device-specific requests to a canonical form, i.e. HTTP requests that may carry information about the device type, the desired language,

Figure 10.2

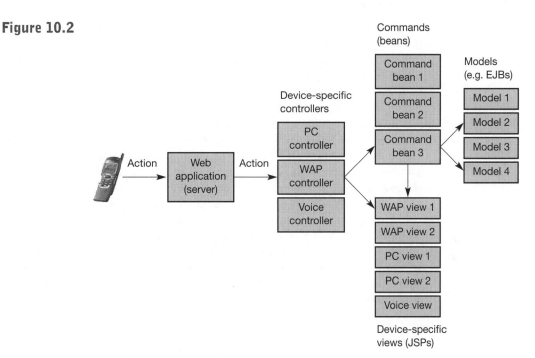

MVC pattern applied to pervasive computing applications

and the desired reply content type, e.g. HTML, WML, or VoiceXML. Examples of gateways in the device connectivity layer are voice gateways with remote VoiceXML-browsers, WAP gateways, and gateways for connecting PDAs. An important function that the device connectivity layer must provide is support of session cookies to allow the application server to associate a session with the device.

The secure access component is the only system component allowed to invoke application functions. It checks all incoming requests and calls application functions according to security policies stored in a database or directory. A particular security state – part of the session state – is reached by authentication of the client using user-ID and password, public-key client authentication, or authentication with a smart card, for example. If the requirements for permissions defined in the security policy are met by the current security state of a request's session, then the secure access layer invokes the requested application function, e.g. a function that accesses a database and returns a bean. Otherwise, the secure access component can redirect the user to the appropriate authentication page. Typically, the secure access component will be implemented as an authentication proxy within a demilitarized zone as shown earlier.

Finally, the output generated by the application logic is delivered back to the user in a form appropriate for the device he or she is using. In the example shown in Figure 10.3, the information to be displayed is prepared by the application logic and passed to the content-delivery module encapsulated in beans. The content-delivery module then extracts the relevant part of the information from the bean and renders it into content that depends on the device type and desired reply content type, for example by calling appropriate JSPs.[2]

The content-delivery module delivers the content generated in the previous step via the device connectivity infrastructure that converts canonical responses (HTTP responses) to device-specific responses, using appropriate gateways. For example, if a user accesses the system via a telephone, the voice gateway receives the HTTP response with VoiceXML content and leads an appropriate 'conversation' with the user, finally resulting in a new request being sent to the server.

The functionality described above can be implemented using a proxy approach or by using an appropriate framework on the application server. In the first case, the proxy will enforce user authentication and authorization checking for protected resources. A servlet base class would have this responsibility in the second case.

Figure 10.3

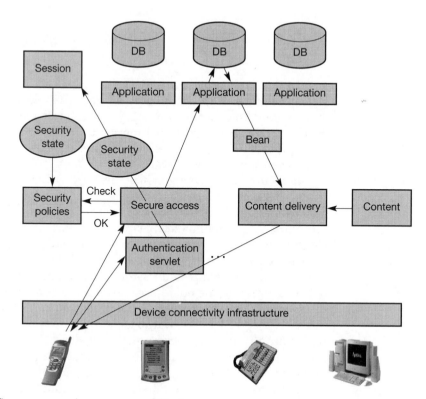

Secure pervasive access architecture

Securing pervasive applications using an authentication proxy

To secure pervasive computing applications, an authentication proxy can be used in combination with a security policy engine. Instead of directly authenticating to Web applications, pervasive computing devices authenticate to the central authentication proxy that enforces a central security policy. Devices may connect directly to the authentication proxy or via an appropriate gateway, depending on the supported protocols. The advantage of this approach is that access rights of users can be managed efficiently at a central place instead of having per-application access policies on individual application servers. The example given in Figure 10.4 shows the flow of messages to authenticate a WAP phone. It depicts the interaction of components the first time the phone sends a request to an application that is secured by the authentication proxy (to keep the picture simple, we have omitted the gateways).

Upon selection of an application function by the user, the device sends a request to the application that is intercepted by the proxy (1). The proxy checks whether a session already exists for the device (2). As this is not the case for the first request, the proxy invokes the appropriate authentication module for the particular device, e.g. the module for form-based authentication using WML forms for the WAP phone (3). The authentication module performs authentication of the user, e.g. for form-based authentication, the module sends a form to the user's device that lets the user

Figure 10.4

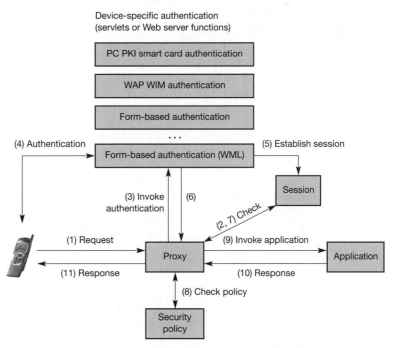

Form-based authentication with a WAP phone (first request)

enter a user ID and password, and then checks them against a credential database to authenticate the user (4). As a result of successful user authentication, a session is established for the user's device (5), and the authentication module returns control to the proxy (6). The proxy checks for a session for the user's device again; this time, a session is present that indicates that the user has been authenticated (7). The proxy gets the user's identity from the session information and uses it to check whether the particular user may invoke the requested action of the application (8). If the security policy allows the access, the proxy invokes the application function (9). The application function returns the result in the response to the proxy (10), which forwards the response to the user's device (11).

For all subsequent requests, processing is much simpler (Figure 10.5). After accessing to the application, the user selects another function. The user's device sends a new request to the application that is intercepted by the proxy (1). The proxy checks whether a session for the device exists, and whether the user has been authenticated (2). As the user has already authenticated himself to the proxy, the check is positive. The proxy gets the user's identity from the session information and uses it to check whether the particular user may invoke the requested action of the application (3). If the security policy allows the access, the proxy invokes the application function (4). The application function returns the result in the response to the proxy (5), which forwards the response to the user's device (6).

Using an authentication proxy has the advantage that the authentication function can be performed in a demilitarized zone by placing a firewall before and after the authentication proxy. Through the outer firewall, requests from external clients can only flow to the proxy. The inner firewall allows only pass requests to application servers that come from the proxy. As a result, all requests targeted to application servers have to

Figure 10.5

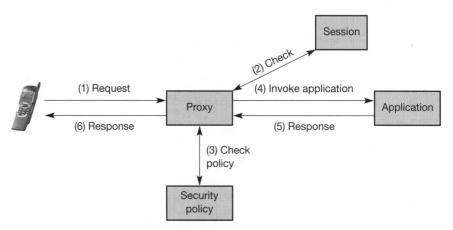

Form-based authentication with a WAP phone (subsequent requests)

pass through the authentication proxy so that it can enforce authentication and authorization of users, and only requests originating from authenticated and authorized users can reach protected Web applications.

Securing pervasive applications using a framework

While the proxy-based approach presented is the most appropriate solution for protecting company websites, a simpler solution can be useful for less demanding scenarios, or to quickly set up pilots. In this section, we outline a simple example of a framework to support secure pervasive applications based on the architecture presented above on a single machine. Note that this framework is intended only for demonstration of the basic concepts, not for use in real solutions. We will use it as a basis for the example application presented in Chapters 11–15.

We assume that the applications to be secured follow either the MVC pattern or the simple JSP-invokes-application-logic pattern. In the first case, a servlet invokes a device-specific controller, which in turn invokes the appropriate methods of the application logic and finally the suitable presentation JSP as a view. The JSP that is invoked depends on the results obtained from the application logic. In the second case, the JSP container invokes a JSP, which may invoke application logic and render the results.

Figure 10.6 shows how a Web application based on the MVC pattern can be secured. To allow for device-dependent authentication protocols, authentication servlets are needed. Before accessing sensitive application functions, the user must authenticate against an authentication servlet, which results in a security state object being added to the session information for that user. Access to sensitive functions of an application is only possible via secure servlets. These servlets obtain the security state for the user, and check whether the particular user may use the desired function under the current security state according to the security policy defined for the particular application. Only if the security policy explicitly allows the operation does the secure servlet invoke the appropriate controller to process the request further.

Figure 10.7 shows how JSP-based applications can be secured in a similar manner. Unlike in the MVC pattern, there is no secure servlet through which all requests have to pass. Instead, each JSP must become a secure servlet. This can be achieved by deriving from a base class that checks whether the user may access the particular JSP under the current security state according to the security policy.

10.4.2 Overview of classes

To allow the securing of applications as described above, the framework provides appropriate base classes for secure servlets, as well as classes that represent security states and security policies. It also defines contracts between the base classes and authentication servlets to specify how these components cooperate.

Figure 10.6

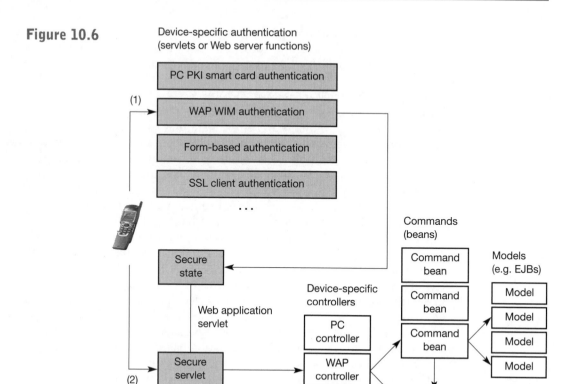

Securing MVC applications

SecureServlet

SecureServlet (**Example 10.1**) inherits from HttpServlet,[2] overwriting the service method. Before invoking the service method of HttpServlet, the service method of SecureServlet uses the SecurityPolicy class (see below) to perform a security check in order to find out whether the user who initiated the current request has the permission to execute the desired function from the device he or she currently uses and with the authentication method he or she used previously to authenticate. The result may be that the user has not yet logged in, that the user has logged in but does not have proper authorization, or that everything is OK. The SecureServlet invokes an appropriate JSP when the login is missing or the user is not authorized for the desired function.

Figure 10.7

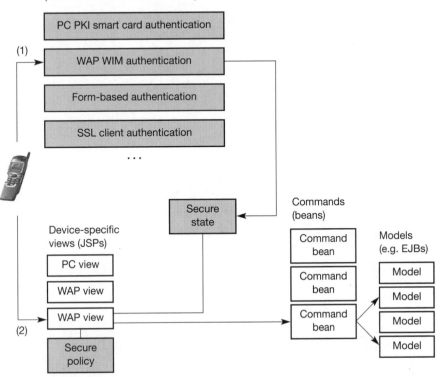

Device-specific authentication
(servlets or Web server functions)

Securing JSP applications

| Example 10.1 | **SecureServlet** |

```
package sample.shop.security;

import javax.servlet.*;
import javax.servlet.http.*;
import java.io.PrintWriter;
import java.io.IOException;
import java.util.Enumeration;

import sample.shop.View;
import sample.shop.auth.AuthStateBean;


/**
 * SecureServlet is the base class for secure multi-mode
   servlets.
```

▶

continued

```
*/
public abstract class SecureServlet extends HttpServlet {
  public final static String ACTION = "Action";

  public void service(HttpServletRequest req,
    HttpServletResponse rsp)
  throws ServletException, IOException {
    if (SecurityPolicy.checkAuthorization (getRole(req),
        getAuthentication(req), getDeviceType(req),
      getApplication(), getAction(req))) {
    super.service(req, rsp);
    } else {
      View.callJSP(getServletContext(),
          "/PVCShop/Security/AccessDenied.jsp", req, rsp);
    }
  }

  public final static String getAction(HttpServletRequest
    req) { return req.getParameter(ACTION);
  }

  public final static String
    getAuthentication(HttpServletRequest req) {
    … get authentication state, e.g. from session …
  }

  public final static String getDeviceType(HttpServlet
    Request req) { … map request's user-agent to device
    type …
  }

  public final static String getRole(HttpServletRequest
    req) {
    … get user's role from request …

  public abstract String getApplication();
}
```

Apart from the `service` method that checks user authorization, the class `SecureServlet` implements four final methods that provide the information needed by the `SecurityPolicy` as a basis for the decision. The `getAction` method extracts the desired action from the incoming request. The `getAuthentication` method obtains the mode of authentication that has been used by the client from which the given request originates. The `getDeviceType` method determines the client's device type from the `user-agent` field in the given request. The `getRole` method determines the user's current role, e.g. by accessing session information.

Finally, the `SecureServlet` class declares an abstract method named `getApplication`. This method must be defined by all servlets that inherit from `SecureServlet` to indicate which application they belong to.

SecureJSP

`SecureJSP` (Example 10.2) inherits from `SecureServlet`. It overwrites the `service` method to intercept all incoming requests, and invokes the `checkAuthorization` method of the `SecurityPolicy` to check whether it may be displayed. If the policy allows the JSP to be displayed, the `service` method calls the `jspService_` method to render the page. As JSPs are usually used only as views, expecting an action parameter in the requests to the secured JSPs is not appropriate. To interoperate with the application/action access pattern supported by the `SecurityPolicy` class anyway, the class `SecureJSP` declares an abstract method named `getAction`, which must be defined by all JSPs derived from this class to specify the action to which displaying the JSP should be mapped.

Example 10.2	**Secure JSP**

```
package sample.shop.security;

import javax.servlet.*;
import javax.servlet.http.*;
import javax.servlet.jsp.*;
import java.io.*;

import sample.shop.View;

/**
 * Base class for secure JSPs.
 */
public abstract class SecureJSP extends SecureServlet
implements HttpJspPage {
  private ServletConfig servletConfig_ = null;

  final public void init(ServletConfig config) throws
    ServletException {
    servletConfig_ = config;
    jspInit();
```

▶

continued

```
      }

final public void service(HttpServletRequest req,
  HttpServletResponse rsp) throws ServletException,
    IOException {
  if (SecurityPolicy.checkAuthorization(getRole(req),
    getAuthentication(req), getDeviceType(req),
    getApplication(), getAction())) {
      _jspService(req, rsp);
    } else {
      View.callJSP(getServletContext(),
        "/PVCShop/Security/AccessDenied.jsp", req, rsp);
    }
  }

protected abstract String getAction();

final public void destroy() {
  jspDestroy();
}

// other methods that JSPs must implement

public void jspInit() {;}

final public ServletConfig getServletConfig() {
  return servletConfig_;
}

public abstract void _jspService(HttpServletRequest req,
  HttpServletResponse rsp)
throws ServletException, IOException;

public void jspDestroy() {;}
}
```

The SecureJSP class provides default implementations for the init and destroy methods so that JSPs can easily be derived from this class just by adding one line with an extends statement at the head of the JSP source file. For the abstract methods prefixed with jsp, the JSP compiler of the application server will generate the appropriate implementations.

Authentication servlets

Our example framework does not provide a base class for authentication servlets, as they can be very different. For example, authentication servlets may be provided for authentication mechanisms using challenge–response methods, smart cards, user identification and password, one-time passwords, etc. However, we define a contract for authentication servlets that requires that they create a SecurityState object and add it to the user's session after successful authentication for use by the framework. In the SecurityState, authentication servlets have to indicate the authentication mechanism used. We present an example of an authentication servlet in Chapter 11.

SecurityState

SecurityState objects (Example 10.3) encapsulate the security state of a session, including information such as the user identification of the user who initiated the session, the authentication method used to log on, and potentially error codes for failed tries. The authentication method attribute of a SecurityState object can have values indicating no authentication, or authentication through user identification and password, smart card, or other means.

Example 10.3	**SecurityState**

```
package sample.shop.auth;

/**
 * This class encapsulates the security state of a
   session.
 */
public class SecurityState {
   public final static int AUT_NONE = 0;
   public final static int AUT_USERID_PASSWORD = 1;
   public final static int AUT_SMART_CARD = 3;
   ...

   public final static int ERR_NONE = 0;
   public final static int ERR_UNKNOWN_USER = 1;
   public final static int ERR_WRONG_CREDENTIAL = 2;

   protected String userID_ = null;

   protected int authState_ = AUT_NONE;
   protected int errorCode_ = ERR_NONE;
```

▶

continued

```
public int     getAuthenticationState() { return
authState_; }
 public int     getErrorCode() { return errorCode_; }
 public String getUserID() { return userID_; }
 public void setAuthenticationState(int value) {
   authState_ = value; }

 public void setErrorCode(int value) { errorCode_ =
   value; }

 public void setUserID(String value) { userID_ = value; }
 }
```

SecurityPolicy

The SecurityPolicy (**Example 10.4**) class encapsulates security policies
for Web applications. It accesses a database that holds authorization
information that determines which roles, authentication modes, and
device types allow access to certain actions of protected Web applications.
The checkAuthorization method takes the user's current role and
authentication mode, as well as the type of device used and the desired
application/action pair, as parameters. It uses a policy database to determine whether the given combination of parameters allows further
processing. If it does, it returns true, otherwise it returns false.

As the SecurityPolicy class consists mainly of a query to find out
whether there is an entry allowing the given combination of parameters
in the policy database, the implementation of the SecurityPolicy class
depends entirely on the database access layer used.

Example 10.4   **SecurityPolicy**

```
package sample.shop.security;

... includes for database access ...

/**
 * SecurityPolicy encapsulates access to the security
policy database.
 */
public class SecurityPolicy {

   ... code to initialize database access ...
```

continued

```
public static boolean checkAuthorization(String role,
    String authentication,
    String deviceType,
    String application,
    String action) {
... Access policy database to check whether a user in
    the given role using the given device type is
    allowed to access the given action of the given
    application. If yes return true, false otherwise ...
}
}
```

10.4.3 Use of the framework

To implement a pervasive application based on the framework presented above, the application developer must implement an application servlet, the application logic, and JSPs to be invoked by the application servlet, and must define a security policy for the application. Appropriate authentication servlets are also required.

All application servlets to be secured must inherit from the class SecureServlet and should not overwrite the service method. Whenever an instance of a servlet derived from SecureServlet receives a request, the service method of the SecureServlet base class is invoked and uses the SecurityPolicy to check authorization of the user. If this check fails, it returns an error. If the authorization check succeeds, the request is processed further by invocation of the service method of SecureServlet's super class HttpServlet, which in turn dispatches the request to the doGet or doPost method, depending on the HTTP method specified in the request.

To use a custom authentication scheme, the application developer has to implement an authentication servlet. If the authentication protocol between the client and the authentication servlet has been executed successfully, the authentication servlet must put a SecurityState object into the session to indicate this fact to application servlets derived from SecureServlet, which may be invoked later within the same session. The interaction between an authentication servlet and secured application servlets accessing the security state established by the authentication servlet is shown in Figure 10.8.

Figure 10.9 gives an example that illustrates how the framework functions. We assume that user authentication has already been performed. The user accesses the server using a WAP phone to perform the ViewAccount action of the application HomeBanking. When clicking the appropriate link, the WAP phone issues a request that passes through a

Figure 10.8

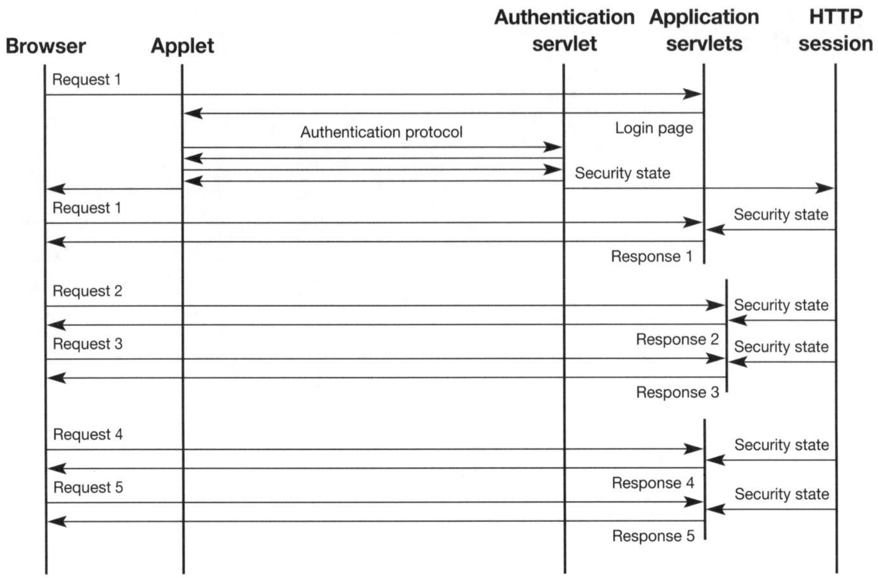

Interaction between the authentication servlet and application servlets via the session object

Figure 10.9

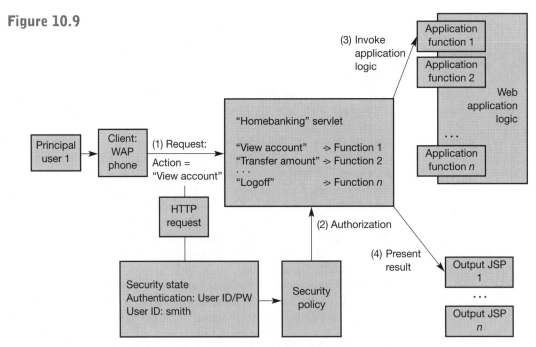

Components used by the secure pervasive access framework

WAP gateway and arrives at the server as an HTTP GET request. The `service` method of the target servlet's base class `SecureServlet` is invoked, gets the `SecurityState` object that has previously been put into the session associated with the request by an authentication servlet, and lets a `SecurityPolicy` class check whether the request should be handled or rejected. In the example, the security policy allows the request to be processed, thus the `service` method of `SecureServlet` invokes the service method of its base class `HttpServlet` to continue processing of the request. As a result, the `doGet` method of the home banking application servlet is invoked and maps the action `ViewAccount` specified in the request to a call to the appropriate methods of the home banking application logic. After obtaining the results from the application logic, the home banking application servlet's `doGet` method invokes the appropriate JSP to present the result to the user in a form suitable for the WAP phone.

10.5 Conclusion

In this chapter we have described an architecture for secure pervasive computing applications based on technologies such as servlets, EJBs, JSPs, and MVC and command patterns. We have presented a simple example framework based on this architecture that illustrates the basic principles. In the following chapters, we will present an example of a pervasive computing application that builds on the basis that we laid here, integrating into the example framework presented above.

References

1. Gamma, E., Helm, R., Johnson, R. and Vlissides, J. (1995) *Design Patterns*. Reading, MA: Addison-Wesley.

2. Sun Microsystems (1999) 'Java Servlet Specification 2.2'.

3. Sun Microsystems, (1999) 'Java Server Pages Specification 1.1.'

11 Example application

In this chapter, we present an example of an application that will be used to show how Java applications that adhere to the architecture presented in Chapter 10 can be extended to support different kinds of device. As an example that is both simple and instructive, we chose a shopping application, including registration, login, a main menu, self-care, purchasing goods, and purchase history. The application is designed for an imaginary Italian restaurant named Uncle Enzo's, which sells via the Internet. In subsequent chapters, we will show how this application can be enabled for access from a PC using smart-card authentication, from WAP phones, from PDAs, and from a voice-only phone via a voice gateway.

11.1 Introduction

In order to demonstrate the technologies presented in the first part of this book, we have invented a scenario for our example application. An imaginary restaurant called Uncle Enzo's specializes in Italian food. Because it is located in a business area, and already has many business customers, it wants to improve the ordering process for the customers.

The first step is to become an e-business and make the menu available for ordering via the Internet, so that people can order pizzas and drinks for take-away or delivery using the PCs in their homes or offices. To improve the payment process in the next step, support for smart cards is added to the application. Customers owning a payment card can now order online and pay securely at the same time, speeding up the processing further.

The availability of smart phones with wireless Internet access demands the next step. Here, the Web application has to be enhanced to handle the differing device capabilities of smart phones. Customers benefit from personalized offerings that allow them to select from their favourites instead of having to browse through the entire menu with a small device.

Including PDAs into the set of client devices further extends the number of potential users of the application. Support for online and offline operation is added in this step. Customers now have the choice between several ways to order the favourite pizza at any time and from any place.

Finally, the application is extended to include ordering over the phone. Instead of handling orders through human operators in a call center, voice recognition and text-to-speech technologies are used to automate the process. Customers can now order from any phone and do not need to have access to a browser any more. Figure 11.1 gives an overview of the final set of devices that can be used to access Uncle Enzo's e-business.

11.2 User interface overview

The user interface of Uncle Enzo's website needs to let new users register and registered users to log in and make purchases. Figure 11.2 gives an overview of the shop's user interface:

- *Registration* allows new users to register by providing their name, address, and payment information. Unlike other functions of the application, registration is only possible from the PC via an SSL connection to protect the consumer's data.
- *The login screen* lets the user authenticate themselves using a device-dependent authentication mechanism. In each case, the user has to provide either user identification and password or a smart card for identification and authentication.
- *The menu* allows the consumer to start shopping, review previous purchases, or to logoff.

Figure 11.1

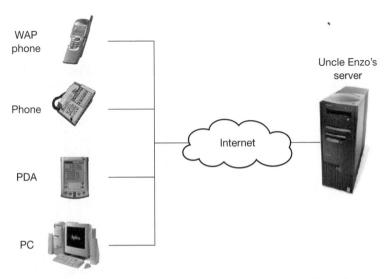

Overview of the devices that can be used to access Uncle Enzo's

Figure 11.2

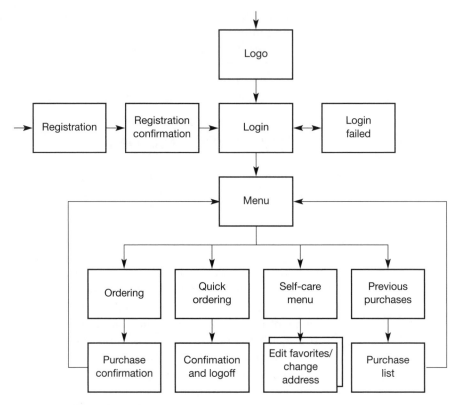

User interface of Uncle Enzo's

- The *ordering* functions let the consumer select the goods he or she wants to buy via a device-dependent user interface. After submitting the selection, the shop application displays a confirmation that it obtained the order and will deliver the goods.

- A function to *review former purchases* displays all the purchases the user has made so far in a device-dependent way. For consumers accessing the shop via a PC, all details of all purchases are displayed at the same time, while for smaller devices, only a limited set of information is displayed at once.

- The *self-care* functionality allows customers to create a personal list of favorites that are used to create a shortlist for quick ordering via WAP as changing the delivery address. As this functionality does not demonstrate concepts or techniques beyond those already demonstrated by other components, we will not describe this part of the system in the remainder of the book.

■ The function to *log off* allows the consumer to end a session with the shop application. After logging off, a new login is required to regain access to the shop.

11.3 Architecture

To implement the shop application, we follow the design patterns presented in Chapter 9. There is one servlet for each group of functions: registration, login, and shopping. As authentication using a smart card and authentication using user identification and password are very different, we use two different servlets to implement these functions. This also allows for other authentication servlets for other authentication modes to be added later.

As we pointed out in Chapter 9, the dialog flows for a particular task may differ, depending on the user's device. Registration can be carried out only from the PC, so we need only one controller for registration. Login must be supported for PCs with smart card, WAP, voice, and PDAs. While the login dialog for WAP, voice access, and PDA is identical, the login dialog for a PC with a smart card, is somewhat different. Therefore, we use one controller for login from the PC using a smart card, and one controller for login from the other devices using user identification and password. The shopping function is more complex than login, and must be optimized for each particular device. Therefore, we decided to use four separate controllers for the shopping function: one for PCs, one for WAP phones, one for voice, and one for PDAs (Figure 11.3).

To encapsulate the application logic, we use the command pattern. For each task, we define a command that can be parameterized using the set methods for the input properties and executed by controllers. After the command has been executed, it can be passed to a JSP to display the result properties. For the shop application, we need commands for registering a new consumer, logging in (using a smart card or user identification and password), listing the items available in the shop, creating a new purchase record, and displaying the last purchase records.

The data that we need to make persistent are registered consumers, available items, and purchases made by consumers. There are many approaches to access persistent data from Java, but one of the most convenient for programmers is object-to-relational database mapping. After defining the types of persistent objects that are needed, and their associations, a tool can be used to generate the Java code for the persistent objects, the database schema to be used to store data for these objects, and the code that connects the Java objects with the database. We will not discuss this topic further, because it is tool specific. The abstraction introduced by employing the command pattern allows for use of any persistence layer without impact on controllers and JSPs.

Figure 11.3

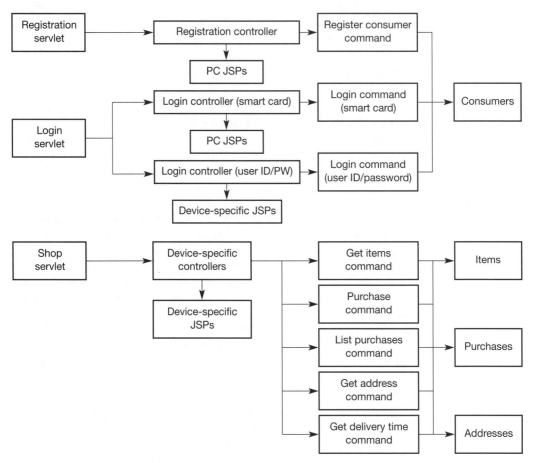

The shop's components

11.4 Implementation

In this section, we give an overview of the implementation of the example application. We present the database schema that the application uses to store data on the server, and the individual components of the application, including servlets, controllers, commands, and JSPs.

11.4.1 Database schema

We designed a simple database schema to manage the product data, user information, and order details for the example application. All products have a unique identification code and are sorted into categories. The relevant category of a product is referenced by a category identification number. Example 11.1 shows an excerpt of the database script used to generate the tables and the information they contain.

Example 11.1   **Database script for the product tables**

```
CREATE TABLE Products (
  itemID            INTEGER NOT NULL PRIMARY KEY,
  categoryID        INTEGER NOT NULL,
  name              VARCHAR(30) NOT NULL,
  description       VARCHAR(90),
  price             INTEGER NOT NULL

  FOREIGN KEY (categoryID) REFERENCES Category
)

CREATE TABLE Category (
  categoryID        INTEGER NOT NULL PRIMARY KEY,
  name              VARCHAR(30) NOT NULL
)
```

User information is stored in a separate table (Example 11.2). A unique number is used to identify each user. However, the users do not have to memorize that number but identify themselves by their chosen user identification and password.

Example 11.2   **Database script for user data**

```
CREATE TABLE UserIDPassword (
  password VARCHAR(30) NOT NULL,
  userID   VARCHAR(30) NOT NULL,

  FOREIGN KEY (consumerID) REFERENCES User
)
CREATE TABLE User (
  userID            VARCHAR(30) NOT NULL,
  lastName          VARCHAR(30) NOT NULL,
  city              VARCHAR(30) NOT NULL,
  country           VARCHAR(30) NOT NULL,
  state             VARCHAR(30),
  addressLine1      VARCHAR(30) NOT NULL,
  addressLine2      VARCHAR(30),
  firstName         VARCHAR(30) NOT NULL,
  zipCode           VARCHAR(30) NOT NULL
)
```

Orders are stored in two tables – one for the general order information (user, order time, delivery time, item count, status) and one for the order details (product item, quantity). The order detail entries are linked to the relevant order via a unique order-identification number. The product items are represented by their product identification code. Example 11.3 is an excerpt from a database script that illustrates the information stored in the order tables.

| **Example 11.3** | **Database script for the order tables** |

```
CREATE TABLE Orders (
  orderID          VARCHAR(40) NOT NULL PRIMARY KEY,
  userID           VARCHAR(20) NOT NULL,
  count            INT NOT NULL,
  status           INT NOT NULL,
  orderDate        DATE,
  orderTime        TIME,
  pickupDate       DATE,
  pickupTime       TIME,

  FOREIGN KEY (userID) REFERENCES Users
)

CREATE TABLE OrderItems (
  orderID   VARCHAR(40) NOT NULL PRIMARY KEY,
  userID    VARCHAR(20) NOT NULL,
  quantity  INT NOT NULL,
  code      CHAR (6) NOT NULL,

  FOREIGN KEY (code) REFERENCES Products,
  FOREIGN KEY (userID) REFERENCES Users
)
```

PDA users are used to performing most tasks offline, and connecting to the network only briefly to synchronize their input with applications in the Internet. When using the database schema with synchronization software such as IBM Mobile Connect, we have to work around a limitation imposed by the synchronization software. All tables stored on the client device must have a primary key column. Because we collect all orders from all users into a single database table on the server, we have to make sure that the specific column is a primary key on both the PDA and the server. For this reason, we use the unique user identification concatenated with the timestamp of the order for the order identification. The primary key in the order items table is the same order identification concatenated with a sequence number. The order items belonging to a specific order can then be found by using the LIKE function in the SQL query statement.

11.4.2 Servlets

In the following sections, we describe the registration servlet, authentication servlets, and shop servlets that are part of the sample application, including the most important fragments of their source code. Before explaining the servlets, we have to introduce a class that allows servlets to determine the devices type from a given request.

Example 11.4 | **Device type mapper**

```
import javax.servlet.http.*;

/**
 * DeviceTypeMapper returns the device type of the client
     for a given request.
 */
public class DeviceTypeMapper {
  public final static int UNKNOWN = 0;
  public final static int PC = 1;
  public final static int WAP_PHONE = 2;
  public final static int VOICE_PHONE = 3;
  public final static int PDA = 4;

  public final static int getDeviceType(HttpServletRequest
   req) {
  String userAgent = req.getHeader("user-agent");

  … return device type for given user agent …
  }
}
```

The device type returned by the getDeviceType method (Example 11.4) is used by the servlets described below to invoke the appropriate controllers for particular client devices.

Shop registration servlet

The shop registration (Example 11.5) servlet only supports registration of users using a PC. For each incoming HTTP request, it checks whether the user agent is a Web browser, and then forwards the request to the controller named `RegistrationControllerPC` if this is the case. For all other device types, it sends back an appropriate HTTP error message.

Example 11.5 | **Shop registration servlet**

```java
import javax.servlet.*;
import javax.servlet.http.*;
import java.io.PrintWriter;
import java.io.IOException;

import sample.shop.Controller;
import sample.shop.beans.ErrorBean;
import sample.shop.DeviceTypeMapper;

/**
 * RegistrationServlet allows new consumers to register
with the shop.
 */
public class RegistrationServlet extends HttpServlet {

  public void doGet(HttpServletRequest req,
    HttpServletResponse rsp)
  throws ServletException, IOException {
  doPost(req, rsp);
  }

  public void doPost(HttpServletRequest req,
    HttpServletResponse rsp)
  throws ServletException, IOException {
    switch (DeviceTypeMapper.getDeviceType(req)) {
    case DeviceTypeMapper.PC:
    RegistrationControllerPC.doProcess(
      getServlet Context(), req, rsp);break;
      case DeviceTypeMapper.WAP_PHONE:
    rsp.sendError(501,
   "Registration not supported for WAP");
    break;
    case DeviceTypeMapper.PDA:
    rsp.sendError(501,
   "Registration not supported for PDAs");
    break;
    case DeviceTypeMapper.VOICE_PHONE:
    rsp.sendError(501,
   "Registration not supported for Voice Phones");
```

▶

continued

```
      break;
      default:
      rsp.sendError(501, "Unknown Device Type");
      break;
    }
  }
}
```

Login servlet

We provide a login servlet (Example 11.6) that supports smart-card-based user authentication from a PC, as well as user authentication using user identification and password from pervasive devices.

The LoginServlet can be used to authenticate users whose user agent is a WAP browser, VoiceXML browser, or PDA-based browser. When it receives a request, it determines the type of the device from which the request originated, and dispatches the request to the appropriate controller. If the request originates from a PC, it invokes the SmartCardLoginController. For WAP phones, PDAs, or voice-only phones, the servlet invokes the PasswordLoginController. For other, unknown devices, it returns the appropriate HTTP error code.

Example 11.6 **Login servlet**

```
import javax.servlet.*;
import javax.servlet.http.*;
import java.io.IOException;

  import sample.shop.DeviceTypeMapper;

/**
 * LoginServlet allows for login using a user ID and
password or a smart card.
 */
public class LoginServlet extends HttpServlet {

  public void doGet(HttpServletRequest req,
      HttpServletResponse rsp)
  throws ServletException, IOException {
      doPost(req, rsp);
  }

  public void doPost(HttpServletRequest req,
      HttpServletResponse rsp)
  throws ServletException, IOException {
```

continued

```
switch (DeviceTypeMapper.getDeviceType(req)) {
  case DeviceTypeMapper.PC :
    SmartCardAuthController.doProcess(
      getServletContext(), req, rsp);
    break;
  case DeviceTypeMapper.WAP_PHONE :
    PasswordLoginController.doProcess
      (getServletContext(), req, rsp);
    break;
  case DeviceTypeMapper.PDA :
    PasswordLoginController.doProcess
      (getServletContext(), req, rsp);
    break;
  case DeviceTypeMapper.VOICE_PHONE :
    PasswordLoginController.doProcess
      (getServletContext(), req, rsp);
    break;
  default :
    rsp.sendError(501, "Unknown Device Type");
    break;
  }
 }
}
```

Shop servlet

The shop servlet (Example 11.7) allows consumers to purchase goods via WAP phones, voice-only phones, PDAs, or PCs, and to review previous purchases from a PC and PDA. For each incoming HTTP request, the servlet checks the user agent header and forwards the request to the appropriate controller, i.e. ShopControllerPC for PC-based browsers, ShopControllerWAP for WAP phones, ShopControllerVoice for voice gateways, and ShopControllerPDA for PDAs.

The ShopServlet extends SecureServlet and is thus accessible only to authenticated users. As described in Chapter 10, SecureServlet overwrites the service method to intercept all requests targeted to servlets derived from it. As a result, ShopServlet only processes a request if the security policy allows execution of the action specified in the request of the servlet's application for the user's role via the user's device.

Example 11.7 Shop servlet

```java
package sample.shop.shop;

import javax.servlet.*;
import javax.servlet.http.*;
import java.io.IOException;

import sample.shop.security.SecureServlet;
import sample.shop.security.Role;
import sample.shop.DeviceTypeMapper;

/**
 * This servlet securely controls all access to the shop.
 */
public class ShopServlet extends SecureServlet {

 public void doGet(HttpServletRequest req,
  HttpServletResponse rsp)
 throws ServletException, IOException {
     doPost(req, rsp);
 }

 public void doPost(HttpServletRequest req,
  HttpServletResponse rsp)
 throws ServletException, IOException {
   switch (DeviceTypeMapper.getDeviceType(req)) {
     case DeviceTypeMapper.PC :
       ShopControllerPC.doProcess(getServletContext(),
       req, rsp);
       break;
     case DeviceTypeMapper.WAP_PHONE :
       ShopControllerWAP.doProcess(getServletContext(),
       req, rsp);
       break;
     case DeviceTypeMapper.PDA :
       ShopControllerPDA.doProcess(getServletContext(),
       req, rsp);
       break;
```

▶

continued

```
        case DeviceTypeMapper.VOICE_PHONE :
            ShopControllerVoice.doProcess(getServletContext(),
               req, rsp);
            break;
        default :
            rsp.sendError(501, "Unknown Device Type");
            break;
    }
  }


  public String getApplication() {
      return "PVCShop";
  }
}
```

11.4.3 Controllers

Controllers process requests by invoking application logic (e.g. via a command), and generate a response by invoking a view (e.g. a JSP) depending on the result returned by the application logic. As most of the controllers we use in this example are device specific, they are explained in detail in the chapters dedicated to the particular devices. In this chapter, we present only the RegistrationController, which allows registration via the PC, and the PasswordLoginController, which is used for multiple devices.

RegistrationController

The RegistrationController (Example 11.8) supports two actions. When invoked with the action GetRegistrationPage, it returns an HTML page with the registration form. When invoked with the actions RegisterNewConsumer, the controller parses obtains the values of the parameters FirstName, LastName, AddressLine1, AddressLine2, ZipCode, City, State, Country, UserID, and Password from the request, and creates an instance of RegisterConsumerCommand using these parameters. By invoking the execute method of the command, it creates a record for the new user in the shop's database.

PasswordLoginController

The PasswordLoginController (Example 11.9) is used by the LoginServlet to allow logon for WAP phones, PDAs, and voice-only phones via a voice gateway using user identification and password. Like all controllers in this example, the PasswordLoginController has a doProcess method that takes the servlet context of the calling servlet and a request/response pair as parameters. The servlet context is required for invocation of JSPs, while the request provides the input to be processed and the response receives the output.

Example 11.8   **RegistrationController**

```
package sample.shop.registration;

import javax.servlet.*;
import javax.servlet.http.*;
import java.io.PrintWriter;
import java.io.IOException;

import sample.shop.Controller;
import sample.shop.View;
import sample.shop.beans.ErrorBean;

/**
 * RegistrationController lets customers register with
the shop.
 */
public class RegistrationControllerPC extends Controller
{
  public final static String ACTION_REG_NEW_CONSUMER =
      "RegisterNewConsumer";
  public final static String ACTION_GET_REG_PAGE =
      "GetRegistrationPage";

  public final static String PARAM_FIRST_NAME =
      "FirstName";
  public final static String PARAM_LAST_NAME = "LastName";
  public final static String PARAM_ADDRESS_LINE_1 =
      "AddrLine1";
  public final static String PARAM_ADDRESS_LINE_2 =
      "AddrLine2";
  public final static String PARAM_ZIP_CODE = "ZipCode";
  public final static String PARAM_CITY = "City";
  public final static String PARAM_STATE = "State";
  public final static String PARAM_COUNTRY = "Country";
  public final static String PARAM_USER_ID = "UserID";
  public final static String PARAM_PASSWORD = "Password";

  public static void doProcess(ServletContext
    servletContext,
      HttpServletRequest req, HttpServletResponse rsp)
```

▶

continued

```
throws ServletException, IOException {
    String action = req.getParameter("Action");

    if (action.equals(ACTION_GET_REG_PAGE)) {
      View.callJSP(servletContext,
        "/PVCShop/Registration/NewConsumerForm.jsp",
        req, rsp);
    } else if (action.equals(ACTION_REG_NEW_CONSUMER)) {
      RegisterConsumerCommand command = new
      RegisterConsumerCommand();
      command.setFirstName(req.getParameter
        (PARAM_FIRST_NAME));
      command.setLastName(req.getParameter
        (PARAM_LAST_NAME));

      command.setAddressLine1(req.getParameter
        (PARAM_ADDRESS_LINE_1));
      command.setAddressLine2(req.getParameter
        (PARAM_ADDRESS_LINE_2));
      command.setCity(req.getParameter(PARAM_CITY));
      command.setZipCode(req.getParameter(PARAM_ZIP_
        CODE));
      command.setState(req.getParameter(PARAM_STATE));
      command.setCountry(req.getParameter(PARAM_
        COUNTRY));
      command.setUserID(req.getParameter(PARAM_USER_ID));
      command.setPassword(req.getParameter(PARAM_
        PASSWORD));
      boolean success = command.execute();
      if (success) {
        req.setAttribute("consumerBean", command);
        View.callJSP(servletContext,
    "/PVCShop/Registration/NewConsumerConf.jsp",
    req, rsp);
      } else {
        ErrorBean errorBean = new ErrorBean(1, "User ID
          already exists");
          req.setAttribute("ErrorBean", errorBean);
          View.callJSP(servletContext,
              "/PVCShop/Registration/Registration
                Failed.jsp", req, rsp);
          }
        }
    }
}
```

| Example 11.9 | **PasswordLoginController** |

```java
import javax.servlet.*;
import javax.servlet.http.*;
import java.io.PrintWriter;
import java.io.IOException;

import sample.shop.Controller;
import sample.shop.View;

/**
 * PasswordLoginController allows for login using user id
   and password.
 */
public class PasswordLoginController extends Controller {
  private final static String ACTION_GET_LOGON_PAGE =
    "GetLogonPage";
  private final static String ACTION_LOGON = "Logon";

  private final static String LOGON_SUCCESS_PAGE =
    "LogonSuccessPage";
  private final static String LOGON_FAILURE_PAGE =
    "LogonFailurePage";

  private final static String USER_ID = "UserID";
  private final static String PASSWORD = "Password";

  public static void doProcess(ServletContext
    servletContext,
                               HttpServletRequest req,
                               HttpServletResponse rsp)
  throws ServletException, IOException {
    // Get the command from the request.
    String action = req.getParameter("Action");

    if (action.equals(ACTION_GET_LOGON_PAGE)) {
      View.callJSP(servletContext,"/PVCShop/Login/
        LoginForm.jsp", req, rsp);
    } else if (action.equals(ACTION_LOGON)) {
      String userID = req.getParameter(USER_ID);
      String password = req.getParameter(PASSWORD);
```

▶

continued

```
SecurityState securityState = new SecurityState();
securityState.setUserID(userID);

PasswordLoginCommand command = new PasswordLogin
  Command();
command.setUserID(userID);
command.setPassword(password);
boolean success = command.execute();
if (success) {
  // Get session to which request belongs
  HttpSession session = req.getSession(true);
  securityState.setAuthenticationState(Security
    State.AUT_USERID_PASSWORD);
  session.putValue(SecurityState.AUTH_STATE_
    BEAN_ID, securityState);

  // Show the main menu after successful login.
  View.callJSP(servletContext, "/PVCShop/Menu/Main
    Menu.jsp", req, rsp);
} else {
  if (command.getErrorReason() == PasswordLogin
    Command.WRONG_CREDENTIAL){securityState.
    setErrorCode(SecurityState.ERR_WRONG_
    CREDENTIAL);
  } else if (command.getErrorReason()==Password
    LoginCommand.UNKNOWN_USER){securityState.
    setErrorCode(SecurityState.ERR_UNKNOWN_USER);
  }
}
  // Show the failure page if login fails.
  View.callJSP(servletContext,"/PVCShop/Login/
    LoginFailed.jsp", req, rsp);
  }
 }
}
```

The `PasswordLoginController` implements two actions – `GetLogonPage` and `Logon`. It expects the action to execute in a request parameter named `Action` (to keep the example short, we omitted the error handling here and at some later occasions).

If the action is `GetLogonPage`, the controller only invokes a view, which invokes a JSP that returns a login form with dedicated markup to the client. If the action is `Logon`, the controller gets user identification and password from the request, initializes an instance of `PasswordLoginCommand` using these data, and executes the command. If the command successfully verifies the given credentials, the controller establishes a security state within the session (see Chapter 10) to indicate that the user has been authenticated. If verification of the credentials fails, the controller determines the reason and invokes the appropriate JSPs to display it to the user.

11.4.4 Commands

As explained in Chapter 9, commands can encapsulate access to the models and act as result containers that can be passed to views. For this example, we implemented commands as beans that have input properties to provide parameters, an execute method, and output properties for obtaining result data. The controllers initialize command beans by setting the required input properties, call the execute method to let the command perform its function, and pass the command beans to the views, which extract and display the contained information. In this section we present the commands used by the example application.

RegisterConsumerCommand
This command allows a new consumer to register with the shop. Before executing the command, the invoking controller must set the input properties. When the command is executed, it generates a new consumer record in the database and fills it with its properties. After execution of the `RegisterConsumerCommand` (Example 11.10), the data that have been written successfully to the database can be retrieved to generate a confirmation.

Login commands
As logging in using a smartcard or user ID and password are different, we need separate login commands. The command for smart-card login is only used for PC clients with a smart card reader, so we will omit it here and present it in Chapter 12. The login command for authentication by user ID and password takes the user identification and the password provided by a consumer as input parameters (Example 11.11).

Example 11.10 **RegisterConsumerCommand**

```
… includes for persistence layer …

/**
 * This command registers a consumer.
 */
public class RegisterConsumerCommand {

… references to objects related to persistence layer …

// Input and output properties
private String firstName_ = null;
private String lastName_ = null;
private String city_ = null;
private String country_ = null;
private String password_ = null;
private String userID_ = null;
private String state_ = null;
private String zipCode_ = null;
private String addressLine1_ = null;
private String addressLine2_ = null;

// Methods to set input proerties
public void setAddressLine1(String value) {
  addressLine1_ = value; }
public void setAddressLine2(String value) {
  addressLine2_ = value; }
public void setCity(String value) { city_ = value; }
public void setCountry(String value) { country_ = value;
  }
public void setFirstName(String value) { firstName_ =
  value; }
public void setLastName(String value) { lastName_ =
  value; }
public void setState(String value) { state_ = value; }
public void setZipCode(String value) { zipCode_ = value;
  }
public void setUserID(String value) { userID_ = value; }
public void setPassword(String value) { password_ =
  value; }

// Execute method
public boolean execute() {
```

▶

continued

```
... code to add user to user database table, depends on
persistence layer ...
 }

// Methods to get output properties
 public String getAddressLine1() { return addressLine1_;
}
 public String getAddressLine2() { return addressLine2_;
}
 public String getCity() { return city_; }
 public String getCountry()      { return country_; }
 public String getFirstName() { return firstName_; }
 public String getLastName() { return lastName_; }
 public String getState() { return state_; }
 public String getZipCode() { return zipCode_; }
 public String getUserID() { return userID_; }
 public String getPassword() { return password_; }
}
```

Example 11.11 **User ID/password login command**

```
package sample.shop.auth;

... imports specific for persistence layer ...

/**
 * This command authenticates a user by checking his user
ID and password.
 */
public class PasswordLoginCommand {
 // Input properties
 protected String userID_ = null;
 protected String password_ = null;

 // Output properties
 protected String errorReason_ = null;

 public final static String UNKNOWN_USER = "Unknown
   User";
 public final static String WRONG_CREDENTIAL = "Wrong
   Password";
```

▶

```
continued    // Methods to set input properties
             public void setPassword(String value) { password_ =
                value; }
             public void setUserID(String value) { userID_ = value; }

             // Method to execute command
             public boolean execute() throws ServletException {
                boolean success = false;

                ... checking of user id and password using persistence
                     layer ...
                ... returns true if user id and password are correct
                     false otherwise ...
                ... sets error reason appropriately if the check fails ...
                }

             // Method to get output property
             public String getErrorReason() {
             return errorReason_;
             }
             }
```

Get items command

This command allows the list of items that are available for purchase in the shop to be brought up. Its input properties allow the specification of characteristics of a subset of items to be retrieved. After executing the command, its indexed output properties provide item information for the specified subset of items available in the shop. As this command does not introduce new concepts, we will omit the source code here.

Order command

This command creates a new order record and associated order item records in the database, using the data provided by the application through the input properties. After execution, the data written to the database are available in the output properties and can be used to generate a confirmation. We will not include the source code of this command here, as it does not introduce any new concepts.

Get purchases command

This command collects all previous purchases for a consumer specified by setting the appropriate input property from the database. If desired, a maximum number of purchases to obtain can be specified in addition. After execution of the GetPurchases command, the consumer's purchases are accessible through the command's output properties. As this command does not introduce any new concepts, we will not include the source code here.

Get address command

This command gets the address information for a particular customer. It takes the user identification number of the customer as an input property. After execution of the command, the user's address information, including street, city, postal/zip code, state, and country, is available through the output properties.

11.4.5 Views

As the views, i.e. the JSPs, used in the shop application are device specific, we present specific JSPs in the chapters dedicated to particular devices. At this point, we describe the mechanism to invoke JSPs depending on user agent information that is contained in each HTTP request (see Chapter 5) and the JSPs for user registration, which is required no matter what device a customer uses to access the ordering functionality of the application. The JSPs for logon and purchasing goods are discussed in subsequent chapters.

User-agent-dependent invocation of Java Server Pages

HTTP defines various header fields that allow transmission of meta information within requests. The fields `accept` and `user-agent` can be used to determine JSPs suited to be invoked for the particular user agent. Example 11.1 shows a method that takes an `HttpServletRequest` object as a parameter and returns the markup type that should be used to answer the request.

Example 11.12 **User-agent-dependent display of views**

```
import javax.servlet.*;
import javax.servlet.jsp.*;
import javax.servlet.http.*;
import java.io.IOException;
public class View {
  public final static String
     getMarkUpType(HttpServletRequest req) {
     String userAgent = req.getHeader("user-agent").trim();

     … Read the property file for mapping user-agents to
        MIME types …
```

▶

continued

```
    // Try direct lookup
    String type = deviceTypes.getProperty(userAgent);
    if (type != null) {
        return type;
    }
    // Try to find the best match using the known properties
      as prefix
    Enumeration names = deviceTypes.propertyNames();
    while (names.hasMoreElements()) {
        String name = (String) names.nextElement();
        if (userAgent.startsWith(name)) {
        return deviceTypes.getProperty(name);
        }
    }
}
```

For this example, we assume that a property file exists that specifies the mapping of user-agent information to markup types to be used for particular user agents. Such a property file might look like that shown in Example 11.13.

Example 11.13 **Mapping of user agents to markup types**

```
# Property File mapping user-agents to markup types
 UP.=WML
Nokia=WML
Wapalizer=WML
SIE-IC35=WML
SIE-S35=WML
R380=WML
Mozilla=HTML
iSiloWeb/1.18\ Windows/32=HTML_PDA
 ...
```

Once we have a method that can determine the markup type to be used for a given request, we can write a method that calls JSPs depending on a user's device, as shown in Example 11.14. Although it results in a duality to a certain extent – the controllers that invoke JSPs via this method may already be device-dependent – device dependent JSP invocation is useful using one controller for devices that share the same flow but require views optimized on a per-device basis.

The method `callJSP` takes a page name, an `HttpServletRequest`, and an `HttpServletResponse` object as parameters. It maps the page name to

Example 11.14 | **User-agent-Dependent JSP invocation**

```
... class View continued ...
  protected void callJSP(ServletContext servletContext,
String pageName,
  HttpServletRequest req, HttpServletResponse rsp)
  throws ServletException, IOException
{
String deviceDependentPageName = null;
String markUpType = getMarkUpType(req);
if (markUpType.equals("WML")) {
  deviceDependentPageName = "/wml/" + pageName;
} else if (markUpType.equals("VoiceXML")) {
  deviceDependentPageName = "/voicexml/" + pageName;
} else if (markUpType.equals("HTML_PDA")) {
  deviceDependentPageName = "/htmlpda/" + pageName;
} else { // HTML is default
  deviceDependentPageName = "/html/" + pageName;
}
// Prevent browsers from caching the dynamic page.
rsp.setHeader("Pragma", "No-cache");
rsp.setDateHeader("Expires", 0);
rsp.setHeader("Cache-Control", "no-cache");
  noCache(rsp);
// Invoke the JSP
servletContext().getRequestDispatcher(device
  DependentPageName) forward(req, rsp);
}
}
```

a device-dependent page name, and invokes the JSP designed for the particular device class. The first step is to obtain the markup type that is required for the user's device using the getMarkUpType method shown above. The code then maps the markup type to a directory name that is appended to the page name as a prefix. As the JSPs we invoke show dynamic data, and should not be cached by browsers or proxies, the code sets the Pragma, Expires, and Cache-Control header fields to the appropriate values. Finally, the callJSP method gets the request dispatcher from the servlet context and invokes the device dependent JSP using the forward method.

Registration Java Server Pages

The registration page asks the user to provide their first and last names, address information, and the desired user identification and password. Figure 11.4 shows the registration page.

Unlike the other pages, the registration page contains no dynamic data. It contains a form with input fields named `FirstName`, `LastName`, `AddressLine1`, `ZipCode`, `City`, `Country`, `State`, `UserID`, `Password`, and `PasswordConfirmation`. The form posts data entered by the user to the relative URL `/servlet/sample.shop.registration.RegistrationServlet`,

Figure 11.4

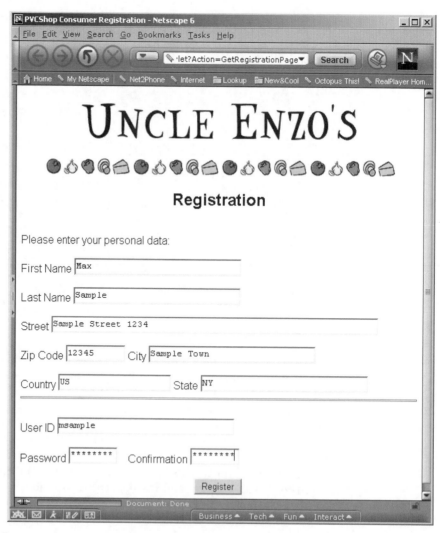

Registration page

setting the controller action to be invoked to `RegisterNewConsumer`. The registration JSP is shown in Example 11.15.

Example 11.15   **Registration JSP**

```
<!DOCTYPE HTML PUBLIC "-//W3C//DTD HTML 4.0
 Transitional//EN">
<HTML>
<HEAD>
 <META HTTP-EQUIV="content-type"
  CONTENT="text/html;charset=iso-8859-1">
 <META http-equiv="Content-Style-Type"
  content="text/css">
 <TITLE> Uncle Enzo's Consumer Registration
    </TITLE>
</HEAD>
<BODY BGCOLOR="#FFFFFF" LINK="#3366CC" VLINK="#55148B"
ALINK="#FF9900">
 <P align="center">
 <IMG src="/images/enzo48.gif" width="456" height="68"
    border="0">
 <BR><BR>
 <IMG src="/images/enzo.gif" width="128" height="30"
  border="0">
 <IMG src="/images/enzo.gif" width="128" height="30"
  border="0">
 <IMG src="/images/enzo.gif" width="128" height="30"
  border="0">
 <IMG src="/images/enzo.gif" width="128" height="30"
  border="0">
 </P>

 <H1 align="center">Registration</H1>

 <BR><BR>
 <FORM name="UserData"
    method="POST"
    action="/servlet/sample.shop.registration.
      Registration Servlet"
>
 <INPUT type="hidden" name="Action"
   value="RegisterNewConsumer">
```

▶

continued

```
Please enter your personal data:
<BR><BR>
FirstName <INPUT name="FirstName" size="30"
  maxlength="30" type="text">
<BR><BR>
LastName <INPUT name="LastName" size="30" maxlength="30"
  type="text">
<BR><BR>
Street <INPUT name="AddrLine1" size="60" maxlength="60"
  type="text">
<BR><BR>
Zip Code <INPUT name="ZipCode" size="10" maxlength="10"
  type="text">
City <INPUT name="City" size="30" maxlength="30"
  type="text">
<BR><BR>
Country <INPUT name="Country" size="20" maxlength="60"
  type="text">
State <INPUT name="State" size="30" maxlength="30"
  type="text">
<BR><HR><BR>
User ID <INPUT name="UserID" size="32" maxlength="32"
  type="text">
<BR><BR>
Password <INPUT name="Password" size="8" maxlength="8"
  type="password">
Confirmation<INPUT name="PWConf" size="8" maxlength="8"
  type="password">
<BR><BR>
<CENTER>
<INPUT type="submit" name="Submit" value="Register">
</CENTER>
</FORM>
</BODY>
</HTML>
```

The registration confirmation page is displayed by the RegistrationController after successful registration of a new user. It shows all data that have been stored in the new user record in the database during the previous step. Figure 11.5 shows the confirmation page.

The registration confirmation JSP (Example 11.16) displays the registration information in the RegisterConsumerCommand instance that has been used to store the new record.

Figure 11.5

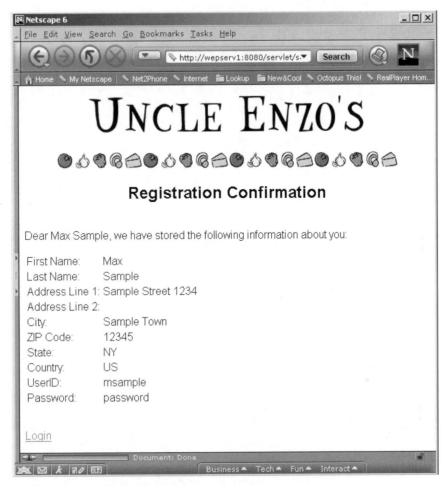

Registration confirmation page

Example 11.16   **Registration confirmation JSP**

```
<!DOCTYPE HTML PUBLIC "-//W3C//DTD HTML 4.0
  Transitional//EN">
<HTML>
<HEAD>
 <META HTTP-EQUIV="content-type"
  CONTENT="text/html;charset=iso-8859-1">
 <META http-equiv="Content-Style-Type"
  content="text/css">
 <TITLE>Uncle Enzo's - Registration conformation</TITLE>
```
▶

continued

```
</HEAD>
<BODY BGCOLOR="#FFFFFF" LINK="#3366CC" VLINK="#55148B"
ALINK="#FF9900">
 <P align="center">
 <IMG src="/images/enzo48.gif" width="456" height="68"
   border="0">
 <BR><BR>
 <IMG src="/images/enzo.gif" width="128" height="30"
   border="0">
 <IMG src="/images/enzo.gif" width="128" height="30"
   border="0">
 <IMG src="/images/enzo.gif" width="128" height="30"
   border="0">
 <IMG src="/images/enzo.gif" width="128" height="30"
   border="0">
 </P>

 <H1 align="center"> Registration Confirmation</H1>

 <BR><BR>

 <jsp:useBean id="consumerBean"
   class="sample.shop.registration.RegisterConsumer
     Command"
   scope="request"
 />

 Dear <%=consumerBean.getFirstName() %>
<%=consumerBean.getLastName() %>,
 we have stored the following information about you:
 <BR>
 <TABLE>
 <TBODY>
 <TR><TD>First Name: </TD>
     <TD><%=consumerBean.getFirstName()%> </TD></TR>
 <TR><TD>Last Name: </TD>
     <TD><%=consumerBean.getLastName()%> </TD></TR>
 <TR><TD>AddressLine1:</TD>
     <TD><%=consumerBean.getAddressLine1()%></TD></TR>
 <TR><TD>AddressLine2:</TD>
     <TD><%=consumerBean.getAddressLine2()%></TD></TR>
 <TR><TD>City: </TD>
     <TD><%=consumerBean.getCity()%> </TD></TR>
<TR><TD>ZIP Code: </TD>
     <TD><%=consumerBean.getZipCode()%> </TD></TR>
```

▶

continued

```
<TR><TD>State: </TD>
    <TD><%=consumerBean.getState()%> </TD></TR>
<TR><TD>Country: </TD>
    <TD><%=consumerBean.getCountry()%> </TD></TR>
<TR><TD>UserID: </TD>
    <TD><%=consumerBean.getUserID()%> </TD></TR>
    <TR><TD>Password: </TD>
    <TD><%=consumerBean.getPassword()%> </TD></TR>
</TBODY>
</TABLE>
<BR>
<P>


<Ahref="/servlet/sample.shop.auth.LoginServlet?Action=
   GetLogonPage"> Login
</A>
</P>
</BODY>
</HTML>
```

The registration confirmation JSP uses the `jsp:useBean` tag to access the `RegisterConsumerCommand` object passed to the JSP by the registration controller. It uses the getter methods of the command object only to obtain the output properties, i.e. it uses only as a view bean. For the user's convenience, we added a link to the login function at the end of the page. The reference points to the servlet `/servlet/sample.shop.auth.LoginServlet` explained earlier, specifying the action `GetLogonPage` in a parameter. When the user clicks on this link, the browser sends a request to the login servlet that returns the login page.

11.5 Summary

In this chapter, we have given an overview of the example presentation that uses the Web technologies presented in Chapter 5 and design patterns proposed in Chapter 9 to create an e-business application that can be accessed from different devices. We have presented device-type-independent servlets and commands, and the controllers and views for customer registration. In the following four chapters, we will explain the device-specific parts of the application that are required to support login and purchasing of goods from PCs, WAP phones, PDAs, and voice-only phones.

12   Access from PCs

In this chapter, we show how the shop application can be extended to allow for access from PCs, using a smart card for authentication via the Internet as presented in Chapter 5. We explain how to implement the required components, including an authentication applet and the corresponding authentication servlet and how to integrate them into the shop application. Finally, we present the controller for PC access and the JSPs that it uses to interact with consumers.

For a general discussion on smart-card application development, see Hansmann *et al*.[1]

12.1 Smart-card-based authentication via the Internet

In this section, we show how authentication via the Internet can be implemented with a public-key smart card. In order to enable customers to perform this method of authentication, they receive a loyalty card with a chip. The card is pre-personalized with a private key for generating digital signatures, and a certificate that contains information about the customer, the public key associated with the customer's private key, and a signature over these data.

The user needs a PC with a connected smart-card reader. When the user tries to access a URI provided by a protected servlet but is not yet logged in, the servlet sends back a login page that contains an authentication applet, parameterized with the URI that was requested. The authentication applet acts as a mediator that enables communication between the smart card and the authentication servlet on the Web server. Figure 12.1 shows the message flow between the components involved in this communication.

In the first step, the authentication applet sends a request to the authentication servlet to get a random challenge. It then prompts the user for the password for the smart card, and gives that password to the card. Once the smart card has obtained and accepted the password, it can be used to generate digital signatures. The applet sends a second request to the card that contains the challenge from the server to obtain a digital signature over that challenge from the smart card. It sends a third

Figure 12.1

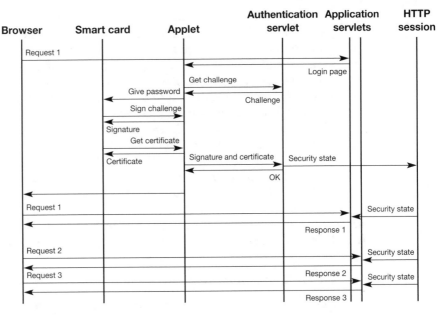

Authentication using a smart card

request to obtain the certificate for the key used to sign the challenge. The authentication applet then sends this digital signature and the certificate to the authentication servlet for verification. If the signature is valid, the authentication servlet adds a security state to the current session to indicate that the user is now logged in; it returns an OK message to the authentication applet. The applet now lets the browser display the URI that was requested. As the authentication state is present in the session at this point, this request and all subsequent requests are served until the session expires.

In order to be able to communicate with the smart card, the authentication applet needs an appropriate Java API, and appropriate driver software must be installed on the user's PC to make the card reader available to applications. On PCs running Windows operating systems, this means that a PC/SC service and a PC/SC device driver[2] must be installed on the PC. Also, the user's Web browser must be enabled for smart-card access, so that applets can obtain access to the smart card. For this purpose, the OCF[3] and a card terminal class for access to the reader have to be made available for the browser by installing the required files in the appropriate browser directory.

Card services that encapsulate the smart card's application protocol are packaged in a JAR file, together with the applets that use them. This JAR file is deployed on the Web application server and will be downloaded when required by a login page.

On the server side, in addition to the application servlets,[4] HTML pages and JSPs,[5] a login servlet must be deployed. This servlet implements the server-side authentication protocol logic and provides a security state upon successful authentication of a user, e.g. by putting it into the HTTP Session. Security-aware application servlets can then access the security state before performing sensitive functions.

When the user logs in, a page with the authentication applet is displayed in the browser. If the smart card requires a password, the authentication applet prompts the user to enter the password, and then provides it to the card before starting the actual authentication protocol. The authentication protocol is executed between the smart card and the authentication servlet, mediated by the authentication applet. If the user is authenticated successfully, the authentication servlet adds a security state to the session, which indicates that the user has been authenticated. Figure 12.2 gives an overview of the architecture.

12.1.1 Implementation

Smart-card-based authentication via the Internet plugs into the login servlet presented in the previous chapter. The LoginServlet receives requests from a Web browser running on a PC, and forwards the request to the SmartCardLoginController. The controller implements the functionality that is specific for smart-card authentication.

Figure 12.2

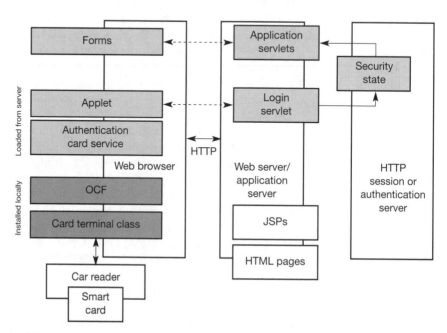

Architecture overview

SmartCardLoginController

The `SmartCardLoginController` (Example 12.1) supports a simple challenge–response based authentication scheme. It provides three actions to implement the server-side part of the authentication protocol:

- *Get Logon Page* returns an HTML page to the browser, which includes the smart-card-authentication applet.
- *Get Challenge* allows authentication applets to obtain a random challenge from the authentication servlet on the server. The authentication servlet remembers the challenge given to a particular client by creating new `SmartCardLoginCommand` instance, presetting the challenge input attribute of the command, and storing the command in the session for later use by the logon action.
- *Logon* allows authentication applets to authenticate after having obtained a random challenge. The authentication applet must provide the identity of the consumer's smart card and the signature created by the smart card. The authentication servlet retrieves the challenge that was given to the particular client, and the certificate that belongs to the consumer's smart card. Using the public key contained in the certificate, the authenticate action verifies the client.

Example 12.1 **SmartCardLoginController**

```
import javax.servlet.*;
import javax.servlet.http.*;
import java.io.IOException;
import java.security.*;

import sample.shop.Controller;
import sample.shop.View;

import sample.shop.HexString;

/**
 * SmartCardLoginController allows for authentication
using smart cards.
 */
public class SmartCardLoginController extends Controller
{

  // Actions implemented by the controller
  private final static String ACTION_GET_LOGON_PAGE =
    "GetLogonPage";
```

▶

continued

```
private final static String ACTION_GET_CHALLENGE =
  "GetChallenge";
private final static String ACTION_LOGON = "Logon";

// JSPs invoked by the controller
private final static String LOGON_SUCCESS_PAGE =
  "LogonSuccessPage";
private final static String LOGON_FAILURE_PAGE =
  "LogonFailurePage";

// Header fields used by the controller
private final static String CHALLENGE = "Callenge";
private final static String SIGNATURE = "Sinature";
private final static String CERTIFICATE = "Certificate";

private final static String SMARTCARD_LOGIN_COMMAND =
 "sample.shop.SmartCardAuthController.
    SMARTCARD_LOGIN_COMMAND";

public static void doProcess(ServletContext
  servletContext,
HttpServletRequest req,
HttpServletResponse rsp)
throws ServletException, IOException
{
  String action = req.getParameter("Action");

  if (action.equals(ACTION_GET_LOGON_PAGE))
  {
    // Return login form with smart card login applet.
    View.callJSP(servletContext,
      "/PVCShop/Login/LoginForm.jsp", req, rsp);
  }
  else if (action.equals(ACTION_GET_CHALLENGE))
  {
   // Create a challenge, store it and send it back to
   the login applet.
try {
  byte[] challenge = new byte[8];
  SecureRandom random =
  SecureRandom.getInstance("SHA1PRNG");
  random.nextBytes(challenge);
```

continued

```
SmartCardLoginCommand command = new
  SmartCardLoginCommand();
command.setChallenge(challenge);
req.getSession(true).putValue(SMARTCARD_LOGIN_COMMAND,
  command);
} catch (NoSuchAlgorithmException e) {
  throw new ServletException("SmartCard Authentication
    Not Available");
  }
}
else if (action.equals(ACTION_LOGON))
{
  // Verify certificate, get public-key, verify
    signature over challenge
  byte[] signature =
    HexString.parseHexString(req.getParameter
      (SIGNATURE));
  byte[] cert =
    HexString.parseHexString(req.getParameter
      (CERTIFICATE));

SmartCardLoginCommand command = (SmartCardLoginCommand)
  req.getSession().getValue(SMARTCARD_LOGIN_COMMAND);
command.setSignature(signature);
command.setCertificate(cert);
boolean success = command.execute();
String userID = command.getUserID();

SecurityState securityState = new SecurityState();
securityState.setUserID(userID);

if (success)
{
HttpSession session = req.getSession(true);
securityState.setAuthenticationState(
SecurityState.AUT_USERID_PASSWORD);
session.putValue(SecurityState.SEC_STATE_BEAN_ID,
securityState);
View.callJSP(servletContext,
"/PVCShop/Menu/MainMenu.jsp", req, rsp);
}
else
{ if (command.getErrorReason()==SmartCardLoginCommand.
  WRONG_CREDENTIAL){
```

▶

continued

```
        securityState.setErrorCode(SecurityState.ERR_WRONG_
        CREDENTIAL);
    }
    else if(command.getErrorReason() ==
      SmartCardLoginCommand.UNKNOWN_USER)
    {

      securityState.setErrorCode(SecurityState.ERR_
        UNKNOWN_USER);
      }
    }
    View.callJSP(servletContext,
      "/PVCShop/Login/LoginFailed.jsp", req, rsp);
    }
  }
}
```

To support smart-card-based authentication, we need a command to verify the certificate sent by the client and – using the public key contained in that certificate – the smart card's signature over a challenge from the server. The signature, certificate and random challenge have to be provided to the command using the setter methods for the appropriate input properties before executing the command.

Example 12.2   **SmartCardLoginCommand**

```
package sample.shop.auth;

import javax.servlet.http.*;
import javax.servlet.*;
import java.rmi.RemoteException;
import java.security.*;
import java.security.cert.*;
import java.io.*;
… includes for persistence layer …

/**
 * SmartCardLoginCommand allows to authenticate a user
using a smart card.
 */
public class SmartCardLoginCommand {
```

continued

```
… attributes/functions for database or LDAP access
depending on the persistence layer used …

public final static String UNKNOWN_USER = "Unknown
  User";
public final static String WRONG_CREDENTIAL = "Wrong
  Password";

public final static PublicKey UNCLE_ENZOS_PUBLIC_KEY =
  null;

// Input properties
protected byte[] challenge_ = null;
protected byte[] signatureBytes_ = null;
protected byte[] certificateBytes_ = null;
// Output properties
protected String userID_ = null;
protected String errorReason_ = null;

// Setter methods for input properties
public void setChallenge(byte[] value) { challenge_ =
 value; }
public void setSignature(byte[] value) { signatureBytes_
 = value; }
public void setCertificate(byte[] value ) {
 certificateBytes_ = value; }

public boolean execute() throws ServletException {
… initialize database access layer of not yet done …

boolean success = false;

try {
  CertificateFactory cf =
   CertificateFactory.getInstance("X.509");
  InputStream inStream = new
   ByteArrayInputStream(certificateBytes_);
  X509Certificate cert = (X509Certificate)
  cf.generateCertificate(inStream);
  inStream.close();

  cert.checkValidity();
  cert.verify(UNCLE_ENZOS_PUBLIC_KEY);

  PublicKey publicKey = cert.getPublicKey();
```

continued

```
Signature signature = Signature.getInstance("SHA-
  1/RSA");
signature.initVerify(publicKey);
signature.update(challenge_);
if (signature.verify(signatureBytes_)) {
userID_ = cert.getSubjectDN().getName();
success = true;
}
} catch (GeneralSecurityException e) {
  throw new ServletException("Invalid Certificate");
} catch (IOException e) {
  throw new ServletException("Signature Verification
    failed");
}
return success;
// Getter methods for output properties
public String getUserID() { return userID_; }
public String getErrorReason() { return errorReason_; }
}
```

In Example 12.2, the `execute` method creates an `X509Certificate` object from the data provided through the `setCertificate` method. It checks the validity of the certificate, and verifies whether it has a valid signature, using the `checkValidity` and `verify` methods of the `X509Certificate` object. If these methods do not reveal any exceptions, then the certificate is valid and authentic.

The next step is to verify the digital signature. The `java.security` package provides the `Signature` class to perform this task. To obtain a `Signature` object, the `getInstance` method has to be used. We assume that our smart cards create digital signatures using secure hash algorithm (SHA)-1 for hashing and the RSA algorithm for creating the signature from the SHA-1 hash. Specifying the algorithm identifier `SHA-1/RSA` results in creation of a matching `Signature` object. To perform its task, the `Signature` object needs an RSA public key that must be passed through the `initVerify` method. Next, it needs the data over which the signature has been generated; it must be provided by one or more calls to the `update` method. Once the `Signature` object has this input, the `verify` method can be invoked with the signature to be verified as a parameter.

If signature verification is successful, then the execute method sets the user identification property to the user identification contained in the customer's certificate and returns `true`. After successful execution of the `SmartCardLoginCommand`, the user identification of the authenticated customer can be obtained using the `getUserID` method.

Authentication applet

The authentication applet is responsible for performing the client-side part of the authentication protocol. It acts as a mediator between the smart card and the authentication servlet at the server, using the authentication card service to let the smart card perform the required operations, and using an HTTP connection to communicate with the authentication servlet. To integrate with the Web application, the applet allows the Web page to specify the following parameters:

- *Authentication servlet URI:* the URI of the authentication servlet to which the applet has to connect to perform the authentication protocol.
- *Success page:* the URI of the page that should be displayed after successful authentication to the server. This is usually the URI originally requested.
- *Failure page:* the URI of the page that should be displayed after failed authentication to the server.

The authentication applet drives the authentication process by performing the following steps:

1. The authentication applet prompts the user to enter the smart card and the PIN. The user inserts the smart card and enters the PIN.
2. The authentication applet passes the PIN to the smart card using the authentication card service's `givePIN` method (see below). If incorrect, it displays a warning and goes back to step 1.
3. The authentication applet requests a random challenge from the authentication servlet on the server via HTTP using the `GetChallenge` action. The server generates a random challenge for the session though which the applet connects and sends it back.
4. The authentication applet receives the random challenge from the server and lets the smart card generate a digital signature over it, using the authentication card service's `generateSignature` method (see below).
5. The authentication applet obtains the signing certificate from the smart card, using the authentication card service's `getSigningCertificate` method.
6. The authentication applet sends the digital signature and the signing certificate to the authentication servlet on the server via HTTP using the `Authenticate` action. The authentication servlet receives the signature and the certificate, validates the certificate, verifies the signature using the random challenge associated with the current session, and returns the result.

7. The authentication applet receives the result from the authentication servlet and disconnects the HTTP connection. Depending on the result, it lets the browser display either the success page or the failure page.

As we are focusing on server-side programming in this book, we will not provide sample code for the authentication applet here. More information on programming applets that access smart cards is provided in Hansmann et al.[1]

Authentication card service

The authentication card service encapsulates the smart cards application protocol data unit (APDU) interface, i.e. it provides a Java API, including certain methods for accessing smart card functions, and performs the conversation with the smart card to allow the smart card to perform the required actions. The authentication card service API includes the following methods:

```
public boolean givePIN(byte[] pin);
public byte[] generateSignature(byte[] data);
public byte[] getSigningCertificate();
```

The first method, givePIN, passes a PIN to the smart card. It returns true if the PIN is accepted by the smart card, otherwise it returns false. The second method, generateSignature, generates a digital signature over the data passed in the byte array data, returning a byte array that represents the digital signature. This function is used by the applet to let the smart card generate a digital signature over the random challenge from the server. The third method, getSigningCertificate, obtains the certificate for the signing key from the smart card, and returns it as an X.509 certificate encoded in a byte array.

12.1.2 Login

The login JSP (Example 12.3) for login with a smart card generates an HTML page that includes an applet for smart-card-based authentication (Figure 12.3).

As explained above, the applet prompts the customer for the smart card's PIN, which is required to activate the smart card for generation of digital signatures.

When the user enters the PIN, and presses the logon button or the return key, the applet initiates communication to the URL specified in the AuthURL parameter. It gives the PIN to the smart card, requests a random challenge from the server, lets the smart card generate a digital signature over the challenge from the server and sends the result to the server for verification as described above. If the server's response is an OK, the applet lets the browser display the URI specified in the SuccessPage parameter; otherwise it points the browser to the `FailurePage` URI.

Figure 12.3

Login screen

Example 12.3 | **Login JSP source code**

```
<!DOCTYPE HTML PUBLIC "-//W3C//DTD HTML 4.0
Transitional//EN">
<HTML>
 <HEAD>
 <META HTTP-EQUIV="content-type"
  CONTENT="text/html;charset=iso-8859-1">
 <META http-equiv="Content-Style-Type" content="text/css"
 <TITLE> Uncle Enzo's - Login </TITLE>
 </HEAD>
```

▶

continued

```
<BODY BGCOLOR="#FFFFFF" LINK="#3366CC" VLINK="#55148B"
  ALINK="#FF9900">
<P align="center">
<IMG src="/images/enzo48.gif" width="456" height="68"
  border="0">
<BR><BR>
<IMG src="/images/enzo.gif" width="128" height="30"
  border="0">
<IMG src="/images/enzo.gif" width="128" height="30"
  border="0">
<IMG src="/images/enzo.gif" width="128" height="30"
  border="0">
<IMG src="/images/enzo.gif" width="128" height="30"
  border="0">
</P>

<CENTER>
   <H1 align="center">Welcome !</H1>
   <BR><BR>
   <APPLET code="sample.shop.auth.LoginApplet.class"
      name="Smart Card Login Applet"
      archive="SampleShop.jar"
      width="500" height="300"
      codebase="/sample/shop/"


>

  <param name=AuthURL
    value="/servlet/sample.shop.auth.LoginServlet">
  <param name=SuccessPage
    value="/servlet/sample.shop.shop.ShopServlet&
      Action=GetMenuPage>
  <param name=FailurePage
    value="/servlet/sample.shop.auth.LoginServlet&
      Action=GetErrPage">
  </APPLET>
  </CENTER>
</BODY>
</HTML>
```

12.2 Ordering goods

After successful login to Uncle Enzo's shop application, the customer can
order food or review the history of previous orders. In this section, we use
use the PC-specific controller for these tasks, as well as the PC-specific
JSPs invoked by this controller (Example 12.4).

Example 12.4 — **Shop controller PC**

```java
package sample.shop.shop;

import javax.servlet.*;
import javax.servlet.http.*;
import java.io.IOException;

import sample.shop.Controller;
import sample.shop.View;
import sample.shop.beans.ConsumerBean;
import sample.shop.auth.SecurityState;

/**
 * ShopControllerPC implements the shopping flow for PC
clients.
 */
public class ShopControllerPC extends Controller {
  public final static String ACTION_GET_MENU_PAGE =
    "GetMenuPage";
  public final static String ACTION_BEGIN_SHOPPING =
    "BeginShopping";
  public final static String ACTION_CHECKOUT = "Checkout";
  public final static String ACTION_FINISH_SHOPPING =
    "FinishShopping";
  public final static String ACTION_VIEW_HISTORY =
    "ViewHistory";
  public final static String PARAM_NUMBER = "Number";
  public final static String PARAM_ITEM_ID = "ItemID";

  public static void doProcess(ServletContext
    servletContext,
                   HttpServletRequest req,
                   HttpServletResponse rsp)
  throws ServletException, IOException
  {
    String action = req.getParameter("Action");
```

▶

continued

```
String userID = ((SecurityState)
  req.getSession().getValue(SecurityState.AUTH_STATE_
    BEAN_ID)).getUserID();

if (action.equals(ACTION_GET_MENU_PAGE)) {
  View.callJSP(servletContext,"/PVCShop/Menu/MainMenu.
    jsp", req, rsp);
}
else if (action.equals(ACTION_BEGIN_SHOPPING))
{
  GetItemsCommand getItemsCommand = new
    GetItemsCommand();
  boolean success = getItemsCommand.execute();
  if (success) {
    req.setAttribute("itemsBean", getItemsCommand);
    View.callJSP(servletContext,
                "/PVCShop/Shop/ItemsList.jsp", req,
                  rsp)
  } else {
    View.callJSP(servletContext,
                "/PVCShop/Shop/LoginRequired.jsp",
                  req, rsp);
  }
}
else if (action.equals(ACTION_CHECKOUT))
{
  OrderCommand checkOutCommand = new OrderCommand();
  checkOutCommand.setUserID(userID);

  int i = 0;
  while (req.getParameter(PARAM_NUMBER + i) != null
        && req.getParameter(PARAM_ITEM_ID + i) !=
          null) {
    checkOutCommand.setNumber(req.getParameter
      (PARAM_NUMBER + i), i);
    checkOutCommand.setID(req.getParameter(PARAM_
      ITEM_ID + i), i);
    i++;
  }

  boolean success = checkOutCommand.execute();
  if (success) {
    req.setAttribute("purchaseBean", checkOutCommand);
    View.callJSP(servletContext,
                "/PVCShop/Shop/PurchaseConfirmation.
                  jsp", req, rsp);
  } else {
```

continued

```
        View.callJSP(servletContext,
                    "/PVCShop/Shop/LoginRequired.jsp", req,
                    rsp);
    }
}
else if (action.equals(ACTION_VIEW_HISTORY))
{
    GetPurchasesCommand getPurchasesCommand = new
    GetPurchasesCommand();
    getPurchasesCommand.setUserID(userID);

    boolean success = getPurchasesCommand.execute();
    req.setAttribute("purchaseVectorBean",
    getPurchasesCommand);
    if (success) {
      View.callJSP(servletContext,
                    "/PVCShop/Shop/PurchaseHistory.jsp",
                    req, rsp);
    } else {
    View.callJSP(servletContext,
                    "/PVCShop/Shop/LoginRequired.jsp", req,
                    rsp);
    }
}
else if (action.equals(ACTION_FINISH_SHOPPING))
{
    View.callJSP(servletContext,
    "/PVCShop/Menu/MainMenu.jsp", req, rsp);
    }
    }
}
```

12.2.1 Menu

After successful login, the main menu (Figure 12.4) is displayed. It allows the consumer to start shopping by selecting the Shop link, to review previous purchases by selecting the Review Purchases link, or to logout using the Logout link.

The first two links point to `/servlet/sample.shop.shop.ShopServlet`, the URI of the shop servlet. These links specify the actions `BeginShopping` and `ViewHistory`, respectively to indicate what the shop controller has to do in order to process the request. The third link points to `/servlet/sample.shop.auth.LogoffServlet`, the URI of the logoff servlet, specifying the action `Logoff`.

The JSP for the main menu is shown in Example 12.5.

Figure 12.4

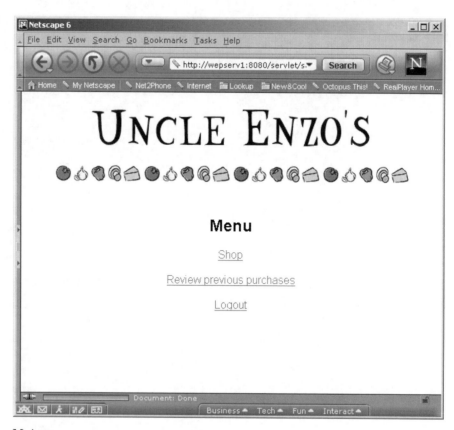

Main menu

Example 12.5 — Main menu JSP

```
<!DOCTYPE HTML PUBLIC "-//W3C//DTD HTML 4.0
  Transitional//EN">
<HTML>
  <HEAD>
    <META HTTP-EQUIV="content-type"
      CONTENT="text/html;charset=iso-8859-1">
    <META http-equiv="Content-Style-Type"
      content="text/css">
    <TITLE>Uncle Enzo's </TITLE>
  </HEAD>
  <BODY BGCOLOR="#FFFFFF" LINK="#3366CC" VLINK="#55148B"
    ALINK="#FF9900">
    <P align="center">
```

continued

```
          <IMG src="/images/enzo48.gif" width="456"
            height="68" border="0">
          <BR><BR>
          <IMG src="/images/enzo.gif" width="128" height="30"
            border="0">
          <IMG src="/images/enzo.gif" width="128" height="30"
            border="0">
          <IMG src="/images/enzo.gif" width="128" height="30"
            border="0">
          <IMG src="/images/enzo.gif" width="128" height="30"
            border="0">
      </P>
      <CENTER>
        <H1 align="center">Menu</H1>
        <BR>
        <A href="/servlet/sample.shop.shop.ShopServlet?
        Action=BeginShopping">
          Shop
        </A>
        <BR><BR>
        <A href="/servlet/sample.shop.shop.ShopServlet?
        Action=ViewHistory">
          Review prevous purchases
        </A>
        <BR><BR>
        <A href="/servlet/sample.shop.auth.LogoffServlet?
        Action=Logoff">
          Logout
        </A>
      </CENTER>
    </BODY>
</HTML>
```

12.2.2 Items list Java Server Page

If the consumer selects the link Shop from the menu, the action BeginShopping is invoked. The PC controller retrieves the list of available items from the shop database, and invokes the appropriate JSP (Example 12.6) to display a form in which these items are listed (Figure 12.5).

Figure 12.5

Items list

The JSP obtains the information about available items from the GetItemsCommand object passed by the controller in the request. The command has indexed output properties that the JSP accesses in a for-loop to create a form with a table of items available in the shop.

Example 12.6 **Items list JSP**

```
<!DOCTYPE HTML PUBLIC "-//W3C//DTD HTML 4.0
  Transitional//EN">
<HTML>
  <HEAD>
    <META http-equiv="content-type"
      content="text/html;charset=iso-8859-1">
    <META http-equiv="Content-Style-Type"
      content="text/css">
    <TITLE>Uncle Enzo's - Items List/</TITLE>
  </HEAD>
  <BODY bgcolor="#FFFFFF" link="#3366CC" vlink="#55148B"
    alink="#FF9900">
    <P align="center">
      <IMG src="/images/enzo48.gif" width="456"
        height="68" border="0">
      <BR><BR>
      <IMG src="/images/enzo.gif" width="128" height="30"
        border="0">
      <IMG src="/images/enzo.gif" width="128" height="30"
        border="0">
      <IMG src="/images/enzo.gif" width="128" height="30"
        border="0">
      <IMG src="/images/enzo.gif" width="128" height="30"
        border="0">
    </P>

    <jsp:useBean id="itemsBean"
                 class="sample.shop.shop.GetItemsCommand"
                 scope="request"
    />
    <H1 align="center">Purchase</H1>
    <BR>
    <P>You can purchase the following items:</P>
    <FORM method="POST" action="/servlet/sample.shop.
      shop.ShopServlet">
    <INPUT type="hidden" name="Action" value="Checkout">
    <TABLE>
      <TBODY>
        <% for (int i = 0; i < itemsBean.size(); i++) {
          %>
          <TR>
            <TD>
```

▶

continued

```
            <TABLE>
              <TBODY>
                <TR>
                  <TD width="75%"><B>
                    <%= itemsBean.getName(i) %>
                  </B></TD>
                  <TD width="15%">
                    <%= itemsBean.getTotal(i).
                      toString() %>
                  </TD>
                  <TD width="10%">
                    <INPUT size="4" type="text"
                      maxlength="4"
                            name="Number<%= i%>"
                              value="0">
                    <INPUT type="hidden"
                    name="ItemID<%= i%>"
                            value="<%= itemsBean.
                            getItemID(i) %>">
                  </TD>
                </TR>
              </TBODY>
            </TABLE>
            <TABLE>
              <TBODY>
                <TR>
                  <TD>
                    <%= itemsBean.getDescription(i) %>
                  </TD>
                </TR>
              </TBODY>
            </TABLE>
          </TD>
        </TR>
        <% } %>
      </TBODY>
    </TABLE>
    <BR>
  <CENTER>
  <INPUT type="submit" name="Buy" value="Buy">
  </CENTER>
  </FORM>
  </BODY>
</HTML>
```

The consumer can specify a certain quantity for each of the desired items, and then purchase these items by pressing the Submit button. The form generated by the JSP posts the data to the servlet with the URI `/servlet/sample.shop.shop.ShopServlet`, specifying the action `Checkout` in a hidden field. In addition to the values entered by the consumer, the form generated by the JSP posts an item identifier for each item, which allows the application logic on the server to identify the items uniquely.

12.2.3 Purchase confirmation

After the consumer has selected their items and pressed the Submit button, the `FinishShopping` action is invoked. The PC controller invokes the business logic to generate and store the purchase order in the database, and invokes the purchase confirmation JSP (Example 12.7) to display the purchase summary for the consumer (Figure 12.6).

Figure 12.6

Purchase confirmation

The purchase confirmation JSP displays the information stored in the `OrderCommand` object after execution. To allow the customer to navigate back to the main menu, it provides a link that points to `/servlet/sample.shop.shop.ShopServlet`, the URI of the shop servlet, specifying the action `FinishShopping`.

Example 12.7   **Purchase confirmation JSP**

```html
<!DOCTYPE HTML PUBLIC "-//W3C//DTD HTML 4.0
Transitional//EN">
<HTML>
  <HEAD>
    <META http-equiv="content-type"
       content="text/html;charset=iso-8859-1">
    <META http-equiv="Content-Style-Type"
       content="text/css">
    <TITLE> Purchase Summary </TITLE>
  </HEAD>
<BODY bgcolor="#FFFFFF" link="#3366CC" vlink="#55148B"
   alink="#FF9900">
   <P align="center">
     <IMG src="/images/enzo48.gif" width="456"
       height="68" border="0">
     <BR><BR>
     <IMG src="/images/enzo.gif" width="128" height="30"
       border="0">
     <IMG src="/images/enzo.gif" width="128" height="30"
       border="0">
     <IMG src="/images/enzo.gif" width="128" height="30"
       border="0">
     <IMG src="/images/enzo.gif" width="128" height="30"
       border="0">
   </P>

   <jsp:useBean id="purchaseBean"
              class="sample.shop.shop.OrderCommand"
              scope="request"
   />

   <H1 align="center">Purchase Confirmation</H1>
```

continued

```
    You have purchased the following items:

    <TABLE>
      <TBODY>
      <% for (int i = 0; i < purchaseBean.size(); i++) {
      %>
        <TR>
          <TD width="80%"> <%=purchaseBean.getItemName(i)
          %> </TD>
          <TD width="10%"> <%=purchaseBean.getItemTotal(i)
          %> </TD>
          <TD width="10%"> <%=purchaseBean.get
            ItemNumber(i) %> </TD>
        </TR>
      <% } %>
      <TR>
        <TD width="80%">Total:</TD>
        <TD width="20%"> <%=purchaseBean.getTotal() %> </TD>
      </TR>
    </TBODY>
  </TABLE>
  <BR><BR>
  <P>We will deliver the food within 1/2 hour.</P>
  <P>
    <A href="/servlet/sample.shop.shop.ShopServlet?Action =
      FinishShopping">
      Back to Main Menu
    </A>
  </P>
  </BODY>
</HTML>
```

12.2.4 Purchase history JSP

If the consumer selects the link Review Previous Purchases from the menu, the PurchaseHistory action is invoked. The PC controller queries the shop database to obtain the list of previous purchases for the consumer, and invokes the purchase history JSP (Example 12.8) to display the list (Figure 12.7).

The purchase history JSP uses two nested loops to display the items for all purchases of a consumer. It obtains the information from the GetPurchasesCommand passed to the JSP in the request when being invoked by the ShopController.

Figure 12.7

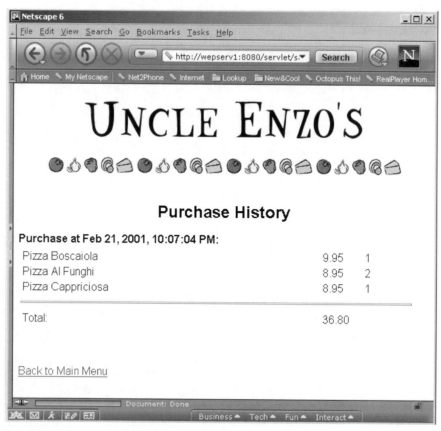

Purchase history screen

Example 12.8 **Purchase history**

```
<!DOCTYPE HTML PUBLIC "-//W3C//DTD HTML 4.0
  Transitional//EN">
<HTML>
  <HEAD>
    <META http-equiv="content-type"
      content="text/html;charset=iso-8859-1">
    <META http-equiv="Content-Style-Type"
      content="text/css">
    <TITLE>Purchase History/</TITLE>
  </HEAD>
  <BODY bgcolor="#FFFFFF" link="#3366CC" vlink="#55148B"
    alink="#FF9900">
```

continued

```jsp
<jsp:useBean id="purchaseVectorBean"
             class="sample.shop.shop.GetPurchases
             Command"
             scope="request"
/>
<P align="center">
  <IMG src="/images/enzo48.gif" width="456"
    height="68" border="0">
  <BR><BR>
  <IMG src="/images/enzo.gif" width="128"
    height="30" border="0">
  <IMG src="/images/enzo.gif" width="128"
    height="30" border="0">
  <IMG src="/images/enzo.gif" width="128"
    height="30" border="0">
  <IMG src="/images/enzo.gif" width="128"
    height="30" border="0">
</P>
<BR>

<H1 align="center">Purchase History</H1>

<% for (int j = 0; j < purchaseVectorBean.size();
  j++) { %>

  <B>Purchase at <%=purchaseVectorBean.getPurchase
    Bean (j).getDate() %>,
  <%=purchaseVectorBean.getPurchaseBean(j).getTime()
    %>:</B>

  <TABLE>
    <TBODY>
      <% for (int i = 0;
              i < purchaseVectorBean.getPurchaseBean
                (j).size();
              i++) {
      %>
        <TR>
          <TD width="80%">
            <%=purchaseVectorBean.getPurchase
              Bean(j).getItemName(i) %>
          </TD>
          <TD width="10%">
            <%=purchaseVectorBean.getPurchase
              Bean(j).getItemTotal(i) %>
```

▶

continued

```
          </TD>
          <TD width="10%">
            <%=purchaseVectorBean.get
               PurchaseBean(j).getItemNumber(i) %>
          </TD>
        </TR>
      <% } %>
      </TBODY>
    </TABLE>
    <HR>
    <TABLE>
      <TBODY>
        <TR>
          <TD width="80%">
            Total:
          </TD>
          <TD width="10%">
            <%=purchaseVectorBean.getPurchase
               Bean(j).getTotal() %>
          </TD>
          <TD width="10%"></TD>
        </TR>
      </TBODY>
    </TABLE>
  <% } %>
  <BR><BR>
  <P>
    <A href="/servlet/sample.shop.shop.ShopServlet?
     Action=FinishShopping"> Back to Main Menu
    </A>
  </P>
  </BODY>
</HTML>
```

12.3 Conclusion

In this chapter, we have revisited Web application programming based on the J2EE technologies, including servlets and JSPs, and the MVC paradigm. We have described how user authentication via the Internet using smart cards works using a pure Java architecture based on the OCF. We have given an overview of the required components, including servlets, controllers, commands encapsulating models, views, and contained applets. Furthermore, we have presented an implementation of the ordering process for the PC, including reviewing the order history.

After reading this chapter, you should know how to implement Web applications that support PCs, and how to secure such applications using smart-card authentication. The following chapters will show you how to extend the example application further in order to also support pervasive computing clients, and will introduce you to the specifics of Web applications for pervasive computing.

References

1. Hansmann, U., Nicklous, M., Schäck, T. and Seliger, F. (2000) *Smart Card Application Development Using Java*. Berlin: Springer.

2. PC/SC Workgroup (1999) 'PC/SC Specification 1.0'.
   http://www.pcscworkgroup.com

3. OpenCard Consortium (2000) 'OCF 1.2 Programmers Guide'.
   http://www.opencard.org

4. Sun Microsystems (1999) 'Java Servlet Specification 2.2'.
   http://www.javasoft.com

5. Sun Microsystems (1999) 'Java Server Pages Specification 1.2'.
   http://www.javasoft.com

13   Access via WAP

In this chapter, we show how the application is extended to allow for access using mobile devices with a WAP browser, especially mobile phones. We describe how the functionality supported for WAP fits into the overall architecture, and we discuss the infrastructure needed to connect mobile devices to Uncle Enzo's application server. We provide some source code fragments for parts of the WAP-specific functionality of the application. Finally, we outline some extensions that improve the speed or usability of Uncle Enzo's shop.

13.1   WAP functionality

Using a WAP device is a convenient way to perform simple interactions with services on the Internet. Unlike a PC, such a device does not require a long time to boot, and as it is often in the user's pocket, it can be used wherever the customer is, even to order a pizza on the way home from work, for example. The idea of supporting ordering via WAP is very attractive for Uncle Enzo's, because no additional personnel are needed for the ordering process. WAP devices can interface directly with Uncle Enzo's server and the ordering system.

Due to the limitations of WAP devices, mentioned in Chapter 6, it is important to optimize applications for usability, and to provide an easy-to-use and efficient user interface. The small displays of WAP phones make offering the full list of menu items unreasonable. Therefore, Uncle Enzo's offers only a short list of menu items. If the customer has previously customized their personal list of favorites, this list is used as a shortlist for WAP, otherwise the chef's recommendation are used as a default. This function is called quick order. Specifying your favorites is only possible using a PC browser, as performing that task with a WAP phone would be too tedious. Also, all administrative functions, such as changing an address or credit card number, can be accessed only from a PC.

As only a subset of the functions that Uncle Enzo's website provides is available for WAP clients, only a part of the dialog flow is relevant for the WAP application. Figure 13.1 shows those parts as highlighted boxes.

Figure 13.1

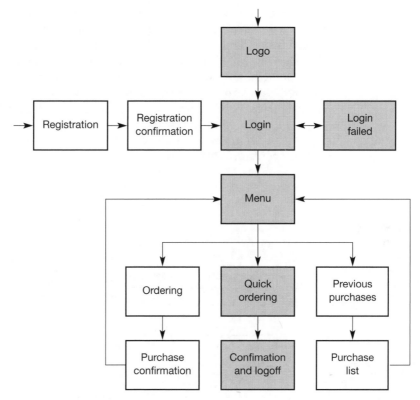

User interface overview

When the customer navigates to the shop, a logo is displayed for five seconds before the login page appears. The user can now use their customer number and PIN to authenticate themselves to the shop application. If the authentication fails, an error page is displayed for five seconds, that the login page is displayed again.

Once the customer has been authenticated, the application displays the quick order list. The customer can select a quantity for each menu item within the quick order list. When the customer submits the order, the application displays a page with the estimated delivery time and the delivery address. The customer can now either confirm or cancel the order.

13.1.1 Integration with the overall architecture

To unfold real value, the Uncle Enzo's WAP interface needs to integrate well with the overall architecture. As a limited subset of the shop functionality is provided via WAP, only a few of the components introduced in the previous chapters are actually used when a customer accesses the system using a WAP phone. Figure 13.2 shows those components as highlighted boxes. Only the login and shopping are enabled for use via WAP. The `LoginServlet` forwards all incoming requests originating from WAP devices to the `LoginController`, which uses the appropriate `LoginCommand` to authenticate users. The `ShopServlet` forwards all requests from WAP devices to the `ShopController` for WAP devices. The `ShopController` for WAP uses the `GetItems`, `Purchase`, `GetAddress`, and `GetDeliveryTime` commands. All JSPs invoked by the `ShopController` for WAP contain WML markup.

Figure 13.2

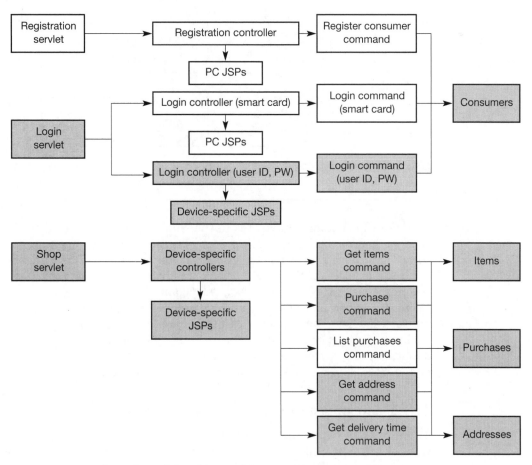

Overview of the shop architecture

13.1.2 Infrastructure

In addition to the standard Internet infrastructure required to deploy classical Web applications, providing access to an application via WAP devices requires a WAP gateway and appropriate dial-in hardware. Businesses that deploy WAP-enabled applications have the choice of either setting up their own equipment for WAP connectivity, or just relying on the services provided by network operators. Usually, network operators provide the dial-in hardware and the WAP gateway for their subscribers, with the advantage that the phones are already preconfigured to access their WAP gateways when they are given to subscribers. As Uncle Enzo's wants to deploy the application as quickly, as possible and with maximum convenience for his customers, the obvious decision is to rely on external WAP gateways provided by network providers. Figure 13.3 shows the resulting topology.

No special equipment is required at Uncle Enzo's site. Requests from WAP phones flow to the WAP gateways of the respective network providers, and are converted into HTTP requests, which flow to Uncle Enzo's application server. The software on the server detects that those requests originate from a WAP device, and returns HTTP responses with the appropriate document type and content to the WAP gateway at the network provider. Finally, the WAP gateway converts the response to a WAP response and sends it back to the device.

13.2 Implementation

In this section, we explain the implementation of the quick order functionality. We start with a brief review of some tools that can be used for the implementation of WAP applications, and parts of the implementation itself. Finally, we give some suggestion for enhancing the application.

Figure 13.3

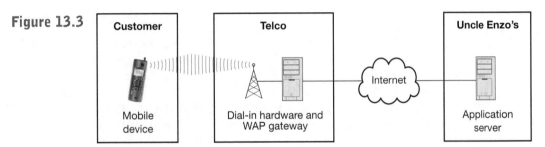

WAP infrastructure

13.2.1 Tools

WML (see Chapter 6), which is supported by today's mobile phones with Internet connectivity, is a language based on XML. It can be edited using standard text editors, XML editors, or WML editors provided with WAP toolkits. As we used very simple JSPs to generate all output for our example application, including the WML pages for WAP, we used a standard text editor rather than an XML or WML editor. However, when designing complex WML pages, it is usually more convenient to create an initial version of the WML pages using a WAP toolkit, as the emulator immediately shows how the WML markup will appear on the phone. A WAP application toolkit can also be used to convert images to the WBMP format required by WAP phones

Once the WML pages have been created, appropriate tools are required to deploy and test them. We used a WAP toolkit, including a WAP emulator, for this purpose. After deploying the Web application, including the JSPs that created the WML markup, we pointed the WAP emulator to the application server to test the application. This is much easier and faster than using real phones, and is sufficient for initial testing. The WAP toolkits usually have the capability to display the WML source for any deck received from the application, indicating any errors, which is helpful for debugging.

Only at the very end of the development process is the WAP application tested on real phones. Notably, because of the differences in form factors, user interface elements, and firmware between the phones on the market, it is not sufficient to test an application with one particular device. Tests with each individual target device are required to assure good usability on each target phone.

13.2.2 Implementation

In this section, we describe the implementation of the ordering process for a WAP browser on a mobile device. We focus on the WAP-specific parts, including the views and the shop controller for WAP. The other components that are involved have already been presented in Chapter 11.

Logo and login
In order to login to the shop via WAP, the customer must point the WAP browser to the URL of the `LoginServlet`, specifying the action `GetLogonPage`, for example `/servlet/sample.shop.auth.LoginServlet? Action=GetLogonPage`. When the `LoginServlet` receives a request from a WAP phone targeted to that URI, it dispatches the request to the `LoginController`, which provides user authentication with user identification and password. In response to the action `GetLogonPage`, this controller invokes a view that displays the login deck.

When implementing applications that operate over slow, wireless networks, it is important to reduce client–server interactions to an absolute minimum. For this reason, the logo and login cards are bundled together in one WML deck, which reduces the number of messages sent between the mobile devices and the server. Example 13.1 shows the WML source of the login deck.

Example 13.1	Login deck, including logo and login cards

```
<?xml version="1.0"?>
<!DOCTYPE wml PUBLIC "-//WAPFORUM//DTD WML 1.1//EN"
"http://www.wapforum.org/DTD/wml_1.1.xml">

<wml>
 <card id="Logo" newcontext="true" title="Welcome">
   <onevent type="ontimer">
   <go href="#Login"/>
   </onevent>
   <timer value="50"/>
   <do type="prev" label=""><noop/></do>
   <p align="center">
   <img src="uncleenzos.wbmp" alt="Uncle Enzos's"/><br/>
   </p>
 </card>

 <card id="Login" title="Uncle Enzo's" newcontext="true">
   <p>
   User ID<input format="*N" name="userID"
     title="User:"/>
   PIN<input format="NNNN" name="password" title="PIN:"/>
   <anchor> Login
    <go method="get"
       href="/servlet/sample.shop.auth.LoginServlet">
       <postfield name="Action" value="Logon"/>
       <postfield name="UserID" value="$userID"/>
       <postfield name="Password" value="$password"/>
    </go>
   </anchor>
   </p>
 </card>
</wml>
```

The WML card named `Logo` displays the image `uncleenzos.bwmp` for five seconds before displaying the login page. The delay is implemented as a timer event with the code `<timer value="50">`. Timer values are measured in tenths of a second. Figure 13.4 shows the logo card displayed on a phone.

The login card prompts the customer for the customer number and PIN. The user identification is a numeric value with variable length, specified by the expression `format="*N"`. The PIN is a four-digit value specified by the expression `format="NNNN"`. The WAP implementation uses numeric rather than alphanumeric user identifications to reduce the number of keystrokes the user has to perform. For example, entering the user ID 'Enzo' with a WAP phone requires 11 keystrokes (33-66-9999-666), but only four keystrokes are needed to enter 0815 as the customer number. For the same reason, we use a numerical PIN instead of an alphanumerical password. Figure 13.5 shows the login card displayed on a WAP phone.

When the customer enters the user identification (customer number) and the PIN, and then selects the login link, the WAP browser creates a `GET` request with the parameters `Action`, `UserID`, and `Password` and sends it to the `LoginServlet`. The `Action` parameter has the fixed value `Logon`, while the other parameters contain the user identification number and PIN, respectively. The login servlet receives the new request and again dispatches it to the appropriate `LoginController`. The controller parses the parameters, and checks the user identification number and

Figure 13.4

Welcome card

Figure 13.5

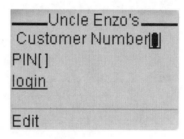

Login card

PIN entered by the customer using the `PasswordLoginCommand`, then displays the quick order page or bad login page, respectively. Example 13.2 shows an excerpt of the relevant code from the `PasswordLoginController` presented in Chapter 11.

Example 13.2   **The login action of the `LoginController`**

```
if (action.equals(ACTION_GET_LOGON_PAGE)) {
View.callJSP(servletContext,
  "/PVCShop/Login/LoginForm.jsp", req, rsp);
} else if (action.equals(ACTION_LOGON)) {
  String userID = req.getParameter(USER_ID);
  String password = req.getParameter(PASSWORD);

SecurityState securityState = new SecurityState ();
securityState.setUserID(userID);

PasswordLoginCommand command = new
  PasswordLoginCommand();
command.setUserID(userID);
command.setPassword(password);
boolean success = command.execute();
if (success) {
  // Get session to which request belongs, create if
    required.
  HttpSession session = req.getSession(true);

  securityState.setAuthenticationState(Security
    State.AUT_USERID_PASSWORD);
  session.putValue(SecurityState.AUTH_STATE_BEAN_ID,
    securityState);

  // Show the main menu after successful login.
  View.callJSP(servletContext,
    "/PVCShop/Menu/MainMenu.jsp", req, rsp);
} else {

  if (command.getErrorReason() ==
    PasswordLoginCommand.WRONG_CREDENTIAL) {
  securityState.setErrorCode(SecurityState.ERR_
    WRONG_CREDENTIAL);
  } else if
```

▶

continued

```
(command.getErrorReason()==PasswordLoginCommand.UNKNOWN_US
  ER){
  securityState.setErrorCode(SecurityState.ERR_
    UNKNOWN_USER);
  }
}
  // Show the failure page if login fails.
  View.callJSP(servletContext,
  "/PVCShop/Login/LoginFailed.jsp", req, rsp);
}
```

As explained in Chapter 10, the `callJSP` method of the `View` class resolves generic URIs to device specific URIs. When processing a request that originates from a WAP device, the URI `/PVCShop/Menu/MainMenu.jsp` is therefore resolved to `wml/PVCShop/Menu/MainMenu.jsp`. Example 13.3 shows the URI of the quick-order JSP.

Example 13.3   The `GetQuickOrderMenu` **action of the shop controller**

```
GetItemsCommand getItemsCommand = new GetItemsCommand();
getItemsCommand.setUserID (userNumber);
success = getItemsCommand.execute();
  if (success) {
  req.setAttribute("itemsBean", getItemsCommand);
  callJSP(servletContext,
    "/PVCShop/Shop/QuickOrderList.jsp", req, rsp);
  } else {
    callJSP(servletContext,
"/PVCShop/Shop/OutOfOrder.jsp",
      req, rsp);
}
```

The bean that contains the menu information is passed to the `QuickOrderList.jsp`. If the login fails, or getting the quick order list fails, the corresponding error JSPs are called.

Quick order
The `QuickOrderList.jsp` (**Example 13.4**) displays the menu where the customer can select the number of items to be ordered. Figure 13.6 illustrates a quick order list.

Example 13.4 **The quick order JSP**

```
<%@ content_type="text/vnd.wap.wml; charset=iso-8850-1"&>

<jsp:useBean id="itemsBean"
class="sample.shop.beans.ItemsBean" scope="request"/>

<?xml version="1.0"?>
<!DOCTYPE wml PUBLIC "-//WAPFORUM//DTD WML 1.1//EN"
"http://www.wapforum.org/DTD/wml_1.1.xml">

<wml>
  <card id="Menu" title="Uncle Enzo's">
   <p>
    Enter Quantity:<br/>
    <% for (int i = 0; i < itemsBean.size(); i++) { %>
    <%= itemsBean.getName(i)%>
     <input format="N" name="<%= itemsBean.getItemID(i)%>
       " title="<%= itemsBean.getName(i)%>"/>
    <%}%>
    <anchor> Order
     <go method="get"
        href="/servlet/sample.shop.shop.ShopServlet">
        <postfield name="Action" value="Checkout"/>
        <% for (int i = 0; i < itemsBean.size(); i++) { %>
          <postfield name="ItemID<%= i%>"
             value="$<%= itemsBean.getItemID(i)%>"/>
     <%}%>
     </go>
     </anchor>
    </p>
   </card>
  </wml>
```

In the quick order list, the customer can enter a single-digit number for each menu item (defined by `format="N"` in the JSP). The link to submit the order is at the end of the list. In our example, the customer orders one insalata Cesare and one pizza calzone (Figure 13.7).

Purchase confirmation
When the customer presses the link to order, the controller servlet invokes the total amount calculation, gets the address of the customer from the persistence framework, and estimates the time needed until the

Figure 13.6

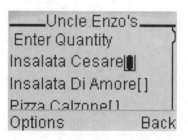

Quick order list

Figure 13.7

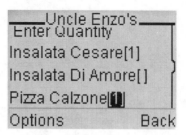

Quick order list with order data

order arrives at the customer's address (Figure 13.8). The estimate of the delivery time is described in the next section.

The customer can now confirm or cancel the order. When the order is confirmed the customer is logged out (Figure 13.9); otherwise, the customer returns to the quick order page.

13.2.3 Application extensions

In this section, we describe some extensions that improve the speed or usability of Uncle Enzo's shop, which are not implemented in the program code shown in this chapter.

Figure 13.8

Purchase confirmation

Figure 13.9

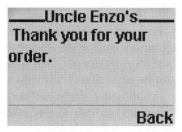

Logoff screen

Alternative authentication mechanisms

The application uses a user identification number and a numerical password for authenticating a customer. This mechanism has the advantage that it will work on any phone, but it is inconvenient for the user. There are two alternatives to this approach:

■ *Customer identification using MSISDN numbers*. Every mobile phone has a unique mobile subscriber integrated services digital network (MSISDN) number that is used by phone companies to identify devices. Most people consider their mobile phone to be a personal device, and therefore want to be identified just by owning the device, rather than typing in user the ID number and password. In this case, users need to provide their telephone number when signing up, which gives the shop a mapping of MSISDN numbers to user ID numbers. If the WAP gateway through which a user connects to the shop application forwards the MSISDN number of the caller, then the shop can use this number for user identification and map it to a user ID.

■ *Customer authentication using WIMs*. In Chapter 6, we presented the notion of WIMs, which allow for secure authentication via the Internet. When WIMs are introduced in future WAP phones, customers owning such phones may be identified using a private key and WAP certificate stored in their WIM. During the registration procedure, the user will have to register a WAP certificate with the shop, which gives the shop a mapping of certificates to user ID numbers. When a customer with a WIM enabled phone logs on to the shop, the shop may send a WML page, including a WMLScript procedure, that lets the WIM generate a signature over a random challenge from the server using the appropriate private key, export the WAP certificate for that key, and sends both signature and WAP certificate back to the server for authentication.

Multipart responses

WAP devices can accept multipart responses (Example 13.5) known from Internet mail. Multipart responses allow servers to chain files and return them to the client in one response. This mechanism can be used to reduce the number of requests that the mobile device sends to the server.

For example, the shop logo and the initial WML deck can be transferred in one response, so that the client does not need to send an additional request to the server to obtain the image referenced in the WML card. The image is transferred to the client together with the logo card.

Example 13.5 **Multipart response**

```
Content-type: multipart/mixed;boundary="--- NEXT PART ---
"
Content-location: http://server/index.wml

--- NEXT PART ---
Content-type: text/vnd.wap.wml

<?xml version="1.0"?>
<!DOCTYPE wml PUBLIC "-//WAPFORUM//DTD WML 1.1//EN"
"http://www.wapforum.org/DTD/wml_1.1.xml">

<wml>
 <card id="Logo" newcontext="true" title="Welcome">
  <onevent type="ontimer">
   <go href="#Login"/>
  </onevent>
  <timer value="50"/>
  <do type="prev" label=""><noop/></do>
  <p align="center">
   <img src="uncleenzos.wbmp" alt="Uncle Enzos's"/><br/>
  </p>
 </card>

 <card id="Login" title="Uncle Enzo's" newcontext="true">
  <p>
   Customer Number<input format="*N" name="user"
     title="User:"/>
   PIN<input format="NNNN" name="pin" title="PIN:"/>
   <a href="/sample/shop/servlet">login</a>
  </p>
 </card>
```

continued

```
</wml>
--- NEXT PART ---
Content-location: uncleenzos.wbmp
Content-type: image/vnd.wap.wbmp


... content of uncleenzos.wbmp ...
--- NEXT PART ---
```

Content parts need to be separated by a delimiter that consists of a unique sequence of characters. This sequence of characters is specified by the boundary attribute within the `Content-type` tag in the header of the document. In our example, the delimiter is `--- NEXT PART ---`. For each part, the tags `Content-type` and `Content-location` are required to enable the WAP gateway to identify the parts correctly.

Use of local images

The WML image tag allows specifying an attribute named `localsrc` that can be used to display images that are predefined by the mobile device. The code below displays a 'smiley' on the browser: `<img src="smiley.wbmp" localsrc="smiley" alt=":-)" />`. If the browser has a built-in smiley picture, it is displayed, otherwise the `smiley.wbmp` is loaded from the server. If the browser does not support graphics, the text `:-)` is displayed.

Input validation using WMLScript

Often, applications need to check whether orders are valid. In our example, at least one menu item must be selected, which is enforced by the structure of the dialog, so that no particular check is required. If an application requires more complicated user input, it is useful to perform sanity checks on user input on the client side to reduce interaction over the network. WMLScript can be used to validate user input on the WAP device itself to reduce the number of network transactions in such a scenario.

13.3 Conclusion

In this chapter, we have described the extension of the application, Uncle Enzo's pizza shop, to support WAP devices. We have covered some of the specific issues that have to be observed in order to implement usable WAP applications. After reading this chapter, you should be able to start experimenting with WAP and start you own application. In the following chapters, we will extend the application further to also allow for access using PDAs and even ordinary telephones via a voice gateway.

14

Access from personal digital assistants

In this chapter, we show how users connecting to the Internet with a PDA can use our example application. The first version of our application will simply synchronize the menu of Uncle Enzo's to the PDA. The user can use this as a reference, and then order via the phone. In the second version, we will use a local database and native application to handle the menu and compose an order. The user will be connected only when synchronizing the data and submitting the order. In the third version, we will use WAP to show the actual menu. The user will be connected while browsing the menu and submitting an order. The chapter concludes with a comparison of the three approaches.

14.1 Extending the example application to personal digital assistants

PDAs give users instant access to personal information-management data, such as calendars and to-do lists. Their operating systems typically also allow the installation of additional applications such as tools and browsers. We will make use of this feature in order to enable users to access the product list of Uncle Enzo's, and to order from the menu.

The device-specific capabilities of PDAs demand special attention to the layout and design of Web pages, or the tools and formats used by client applications. In this chapter, we present three implementations, each tailored for one of the device-connectivity classes described in Chapter 8. Figure 14.1 gives an overview of the necessary changes required in the Web application running on Uncle Enzo's server. The highlighted components have to be extended in order to add the necessary support for PDAs.

14.2 Implementation for synchronized devices

In the first implementation, we will allow the user to download Uncle Enzo's entire menu to the mobile device where it can be used for reference when compiling an order. The actual ordering cannot be made through the PDA, but has to be done using a phone, for example.

Figure 14.1

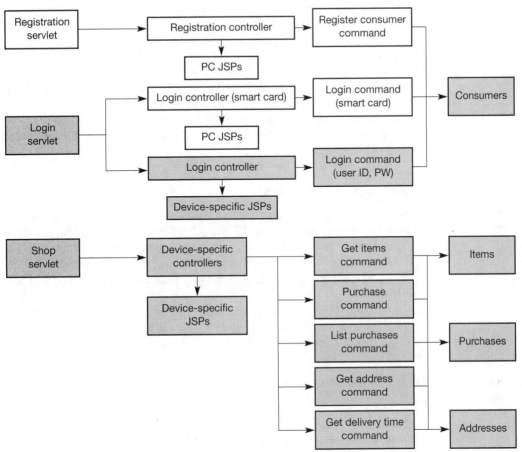

Integration of PDA access into Uncle Enzo's

14.2.1 Tools

We could use a simple database application that includes a viewer for the PDA to display the menu for Uncle Enzo's. Several of these applications are available, and some of them are freeware. They allow a simple database that can be browsed through static forms to be defined. However, that will look as boring as a database table: images will be missing, and navigation will be limited to the features offered by the application.

We need something that supports images as well as hypertext links. Therefore we use an electronic book format for the menu and download the document to the PDA. Currently, there are many proprietary standards for each PDA platform but no widely used open standards for electronic documents. On the Palm OS platform, for example, there are a dozen or so different e-document applications with mostly incompatible formats. For an overview of document readers for Palm OS, see Streitelmeir *et al.*[1] Only a few of these applications are available on multiple platforms. We have chosen the iSilo[2] reader for our first implementation. The advantages of the iSilo application are that it supports a markup language similar to HTML, it is able to convert HTML pages, and it allows documents to be downloaded directly from the Web. It also features good compression, which reduces the size of the document when stored on the PDA. A free client application for Palm OS is available for download.

14.2.2 Application design

Figure 14.2 gives an idea of the complete solution. The user installs the iSiloWeb application on the PC and the iSilo client application on the PDA. A new channel has to be configured once, which is then used to update the data from the Web shop whenever needed. When the PDA is connected to a networked PC, the HTML pages are transferred to the PC and converted to the internal iSilo format. After that, they are synchronized to the PDA in a single file. Afterwards, the PC and the network connection are not needed any more. The user can now access the pages through the iSilo client application.

14.2.3 Menu structure

The menu structure shown in Figure 14.3 will follow the model we designed for the HTML version of the shop, but it leaves out the favorites list and the ordering mechanism (as well as registration, login, and self-care). Only the complete product list can be displayed. This implementation is designed for users who do not connect to the Web shop often, and want to keep the product list on their device for reference only. No personal user data are stored, and no registration process will be necessary. That means that no user login is necessary, but also that there is no way to maintain a favorite quick-order list.

Because of the small displays on PDAs, it is essential to simplify navi-

Figure 14.2

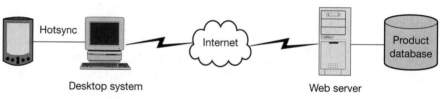

Implementation for synchronized devices

Figure 14.3

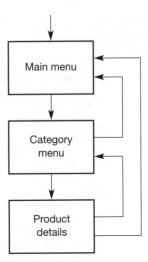

Menu structure for synchronized devices

gation by displaying the products in categories. In this way, the desired product can be found quickly without the need to scroll through long lists. To keep the pages small, the description for each product is available on a separate page, which can be reached through a link.

14.2.4 The data

We have prepared a new set of pages for PDAs connecting to our server. The pages are still composed in HTML format, but with a limited set of tags and with small images. They can be viewed by standard browsers, but they are designed specifically for the smaller screen of a PDA. The Web shop server detects the desired markup format for use on a PDA by looking at the user agent string. The iSiloWeb tool, for example, places the user-agent string `iSiloWeb/1.18 Windows/32` in HTTP requests. However, this is not absolutely necessary for this implementation to work, because the tool can also handle scaling of images and filtering of HTML.

We assume that the user has installed the iSilo client application on the mobile device. The pages are received and downloaded to the PDA using a networked PC running the iSiloWeb tool. This tool allows a channel to be defined that represents a collection of pages from either the local file system or the Web. All the user has to do is to configure the channel with the URL and select the options for conversion to the iSilo format. We have selected to include images and to recursively include pages up to a maximum depth of two levels. After that, the pages are loaded from the Web and converted to the internal, compressed iSilo format. During the next local synchronization, they will be copied to the user's Palm OS device.

Figure 14.4

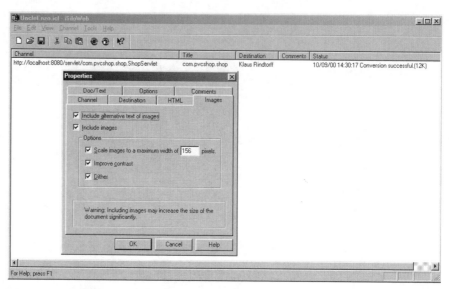

The iSiloWeb tool

Figure 14.4 shows the iSiloWeb tool during channel configuration.

Once transferred to the device, there is no need to have the PDA connected to a networked PC. The pages are available locally on the PDA and can be browsed using the iSilo client application.

14.2.5 The look and feel

When displayed on a PDA screen, the HTML pages will look different to those displayed on a PC browser. They usually lack color, the exact rendering is different, and the font size may vary. One limitation that is particularly unsatisfying is that most tools that convert HTML to an internal PDA format cannot handle tables; instead they place each table cell on a separate line.

The first screen of the Web shop contains the main menu of Uncle Enzo's (Figure 14.5). It displays the available product categories to select from. At the bottom of the picture, the iSilo navigation controls are visible. The Next button allows the user to switch to the next replicated channel. The arrows are used to move through the available pages. The right-hand button is labelled with the current position within the page given as a percentage value, and can be used to jump to another position on the same page.

From here, the user can select one of the categories to browse through the offerings and compile an order. Figure 14.6 shows the client application on the Palm.

Figure 14.5

The main menu for synchronized devices

Figure 14.6

Browsing through a category

At any time, the user can link back to the main menu. For more information about each of the available offerings, the user can select it and is then taken to a separate page presenting more details (Figure 14.7).

14.2.6 Implementation

First, we created the menu using a standard HTML editor. Then we verified that no HTML tags were used that the client viewer cannot handle. Scaled-down versions of the images are embedded at the top and bottom

Figure 14.7

Product details view

of the page. The table is displayed without a border, and all elements on this page are centered.

The static HTML source could be stored as is on the Web server. In this case, it will have to be changed whenever the menu is updated, e.g. when a particular price changes. Worse, we would have to create a separate page for each product item, which would be difficult to administrate. Therefore, instead of using and maintaining static HTML code, our Web shop uses servlets and JSPs to generate the markup. In our sample scenario, the product data are inserted into a page template that is contained within the JSP code (Example 14.1). This allows the product data to be kept in a separate database that is easy to maintain.

14.2.7 Discussion

The client application is relatively small with a footprint of about 85 KB. This is still a relatively large application for Palm OS, but given the fact that it can be used also to view other documents, the size is acceptable. The memory requirements for the data are low, due to the compression method used. No other software is required on the PDA for this implementation.

So far, this application looks and is simple. There is no interaction between the mobile device and the Web shop once the menu has been downloaded. All the user can do is use the hypertext document to browse through the menu. When the Order link is selected, the phone number for Uncle Enzo's pizza shop is displayed. The application runs completely disconnected.

Example 14.1	**JSP code for the main menu**

```
<!DOCTYPE HTML PUBLIC "-//W3C//DTD HTML 4.0//EN">
<HTML>
  <HEAD>
    <META HTTP-EQUIV="content-type"
      CONTENT="text/html;charset=iso-8859-1">
    <TITLE>Uncle Enzo's</TITLE>
  </HEAD>
  <BODY BGCOLOR="#FFFFFF" LINK="#3366CC" VLINK="#55148B"
   ALINK="#FF9900">
  <jsp:useBean id="menuListBean"
    class="sample.shop.shop.GetMenuListCommand"
    scope="request"/>

  <CENTER>
  <IMG SRC="/enzo13bw.gif" HEIGHT=16 WIDTH=123>
  <H3>Our menu</H3>
  <TABLE><TBODY>
    <% for (int i = 0; i < menuListCommand.size(); i++)
       %>
    <% { %>
    <TR><TD>
      <A href="/servlet/ShopServlet?Action=
        ShowItems&CategoryID=<%=
        menuListCommand.getCategoryID(i) %>">

      <%= menuListCommand.getName(i) %></A>
    </TD></TR>
    <% } %>
  </TBODY></TABLE>
  <IMG SRC="/veggies.gif" HEIGHT=23 WIDTH=126>
  </CENTER>
  </BODY></HTML>
```

The advantage of this approach is that it is so simple that every user with the iSilo tool can easily get the menu from Uncle Enzo's – and hopefully order many pizzas. The user does not need an online connection, and they can access the data at anytime without network delays.

The disadvantage of this approach is that Uncle Enzo's will have to deal with orders based on outdated data. If users do not update the channel from time to time, they will not receive menu updates. This is a significant problem for a Web shop, so we will attempt to improve the situation.

14.3 Implementation for intermittently connected devices

The second implementation of PDA access to the example application allows the user to download Uncle Enzo's menu to the mobile device, where it can be used for reference when compiling an order. However, new orders are also transmitted directly from the PDA to Uncle Enzo's Web shop, and during the synchronization the PDA database is updated.

14.3.1 Tools

There are two important components required for this approach. First, there has to be a synchronization mechanism for the data. The task of this component is to replicate the product database from the server to the PDA, and to make sure that it is kept up to date. It will also be used to transfer the orders from the PDA, back to the server. We use the IBM Mobile Connect Synchronization Server for this task.[3]

The second component is a database engine for the PDA. IBM DB2 Everyplace[4] or Oracle Lite DBMS[5] are available for most PDA platforms, and provide a local data store in the form of a relational database. In our example, we use the DB2e database to store the complete menu for Uncle Enzo's. For the sake of simplicity, we also use it to implement the handling of orders.

The Personal Application Builder is a tool available with DB2 Everyplace that automates the generation of client applications. Figure 14.8 shows the development environment of the Personal Application Builder. It allows forms to be designed using a visual builder, and handles the creation of the SQL statements to access the database. The tool automatically generates C code from the form description that is subsequently compiled using the GNU compiler to native code for Palm OS. The supported set of controls is sufficient to create form-based applications, but it imposes several limitations on the design of the user interface. If the data to be displayed and modified cannot be taken straight from a database, but require additional computations, C code scripts can be embedded into the form designs that are run when certain events occur. More elaborate scripting requires the generated code to be edited manually.

The implementation described in this section is implemented in C++ using the Metrowerks CodeWarrior development environment for Palm OS.[6] On the one hand this requires some knowledge of the platform, but on the other hand it allows us to optimize the usability of the application. A C++ library has been written that automatically generates the SQL statements to retrieve data from the local database, and to display them using the table control from Palm OS. Figure 14.9 shows the integrated development environment of the Metrowerks CodeWarrior.

Figure 14.8

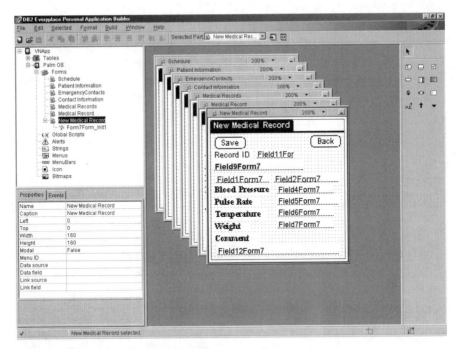

DB2e Personal Application Builder

Figure 14.9

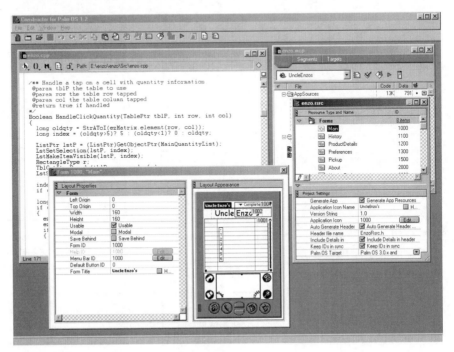

Metrowerks development environment

14.3.2 Application design

Figure 14.10 shows the components used, and how they relate to each other. The PDA connects to the synchronization server via a modem. The synchronization server has access to a relational database via a database server. It processes the updates between the product list stored on the server and the local copy on the client. An event is used to trigger the order handling on the server, and to update the order database.

14.3.3 The menu structure

The possibility to update the data stored on the mobile device allows us to transmit orders to the Web shop and maintain a favorite order list. This requires a proper user authentication, so that all personal data can be kept confidential. Because the synchronization server already performs a user authentication, no login screens need to be added. Figure 14.11 shows the menu structure of the application.

Figure 14.10

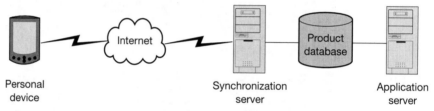

Personal device

Synchronization server

Application server

Implementation for intermittently connected devices

Figure 14.11

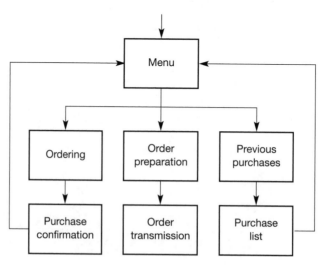

Menu structure for intermittently connected devices

14.3.4 The data

The product data are stored in a relational database accessed by the synchronization server. In this way, the menu prices, categories, and descriptions are easy to maintain. It is even possible to include personalized data for each user. For example, special prices for selected customers may be generated based on individual rebates.

The relational database scheme used in our example defines tables for the products and the categories. Orders are stored in separate tables, one for the order details and one for the order items. Each product is given a unique identification number that is used as a key in the product and order items table.

14.3.5 The look and feel

After the user has configured the Mobile Connect client application with the synchronization server address, the user identification, and password, the PDA is ready to receive the menu (Figures 14.12 and 14.13). During the first time the user connects, the complete database is replicated to the device. During all following connections, only incremental updates will be sent.

When the user starts the client application, it will display the menu. The application offers views for the complete menu, the current order, and individual categories. The user can tap on the quantity column to change the number of items to be ordered (Figures 14.14 and 14.15).

If the user taps on the quantity column in front of the product description, a pop-up menu is displayed where the desired order quantity can be selected. When the product description is selected, a dialog presenting the product details is shown, for example the price and a short description of

Figure 14.12

Synchronization server configuration

Figure 14.13

User configuration

Figure 14.14

Main view

Figure 14.15

Category selection

the product. The user selects the desired quantity, and adds the item to the order list (Figures 14.16 and 14.17).

After the order has been compiled, it is prepared for transmission. The user is prompted for the desired pick-up date and time. Then the internal order database is updated with the entries representing the ordered items and one entry representing the complete order (Figures 14.18 and 14.19).

During the next synchronization process, triggered by the application, the new entries will be sent to the server for handling. At the same time, updates for the product list and the status of previous orders are received (Figures 14.20 and 14.21).

An order history view lists all previously stored orders and their current status. The user can check the order status for pending orders, and have old entries removed from the list (Figures 14.22 and 14.23).

Figure 14.16

Quantity pop-up menu

Figure 14.17

Product details dialog

Figure 14.18

Ordering view

Figure 14.19

Delivery details dialog

Figure 14.20

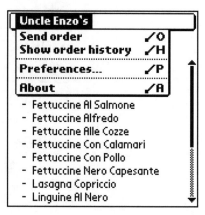

Application menu

Figure 14.21

Order preparation

Figure 14.22

Order transmission

Figure 14.23

Order history view

To complete the process, and to make optimal use of the synchronization capability, the user may even receive a new entry for the date book if a pick-up order has been placed for a specific date. This can be achieved by configuring the Mobile Connect Server to create and replicate date book entries from records of accepted orders in the order database. The user will find a reminder to pick up the order at the given date in the date book application of the PDA.

14.3.6 Implementation

Example 14.2 shows a code snippet from the client application on the PDA. It is included only to give an example for PDA programming, not to illustrate the implementation of this particular application. In the code, we use several methods from an application library to simplify the handling of SQL statements and result sets. The static instances represent the current database view, SQL result set, and table control. Example 14.2 shows how a tap on the quantity column in the current product view is handled.

Configuring the synchronization server

The synchronization server is configured to replicate the product table and the user identification table to the client. The latter is filtered so that only the name of the user currently connected is sent to the device. In this way, the application knows who the current user is without prompting or the need for configuration. Unfortunately, there is currently no API available to query or modify the synchronization server settings. The order and order item tables are replicated in both directions; again, they are filtered so that only the orders for the current user are synchronized. In this way, the new orders reach the server, and the status of old orders is updated on the client device. Instead of giving each user a separate database, we collect all orders into a single database. That avoids manual configuration, and simplifies the administration. Figure 14.24 shows the configuration of a database action on the Mobile Connect Server.

Handling an order

When an order arrives at Uncle Enzo's Web shop, it will show up as an update to the order database. Of course, it is not practical to have somebody watching the database all the time for new entries. Therefore, we need a mechanism that tells us about the new order. This is available in the form of database triggers. The synchronization software already supports triggers. We will use the event generated when inserting a new row into the order details table to trigger the processing of a new order. Mobile Connect allows a Visual Basic Script to handle events to be defined (Example 14.3). We use it only to start a small Java application that handles the database updates.

Example 14.2 | **Code snippet from the implementation for Palm OS**

```
/** Handle a tap on a cell with quantity information.
@param tblP the table to use
@param row the table row tapped
@param col the table column tapped
@return true if handled
*/
Boolean HandleClickQuantity(TablePtr tblP, int row, int
col){
  long oldqty = StrAToI(ezMatrix.element(row, col));
  long index = (oldqty>5)? 5 : (oldqty<1)? 0 : oldqty;
  ListPtr lstP = (ListPtr)GetObjectPtr(MainQuantityList);
  LstSetSelection(lstP, index);
  LstMakeItemVisible(lstP, index);
  RectangleType r;
  TblGetItemBounds(tblP, row, col, &r);
  LstSetPosition(lstP, r.topLeft.x, r.topLeft.y);
  index = LstPopupList(lstP);
  if (index < 0) return false; // nothing selected
  long newqty = index; // starts with 0
  if (newqty != oldqty){
    ezDB2e.bindLong(1, &newqty);
    ezDB2e.bindString(2, ezMatrix.element(row, 2));
    if (ezDB2e.update(&ezSqlUpdateQuantity) ==
        SQL_SUCCESS){
      // check if we must reload the table
      if (ezView.sql != &ezSqlSelectOrders){
        ezMatrix.setElement(row, col, newqty);
        ezTable.refresh();
      }
      else ezTable.reload(&ezDB2e);
    }
  }
  return true;
}
```

The order processing will check for the integrity of the new order, and then process it. The user name is available from the session information supplied by the synchronization server. All orders for the current user are enumerated and their status checked. For each new order in the order details table, the table with the order items is consulted and the number of items is compared with that in the order identification. Then the actual

Figure 14.24

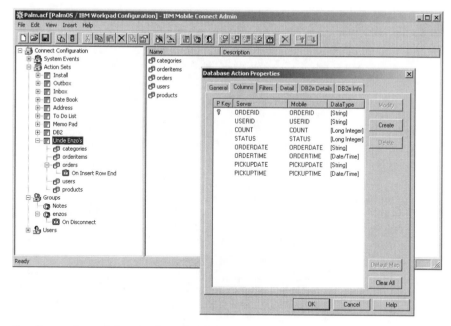

Configuration of the synchronization server

order handling is started (Example 14.4). In our case, we simply print the fact that a new order has arrived, and list all items belonging to it.

When an order is delivered to the customer, the status of it needs to be updated in the database. This should be done based on the result of the delivery process. We will not look at this process in detail within the scope of our example. The order handling used in our implementation simply promotes all accepted orders from status Pending to status Completed when checking for new entries.

Example 14.3   **Visual Basic Script to start order processing**

```
'call JAVA application to handle new orders
Dim command
command = "java Order " & SessionInfo.User \
        & " " & Connect.DBServerUser \
        & " " & Connect.DBServerPassword \
        & " >>order.log"
If Connect.System(command)=0 Then
  EventInfo.Handled = False
End If
```

Example 14.4   **Order handling**

```java
import java.sql.*;
public class Order {
  public static void main(String[] args){
    String dbUrl = "jdbc:odbc:enzo";
    String name = args[0];
    String user = args[1];
    String password = args[2];
    try {
      Class.forName("sun.jdbc.odbc.JdbcOdbcDriver");
      Connection c = DriverManager.getConnection(dbUrl,
      user, password);
      Statement s = c.createStatement();
      ResultSet orders = s.executeQuery("SELECT
       ORDERID,STATUS,COUNT" + " FROM ORDERS WHERE
       USERID='" + name + "'");
      while (orders.next()){
        String orderid = orders.getString("ORDERID");
        int status = orders.getInt("STATUS");
        int count = orders.getInt("COUNT");
        switch (status){
          case 1: {
            ResultSet items = s.executeQuery("SELECT
                COUNT(*)" + " FROM ORDERITEMS WHERE
                ORDERID LIKE '" + orderid + "%'");
            if (items.next()) {
              if (items.getInt(1) == count) {
                System.out.println("Order " + orderid +
                " accepted");
                Statement u = c.createStatement();
                u.executeUpdate("UPDATE ORDERS SET
                    STATUS=2 WHERE ORDERID='" + orderid
                    + "'");
                u.close();
              } else {
                System.out.println("Order " + orderid +
                  " is inclomplete");
                Statement u = c.createStatement();
                u.executeUpdate("UPDATE ORDERS SET " +
                  " STATUS=3 WHERE ORDERID='" +
                  orderid + "'");
                u.close();
```

▶

continued

```
                  }
                }
                break;
              }
              case 2: {
                ResultSet items = s.executeQuery("SELECT * " +
                    FROM ORDERITEMS" + " WHERE ORDERID LIKE
                  '" + orderid + "%'");
                System.out.println("Handling order " +
                    orderid);
                while (items.next()) {
                  System.out.println(" - ordering " +
                      items.getString("code"));
                }
                Statement u = c.createStatement();
                u.executeUpdate("DELETE FROM ORDERITEMS " +
                    WHERE ORDERID LIKE '" + orderid +
                    "%'");
                u.executeUpdate("UPDATE ORDERS SET
                  STATUS=4 " +
                    WHERE ORDERID='" + orderid + "'");
                u.close();
                break;
              }
              case 3: System.out.println("Order "+orderid+"
                  rejected"); break;
              case 4: System.out.println("Order "+orderid+"
                  completed"); break;
            }
          }
          s.close();
        } catch(Exception e) {
        System.out.println(e);
        e.printStackTrace();
        }
      }
    }
```

Example 14.4 shows the simple Java application that is triggered by the synchronization process to search the database for new orders and handle the promotion of the order status. To test the complete application, the product list is downloaded to the device. If a local copy of the data is available in comma-separated values (CSV) format, then the conversion and installation can be accomplished easily with a tool that is available with DB2e. The resulting PDA configuration is saved, and can be used by the Metrowerks CodeWarrior debugger. The order processing is tested using the emulator running on a networked PC.

14.3.7 Discussion

The client application is very small, with a footprint of only 28 KB. However, the database runtime software and the synchronization software together add another 200 KB. This is a lot of memory for current Palm OS devices with 2–8 MB of memory. Nevertheless, this is still acceptable because the database engine and the synchronization software can also be used by other applications. The memory requirements for the data stored in the database are not much higher than those for the native database format, and so are also acceptable.

The transmission of orders from the PDA to the server is based on simple database synchronization. There is no privacy and no concept of a transaction here. If an order is lost or corrupted by a broken connection, there will be problems. The integrity of the order database is at stake, and there will be an unhappy customer. Our implementation can be improved by using a transaction-oriented messaging system, for example MQ Everyplace.[7] The MQ Everyplace client application on the PDA will handle the transmission of the order, and can be used to guarantee the delivery of the message to the server.

The advantage of this approach is that we now have a way to update the product data from our Web shop whenever the customer connects to the synchronization server. This will happen at least for every order sent from the PDA. Nevertheless, there is still a problem if the price of an item changes between the last synchronization and the next order – that's why there is a disclaimer in the order dialog. Users with high connection costs will be happy that the application does not need a permanent network connection: it will be online only when exchanging product and order data. Uncle Enzo's will like it because the user has access to the menu at any time. Furthermore, this approach allows the highest degree of customization. Since we are using native code, it is possible to use all features of the underlying PDA operating system. This can be used, for example, to create an individual user interface that goes beyond what can be done with the standard controls available for Web pages.

The disadvantage of this approach is that we need a special application for each PDA we want to support. Since Uncle Enzo's is certainly not in the application provider business, and connection costs are constantly decreasing, we should try to find a way to improve this solution. In fact, there is a way, and, as we will illustrate, it will be even simpler than the previous two solutions have been.

14.4 Implementation for connected devices

The goal of the third implementation is to give the most up-to-date view of the menu available at Uncle Enzo's, and to make it as device independent as possible. This means that we will have to make a few compromises regarding the user interface because it has to be the same on all available PDA platforms.

14.4.1 Tools

We will use a browser on the PDA to access Uncle Enzo's Web server. With a choice of HTML- and WML-based browsers, we decided to use WML for this implementation. WML gives us all the required formatting and controls needed, and has the additional advantage of being ideally suited for wireless applications. For our application, we used the KBrowser from 4thpass.[8] This supports graphics, and is available for several platforms. Although the KBrowser supports WMLScript, we will not need it for our application.

14.4.2 Application design

Figure 14.25 shows how the PDA connects to the Web shop server, and receives back WML pages. A modem or a phone with a infrared beam connection is used to connect to a WAP gateway, which handles the conversion between HTTP and WAP. All Web pages are available from the Web server in WML format, and all images are encoded in the WBMP format. The Web server connects to the product database and renders the data using JSPs.

Figure 14.25

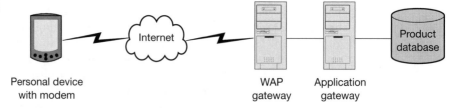

| | | | | |
| Personal device
with modem | | WAP
gateway | Application
gateway | |

Implementation for connected devices

14.4.3 Menu structure

The menu structure for this implementation is very similar to the PC version, since both use a browser to access the Web shop. After an initial login, the favorite order quick list and the complete menu can be displayed. Because PDAs offer an easy way to enter text, the user name and password may both be alphanumeric. Once again, it is essential to sort the product items into categories to keep the number of items per page small. This reduces the need to scroll through long lists in order to find the desired product. Figure 14.26 shows the menu structure of the application.

14.4.4 The look and feel

The appearance of the WML-based solution is similar to the sample application presented in Chapter 13. However, the graphics and layout are adapted to the display capability of the PDA. The screen resolution of popular devices in use today ranges from 160×160 to 640×240 pixels.

Figure 14.26

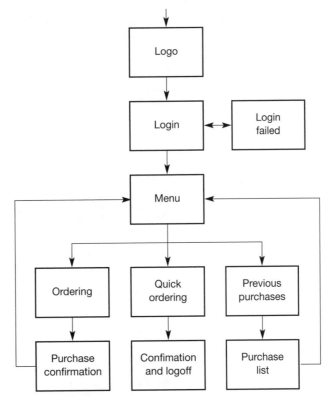

Menu structure for connected services

Those devices with larger screen size often also offer gray-level or color displays. We will target the smaller size, and will use only monochrome graphics, so that our implementation will work with all devices.

After login to the Web shop, the main menu is presented to the user. The favorite choices are immediately available. All other product items are sorted into categories for quick access. When the order is complete, it is sent to the Web server of Uncle Enzo's for processing. An immediate confirmation is sent back to the PDA after receiving the order. Figures 14.27 and 14.28 show how the user can access the web shop using the KBrowser.

Figure 14.27

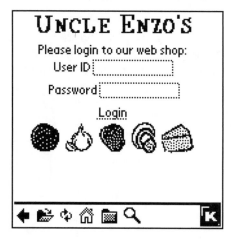

Accessing the Web shop using the KBrowser

Figure 14.28

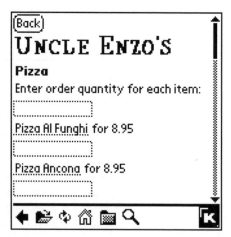

Compiling an order using the KBrowser

14.4.5 Implementation

Of course, the Web server has to be prepared to deliver WML instead of HTML. It can detect the browser used by checking the user agent string that is part of each HTTP request. If it detects that a WML browser is used, the server will switch from HTML to WML markup generation by calling the appropriate set of JSPs. To test the WML pages, and to convert the graphics, we use the Nokia WAP Toolkit. First, all graphics have been converted into the WAP-specific WBMP format. Figure 14.29 shows the conversion using the Nokia WAP Toolkit.

The layout of the WML pages from the sample application in Chapter 11 has been modified for the larger screen size available on PDAs. The JSPs are modified to include slightly larger bitmaps. The text for messages, buttons, and user guidance can now be longer than for smart phones. The formatting does not usually need many changes, and the order handling is identical to that in the WAP implementation. Example 14.5 shows the WML page source returned by the Web shop to a connecting PDA for login. Because PDAs allow text entry, there are no changes required for the login procedure. The resulting WML page is shown in Figure 14.27.

Example 14.6 shows a modified JSP that displays one of the product categories from Uncle Enzo's Web shop. Figure 14.28 shows the resulting WML page displayed by the KBrowser.

Figure 14.29

Conversion to the WBMP format

Example 14.5	**WML Source of the login procedure for PDAs**

```xml
<?xml version="1.0"?>
<!DOCTYPE wml PUBLIC "-//WAPFORUM//DTD WML 1.1//EN"
"http://www.wapforum.org/DTD/wml_1.1.xml">
<wml>
  <card id="Logo" newcontext="true"
    title="Welcome to
     Uncle Enzo's">
    <onevent type="ontimer"> <go href="#Login"/>
    </onevent>
    <timer value="50"/>
    <do type="prev" label=""> <noop/> </do>
    <p align="center"> <img src="enzo13.wbmp"
      alt="Uncle
       Enzos's"/> </p>
    <p align="center"> Welcome to our web shop! <p/>
    <p align="center"> <img src="veggies.wbmp" alt=""/>
    </p>
  </card>
  <card id="Login"
    title="Uncle Enzo's"
        newcontext="true">
    <p align="center"> <img src="enzo13.wbmp"
        alt="Uncle Enzos's"/> </p>
    <p align="center"> Please login to our web shop: <p/>
    <p align="center">
      User ID <input format="*C" name="userID"
          title="User ID"/> <br/>
      Password <input format="*C" name="password"
          title="Password"/> <br/>
      <anchor> Login
        <go method="get"
          href="/servlet/sample.shop.auth.LoginServlet">
          <postfield name="Action" value="Logon"/>
          <postfield name="UserID" value="$userID"/>
          <postfield name="Password" value="$password"/>
        </go>
      </anchor>
    </p>
    <p align="center"> <img src="veggies.wbmp" alt=""/>
    </p>
  </card>
</wml>
```

Example 14.6 **Modified JSP with WML markup for PDAs**

```
<%@ content_type="text/vnd.wap.wml; charset=iso-8850-1"&>
<jsp:useBean id="itemsBean"
class="sample.shop.shop.GetItemsCommand" scope="request"/>
<?xml version="1.0"?>
<!DOCTYPE wml PUBLIC "-//WAPFORUM//DTD WML 1.1//EN"
"http://www.wapforum.org/DTD/wml_1.1.xml">
<wml>
    <card id="Quick" title="Uncle Enzo's Quick Order">
      <p align="center"> <img src="enzo13.wbmp"
        alt="Uncle
        Enzos's"/> </p>
      <p> Enter the desired quantity for each item: <br/>
        <% for (int i = 0; i < itemsBean.size(); i++) %>
        <% { %>
          <%= itemsBean.getName(i) %>
            <input format="N" name="<%=
            itemsBean.getItemID(i)
          %> " title="<%= itemsBean.getName(i) %>"/>
        <% } %>
        <anchor> Order
          <go method="get"
            href="/servlet/sample.shop.shop.ShopServlet">
            <postfield name="Action" value="Checkout"/>
            <% for (int i=0; i<itemsBean.size(); i++) %>
            <% { %>
              <postfield
              name="<%= itemsBean.getItemID(i) %>"
                value="$<%= itemsBean.getItemID(i) %>"/>
            <% } %>
          </go>
        </anchor>
      <p align="center"> <img src="veggies.wbmp" alt=""/>
      </p>
    </card>
</wml>
```

Finally, the device-detection logic in the Web application is extended to
accept the new WML browser class for PDAs from the user agent string
in the HTTP request. To test the application, the Palm emulator running
on a networked PC can be used. In contrast to the scenario using WAP
phones, there are no visible differences between the rendering on the
emulator and on the physical device, thus the PDA emulator is sufficient

for the initial testing. However, to guarantee the usability of the implementation, testing with a real device is still necessary.

14.4.6 Discussion

The size of the client application is 86 KB. This is for the WML browser alone. No internal database is required on the PDA because all data remain on the server, and are sent to the PDA when necessary. Orders are compiled and handled while connected to the server. The advantage of this approach is that the latest data will always be available. On the other hand, it also means that nothing is kept on the PDA, and that there is no way to check the history or status of recent orders unless the PDA is online and the Web server application is extended to support this.

Using HTML markup instead of WML markup for this implementation would limit the number of formats and tools necessary, and would thus decrease its complexity. However, this requires the availability of an HTML-capable browser on the PDA. If that browser supports only a subset of HTML, it will still require the Web server to handle access via PDAs separately by generating an appropriate HTML subset and a suitable layout for the smaller PDA displays.

14.5 Comparison

If we compare all three implementations demonstrated in this chapter, we can see how they fall into three application categories:

- offline (first implementation)
- intermittently connected (second implementation)
- connected (third implementation).

The first implementation requires no effort on the server side, but it is most dependent on the tools available for the PDA. The second application requires the most effort on the PDA side, but it allows the highest degree of customization. The third implementation is the most portable on the PDA side, but it requires the Web server to support PDA specific markup. The properties and benefits of all three approaches are summarized in Table 14.1.

Table 14.1	Comparison of the three implementations		
	Implementation for synchronized devices	**Implementation for intermittently connected devices**	**Implementation for connected devices**
Tools used	iSilo and iSiloWeb	Metrowerks CodeWarrior	KBrowser
Client data format	Proprietary document format	Proprietary database format	Not applicable
Client application	Special viewer for the relevant PDA operating system	Native application for the PDA operating system	Standard WAP browser
Data sharing	None	Standard SQL API	Not applicable
Data synchronization	Using a networked PC and special tool	Network connection	Not applicable
Data actuality	Initial replication without enforced updates	Initial replication with regular updates	No replication, but immediate access to data
Connection	One-time connection for initial replication	Regular connections to synchronize data	Permanent connection during application use
Data source	Any Web server	Synchronization server with database access	Dedicated Web server and WAP gateway

References

1. Streitelmeir, J. Clark, J. and Brandwein, E. (2001) 'Official gadgeteer hands on review: Doc readers for Palm OS PDAa'.
http://www.the-gadgeteer.com/docreaders-review.html

2. iSilo. http://www.isilo.com

3. IBM. 'Mobile Connect Version 2.41'.
http://www-3.ibm.com/pvc/products/mobile_connect/index.shtml

4. DB2 Everyplace: http://www-4.ibm.com/software/data/db2/everyplace/

5. Oracle. 'Oracle 8i Lite'.
http://www.oracle.com/ip/deploy/database/8i/8ilite/index.html

6. Metrowerks. 'CodeWarrior for Palm OS'.
http://www.metrowerks.com/products/palm/

7. IBM. 'MQ Series Everyplace':
http://www-4.ibm.com/.software/ts/mqseries/everyplace

8. 4thpass.'KBrowser'. http://www.4thpass.comkbrowser/index.html

15

Access via voice

With the steadily increasing computing power of PCs, and advances in voice-recognition research, speech-recognition and speech-synthesis software has now reached a quality acceptable for commercial use. We described fundamentals of speech recognition and speech synthesis in Chapter 7. In this chapter, we explain how an e-business application can communicate with users over a normal telephone line, and how a voice gateway will be used by our application for speech recognition and text-to-voice generation. We will present the JSPs and the VoiceXML pages needed for interacting with the voice gateway.

15.1 Extending the example application to voice access

Most of Uncle Enzo's customers are not using PCs or PDAs to order their pizza. They just place their order using the wire-line or mobile phone. This is convenient for the customers, but as it is not automated, it is expensive for Uncle Enzo's. Therefore, Uncle Enzo's wants to enhance their automatic pizza ordering service with a speech-controlled interface for telephone access.

To integrate access via a normal telephone, some components of our example application architecture need to be enabled for voice access. We show how the application architecture is enabled for voice access, and explain the controllers and JSPs needed for voice access. We then explain how a voice gateway is used together with our application.

Because the voice interface has a very low bandwidth compared with graphical displays, we are using the same quick ordering mechanism that we introduced in Chapter 13. This allows the user to pick a favorite item, rather than listening to the complete menu.

15.1.1 Integration in the overall architecture

Figure 15.1 shows the overall architecture. The highlighted components are added to the example system: the login JSP for voice, the controller servlet for accessing the shop via voice, and the JSPs for rendering the shop information in VoiceXML for output to the user.

15.1.2 Infrastructure

In addition to the standard infrastructure required to deploy Web applications, enabling Web applications for access using voice input/output through ordinary phones requires additional equipment. A voice gateway is used to connect a normal phone to the example application. Figure 15.2 shows how the voice gateway fits into the Web shop architecture.

Figure 15.3 shows the interaction between the voice gateway and the application server in detail. The voice gateway runs the voice browser,

Figure 15.1

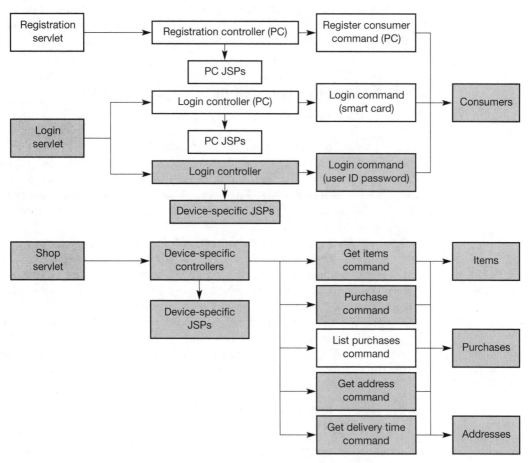

Integration of voice access into the application

Figure 15.2

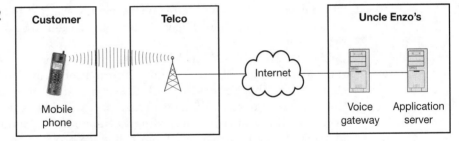

Voice access infrastructure

Figure 15.3

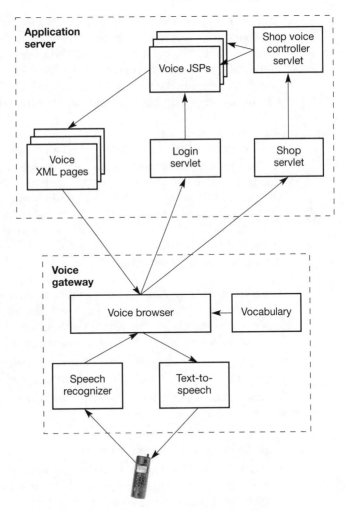

Voice gateway architecture

which communicates with a telephone via a voice-recognition module and a text-to-speech module. The voice browser is the interface to the application server.

Like HTML pages, VoiceXML pages can be generated dynamically on the server, using JSPs that render information provided by servlets. As explained in Chapter 7, VoiceXML files can contain grammars to increase the recognition rate. If a grammar is available, the voice browser processes the user input according to the defined grammar. The recognized sentence is forwarded from the voice browser to the responsible servlet on the application server side.

15.1.3 User Interface

The user interface for voice is very different from the user interfaces for the other access paths presented earlier, as it contains no graphics or text. Instead of HTML or WML pages, the user interaction flow is based on VoiceXML pages. In this section, we give an overview of voice interface design principles, then show the flow of the different VoiceXML pages, and finally give a dialog example for ordering with voice.

Voice user interface design principles
The voice user interface differs from a graphical user interface in several ways. First, voice is sequential, and scrolling back to the information heard before is not as easy as with a display. In addition, the bandwidth of the voice channel is very limited (<15 characters/second). Because automated speech recognition is a difficult task, the voice user interface needs to be tailored towards the capabilities required by the speech-recognition system. The following design principles can help to produce a voice user interface with high usability:

- *Limit choices in dialog*. The number of choices in a dialog should be less then five, as most users cannot remember more then five items. This also results in a small and efficient grammar for the speech recognition engine, with high recognition rates.
- *Grammars*. Use grammars whenever possible to allow for high recognition rates and high recognition speed.
- *Distinct keywords*. Use keywords that do not sound similar to get high recognition rates.
- *Key entry*. Use key entry for selection if possible, as keys are transferred with a high reliability.
- *'Bark in'*. Enable the user to say a command while the system generates text-to-speech output. This enables experienced uses to make shortcuts in the voice menu.

- *Pre-recorded voice.* Use pre-recorded words or sentences whenever possible to make the text-to-speech output more understandable.
- *Dialects.* Be aware of dialects when choosing grammars and keywords. When a system is used locally (e.g. in a specific town), it can be useful to train the system to the local dialect.
- *Personalized user interface.* Enable the user to personalize the voice interface so that the choices are minimized (e.g. have a default delivery address).

In our example we will use limited choices, grammars, key entry, and the ability to personalize the user interface.

User interface overview

Figure 15.4 shows which parts of the user interface of the overall architecture are used for voice. The voice application starts directly with the login page. The quick ordering concept discussed in relation to WAP is used (give out the favorite items for quick ordering), but it is also possible to make an order from the menu.

Figure 15.4

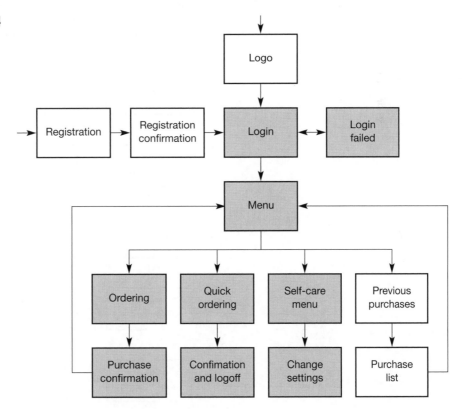

User interface overview

The VoiceXML flow displayed in Figure 15.5 shows the user interface script for the voice application in more detail. In our example, only one item can be ordered per order request. This limits the size of the example, and complete VoiceXML pages can be shown.

The first page is a static login page, where the customer, named Anna in our example, must enter her customer number and PIN. If the PIN number is incorrect, she gets the login page again, otherwise the system displays the quick order page. As mentioned before, voice is an interface with a very low bandwidth, therefore the data to be transmitted must be tailored towards easy and fast ordering. The application therefore uses the quick ordering mechanism. It will first list Anna's favorite pizzas, then allow her either to choose one of them or request to order from the menu. If she wants to order from the menu, she is directed to the menu order page. Both dialog flows join at the confirmation page, where Anna must confirm her order. If she does not confirm the order, she gets back to the quick order page. After confirming the order, she can either choose to have the order delivered to her usual address, or she can provide a different address. Finally, all delivery information is summarized, and Anna is asked for a final confirmation.

VoiceXML can provide different levels of error handling. Frequently, the recognition engine may not properly recognize the words spoken.

Figure 15.5

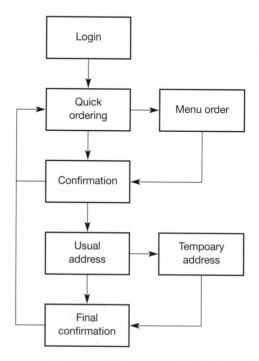

VoiceXML flow

Therefore, the first error message is normally only a very short one to save bandwidth. If the error occurs a second time, the user may need more help, and a more exhaustive help text is spoken. This mechanism is also shown in our VoiceXML example code (Example 15.1).

User interface example

Example 15.1 shows an example login and ordering of a registered user. On the left is Uncle Enzo's pizza ordering service, and on the right is Anna, our customer who wants to order a pizza.

Example 15.1 | **Ordering by voice**

Uncle Enzo's ordering system	Customer Anna

'Welcome to Uncle Enzo's pizza ordering service!'
'Please enter your customer code.'

    Anna enters her customer code via the phone keyboard.

'Thank you. Please enter your PIN code.'

    Anna enters her PIN code via the phone keyboard.

'Your favourite items are:'
'Number one: Pizza Al Funghi'
'Number two: Pizza Hawaii'
'Number three: Pizza Pompeii'
'Number four: Spaghetti Primavera'
'Number five: Pizza Margherita'
'Which one would you like to order?'

    'I would like to have number three.'

'You have chosen Pizza Pompei for nine dollars ninety-five cents.'

'Is that correct?'

    'Yes.'

'Should the pizza be devlivered to the usual address in California?'

    'Yes, please.'

'Your pizza will be delivered in twenty minutes to Los Angeles, Hollywood Boulevard number twenty. Is that your order?'

    'Yes.'

'Thank you, Anna.'

The ordering consists of several steps:

1. *Login*. The user must enter the customer number and PIN via the keyboard of the phone to enable the system to identify and authenticate the customer. The system checks the entered customer number and PIN against the customer database. If the customer number and PIN are correct, the system proceeds with the ordering dialog, otherwise it prompts again for customer and PIN.

2. *Ordering*. After successful authentication, the customer gets their personal five favorite pizza and pasta meals to choose from. Now the customer can order one of the five by telling the ordering system the chosen number, or she can ask to order from the menu.

3. *Confirming the order*. The system now repeats the order, tells the customer the price of the ordered pizza, and asks for confirmation.

4. *Delivery address*. The ordering system wants to know where to deliver the pizza. It first asks if it should be delivered to the usual address. This means that the customer does not have to enter the delivery address for each order. Optionally, the customer can give a different address for this particular order.

5. *Final confirmation*. The system tells the customer how long delivery will take, and where the pizza will be delivered to. It asks for a final confirmation to process the order.

15.2 Implementation

With the implementation explained below, a customer can call Uncle Enzo's pizza service on the phone and order a pizza. The ordering process and the interaction with the customer is done automatically using voice-recognition and text-to-speech technology. The implementation is based on JSPs. It provides VoiceXML pages that are processed by the voice gateway when interacting with the customers.

15.2.1 Tools

We use IBM's Websphere Studio with the Voice Server SDK plug-in as a test environment. This environment allows VoiceXML applications embedded into normal Web applications to be tested. It also offers support for interactive generation of VoiceXML pages.

15.2.2 Commands

The voice application uses the same commands as the WAP application described in Chapter 13. It features a numeric login and password, uses the quick ordering mechanism, and confirms the delivery address and delivery time. Refer to Chapter 11 for a description of these commands.

15.2.3 Controllers, Java Server Pages, and VoiceXML pages

To give an idea of how voice can be integrated into Web applications, some code fragments are shown in this section. Because the VoiceXML part is the main difference of the voice application, compared with the WML application, the VoiceXML pages are shown in more detail.

Controllers and Java Server Pages
As explained in Chapter 11, controllers process requests by invoking application logic (e.g. via a command), and generate a response by invoking a view (e.g. a JSP) depending on the result returned by the application logic.

For login to the system via voice, the same `LoginServlet` and `PasswordLoginController` are used as for login via WAP. Example 15.2 shows the relevant part of the `PasswordLoginController` class. It provides a generic URI `/PVCShop/Menu/MainMenu.jsp` for invocation of the menu JSP that is mapped to real URIs by the `callJSP` method. The mapping depends on the client device type. In the case of a voice telephone connected via a voice gateway, the URI `/PVCShop/Menu/MainMenu.jsp` is mapped to `/voicexml/PVCShop/Menu/MainMenu.jsp`.

Example 15.2 | **The login action of the PasswordLoginController**

```
if (action.equals(ACTION_GET_LOGON_PAGE)) {
    View.callJSP(servletContext,
"/PVCShop/Login/LoginForm.jsp", req, rsp);
    } else if (action.equals(ACTION_LOGON)) {
    String userID = req.getParameter(USER_ID);
    String password = req.getParameter(PASSWORD);

    SecurityState securityState = new SecurityState ();
    securityState.setUserID(userID);

    PasswordLoginCommand command =
    new
      PasswordLoginCommand();
    command.setUserID(userID);
    command.setPassword(password);
    boolean success = command.execute();
    if (success) {
```

▶

continued

```
                            // Get session to which request belongs, create
                               if required.
                            HttpSession session = req.getSession(true);

                            securityState.setAuthenticationState
                              (SecurityState.AUT_USERID_PASSWORD);
                            session.putValue(SecurityState.AUTH_STATE_BEAN_ID,
                               securityState);

                            // Show the main menu after successful login.
                            View.callJSP(servletContext,
                              "/PVCShop/Menu/MainMenu.jsp", req, rsp);
                          } else {
                            if (command.getErrorReason() ==
                              PasswordLoginCommand.WRONG_CREDENTIAL) {

                            securityState.setErrorCode(SecurityState.
                              ERR_WRONG_CREDENTIAL);
                            } else if (command.getErrorReason()
                            ==PasswordLoginCommand.
                            UNKNOWN_USER){

                              securityState.setErrorCode(SecurityState.
                              ERR_UNKNOWN_USER);
                            }
                          }
                          // Show the failure page if login fails.
                          View.callJSP(servletContext,
                            "/PVCShop/Login/LoginFailed.jsp", req, rsp);
                        }
```

The quick order JSP is implemented as shown in Example 15.3.

This JSP generates a list of the customer's favorite items. The customer can choose one of these items, or can get to the menu ordering via the Menu command. The hidden `ItemIDs` can be achieved with a grammar when using VoiceXML. The recognized word is then replaced with the value in the brackets (e.g. 'one' with the value of `itemBean.getItemNumber(1)`).

In our example, only one item can be ordered at a time. Therefore, the `ItemID` for the checkout action can be fixed to `ItemID1`, and no quantity is qualified. Hence the `ShopServlet takes` one as default ordering quantity.

The VoiceXML code is explained in detail below.

Example 15.3	**Voice quick order JSP**

```
<%@ content_type="text/vnd.voice.vxml; charset=iso-8850-
1"&>
<jsp:useBean id="itemsBean"
class="sample.shop.shop.GetItemsCommand" scope="request"/>
<?xml version="1.0"?>
<vxml version="1.0">
  <form>
    <block>
    Your favourite items are:
<% for (int i = 0; i < itemsBean.size(); i++) { %>
       Number <%= i %>: <%= itemsBean.getName(i)%>
<%
    }
%>
    </block>
    <field name="ItemID1">
    <prompt timeout="4s"> Which one do you like to
      order? </prompt>
    <grammar type="application/x-jsgf">
      One {<%= itemBean.getItemNumber(1) %>} |
      Two {<%= itemBean.getItemNumber(2) %>} |
      Three {<%= itemBean.getItemNumber(3) %>} |
      Four {<%= itemBean.getItemNumber(4) %>} |
      Five {<%= itemBean.getItemNumber(1) %>} | Help |
        Menu
    </grammar>
    <catch event="nomatch noinput help" count="1">
        Please say the number of your favourite Pizza
          or Menu to order from menu.
    </catch>
    <filled>
      <if cond="SelectedItem == 'Menu'"/>
        <submit
next="/servlet/sample.shop.shop.ShopServlet?Action=GetMain
Menu"/>
      <elseif cond"SelectedItem == 'Help'"/>
        <submit
next="/servlet/sample.shop.shop.ShopServlet?Action=GetHelp
""/>
      <else/>
        <submit
next="/servlet/sample.shop.shop.ShopServlet?Action=Checko t"
```

continued

```
namelist="ItemID1" />
        </if>
    </field>
  </form>
</vxml>
```

VoiceXML files
VoiceXML consists of two parts: the grammar files and the VoiceXML pages. The VoiceXML grammars are based on JSGF (see Chapter 7). They help to narrow down the possible answers for the speech recognizer.

Example 15.4   **Confirmation grammar**

```
#JSGF V1.0;
grammar confimation;
public <confirm> =  Yes | No | Help;
```

The confirmation grammar (Example 15.4) is used whenever the customer must confirm something (e.g. the chosen pizza). In addition to 'Yes' and 'No' the customer can always ask for help.

The item grammar (Example 15.5) is used when the customer wants to choose an item from the complete menu. In contrast to the list of five favorites, in which the customer only says a number, here the customer

Example 15.5   **Item grammar**

```
#JSGF V1.0;
grammar item;
public <items> = <antipasti> | <salads> | <soups> |
<pizza> | <pasta> | <chicken> | <veal> | <fish> |
<desserts> | <beverages>;

private <pizza> =  Pizza <pizzatype> | <pizzatype>;

private <pizzatype> = Al Funghi | Ancona | Boscaiola |
Cappriciosa | Capri | Carbonara | Frutti Di Mare |
Gamberetti | Hawaii | Magherita | Pompeii | …;

private <pasta> = Canelloni Al Forno | Spaghetti
Primavera | …;

private <salad> = Insalata <saladtype>;

private <saladtype> = Cesare | Dellorto | Di Amore |
Mista | Tricolore | de Mediterraneo;
```

must say the name of the item. Therefore, all available items must be listed in that grammar. To keep the example code short, only a few items were listed. One notable entry is that for 'pizza'. This allows the prefix 'pizza' to be added to any pizza, or for just the name of the pizza to be spoken. Pizza names are not normally in the dictionary of the voice gateway, so the Italian words need to be added.

The VoiceXML pages are used to render the Web shop information to speech output and recognize the voice input.

Example 15.6	Login VoiceXML

```xml
<?xml version="1.0"?>
<vxml version="1.0">
  <form>
    <block>
      Welcome to the Uncle Enzo's pizza ordering
        service!
    </block>
    <field name="UserID" type="DTMF">
      <prompt> Please enter your customer code.
      </prompt>
      <catch event="nomatch noinput help" count="1">
      Please enter your customer code via keyboard.
      </catch>
      <catch event="nomatch noinput help" count="2">
      Please enter the customer code you received at
      registration time with your telephone
      keyboard.
      </catch>
    </field>
    <field name="Password" type="DTMF">
      <prompt> Thank you. Please enter your PIN code.
      </prompt>
      <catch event="nomatch noinput help" count="1">
      Please enter your secret PIN code via keyboard.
      </catch>
    </field>
    <block>
      <submit
next="/servlet/sample.shop.auth.LoginServlet&Action=Logon"
namelist="UserID Password" />
    </block>
  </form>
</vxml>
```

The login VoiceXML page (Example 15.6) handles the login via voice. It speaks out the welcome text, and then asks for the customer number. As an example of how to handle **unrec**ognized words, this example uses `catch` statements. After the first **unk**nown word, the `count=1` catch statement is executed. In this case, only a small amount of information is given to the customer on how to enter the customer number. If the customer still doesn't enter a number, the catch statement with `count=2` is executed, giving the customer an exhaustive explanation on what to do.

After the customer has entered their number (this is indicated by the `type=DTMF` flag), they are asked for their secret PIN to authenticate themselves to the system. Both numbers are given to the `Login` servlet for verification. After verification, the servlet dynamically generates the customer specific `order.vxml` page for ordering pizza, shown in Example 15.7.

Example 15.7	**Order VoiceXML**

```
<?xml version="1.0"?>
<vxml version="1.0">
  <form>
    <block>
      Your favourite items are:
      Number 1: Pizza Al Funghi
      Number 2: Pizza Hawaii
      Number 3: Pizza Pompeii
      Number 4: Spaghetti Primavera
      Number 5: Pizza Margherita
    </block>
    <field name="Item1">
      <prompt timeout="4s"> Which one would you like to
       order? </prompt>
      <grammar type="application/x-jsgf" />
        One {17} |
        Two {21} |
        Three {42} |
        Four {13} |
        Five {25} | Help | Menu
      </grammar>
      <catch event="nomatch noinput help" count="1">
          Please say the number of your favourite Pizza
          or Menu to order from menu.
      </catch>
      <filled>
      <if cond="SelectedItem == 'Menu'"/>
```

continued

```
            <submit
next="/servlet/sample.shop.shop.ShopServlet?Action=GetMain
Menu"/>
        <elseif cond"SelectedItem == 'Help'"/>
          <submit next="/servlet/sample.shop.shop.
            ShopServlet?Action=GetHelp""/>
          <else/>
            <submit next="
servlet/sample.shop.shop.ShopServlet?Action=Checkout"
namelist="Item1" />
        </if>
        </filled>
      </field>
    </form>
</vxml>
```

The ordering VoiceXML page lists the customer's favorite items, then asks for a choice. The `if` statement checks whether the keywords 'Menu' or 'Help' was said. If so, the corresponding VoiceXML page is called, otherwise, the `Order` servlet is called with the `ItemID` of the chosen pizza.

The choice grammar allows the customer to choose a favorite pizza. Therefore, it consists of the words 'one' to 'five'. As explained above, the numbers are replaced with the hidden `ItemID` value, which the system needs to identify the item.

Now, the `Order` servlet produces a new dynamic VoiceXML page with the price of the ordered item and the dialog for getting the address. The above examples show the principles of how to create voice access and how the voice interface interacts with the backend system.

15.2.4 Application extensions

The above application was simplified to help understanding and produce small VoiceXML pages. Nevertheless, the voice application shows the basic elements needed in a real-world voice scenario, including JSPs and error handling. Some potential extensions of the application are discussed below.

Multiple item ordering
The restriction for ordering only one item was applied to keep the VoiceXML code short. It is easy to extend the ordering VoiceXML page to ask for the quantity of an ordered item, and whether the customer wants to order additional items.

Special offers

In addition to the preselected favourite items, Uncle Enzo's could offer the customer a special pizza of the day. The following code fragment, which needs to be inserted into the order JSP, would achieve this:

```
<jsp:useBean id="offerOfTheDayBean"
class="sample.shop.shop.GetOffersOfTheDayCommand"
scope="request"/>
...
Number 6, Pizza of the day:
<%= offerOfTheDayBean.getName() %> for only
<%= offerOfTheDayBean.getPrize() %>
```

The `offerOfTheDayBean` encapsulates the access to the database, where the offer of the day and the special price are stored.

Bonus system

As the customer data are stored in a database, the customer record could easily be enhanced with a field for bonus points. This would allow Uncle Enzo's to offer a bonus pizza after, say, ten received orders.

Registration via the phone

For simplicity, our example allows registrations with Uncle Enzo's only via the PC. There is no technical reason why customers could not register over the phone. The customer would have to spell out the critical information, such as name and address, as the voice-recognition system has no helping grammar for understanding names and addresses.

15.3 Conclusion

In this chapter, we have given an introduction to voice-enabled Web applications. We have presented the basic principles, including the functions provided by a voice gateway to connect phones to servers. We have shown how the example application, Uncle Enzo's shop, can be extended to support voice as an additional access mode. After reading this chapter, and using the referenced information provided in Chapter 7, you should now be able to start implementing your own voice-driven applications.

Conclusion

In Part 2 of this book we have presented technologies for implementing pervasive computing Web applications, including the most relevant components of the Java 2 Enterprise Edition, XML technology, and Web services technology. An architecture for pervasive Web applications based on these technologies has been presented, and an example of a Web application was given that can be accessed via PCs, WAP phones, voice, and PDAs based on this architecture. For each access mode, we have shown how to implement the relevant application part, using servlets, controllers, command beans, and JSPs to create the particular markup types. After reading this part, you should have the overview and hands-on information to create your own pervasive computing applications using state-of-the-art technology.

Appendix

Frequently used abbreviations

ADSL	Asymmetric digital subscriber line
AES	Advanced Encryption Standard
AMPS	Advanced mobile phone service
APDU	Application protocol data unit
API	Application programming interface
AWD	Abstract Window Toolkit
C#	C Sharp programming language
CAPI	Cryptographic application programming interface
CC/PP	Composite capability/preference profile
CD	Compact disk
CDF	Channel definition format
CDMA	Code division multiple access
CDPD	Cellular digital packet data
CERN	European Center for Nuclear Research
cHTML	compact Hypertext Markup Language
CLDC	Connected limited device configuration
CoG	Chip-on-glass

CORBA	Common object request broker architecture
CPU	Central processing unit
CSV	Comma-separated values
DES	Data Encryption Standard
DHCP	Dynamic host configuration protocol
DHTML	Dynamic Hypertext Markup Language
DOM	Document object model
DRAM	Dynamic random-access memory
DSA	Digital signature algorithm
DSS	Digital signature standard
DSTN	Dual-scan
DTD	Document type definition
DVD	Digital versatile disk
EEPROM	Electrically erasable and programmable read-only memory
EJB	Enterprise Java Bean
ETSI	European Telecommunications Standardization Institute
FAR	False accept rate
FRAM	Ferroelectric random-access memory
FRR	False reject rate
GBDE	Global Business Dialog on Electronic Commerce
GENA	General event notification architecture
GNU	GNUs, not UNIX
GPS	Global positioning system

GPRS	General packet radio service
GSM	Global system for mobile communications
HSCSD	High-speed circuit-switched data
HTML	Hyper Text Markup Language
HTTP	Hypertext transfer protocol
HTTPS	Hypertext transfer protocol over SSL
ICC	Integrated circuit card
ICMP	Internet control message protocol
IDEA	International Data Encryption Algorithm
iDEN	Integrated digital enhanced network
IDL	Interface definition language
IESC	Internet Engineering Steering Committee
IETF	Internet Engineering Task Force
IFD	Interface device
IIOP	Internet inter-orb protocol
IP	Internet protocol
IPv6	Internet protocol version 6
IR	Infrared
IrDA	Infrared Data Association
IrMC	Infrared Mobile Communication
ISO	International Organization for Standardization
ISP	Internet service providers
ITU	International Telecommunication Union

J2EE	Java 2 Enterprise Edition
J2ME	Java 2 Micro Edition
J2SE	Java 2 Standard Edition
JAR	Java archive file
JDBC	Java database connectivity
JMS	Java message service
JNDI	Java naming and directory interface
JSGF	Java speech grammar format
JSML	Java Speech Markup Language
JSP	Java server page
JTA	Java transaction application programming interface
JTS	Java transaction service
JVM	Java virtual machine
LAN	Local area network
LCD	Liquid crystal display
LCoG	Liquid-crystal-on-glass
LDAP	Lightweight directory access protocol
LEP	Light-emitting polymer
Li	Lithium
MAC	Message authentication code
MAL	Mobile application link
MathML	Mathematical Markup Language
MFC	Multifrequency coding
MIT	Massachusetts Institute of Technology

MMU	Memory management unit
MRAM	Magneto-resistive random-access memory
MSISDN	Mobile subscriber integrated services digital network
MVC	Model–view–controller
NBS	National Bureau of Standards
NCSA	National Center for Supercomputing Applications
NiCad	Nickel–cadmium
NiMH	Nickel–metal hydride
NIST	National Institute of Standards and Technology
OBEX	Object exchange
OCF	Open Card Framework
ODBC	Open Database Connectivity
OHG	Operator Harmonization Group
OLED	Light-emitting organic diode
ORB	Object request broker
OSGi	Open service gateway initiative
OSI	Open system interconnect
OTP	Over-the-air provisioning
PAP	Push access protocol
PC/SC	Personal computer/smart card interface
PDA	Personal digital assistant
PDC	Personal digital cellular
PHS	Personal handyphone system
PIM	Personal information management

PIN	Personal identification number
PKCS	Public-key cryptography standard
PKI	Public-key infrastructure
PLMN	Public land mobile network
POP3	Post office protocol
PPG	Push proxy gateway
PPP	Point-to-point protocol
PSA	Personal speech assistant
PSD	Personal security device
PSTN	Public switched telephony network
RAM	Random-access memory
RDF	Resource description framework
RF	Radio frequency
RFC	Request for comments
RMI	Remote method invocation
ROM	Read-only memory
RPC	Remote procedure call
RTSJ	Real-Time Specification for Java
SAX	Simple application programming interface for XML
SGML	Standard generalized markup language
SHA	Secure hash algorithm
SIM	Subscriber identity module
SMIL	Synchronized Multimedia Integration Language

SMS	Short message service
SOAP	Simple object access protocol
SQL	Structured Query Language
SRAM	Static random-access memory
SSDP	Simple service discovery protocol
SSL	Secure sockets layer
SyncML	Synchronization Markup Language
TAN	Transaction authorization number
TCP	Transport control protocol
TDMA	Time division multiple access
TLS	Transport layer security
UDDI	Universal description, discovery and integration
UDP	User datagram protocol
UID	User identifier
UMTS	Universal mobile telecommunications system
UPnP	Universal plug-and-play
URI	Uniform resource identifier
URL	Uniform resource locator
Ut-RAM	Uni-transistor random-access memory
VCR	Video cassette recorder
VLIW	Very long instruction word
VM	Virtual machine
VML	Vector Markup Language

VoiceXML   Voice Extensible Markup Language

W3C   World Wide Web Consortium

W-CDMA   Wide-band code division multiple access

WAE   Wireless application environment

WAP   Wireless application protocol

WBMP   Wireless bitmap

WBXML   Wireless Binary Extensible Markup Language

WCMP   Wireless control message protocol

WDP   Wireless datagram protocol

WIM   Wireless identification module

WML   Wireless Markup Language

WPKI   WAP public key infrastructure

WSDL   Web Services Definition Language

WSP   Wireless session protocol

WTLS   Wireless transport layer security

WTP   Wireless transaction protocol

WWW   World Wide Web

XAML   Transaction Authority Markup Language

XHTML   Extensible Hypertext Markup Language

XML   Extensible Markup Language

XSD   XML schema definition

XSL   Extensible Stylesheet Language

Index